NEW ORLEANS AND THE TEXAS REVOLUTION

EDWARD L. MILLER

New Orleans

AND THE

Texas Revolution

Foreword by Archie P. McDonald

Texas A&M University Press
College Station

The paper used in this book meets the minimum requirements of the American
National Standard for Permanence of Paper for Printed Library Materials,
z39.48-1984. Binding materials have been chosen for durability.
∞

LIBRARY OF CONGRESS CATALOGING-IN-PUBLICATION DATA

Miller, Edward L.
    New Orleans and the Texas Revolution / Edward L. Miller.—1st ed.
        p. cm.
    Includes bibliographical references (p.   ) and index.
    ISBN 1-58544-358-1 (cloth : alk. paper)
    1. Texas—History—Revolution, 1835–1836.   2. New Orleans (La.)—
History, Military—19th century.   3. Texas—Politics and government—
1835–1836.   4. New Orleans (La.)—Politics and government—19th century.
5. Texas—History—Revolution, 1835–1836—Finance.   6. New Orleans
(La.)—Economic conditions—19th century.   7. Capitalists and financiers—
Louisiana—New Orleans—History—19th century.   8. Businessmen—
Louisiana—New Orleans—History—19th century.   I. Title.
    F390.M73 2004
    976.4'02—dc22

                                                        2004001179

For my wife, Marie

TABLE OF CONTENTS

FOREWORD

During the statewide sesquicentennial commemoration in 1986, the annual meeting of the Texas State Historical Association featured eclectic sessions that celebrated aspects of Texas's varied culture over the 150 years since its separation from Mexico. I remember leading the singing of "Texas, Our Texas" at an elaborate birthday party that included a gigantic birthday cake with sparklers and presenting a paper on William B. Travis, commander of the Alamo, which remains the crucible of Texas history.

When the meeting closed on Saturday, several of us drove to Winedale for a follow-up seminar hosted by Jenkins Garrett of Fort Worth. After an excellent meal and during what would have been "cigar time" in a more Victorian setting, Garrett asked each of about twenty lay and professional historians their opinion of what made Texas unique.

Later responders had the advantage of more time to ponder the question, which in any event does not have a single, always correct, answer, but what was notable was that the majority of the responses involved the Texas Revolution.

That "revolution" captures the interest of Texans as much today as it did in 1986, or even 1936, when we were likely more interested in promoting tourism as economic development than we were in history itself. The best-known icons of the revolution define much of Texas's history. These include the reconstructed façade of the chapel of the Mission San Antonio de Valero, better known the world over as the Alamo, which was emulated in small-town storefronts for a century. Picture William Barret Travis drawing a line as real as it was imaginary, for every defender knew the consequence of remaining within the Alamo's walls. And recall the several score and more movies that focus on the Alamo or its aftermath.

The Texas Revolution interests scholars more than any other aspect of the state's history. Eugene C. Barker wrote of the revolution's causes nearly a century ago. Distinguished historians and writers such as William C. Binkley, William Wharton, Walter Lord, Lon Tinkle, and Ben Procter, whose monograph on the battle of the Alamo remains a best-seller, keep its historiography ever green. Bill Groneman and James Crisp still dispute the details of a controversy that Dan Kilgore raised in the 1980s. The late but learned publisher-scholar John H. Jenkins provided us with ten volumes of the *Papers of the Texas Revolution* so that all can have access to these primary sources.

Edward L. Miller has recently presented still another view of the revolution. His *New Orleans and the Texas Revolution* has been a decade or more in the making. At a meeting of the East Texas Historical Association in Nacogdoches, we first discussed his interest in the New Orleans Greys, two companies recruited in New Orleans in the fall of 1835 to join the fight in Texas. The setting was appropriate, for Nacogdoches's cosmopolitan citizen Adolphus Sterne played a prominent role in recruiting the New Orleans Grays, then hosted an elaborate welcoming banquet for them when they reached Texas en route to ill-fated destinies at the Alamo or Goliad. It was my pleasure then to encourage Ed in his research and now to commend him on its yield.

Miller's study has broadened from the Grays to the larger issue of the role New Orleans played in events in Texas history. The Crescent City commanded the ingress of the world to the interior of America and America's egress to the world. New Orleans was the primary launching point for approaching any Texas port by open sea or river with immigrants or trade goods, and it was also the conduit of its exports when they were developed.

New Orleans, even if it appears out of the way geographically, was on the way to Texas for so many because of the city's command of access, finance, and supplies. New Orleans was also a haven for exiled Spanish and later Mexican nationalists and was the launching pad for filibustering expeditions, some of which became successful revolutions. It was simply a crossroads of people and products, and those who commanded it largely controlled what occurred around it—especially in Texas and especially during the days of revolution.

Ed Miller has studied this New Orleans-Texas connection more than anyone else. I applaud him for the effort and trust that others will profit from it as well.

ARCHIE P. McDONALD
EAST TEXAS HISTORICAL ASSOCIATION

ACKNOWLEDGMENTS

Little could I imagine how important my involvement in historical reenacting would be in the writing of this book. The genesis for this work started with a simple effort—as a reenactor—to determine the image of the uniform of the New Orleans Greys and eventually the details of the lives of these men. My search ultimately led me to more intriguing discoveries as I stumbled upon sources and documents that had been ignored or overlooked, offering new insights into the powerful influence of the New Orleans' commercial community on the events of the Texas Revolution. The impression of self-sacrificing merchants rushing to the aid of their Texian kinsmen can no longer be fully accepted; rather, these new sources paint a much different picture of intriguing alliances and hidden commercial and political agendas affecting the events in both Texas and Mexico in the 1830s.

Five people in particular deserve special recognition in making this work a reality. Archie McDonald, my former history professor and an eminent historian, offered sage advice from the beginning, and I offer my thanks for his graciously written foreword. Robert "Bob" Benavides was an invaluable advisor, editor, and research colleague. His translation of the December 11, 1835, issue of *El Mosquito Mexicano* provides an important part of this overall work. It is available for viewing or printing via a link at http://www.tamu.edu/upress/BOOKS/2004/miller.htm. Mrs. Sherrie Pugh, Archivist of the Adjutant General's Military Library and Museum, Jackson Barracks, New Orleans, was my pilot and consultant in New Orleans. I will always remember my visits with both her and her husband, Colonel John Pugh, with deep fondness. Special thanks go to Gary Foreman, of Native Sun Productions, and his staff, who designed the maps and the poignant imagery for the book's cover. Thanks also go to the staff of Texas A&M University Press for their patience and encouragement over the past several years as we corresponded on this project.

The following friends, family, and colleagues also deserve recognition for their valuable contributions: Ollie and Mary Lou Moye; Cyndi Gutierrez;

Dr. Bill Schultz; Kevin R. Young; Linda and Mitch Burd; Edmund Christy; Richard O. Cook; Clayton Borne III; Henry Thibadeaux; George Anglada III; Carlos Marbán; Bill Davis; Mitzi Agnew, Cathy Kelly, Diane Pais, Mark and Denise Baughman, and other members of the Kitty Hawk Middle School administration and staff, Robert Carrier, Phillip De La Peña, and John Bryant, deceased.

A number of archivists and librarians also deserve my heartfelt appreciation for their assistance: Sally Reeves, director of the New Orleans Notarial Research Archives; Eleanor Burke, her assistant; Wayne Everard, New Orleans Public Library; archivists John Anderson, Jean Carefoot, and Donaly Brice, Texas State Archives, Austin, Texas; Frank Faulkner, Josephine Myler, Clarrissa Chavira, and Linda Hachet, San Antonio Public Library; Cathy Herpich, former director of the Daughters of the Republic of Texas Library; Jeanette Phinney, Rusty Gaméz, and Warren Stricker of the Daughters of the Republic of Texas Library; Sally Spier Stassy, Williams Research Center, Historic New Orleans Collection; Michael Hironymous, Nettie Benson Latin American Collection, University of Texas at Austin; Barbara Smith-LaBorde, Center for American History, University of Texas at Austin; Galen Greaser, Archives Division, Texas General Land Office; Elaine B. Smith, Hill Memorial Library, Louisiana State University; Dennis Medina, University of Texas at San Antonio Special Collections; Wilbur Meneray, Howard-Tilton Library, Tulane University; Barbara Mechell, Grand Lodge of Texas Masonic Library; the staff of the Grand Lodge of Louisiana; Dr. Florence Jumonville, University of New Orleans Special Collections; Kathryn Page, Louisiana State Museum, New Orleans; the staff of the East Texas Research Center, Stephen F. Austin State University, Nacogdoches, Texas; the staff of the Elizabeth Huth Coates Library, Trinity University, San Antonio; the staff of the Rosenburg Library, Galveston; and the staff of the Hermann-Grima Historic Site in New Orleans.

Last but not least, my wife, Marie, deserves the greatest expression of gratitude. She was always there to support and encourage me. She endured being a "research widow" on too many vacations. I also hope that my sons, Aaron and Marshall, will learn through my experience that tenacity and endurance are always essential for success in life.

NEW ORLEANS AND THE TEXAS REVOLUTION

INTRODUCTION

History is full of ironies. In December, 1835, John K. West, president of the Louisiana State Marine and Fire Insurance Company in New Orleans, along with a host of other insurance company presidents, issued a protest to New Orleans District Attorney Henry Carleton urging him to stop the arming of the Texian schooner *Brutus* by Texian agents. Their concern was that the schooner, once released into the Gulf of Mexico, would prey on Mexican shipping. Because their insurance companies were the chief insurers of Mexican cargo leaving New Orleans, they believed their investments would be threatened. Their concerns were justified. The fledgling Texian state government, now in open rebellion against the centralist government in Mexico, issued letters of marque and reprisal to privateers to attack ships headed for Mexican ports.[1]

A group of New Orleans merchants was behind the venture. In October merchants from the American district of the city held a public meeting to garner citywide support for the Texian rebellion. Volunteers were recruited to march to Texas, and Mexican exiles, under the leadership of General José Antonio Mexía with some of these volunteers, left a month later to attack Tampico in the name of federalism. Texian agents had approached at least one of the merchants, William Christy, to sell Texas land for funds to finance the outfitting of the *Brutus*.[2]

The irony of West's protest was that, twenty-one years earlier—in 1815—he was a member of a loosely organized conglomerate of lawyers and merchants known as the New Orleans Association, which was involved in financing parts of the Hidalgo revolution in Mexico. West had outfitted several ships to prey on Spanish shipping for many of the same reasons the *Brutus* was being outfitted to prey on Mexican shipping.[3]

Possessing threads of similarity, both groups of merchants—the New Orleans Association and the Committee on Texas Affairs in New Orleans—were loosely organized confederations of merchants who possessed in part an agenda to politically change the region for speculation and commercial exploitation.

Other plans and other groups would later use New Orleans as a staging point for schemes and expeditions, many with the purpose of targeting Latin American countries for many of the same reasons. The 1840s and 1850s would see new expeditions, but as foolhardy as some of them might have been, New Orleans money almost always figured into the equation. In the case of the New Orleans Association (1815) and the Committee on Texas Affairs in New Orleans, both were clear examples of the cyclical nature of political interference into the affairs of Mexico and the Caribbean by Southern commercial interests via various filibustering groups using New Orleans as a staging point and merchant money to carry out those concerns. In 1815, The New Orleans Association supported the Magee and Gutierrez expedition. In 1835 the Committee on Texas Affairs supported various groups of American volunteers going to Texas. By far one of the best-known groups was the New Orleans Greys. The 1835 committee was also American in scope and played down any alliance with exiled Mexican federalists in the city. In 1815 West looked primarily to privateering in the Gulf as his reward. Several on the Committee on Texas Affairs looked chiefly to East Texas lands for theirs.

New Orleans was the resource point for supplies and volunteers, and financing came from or through the city's wealthy cotton merchants. For a conflict that lasted only six months, the Texas Revolution had much greater significance in terms of its long-range effect on the North American continent. It was no secret that Jackson had an interest in Texas. Evidence also points to collusion between Sam Houston and President Andrew Jackson, and Houston's friendship with New Orleans committee chair William Christy assured New Orleans of American commercial support for revolution.

Despite the protests of prominent Creole merchants who had commercial ties to Mexican trade, not enough evidence could be gathered to indict anyone for the act of launching the *Brutus*. Events were already in motion in Texas and New Orleans. The contrast to West's experience however was that the merchants who were aiding the Texians had little desire to assist exiled federalist Mexicans who also wanted to overthrow a centralist government. It would not be long before their true intentions were revealed. In essence, New Orleans plans in 1835 and 1836 were not to rescue Texas from a centralist despot, but rather were an American attempt to seize Texas from Mexico altogether. Issues of legality would be raised as it would in future expeditions, but each time the U.S. government offered little in prevention of the act except when it affected American shipping.

New Orleans money for exploitation and speculation, proximity to the Gulf of Mexico, and a growing hunger for American expansion drove the events in Texas. A predominately American population in Texas and a Texian leadership that had grown impatient with the political instability in Mexico City served only to hasten the vision of those in New Orleans who longed to see Texas wrested away from Mexico and its lands exploited.

1 § NEW ORLEANS IN 1835

In 1835 the editor of the New Orleans *Bee* proclaimed, "That New Orleans will rival New York in a few years, we have every reason to conclude from great facilities of intercourse and trade every year—almost [every] month—becoming developed. There is very little doubt of the New Orleans and Nashville railroad being completed in 3 or 4 years; and that will open a direct communication with Mississippi and Tennessee—which will doubtless be continued to Richmond and the railroads in the eastern states. By this route, New Orleans may command the whole of the sugar produce of the country; all of the cotton west of Georgia, all the tobacco south of Ohio and Pennsylvania, west of the Shenendoah." [1]

The editor's optimistic prediction in August, 1835, concerning New Orleans's commercial future was indeed reflective of a boom already taking place in the mid-1830s. New Orleans was a thriving bustling port on the Mississippi River, and by 1834 the port had become the leading export city in the United States. The raft of debris, logs, and mud that had congested the Red River traffic to Natchitoches was beginning to be cleared by mid-1835, providing easier trade with the northwestern part of the state and East Texas. By July, 1835, 130 miles of the Red River had been cleared, allowing five steamboats to conduct packet service between Natchitoches and New Orleans. New Orleans exporters and importers carried on a respectable trade with Mexican ports such as Brazoria, Galveston, Matamoros, and Tampico, and to the Caribbean ports of Havana and Port au Prince. [2]

The driving force of the New Orleans economy was the export of cotton. The factor, or commercial merchant, provided the support structure for the bailing, storage, shipment, pricing, and financing of the cash crop. [3] Robert E. Roeder states that the merchant "constituted an independent force in the life of the Southwest, subordinate neither to the planter, nor to the domination of other commercial centers. Through their control of the channels of credit, particularly, the merchants can, in fact, be considered as having been the single most important force in directing the economic development of the Southwestern Cotton Kingdom."[4] In the case of cotton and sugar, factoring was an essential commercial process by which crops made it to market and the planters received their payment. The factor extended credit to the planter in anticipation that the planter's crop would be sold so that the planter could receive needed supplies and slaves to increase his operating capital to increase production for the next growing season. The majority of the cotton exported from New Orleans was shipped to Liverpool, England, rather than to U.S. ports such as Boston and New York. In fact, rates of exchange and prices of other goods were directly affected by the price of cotton. As the price went up or down on the Liverpool import markets, so did the prices of goods the planters bought.[5]

The commercial merchant made his money by charging usually a $2^1/2$-percent commission for his services, which were taken from the planter's total profit and proceeds. The planter was also charged interest on any balances for purchases of any supplies and equipment until the planter's next crop came through. Any clothing and supplies would often be bought from wholesale grocery, dry goods, and clothing merchants. Much of the ready-made clothing available in New Orleans was imported from New York, and daily advertisements in New Orleans newspapers promoted clothes for the planter.[6] One such firm, Frost and Company, advertised as follows:"Having been to the North, and made arrangements with the manufacturers, will continue to receive in addition to their Stock now on hand, a large and complete supply of Boots, Shoes and Brogans, adapted to the country trade and plantation use."[7]

New Orleans exported cotton and imported just about everything else. Much of the foodstuffs and tobacco was sent downriver from the West or from Cuba and Mexico to New Orleans, only to be resold to planters in the region. Reports were usually sent to the planter twice a year updating the planter's debts, charges, credits, and current balance if any. The commercial merchants established a clientele of planters from specific areas from which they obtained cotton shipments. Seven factoring houses controlled over eighty percent of the cotton shipments coming into New Orleans in 1835 and 1836. The other factoring houses were smaller, but shipment lists still indicate that they received a respectable share of the market.[8]

In contrast, the sizable sugar market in New Orleans in the 1830s, more than fifty percent of the Louisiana sugar crop, according to J. Carlyle Sitterson, "was either sold'on plantation' or shipped directly to other towns. Sugar buyers from Cincinnati, Louisville, St. Louis, Pittsburgh, and other cities frequently went to Louisiana plantations to purchase entire crops." Sugar was a crop consumed by many of the inhabitants of the Western United States, and from 1834 through 1861 49.1 percent of the Louisiana crop was consumed by westerners. In contrast, only 20 percent of Louisiana sugar found its way to merchants or refiners in New Orleans. The sugar factor in New Orleans was not altogether different from the cotton counterpart. The factor's responsibility was to hold the planter's hogsheads of sugar in storage until the market was the best in which to sell. In addition to the factor's $2^1/_2$-percent commission, the planter could also expect to pay storage costs and insurance premiums for the transport of the sugar.[9]

With the complex factoring system of shipping both sugar and cotton into New Orleans and with strong cotton crops in the early 1830s, by 1835 the city could boast that banking was also a big business. For all intents and purposes, the factor was the banker for the planter, and many complained that the commercial merchant monopolized the city's credit. Some expressed concern that the broker's control of the state's banking capital and resources also limited Louisiana's ability to diversify its economy to invest in manufacturing and industry.[10]

The factor established credit with New Orleans banks and in turn extended credit to the planter for supplies and capital, and when the factor received bills of exchange, or bills of sterling from English buyers, from the sale of cotton, he sold the bills to local New Orleans banks to pay off his debts. The banks in turn would sell the bills "to other merchants in New Orleans for reuse in cotton purchasing or for making payments in the North or Europe."[11] Brokers such as Thomas Fellows, J. D. Beers, G. R. Stringer, Palfrey and Company, Hermann and Sons, Edward Gottschalk, and Maurice Barrett Sr., also established exchange houses to handle the circulation of these bills of exchange. Very little hard currency was circulated in the factoring system, and the commercial merchant served as the middleman to keep the flow of goods moving from planter to textile mills in New England with bills of exchange and promissory notes being the primary means of payment.[12]

With the growing cotton markets in the South in the early 1830s and with increased internal improvements in New Orleans, the state of Louisiana chartered twelve new banks, virtually all of them headquartered in New Orleans.[13] The *Niles Register* reported that New Orleans banking capital, which was $5,665,980 in 1830, soared to $27,172,145 in 1835, an increase of 479 percent in just five years, hardly keeping pace with banking capital demands for the production of sugar and cotton.[14] Improvement banks that were chartered to build railroads, light the city, or dredge canals were also given banking privileges to make the company stock look more attractive to investors. George Green points out, "An improvement bank's issues of notes and deposits could also provide a source of funds to support its construction project, especially at first, when expenses were high and capital subscription was incomplete."[15] According to Merl Reed, however, Louisiana improvement banks "followed the profit motive rather than meaningful investment outlets. Improvement companies endowed with banking privileges neglected their improvements to concentrate on banking and wild speculation in government land and town lots."[16] This irresponsible practice hastened the panic of 1837, which devastated the Louisiana economy.

The business season usually ran from November through June because many of the citizens who could afford to left the city during the summer months, which were associated with disease and death.[17] Several contemporary references named the months of June, July, and August as the "sickly season." Both cholera and yellow fever had ravaged the city in 1832 and 1833. Theodore Clapp, a Presbyterian minister of the Church of the Messiah, recalled, "On the evening of the 27th of October, it [the cholera epidemic] had made its way through every part of the city. During the ten succeeding days, reckoning from October 27 to the 6th of November [1832], all the physicians judged that, at the lowest computation, there were five thousand deaths—an average of five hundred every day. Many died of whom no account was rendered."[18] The incoming floods of immigrants seem to have been the population segment of the port city that was the hardest hit in terms of disease. These newcomers, many of whom were Irish, not only bore the brunt of disease, but also had to take the low-paying, hard-labor jobs—building the railroads, paving streets, and dredging the canals. For some jobs, many immigrants had to compete with slave labor in New Orleans. Ambrose Fulton recalls one instance in which a riot broke out over the hiring of a mulatto man rather than a white craftsman to supervise the finishing work on the St. Charles Theater in 1835.[19]

Not all of the transients were European immigrants, however. Reverend Clapp called these sometimes-homeless transients who had come to New Orleans for work, crime, or fortune the city's large "floating population."[20] Jerome Bayon commented in September, 1835, "We cannot indeed hide it from the public that there are not less than 500 or 600 persons now in the city, that have been spewed out of the different counties of Mississippi and parishes of Louisiana; that have no legitimate means of support, and that are anxious to engage in riot where plunder may be made. These nightly leave their traces on the ships and craft on the river, and the houses in the remote limits of the city and they harbor by day under or about the wharves, or the swamp—and go abroad at night for their prey."[21]

The flood of immigrants from Europe in the 1830s alarmed some Americans. The new arrivals were useful as a source of cheap labor, but those foreigners who affiliated with their own national and ethnic brethren, rather than being assimilated into American society, were increasingly viewed as a political threat to established American society and government. Nativists viewed their cause as preserving American institutions and called for tighter immigration and enfranchisement laws. Not unique to New Orleans, the nativist movement also had organizations in New York and Philadelphia, both of which cities had large immigrant populations.[22] Much of the anti-immigrant fervor in New York and other cities had a strong anti-Catholic message as well. At least in New Orleans, however, with its strong Catholic Creole population, this part of the nativist message remained noticeably quiet, while the issues of foreign political affiliations and the preeminence of natives over naturalized citizens in government positions became divisive concerns in 1835 New Orleans. Politically, the Democratic party had been very successful in courting the Irish vote during the 1835 New Orleans alderman elections, with several candidates in the city making naturalization and the immigrant matter their major campaign focus.[23]

Several New Orleans leaders and businessmen launched attacks on the new Whig governor, Edward D. White, and his nominations of naturalized and nonnative Americans to government positions. The Louisiana Native American Association, organized in early April 1835 because of these attacks, held meetings that spawned the resolutions and accusations against the governor. According to John Gibson, editor of the *True American*, the association originated from a published letter expressing support for amending the naturalization laws on July 4, 1835.[24] The letter was written to a New York committee of the Native American Association. In August, 1835, Gibson declared that he had founded the Louisiana Native American Association in July after his return from a trip: "The first step in the whole proceedings was taken on the 28th of July when he [Gibson] proposed his plan to a meeting of some twenty or thirty friends."

Notable New Orleans citizens, such as notary public and attorney William Christy; James H. Caldwell; and Dr. J. S. McFarlane, surgeon of the city's Marine Hospital and alderman of New Orleans's first district, became early proponents of the association. As the unofficial newspaper for the group, the *True American* also published their first pamphlet, *Address to the Public Authorities of the United States by the Native American Association*, in January, 1836. After an eventful meeting on April 3 at Banks's Arcade, with William Christy identifying himself as the president of the group, the association published a scathing denunciation and censure of Governor White's nomination practices. Jerome Bayon, the editor of the *New Orleans Bee*, later quoted Christy as stating that the organization's main message was "that native born Americans should be appointed to office in preference to foreigners."[25] The minutes and resolutions of the meeting at Banks's Arcade and Christy's denunciation of Governor White were published in the *True American* and other city papers. Bayon refused to publish the resolutions in the *Bee* but allowed them to be published in *L'Abeille* on April 11, obviously making sure the Creole population received the details of the meeting. Both Bayon of the *New Orleans Bee* and J. C. Pendergast, editor of the *Louisiana Advertiser*, unleashed editorial denunciations of the Louisiana Native American Association and William Christy.[26]

As the *True American* became the unofficial paper of the Louisiana Native American Association, Bayon's *Bee* and Pendergast's *Louisiana Advertiser* became its opponent. Throughout the rest of 1835 Bayon relentlessly brought negative attention to the association: "It is high time that all naturalized citizens should be awakened to the dangers threatening them, by their inveterate foes of the alias party.... The Native American association has proscribed naturalized citizens, less than 25 years resident in the country.—Well, how would they like [it if] these proscriptive terms were turned against themselves; and that native Louisianans resolved that no citizen of another state should be entitled to office, without 25 years in this state? ... Many members of that organization have resided here but 2 or 3 years; and some of them 12."[27]

Bayon also criticized the secretiveness in which the association operated. Throughout these ongoing attacks by his paper, he singled out William Christy and James H. Caldwell, questioning their motives and interests within the group. Bayon accused Caldwell of actually secretly owning the *True American* and writing some of its nativist content. Caldwell published the following letter in the *Bee* on August 10:

Mr. Bayon,

Sir—You will please to contradict a statement in your paper of the 10th inst. I am not the proprietor of the True American; I have not the smallest interest, nor have I ever had, in that or any other newspaper, except as an annual subscriber.

JAMES H. CALDWELL.

New Orleans, August 10th, 1835.[28]

Nevertheless, Bayon appealed to "popular or prevalent belief" that Cald-well had "procured funds to establish it [the *True American*]; his having been known in the sheriff's court as security for its editor." Bayon went on to say that if they were wrong, he was glad, but he would not support Caldwell for "any public gratitude or favors." In one editorial Bayon referred to the Louisiana Na-tive American Association as the "Hotspur Humbug society," and in another editorial he relegated the association to a "pseudo corps" used for electioneering the candidacy of James H. Caldwell for mayor of New Orleans and William Christy as a Louisiana gubernatorial candidate. Gibson referred to Bayon and Pendergast as "foreign editors" and continued to publish retorts and commen-tary on the growing flood of foreigners: [29]

> The foreigners who come among us yearly, by thousands, will long keep down the genuine spirit which would make us truly a nation. *Millions* of them are amongst us who look to some distant country, the manners and government of which differs entirely from our own, for the reminiscences of *home*, and for the glory they have to boast of. *Their* father-land is *their* first love, and its glory is the pride of their hearts and the never failing theme of their tongue. This they cannot deprive themselves of, and they would be wretches if they could. Their American feeling then, if they have any, is mixed with a foreign one, which from its very nature must pre-dominate. Thus it is that instead of being Americans, a great portion of the nation are Irishmen, Englishmen, Frenchmen, Germans, etc., who, in-stead of having every feeling centered in this country, have at least half of their hearts on the other side of the Atlantic, and who are habituated to customs derived entirely from foreign countries.[30]

Strangely, William Christy published a letter in the *Bee* on October 8, deny-ing any affiliation with the Louisiana Native American Association:

> I answer emphatically that I do NOT [Christy's uppercase letters] be-long to the Native American Association in this city; and that I have no more to do with getting it up, than you [Bayon] had. . . . It is true however that I have my own—and perhaps peculiar—opinions on this subject; which I am sure would be approved of by every intelligent foreigner who might hear them; and I shall on all proper occasions communicate them freely to those who may wish to hear and judge for themselves.[31]

The association's 1836 pamphlet identified only Dr. J. S. McFarlane as the corresponding secretary, but in 1839 a new pamphlet, titled *Address of the Louisiana Native American Association, to the Citizens of Louisiana and the Inhabitants of the United States*, listed Christy's name along with ninety-nine other men who expressed support for the cause. Beverly Chew, T. R. Hyde, J. W. Stanton, Jedediah Leeds, Abijah Fisk, and many other prominent businessmen endorsed the tenets of the group. Jacob Wilcox, who was one of the $10,000 investors in the second Texas loan to the beleaguered Texas government, and Thomas Toby, a businessman and Texas agent, were also signers of the 1839 pamphlet. Evidence shows that Christy was involved with the association from the beginning, and one can only speculate why he made such an emphatic denial of his involvement. Regardless of his motives for his attendance at several of the meetings of the Louisiana Native American Association, Christy apparently underestimated the political backlash that he and others would receive at the hands of Jerome Bayon in the *Bee* and Pendergast in the *Louisiana Advertiser* and sought to use the denial as damage control.[32]

The Louisiana Native American Association polarized the Creole and American populations. In February, 1836, a new group, the Louisiana Loyal American Association, was organized to counter the nativist's influence. The association, consisting mostly of Creole leaders, such as Louisiana Senate President Jacques Dupré of St. Landry parish; B. Marigny; Adolphe Mazureau, Louisiana attorney general; J. J. Mercier; Octave de Armas; Pierre Soulé; General Plauché; and Jerome Bayon all became association members. In addition, Americans John H. Holland and Martin Gordan also joined. Despite the efforts of this new group to check the message of the nativists, the damage had been done.[33]

The message of the Louisiana Loyal American Association was equally polarizing. The "Loyal Americans" accused the nativists of disrupting the public peace with their incendiary rhetoric against foreigners. Gilbert Leonard was elected president of the group, and New Orleans Marshall John H. Holland and Jacques Dupré were elected vice presidents. John Gibson's *True American* had become the mouthpiece for the nativists, and Jerome Bayon's *Bee* now became the mouthpiece for the anti-nativists. Throughout the rest of the year, both newspaper editors sparred over their competing messages. The ill feelings added fuel to the already tense political situation between the Creole population and the Americans, led by Christy, Gibson, and Caldwell.

Finally in March, after years of ethnic tensions between the Creole population and the American quarter, the city government was divided into three municipalities. Americans on the city council (such as James H. Caldwell and

James McFarlane) had accused Creole leaders on the council of stonewalling projects that would have benefited the American district, and Creoles blamed James Caldwell for undermining the influence of Creole culture by introducing a theater in the American district, thus ruining the Théâtre d'Orléans. Caldwell was accused of underwriting John Gibson's pronativist *True American,* and William Christy was accused not only of being a founding member of the group, but also of using the group for his own political aspirations. The Louisiana Native American Association served as the final catalyst to separate the city government. Though the new municipal government seemed to temporarily settle the political feud between the old city and the American district, the growing commercial power of the latter continued to outpace the once-dominant French and Spanish Creole commercial interests. The growing Texas issue would become just another wedge between the two forces in the city.[34]

Proslavery meetings were also held in August, 1835, bringing attention to the growing abolitionist threat in the North. Reports were circulated that abolitionists had infiltrated the South and the city to foster slave uprisings. Safety committees were formed in several rural parishes in order to route abolitionist gamblers, and citizens were warned to be watchful of mysterious persons, such as one who had arrived from Cuba assuming "the garb of a jesuit [*sic*] or priest and is said to be at the convent."[35] A meeting was held in the Arcade Coffee House at Banks's Arcade on August 10, 1835, to discuss measures on how to combat the threat of abolitionism in the South. William Christy, undaunted at that time by the negative publicity received from his nativist interests, was named as chair of the meeting and, after a stirring speech by New Orleans attorney Randall Hunt, appealed for cool heads. The assembly approved amendments to request the enforcement of existing slave laws and appointed A. B. Roman, L. Millaudin, D. Frieur, J. W. Breedlove, and J. B. Plauché to assist Christy in "carrying into effect the object of this meeting."[36] Jerome Bayon, weary of the numerous Native American meetings and the antiabolitionist assembly, called on his newspaper brethren to use discretion in publishing any further notices for meetings of any kind.[37]

In 1835 New Orleans had a resident population of 70,000 and a transient population exceeding 40,000. The Creole population, residents of Spanish descent, including Canary Islanders, Cubans, and West Indians along with the French Creoles, maintained an Old World culture unique and foreign to that of the bustling, rough Americans. In 1836 New Orleans was divided politically into three districts to accommodate the political rivalry between the groups. The area between Esplanade and Canal Street was the Old City, or the Creole

French and Spanish section traditionally known as the *vieux carré*. Canal Street and upriver, including Magazine, St. Charles, Julia, and Camp Streets, extended westward and northward and became known as the American district, traditionally called the Faubourg St. Mary. This suburb was developed out of the original Gravier estate, for which Gravier Street was named. Magazine Street, originally known as Calle de Almazón, was named for the warehouses, or magazines, in which Kentucky tobacco was stored in the days of General James Wilkinson.[38]

By the 1830s, the American district was increasingly becoming the center of commercial activity in the city, and Faubourg Marigny became the melting pot of the middle class. Many of the municipal improvements were started in this area. A large part of the city was lighted with gas, and with mixed results many of the sidewalks and streets were paved in the 1830s.[39] William Christy also started a project of transporting stones from Kentucky to be used in paving the streets. The city council approved the project only to see Christy mysteriously cancel the contract.[40] New Orleans experienced an explosion of building construction. Many new bank buildings were built in the city, and in the American sector large impressive structures, such as the St. Charles Theater and Banks's Arcade, were classic examples of the city's wealth.[41]

The St. Charles Theater was one of several theaters built by James H. Caldwell in New Orleans, Cincinnati, Nashville, and Mobile. The St. Charles Theater, however, was considered one of the most impressive theaters of its day. Descriptions of it tell of a massive chandelier "twelve feet in height, thirty-six feet in circumference, weighing 4200 pounds, and illumined with 176 gas lights." It had opulent viewing boxes and a stage that was ninety-six feet wide.[42]

Banks's Arcade was built in 1833 by Charles F. Zimpel, architect, engineer, and surveyor. It took up the entire front of Magazine Street between Gravier and Natchez Streets. Standing three stories high, its brick, red in color, was supposedly used originally as ballast on French ships. It was also believed that the brick was unique to Banks's Arcade and the Pontalba buildings on Jackson Square. The arcade, or alley, was located in the center of the building, splitting the building lengthwise, and was covered over by a glazed glass roof that extended from Gravier to Natchez Streets. It was an impressive edifice, providing a large meeting room and storage on the second floor, which eventually housed the Washington Guard's equipment and gear. The main entrances opened onto both Natchez and Gravier Streets. The middle of the first floor opened onto Magazine Street, and the back door opened into the Arcade. John Gibson described the Arcade Coffee House, which was owned by John Brainard, as

100 feet long, 60 feet wide, and 35 feet high:[43] "It was handsomely adorned by pictures, engravings, etc., and from its size; and the gallery, which surrounds the upper story, is well calculated, and frequently used for public meetings. Five thousand persons can be here assembled without inconvenience."[44]

Brainard's coffeehouse was the site of many public meetings, including several pro-Texas meetings during the Texas Revolution. Several business offices were also located in Banks's Arcade. William Christy's notarial office was located there in 1835. Putnam Rea's *Commercial Bulletin* was on the corner of Gravier and Magazine Streets. Auctions were held there, as in the case of the auctioning off of a sugar plantation along with its working capital and slaves on May 15, 1835. Auctioneers Flower and Cenas had their offices in the complex on Magazine Street. Merchants could even get a shave and a haircut at Phellan and Fedings's hairdressing salon in the arcade. John Gibson's printing office rented the Natchez and Magazine Street corner starting in December, 1835, and published the *True American*, which would become the unofficial newspaper of the Louisiana Native American Association.[45]

Private apartments were located on the third floor. Not too long after its completion, the Arcade received some unwanted publicity. In 1835 two men were viciously murdered in one of the residential sections: "The mangled corpses presented a hideous spectacle of butchery."[46]

New Orleans also became one of the largest centers for militia organizations in the South. Strong ethnic affiliation, fraternity, putting down riots, maintaining civil order, and the potential danger of slave uprisings spurred the formation of these groups. The New Orleans newspapers were dotted with notices of drills, which usually took place on Sundays. Many of these units such as the Voltegeurs, the Chasseurs à Cheval d'Orléans, the Cazadores d'Orléans, and the Grenadiers d'Orléans fashioned themselves after Napoleanic line companies and adopted colorful uniforms. In many Southern cities like New Orleans, volunteer companies were made up of the wealthy, who could afford to have a uniform made. The variety in color caused one observer to comment, concerning the Louisiana Legion, "It is to be regretted that the Legion did not adopt the same uniform for all its companies." The Louisiana Legion was the largest of the New Orleans militia organizations and was composed of many of the city's Creole leaders. The Washington Guards were a part of the legion, and their armory was housed at Banks's Arcade as early as November, 1835.[47]

The slave population in New Orleans was estimated to be approximately half that of the white population. Slave uprisings were always a concern. In one instance, in 1836, two New Orleans constables were nearly lynched for interfering in one militia's afternoon target practice. Two slaves were given the dubious task of carrying the target from the firing site. As the two rested while waiting for the company to catch up with them, along Tchoupitoulas and Gravier Streets behind Banks's Arcade, two city constables, observing the two slaves carrying a mysterious painted sign, confronted them regarding their reason for being there. The startled slaves ran away, leaving the painted target behind. The constables, not aware of what the painting was used for, destroyed it on the spot just as the militia company marched up. Seeing the constables destroying their target, the company nearly lynched the pair on sight. A council hearing was called in response to the incident. After reviewing the case, the council ruled in favor of the constables. The sign, which the two slaves were commissioned to carry as the official target of the militia company, was a life-sized painting of a runaway slave, clearly reflective of one of the militia's recognized purposes in New Orleans.[48]

The United States, which was fifty-nine years old in 1835, was a flourishing young republic; yet it was also a nation with many divisive issues that threatened its unity. A spirited decade, the 1830s witnessed the beginning of William Lloyd Garrison's abolitionist movement against the South's "peculiar institution." President Andrew Jackson had just won his second term of office in 1832, having weathered a stormy first term with tariff and banking issues. The Whigs, the opposition party, made up chiefly of wealthy businessmen and planter-class members of the country and disillusioned Democrat-Republicans, experienced local political success in Louisiana with the 1834 election of Edward Douglass White as Whig governor. The Louisiana congressional delegation and much of the state legislature also became Whig in 1834.[49] The planter class of Louisiana, the sugar cane interests in the southern part of the state near New Orleans, and the state's cotton interests had voted as a block against Jacksonian support for tariffs. The city of New Orleans, which would always be linked to Jackson's fame as the "Hero of the Battle of New Orleans," continued to vote a majority for Jackson and the Democratic party in the 1830s.[50]

As New Orleans entered the fall of 1835, it did so with hopes of a bright future of growing commerce and trade. The panic of 1837 was still two years away. The optimism the citizens felt was tempered somewhat by concerns about the growing political divisions resulting from the spring and summer antiforeign rhetoric of the Louisiana Native American Association and the paranoia over the threat of abolitionists infiltrating the city. Jerome Bayon, however, observed the city on October 12, 1835, as the new business season came alive, that "[m]any of the citizens are daily returning; and many strangers have already arrived.

Commodities imported coastwise begin to cover the levee and block up the streets. The business has not yet fairly set in for the trade from the interior, in sugar and cotton, although supplies of each have been received, equal in quality and exceeding in quality in crops of the preceding year. . . . Few cases of summer fever remain among our citizens; and the weather has become wintry cold, yet generally salubrious, for those who have not the foolhardiness to continue their summer clothing. Every circumstance presents flattering prospects for the city of New Orleans, in its march to successful greatness." [51]

The city also became the center of controversy over the revolution brewing in Texas. In the same column of the *Bee* in which Bayon wrote his optimistic assessment of the upcoming business season, he also published several articles titled "War in Texas." Having been the launching point for several revolutionary expeditions into Mexico, the Caribbean, and Latin America, the city witnessed another filibustering scheme in the making. Pirating activity had made the Texas coast a base of operations. Revolution was brewing in Texas once again.

2 § *ANFICTIONES*

As editors Jerome Bayon of the New Orleans *Bee* and J. C. Pendergast of the *Louisiana Advertiser* waged a media war against the Louisiana Native American Association and John Gibson's *True American*, the former vice-president of Mexico, Valentín Gómez Farías, his wife, a daughter, three sons, and one elderly servant were leaving their home in Mexico City. After nearly a year-long journey during which another son was born, the family finally embarked from Matamoros in August, 1835, bound for New Orleans.[1] At the end of an extremely trying voyage, in which one of Gómez Farías's sons was nearly lost, the family quietly arrived in the bustling port of New Orleans. The weary family members must have been relieved at the sight of dry land.

THE NEW ORLEANS–MEXICAN CONNECTION

Mexico's political history had been just as turbulent as Gómez Farías's journey to New Orleans. The Mexican political system had its origin in Spanish royal authoritarianism, and Mexico's independence was won in a less-than-unified front. The monarchy of Agustín de Iturbide, which lasted only a year, was a short-lived experiment in establishing a Mexican monarchy in the image of its Spanish predecessors. Mexico's revolutionary leaders were split into conservative (or centralist), royalist, and liberal federalist political factions; from the start, military revolts, exile, imprisonment, executions, and media attacks were commonplace in Mexican politics in the 1820s and 1830s. The forming of a federal republic in 1824 established an uneasy alliance that endured through the end of Guadalupe Victoria's term of office. Even though the Mexican government was by design a constitutional federal republic, the country did not unify politically.[2]

With the expulsion of many Spanish royalists in Mexico in the late 1820s, centralists and liberal federalists were left to vie for political control. The conservatives, or centralists, wanted to maintain a strong central government and preserve the privileges of the Roman Catholic Church, the military, and the *hombres de bien*, or the landed gentry, of Mexico. The liberal federalists looked to the United States political system as their inspiration for the blueprint of Mexican government and society. The Mexican liberals—Valentín Gómez Farías, José María Luis Mora, Lorenzo de Zavala, José Antonio Mexía, and Antonio López de Santa Anna—anchored their political ideals in regional control, preserving and protecting local government, and decentralizing the national government.[3]

Fragile governments changed hands at least six times in the tumultuous period of the late 1820s and early 1830s. Finally, in 1833 Antonio López Santa Anna, a national hero who became known as the hero of Tampico, was elected as a federalist. Rather than taking the reigns of power, he returned to his hacienda, unable to take office because of illness. Gómez Farías, Santa Anna's elected vice-president, was sworn in and immediately took the reigns as chief executive in March, 1833. The takeover by the liberal federalists under Gómez Farías marked a decided change in Mexican politics. To the dismay of conservatives, the Gómez Farías administration brought about sweeping, aggressive reform as part of a movement to diminish the power and privileges of the Catholic church despite the fact that the constitution of 1824 had made it the official religion of the land. Unessential church property was confiscated and sold; missions were secularized, and the mandatory tithe to the church was suspended. Gómez Farías's administration also set out to secularize education.[4]

Gómez Farías was known as a man of principle. Former United States ambassador to Mexico Waddy Thompson stated, "the only fault imputed to him [Gómez Farías] is that he is too much an 'exaltado,' that he carries his ideas of liberty to an extent impracticable in Mexico." George Hammeken, who lived in Mexico City in the 1830s and was a friend of Stephen F. Austin, described Gómez Farías as "one of the most disinterested Liberals in Mexico, but is at the same time as obstinate and stubborn as a mule." George Farías described Gómez Farías as "a man of admirable integrity but too optimistic to be a successful statesman. He was, however, an enemy of the Catholic Church." Known to have a bad temper, Gómez Farías was often referred to as "Gómez Furious." Gómez Farías could also hold a grudge, and it was no secret that he did not like Stephen F. Austin. His dislike for Austin stemmed from a tense meeting between the two in October, 1833. Impatient and frustrated at trying to secure Texas statehood, Austin had told Gómez Farías that the Texans might take matters into their own hands if the government did nothing to support the proposal. Gómez Farías reportedly took great offense at Austin's outburst. To make matters worse, Austin wrote a letter to the *ayuntamiento* (mayor and alder-persons) in San Antonio de Bexár, encouraging them to go ahead with plans to establish a separate state. Mexican leaders in San Antonio turned Austin's letter over to the Mexican authorities, who viewed letter as treasonous. They formed a similar opinion of a paper Austin had written to a friend in Mexico City, in which he stated that "It was the duty of Texas to separate from Mexico if there was no other mode of saving that country from ruin." Gómez Farías had Austin arrested and imprisoned in Mexico City for eighteen months.[5]

The federalists relied on the civic militias to neutralize the established army. Visible symbols of the states' sovereignty, the civic militias were organized in 1827 to counter the power of the established army, and at the expense of the regular army, Gómez Farías's administration set out to strengthen the militias even more. In 1833 the western Mexican states (Querétero, Morelia, Jalisco, San Luís, and Durango) proposed a loose confederacy calling for a militia of 10,500 men—specifically not associated with the regular army—to protect the coalition. Gómez Farías was supportive of the plan. Santa Anna, however, abolished the plan before it could be implemented. C. A. Hutchinson points out that the proposed confederacy was a result of the distrust of the established military in these states, and this event may have been one of the first signs of differences between Santa Anna and Gómez Farías.[6]

Much of Gómez Farías's political support lay in the state legislatures, especially in the western and northeastern states of the republic. In the case of Coahuila y Texas, under the leadership of Agustín Viesca, his brother José María Viesca, José Antonio Navarro, Gaspar Flores, and Victor Blanco, the liberal Coahuila leaders implemented tolerant colonization policies that benefited an increasingly Anglo-American Texas. The Coahuila y Texas leaders openly sought the Southern cotton interests, especially in New Orleans, attempting to lure capital, money, and settlers to Texas. Liberal land policies and a special exemption for slaves offered Southerners the opportunity to make Texas a cotton empire much like Louisiana or Mississippi. Even though slavery was abolished in Mexico in 1829, Texas received an exemption that allowed its citizens to keep their slaves.[7]

In June, 1833, the Mexican Congress enacted the *ley del caso* (law of the case), which sentenced fifty-one prominent Mexicans who were not supporters of the sweeping radical changes to six years of exile. This was a major political misstep for Gómez Farías's administration. This persecution of the political enemies of the radical reforms horrified and alienated the mostly non-Indian, elite hombres de bien. Many politicians, from the municipal governments to the court system, were removed from their jobs, and many were attacked in federalist newspapers for opposing the Gómez Farías government.[8]

Because of his absence from the capital, Santa Anna had detached himself from the reforms of the Gómez Farías administration. Santa Anna spent much of his time away, either at his hacienda or putting down revolts. Conservatives exploited this by appealing to Santa Anna as the savior of the status quo. They sent reports to him of the atrocities of the liberal reforms. In April, 1834, Santa Anna reentered Mexico City, and by June he had the congressional doors locked and guarded. He adopted the *pronuncimiento* of Cuervavaca, which established him as the "protector" of the republic. It is not altogether clear why Santa Anna turned on his own party, but it is possible that, in gauging public opinion from reports received at his hacienda from the centralists and conservatives, he may have realized that Mexico was just not suited or ready for a government based upon the American political system. Alternatively, he may have become convinced that the radical reforms of his vice-president were indeed too radical and were occurring too quickly. Other historians, not as complimentary of Santa Anna's motives, view his change as an opportunity for him to regain the flattering plaudits of the people at the expense of his friends and political allies. By modifying and then ultimately dismantling the radical reforms of Gómez Farías's administration, Santa Anna would again become a national hero with a conservative-centralist alliance that would take over the reins of power.[9]

Weary of the intrigues and revolts of Mexican affairs of state, Gómez Farías had originally made plans to leave politics and possibly take up ranching. He made a one-thousand-peso down payment on a ranch in Chihuahua, but by 1834 he appeared to become more set on leaving the country altogether. In April, 1834, Gómez Farías requested permission to leave Mexico and also asked for a one-year salary in advance. He left Mexico City with his family on September 8, 1834, with his wife, then eight months pregnant. They traveled back to his home state of Zacatecas, where they stayed at Hacienda Cedros, near the town of Mazapil, in the northeast part of the state. Here, while he waited for the advance on his salary, he relied on the charity of friends, mainly Antonio Garay, his former minister of finance. He finally received the discouraging news, however, that the newly instated centralist congress had officially removed him from office on January 28, 1835, thus denying him the requested advance. Hearing rumors that he was a hunted man, Gómez Farías and family traveled on to Parras, where he stayed with fellow liberal and Coahuila y Texas governor Augustín Viesca. Viesca had offered Gómez Farías eleven leagues of Texas land in return for taking Viesca's children with him to the United States.

There is no evidence that Gómez Farías ever attempted to secure the land, and Viesca's children did not go with Gómez Farías to New Orleans.[10]

Gómez Farías traveled with Governor Viesca to Monclova in April. Upon hearing that bands of soldiers were waiting for him, Gómez Farías took a diversionary route and had to be secretly led into the city.[11] Even though he had obtained official letters from interim president Miguel Barragán and Santa Anna permitting his safe travel out of the country, military leaders in the region were suspicious of his presence and, more specifically, of his delay in leaving the country. General Martín Perfecto de Cós, commandant general and inspector of the eastern interior states, was given orders to prevent Gómez Farías from traveling through Texas "[b]ecause the Texans might unjustly use Mr. Farias' name in their uprising and thus compromise him."

Since Gómez Farías's prolonged stay in the state was contributing to local unrest, Cós courteously wrote to Gómez Farías warning him to keep the peace. Gómez Farías assured General Cós that he merely intended to travel first to Monclova with Governor Viesca and then to Matamoras and that his plans did not include revolt or unrest, especially in Texas. Gómez Farías and his family cautiously left Monclova on May 23 and arrived in Monterrey on May 31, again amid reports that Gómez Farías was going to be imprisoned and possibly even taken back to Veracrúz. Nevertheless, he and his family went on to Matamoros and arrived there in late July. Rumors continued to circulate back to Gómez Farías that his enemies wanted him imprisoned—or worse—dead. Thus, fearing for his family's safety, on August 12 Gómez Farías paid for passage to New Orleans on the eighty-four-ton schooner *Watchman*.[12]

Only a few days before Gómez Farías's arrival, Stephen F. Austin had left New Orleans to go to Brazoria after eighteen months of imprisonment, ironically at the hands of vice-president Gómez Farías. Austin also had a harrowing journey from New Orleans to Brazoria. A Mexican patrol ship, the *Correo*, attacked the *San Felipe*, the schooner on which Austin traveled. Captain Hurd, captain of the *San Felipe*, was able to capture the *Correo* and its crew after a short skirmish. He arrested the captain of the *Correo*, Captain Thompson, and took him to New Orleans to await trial.[13] It is not known whether anyone was at the docks to welcome Gómez Farías to New Orleans, but certainly he and his family wasted no time in getting established.

Gómez Farías had three thousand pesos waiting for him as a line of credit from the prestigious commercial establishment of Hermann and Company on St. Louis Street. Antonio Garay had made these arrangements for Gómez Farías, who immediately found a residence at the corner of Esplanade and

Dauphine Streets and hired a tutor for his children.[14] A few days later an anonymous newspaper article made known Gómez Farías's exile, so both fellow exiles and enemies knew he had arrived in New Orleans. While in New Orleans, Gómez Farías missed the simple comforts of home. He wrote to Juan Roland in 1837 that New Orleans did not have the chili peppers that he depended on for his digestion: "I have an appetitive and an amazing digestion. The use of chili suits me perfectly, but as this article is scarce here, so that I will not lack it, I request you send me a little bit of dried chili piquín, and a little bit of tomato that is grown in Saltillo."[15]

Former governor of Mexico and earlier a Yucatán representative to the Spanish Cortés as well as former ambassador to France, Lorenzo de Zavala had resigned his post on August 30, 1834, when he received word that Santa Anna had dissolved congress. Lorenzo de Zavala also arrived in New Orleans by July 13, 1835, having left New Orleans only a month before Gómez Farías's arrival to go on to Brazoria. Zavala had visited New Orleans on several occasions. An admirer of North American government and culture, Zavala observed New Orleans in 1830 as a bustling port that had mosquitoes and yellow fever as obstacles to becoming a great city.[16]

Zavala, however, added that the newly passed, stricter slave laws in Louisiana fostered "antiliberal laws," which suppressed freedom of speech, freedom of press, and the education of slaves in the South. He also observed that some of the very lawmakers who had made these strict slave laws also maintained quadroon mistresses "with whom they would bind themselves in the sacred bonds of matrimony if an invincible prejudice did not interpose itself to prevent such unions."[17] Zavala admitted, however, that the Louisiana sugar plantation system was much more advanced than that in Mexico, "[a]nd the ease of export and locomotion, with the advantage that the planters have and cultivating with slaves, makes it possible for them to sell their sugar at very low prices."[18]

While in New Orleans in 1821, Zavala had affiliated with a York Right Masonic lodge. Rosters of Concorde Lodge number 3 show that Zavala had joined this lodge on his December, 1821, trip. The meeting place for the lodge was on Dauphine Street, between Ursulines and Hospital (now Governor Nicholls) Streets.[19] Notable members of this lodge were General James Wilkenson (of Aaron Burr conspiracy fame); Henry Reug, later a Nacogdoches merchant and land speculator; Auguste Davesac, a member of the New Orleans Association, who supported several filibustering expeditions and brother-in-law of Edward Livingston; and Warren D. C. Hall, filibuster and close friend of James Bowie.

Hall later became an officer in the Texas army and was a prominent resident of Brazoria, Texas.[20]

When he was in Mexico City, Zavala had been the Worshipful Master of La Venerable Logia "La Independencia, no. 3," and was a fellow Masonic officer with General Vicente Filisola and Juan de Dios Maygorga (Guatemalan minister to Mexico). Agustín Viesca, future governor of Coahuila y Texas, was also listed with Zavala as a member of a Mexico City lodge in 1830. Viesca was also the first Worshipful Master of Luz Mexicana Lodge, also a York rite lodge. During the Spanish period, many Spaniards of higher rank became Scottish rite Masons ("rito escosé") and brought their craft to Mexico. The Scottish rite gained early influence in Mexico, mainly from French Masons. The earliest known lodge was established in Mexico in 1806, and Father Hidalgo y Castilla and other revolutionary leaders were reportedly members. In 1816 and 1817, the Grand Lodge of Louisiana established lodges in Veracrúz and Campeche. It is not known, however, what rite these lodges practiced. In 1824 the Grand Lodge of Pennsylvania established a lodge in Alavarado, in Veracrúz.

Joel R. Poinsett, United States ambassador to Mexico, introduced York rite Masonry ("Rito Yorkino") in Mexico City. He petitioned the Grand Lodge of New York, and by 1826 at least three York rite lodges were established: La Libertád number 1, La Federación number 2, and La Independencia number 3. The Scottish rite Masons, who tended to be from Mexico's aristocratic classes, viewed Poinsett's Masonic involvement as foreign interference in Mexican political affairs. Many of the members of the three York rite lodges affiliated along political lines—the liberal federalists becoming York rite Masons, or *yorkinos*, and the centralists gravitating toward the Scottish rite lodges. In the late 1820s Mexican Freemasonry became the battleground on which federalists and centralists vied for power in the Mexican government. The escosé party was eventually able to get U.S. Ambassador Joel Poinsett recalled, and by 1827 secret societies, namely the Masons, were outlawed in Mexico. Masonic lodges continued to meet in secret, and the liberal federalists, or yorkinos, formed themselves into amphictyonic councils. José María Lafragua, a Mexican lawyer, wrote of the formation of these secret groups of yorkinos called *anfictiones* in 1835. Lafragua stated that the name was chosen to give the secret societies a loftier sound.[21]

Freemasonry in New Orleans, on the other hand, developed secretly in the late 1700s. Most lodges were formed under the sponsorship of American Orients, namely the Pennsylvania, South Carolina, and New York Orients. Perfect

Union Lodge number 29 was the first to be organized, and Etoile Polaire (Polar Star), a French rite lodge, was organized soon afterward. By 1812 seven Louisiana lodges were organized into the Grand Lodge of Louisiana. By the 1830s several New Orleans lodges were located within approximately five city blocks of each other. By 1834 Perfect Union Lodge number 29 met on Rampart Street, between Maine and St. Phillip Streets; Etoile Polaire Lodge met on History Street near St. Claude; Concorde Lodge number 3 met on Dauphine Street, between Ursulines and Hospital Streets. The membership of the New Orleans Masonic lodges reflected the immigration patterns of the city's people. Germans, Jews, royalist Spaniards, Mexican liberals, and Santo Dominican exiles all found a welcome fraternity with their Masonic brothers, and for many it provided a network of commercial opportunities that might otherwise have been impossible to attain.[22]

During the first decades of the 1800s, New Orleans served as a key economic market for goods and supplies from Mexico, either clandestine or otherwise. With the political vacuum in Texas as a result of revolutions in Europe and Mexico, Galveston Island became a clearinghouse for piratical activities, namely, the trafficking of African slaves into New Orleans. Louis Aury and Jean Lafitte used the island as their base of operations from 1816 to 1821. Some New Orleans revenue agents colluded with Aury and Lafitte's men in the trade by selling the slaves in New Orleans markets. By the late 1700s Spanish cattle, sheep, horses, and mules were driven to New Orleans markets from Texas, usually in the fall of the year. Even after Mexico won its independence in 1821, New Orleans and Natchitoches merchants were accused of aggravating Indian problems in Texas by buying stolen horses from Texas Indians in return for American goods and arms. Some were even accused of participating with the Indians in raids into Texas.[23]

New Orleans also became a haven for exiled revolutionaries and scheming filibusters. Manuel Herrera, a republican exile, fled to New Orleans, hoping to draw American support for his cause. Instead, he got lost in the political intrigue of the city and lost many of his funds. Felíx Trespalacios, James Long, and Benjamin Milam also received financial support for their filibustering activities. The New Orleans Association, a conglomerate of New Orleans business interests, provided financial backing in the early 1800s for several expeditions.[24] Other business groups continued to carry out clandestine expeditions into Latin America through the end of the antebellum period.[25]

By 1835 Brazoria and other Mexican ports were carrying on a modest trade with New Orleans. The *New Orleans Price-Current and Commercial Intelligencer* reported that 917 bales of Texas cotton were imported from Texas during the 1833–1834-business season, while 3,084 bales were imported from Texas during the 1834–1835 seasons. Tejano leaders had visited New Orleans in 1830, and Ramón Musquiz, a Tejano leader, reported in 1831 that because New Orleans trade would benefit Texas, it should be encouraged for the export of cotton. In an economy dominated by commercial and private paper as its primary currency, much needed specie in the form of doubloons and reales were shipped to New Orleans from Mexican ports in exchange for dry goods. One shipment of specie from Tampico and Tuspán amounting to $240,000 arrived on July 22, 1835, and another shipment of $200,000 was eagerly expected. With the political struggle going on in Mexico, especially with the federalists trying to maintain a consistent hold on the Mexican government, the city's newspapers paid considerable attention to the events in Mexico and Texas throughout the 1833–1835 period. With merchants such as E. W. Gregory, William Bryan, E. J. Forstall, and José María Cabellero making regular shipping runs to Mexican ports, the events in Mexico captured anxious attention.[26]

In 1829 and 1830, after the failed Spanish invasion at Tampico, the Mexican government exiled many Spanish Mexicans, many of whom went to New Orleans. Many families were left destitute in a foreign city. The Mexican congress finally sought to send relief for them and to transport them to Texas, where they could settle. By the middle of 1835 the city had once again become a haven for Mexican political exiles, this time liberal federalists. Gómez Farías, who was partly responsible for the exile of hundreds of Spanish Mexicans to New Orleans, was now exiled to New Orleans himself, destitute and forced to depend upon his friends for support.[27]

On September 9, the *Bee* announced Gómez Farías's arrival in New Orleans. He was hailed as the champion of liberal republican principles, and the newspaper article briefly chronicled his administration's attempts in 1833 to reduce the privileges of the Catholic church and the military in Mexico. Santa Anna was denigrated as a military dictator. The article also mentioned Gómez Farías's original intent of settling in Texas and explained that because of the threats made by his enemies, he and his family had been forced to come to New Orleans instead. José Antonio Mexía met with Gómez Farías immediately after the latter's arrival. Mexía had been in New Orleans since October 19, 1834, residing at 62 Great Men Street in Faubourg Marigny. Mexía gave his wife, Carlotta Walker Mexía, power of attorney in April, 1835, which was filed through New Orleans notary public Octave de Armas, which indicates that his wife and family had probably arrived with Mexía in October, 1834. Carlotta was English

José Antonio Mexía, portrait as a Mexican officer. Painted by Antonio Serrano, 1828. Courtesy of Bancroft Library, University of California, Berkeley.

and was known for her spirited involvement in her husband's military and po-litical career.[28]

Mexía had been a Mexican general and had become an agent of the Gal-veston Bay and Texas Land Company, a conglomerate of businessmen and lawyers in New York and New Jersey who had bought out the empresario con-tracts of David G. Burnet, Joseph Vehlein, and Zavala. Samuel Swarthwout, a major stockholder of the company and no stranger to Texas, was prosecuted in the early 1800s in the Burr conspiracy.[29] James T. Mason, Anthony Day, George

Curtis, William H. Sumner, and Lorenzo de Zavala were also major stock-holders in the company.[30]

Sometime before Gómez Farías's arrival, Mexía had been honored at a breakfast at which he spoke to a crowd of notable New Orleans businessmen at a local restaurant called Marty's, at 145 Chartres Street, near Hewlitt's Exchange. This particular breakfast was sponsored by one of New Orleans Louisiana Legion's militia units, the Chasseurs. Newspaper editor R. M. Carter recalled that Mexía "was toasted in some complimentary way for his exertions in Mexico," and Mexía then made a speech to the packed restaurant. Former Louisiana governor A. B. Roman, Beverly Chew, Louisiana's Attorney General Mazureau, General Plauché (commander of the Louisiana Legion), and William Christy were some of the notable figures present.[31]

The Mexican federalist exiles were not left alone in New Orleans. The Mexican consulate, located at 79 Barracks Street, which was also the residence of Consul Pizarro Martinez, was only a few blocks from where Gómez Farías and his family lived, and Mexicans loyal to the centralist government apparently spied on both leaders. The antifederalist newspaper *El Mosquito Mexicano* printed a letter from "Tomás" in New Orleans to his friend "Pedro" in Mexico City, describing several secret meetings that took place in New Orleans between Gómez Farías, Mexía, and Louisiana capitalists. Cecil Alan Hutchinson, noted biographer of Valentín Gómez Farías, has written extensively on these meetings to address the "Black Legend," which grew out of the writings of Father Mariano Cuevas in the 1920s. Cuevas, who wrote an extensive history of the Catholic church in Mexico, portrayed Gómez Farías as a traitor and used *El Mosquito Mexicano* issue as his main source of evidence.

Abstracts of two secret meetings were enclosed with the letter. The meetings were called anfictiones—the name the yorkinos gave their secret meetings in Mexico City.[32] Patterned after the ancient Greek democratic councils, the writers of the American Federalist Papers used the amphictyonic councils as a model for federalist political theory.[33] "Tomás" had been present at the meetings, and the newspaper published his letter and abstracts in the December 11, 1835 issue (see the complete translation of the December 11, 1835, *El Mosquito Mexicano* issue at http://www.tamu.edu/upress/BOOKS/2004/miller.htm). *El Mosquito Mexicano* started this issue with an introduction to the documents, laying full blame on Mexía as the main conspirator and Gómez Farías and Zavala as co-conspirators.[34]

The first of three documents was the letter from "Tomás" to his friend

"Pedro." Tomás started by encouraging his friend with the news of General Mexía's plans for invading Tampico. Once the plans were initiated, he predicted that Mexía would invade Tampico first and then make his way southward, and by the next year, Mexico would be a federalist republic again.[35]

Tomás went on to say that the abstracts must be kept secret, "especially from the "profane" (non-Masons) and even from those hh (**) (Masonic brothers) who are not trusted mason's trowels." Tomás was also undecided whether he would join Mexía or Stephen F. Austin in Texas. He thought he could help the latter more since Austin "is a little hesitant and chokes in shallow water."

The first meeting took place on September 3 at 103 Ursulines. According to Tomás, Mexía briefed both Gómez Farías and a group of Louisiana capitalists and leaders on the plan. Mexía promised to exchange Texas lands for Louisiana money and supplies for the impending invasion. He even went a step further by suggesting that Texas would become a member of a new "republic of the South" that would essentially become part of Louisiana.[36] The Louisiana capitalists who were present to hear Mexía's plan reflected the South's aims of annexing Texas as a part of Louisiana.

Gómez Farías, speaking in Spanish, doubted whether the people would support the plan due to the strong influence of the priests, friars, and grand proprietors. He stated that, "Although in reality, no damage will be done to the Mexican nation but losing a territory that it could not populate, this dismemberment will always be painful and will not be easy, particularly now, to make the great majority understand that this same dismemberment is only apparent in temporary since, in the end, the states of the South have to come to form one single federated nation." [37]

Gómez Farías went on to suggest that maybe Mexía should consider postponing the expedition or at least just accept the loans at five percent per month without promising Texas lands. Mexía chided Gómez Farías for his hesitation and admonished him to "[r]emain resolute regarding what he [Mexía] would have to do, and if he were going to walk around with doubts and fears, they could all go to the Devil." [38] Gómez Farías hesitatingly agreed to support the plan.[39]

The second meeting, which took place at the same address, convened the very next night, starting at eight o'clock and concluding at one-thirty in the morning. This time the attendees established the specific articles of the plan, and a two-thirds majority vote approved seven of the articles:

1. Gómez Farías, Mexía, and Zavala will be the supreme directors of the undertaking.

2. Gómez Farías will be the "judge for the Republic," especially with regard to the treason of Santa Anna, and Mexía and Zavala will also become judges when they reunite.

3. Mexía will be the general-in-chief of the federal army, and recruitment will come from Louisiana and the Mexican state civil militias.

4. Zavala will be director and chief of the Texas colonists, and he will organize them militarily while General Mexía occupies Tampico.

5. Gómez Farías, Mexía, and Zavala will become "supreme directors" and will establish the federalist system in Mexico; Santa Anna and his ministers will be executed.

6. The legislatures and governors that had existed in March, 1834, will be reestablished and reinstated.

7. Mexía planned to submit seven petitions to the reinstated congress to reestablish a reformed constitution of 1824 to exile those who opposed the reforms, confiscate church wealth and property, secularize all monasteries and convents, guarantee to Mexicans the freedom to worship, to redistribute property, and to establish an alliance with the United States of the North, especially with Louisiana.

The pact was sealed thus: "Amphictyonic Council of New Orleans, September 6, 1835; signed by V. G. Farías, J. A. Mexía, followed by 37 signatures."

At first glance, the abstracts and plans of these meetings appear to be merely the propaganda of an antifederalist newspaper attempting to ruin the political reputation of Gómez Farías. The issue of selling Texas to the United States was a red flag for Mexico in the 1820s and 1830s. As a part of a propaganda campaign, both President Vicente Guererro and José María Tornel had also been accused of attempting to sell Texas to finance government loans. It was no secret either that the United States had expressed an interest in acquiring Texas since the time of Thomas Jefferson's administration.[40]

Southerners had been eyeing Texas as an extension of the cotton kingdom since the early 1800s. Stephen F. Austin remarked in 1829 to Governor Augustín Viesca that he predicted that the Southern states would eventually secede from the United States. Ramón Musquiz, jefe politico of San Antonio de Béxar, wrote to the governor of Coahuila y Texas on March 11, 1833, discussing the affairs in Texas. He predicted that the Southern states would attempt to secede from the United States and "[t]he acquisition of Texas or its attachment to them when they make their attempt, would enlarge the territory belonging to the new government and because [of] this one acquisition or attachment, the new state would doubtless gain greater wealth than it would receive from the other states."[41]

The *Gazeta Constitucionál de Nuevo León* published several articles believed to have been written by Nicolás Bravo and devoted to the current state of Mexico in 1829. In the November 29 issue, Bravo stated that Louisiana and Arkansas had a vested interest in acquiring Texas for several reasons, namely for security. Louisianans and Arkansans wanted to keep Texas from becoming a haven for debtors, malefactors, and fugitive slaves; second, the United States wanted the natural resources of Texas, including the land for farming.[42] Stephen F. Austin also believed that Louisiana had a vested interest in what happened to Texas. Writing to his cousin Mary Austin Holly from New Orleans in August, 1835, Austin stated that, "It is very evident that Texas should be effectually, and fully, Americanized—that is—settled by a population that will harmonize with their neighbors to the East. . . . Texas must be a slave country. It is no longer a matter of doubt. The interest of Louisiana requires that it should be. A population of fanatical abolitionists in Texas would have a very dangerous and pernicious influence on the overgrown slave population of that state.[43]

The union of Texas with other northern Mexican states into a separate federalist coalition was not a new idea. As early as 1833, writings defiantly appeared discussing the plan. In an essay believed to be written by Samuel May Williams, the idea of a separate coalition of Mexican states was already being promulgated: "When a Texas will have fifty or sixty thousand souls (and that will surely happen in three or four years), when they have appointed their judges and magistrates, founded villages and counties and introduced commerce, it will declare itself independent from Mexico and even will invite Coahuila, Chihuahua, Sonora, and S——, San Luis Potosi, New Mexico, to form a republic really free and a separate coalition. . . . It will say to these states, abandon that corrupted and venal Mexico, a daughter of the Old Spanish, a slave of the militarists and of the clergy, and come with us to make a great federation of the American Republic. The U.S. of the North will be a country prosperous and happy, enjoying the blessings of the presidency in a true liberty."[44]

In light of the plan to turn Texas over to Louisiana capitalists, another question is whether Gómez Farías was a traitor, as Mariano Cuevas supposed. Hutchinson believes the answer lies in examining Gómez Farías's letters and writings before and after the secret meetings to glean any reference to his views on Texas. In the voluminous extant correspondence of Gómez Farías there appears to be no indication that he supported this pact. He personally had Austin imprisoned for his letter to Texian leaders. Gómez Farías reassured interim president Barragán that his record in dealing with Austin's rashness over Texas statehood was indicative of his loyalty.[45] It is very likely that there were secret meetings between Mexican federalists and Louisiana capitalists. It is also very possible that Gómez Farías was indeed at the secret meetings, and the point that he questioned both the timing of Mexía's plans and the sale of Texas lands to Louisiana capitalists lends the story an element of believability. Gómez Farías's response indicates that he was not completely supportive of the plans of the New Orleans amphictyonic council; therefore, his response would have been consistent with his writings before and after the secret meetings.[46]

Though the financial support was from American supporters, plans laid out in both amphictyonic meetings were exclusively Mexican and proposed the eventual reestablishment of the federal system in Mexico. Evidently, the idea of turning over Texas lands for a new republic of the South must have dazzled the eyes of the Southern capitalists. Hutchinson, as well as Cuevas, also assumes that the secret meetings were actually Masonic gatherings. In fact, Hutchinson believes that the 103 Ursulines address was "The meeting place of Concorde Lodge number 3. A York rite lodge to which Lorenzo de Zavala seems to have belonged."[47] In the 1950s Hutchinson attempted to locate records for this lodge but was unsuccessful. Father Mariano Cuevas also attempted to locate records for the secret meetings through the Grand Lodge of Louisiana in New Orleans but also failed.[48]

As late as the 1960s, the "black legend" of the treachery of Gómez Farías and his supposed involvement with New Orleans Masons continued to be perpetuated in Mexico. In 1964 Salvador Borrego, in the spirit of Father Cuevas's 1927 allegations, wrote *América Peligra* (*America in Danger*), a book in which he referred to New Orleans in the 1830s as the "[f]oreign capital of Mexico's Masonry."[49] Borrego states that the documents of the secret amphictyonic meetings "appear" in the Grand Lodge of Louisiana and were published as abstracts in the December, 1835, issue of *El Mosquito Mexicano* in both Mexico City and Puebla. He asserts that the Grand Lodge of Louisiana, headquartered in New Orleans, was behind the York rite movement in Mexico in the 1820s and 1830s and that all orders came from the Grand Lodge. Manuel Gómez Padraza, a Mexican York rite leader, was "[t]he founder of the amphictyonic lodges"[50] and had been exiled to New Orleans earlier. Lorenzo de Zavala was "the spiritual father of the anti-Mexicans," and Gómez Farías went to New Orleans "in search [of] support" and new "lights." Borrego's assertions are that the treachery of the amphictyonic meetings was clearly and simply a Masonic conspiracy and that these gatherings were identified in New Orleans in 1835 as York rite Masonic meetings.[51]

In 1999 the author of this book received permission to research Grand Lodge records for any accounts of these secret meetings. Although the staff members of the Grand Lodge of Louisiana in Alexandria was helpful in attempting to find any information for this time period that might shed light on the amphictyonic council, they were unable to find any reference to the meetings or any direct Masonic involvement with Mexía's scheme. Original rosters of many of the New Orleans lodges were found, and the names of many leading New Orleans citizens were listed on the rolls of several Masonic lodges. The original records of these secret meetings in September, 1835, would still be available if indeed they ever existed and were Masonic accounts.

One discovery was made, however, from the annual rosters concerning the lodge location of Concorde Lodge number 3. From the early 1820s through the 1840s the annual rosters show consistently that the address was never on Ursulines Street. In addition to the annual Masonic rosters of this particular lodge, New Orleans city directories, city maps (specifically Zimpel's 1834 New Orleans city map), and John Gibson's 1838 map all indicate that the meeting place was on Dauphine Street, close to the 103 Ursulines address, but never actually on Ursulines.[52] Hutchinson's assumption that the 103 Ursulines address was a Masonic lodge was erroneous. The 103 Ursulines address and the meeting location for Concorde Lodge number 3 were not the same, and 103 Ursulines was simply a private residence.

A mystery then arises as to who lived at the Ursulines address. Whoever lived at that house evidently knew the meetings took place there. François Correjoles built the Creole cottage in the early 1800s, and the residence actually consisted of two cottages, 101 and 103 Ursulines, separated by a full wall extending to the crest of a common roof, much like a modern-day duplex. The bungalows were mirror images of each other, consisting of three rooms on the first floor. Each room measured approximately sixteen feet square, with the front room designated as the formal parlor; the two rooms to the back of the house served as additional parlors and dining rooms. Each room had a fireplace with either the same or very similar mantle designs. The bedrooms were located upstairs and were reached by an internal stairway from inside the back parlor.

The owner of the property at the time of the secret meetings was Jacques Dupré. From Opalousas in St. Landry parish, Dupré was one of the largest cattle ranchers in Louisiana. He was also a politician, serving as president of the Louisiana senate, and interim governor after the death of Governor Derbigny in 1829. Dupré was a state senator for his parish until his death in 1846. He bought the property from François Dufour in March, 1833, and it is unclear whether Dupré ever resided at 103 Ursulines or lived somewhere else in the city since he also owned several other properties, mainly in the old city. It is also puzzling why this address was chosen for the meetings. No apparent Texas or Mexican connection was found with Jacques Dupré other than his ranching interests in Louisiana; he probably looked to Texas for the buying of range cattle. Opelousas was one of the key settlements in central Louisiana on the road from southeast Texas to New Orleans. No apparent Masonic connection with Dupré was found either. Although he may have been affiliated with Humble Cottage Lodge in Opalousas, there are no apparent records that Dupré had any Masonic membership with the Opalousas lodge or any of the New Orleans lodges in this period.[53]

Why the 103 Ursulines address? Perhaps simply the fact that it was a less-than-conspicuous meeting location. The cottage was in a middle-class neighborhood in the old city where washerwomen, tinsmiths, grocers, and dry good stores could be found.[54] In a three-block area around the address, many of the residences were listed as the homes of free women of color. In the 1834, 1835, and 1838 city directories no one is identified as living at 103 Ursulines. In 1838 a tinsmith, John Peters, is listed at the 101 Ursulines address.[55]

It is possible that the Masons of the New Orleans lodges were in fact involved in the secret meetings since many of them were also leading businessmen of the city. Many prominent leaders who were mentioned as attending the breakfast in Mexía's honor earlier that year were Masons, but documentary proof of direct Masonic involvement with the secret meetings continues to be elusive.

The New Orleans Masonic tradition also attributes a story to private meetings that took place at this same 103 Ursulines residence between Stephen F. Austin and "thirty-three Masons" to discuss plans for a revolution in Texas. Again no conclusive or substantial documentation has been found to confirm that such a Masonic meeting actually took place, although Austin certainly met with New Orleans leaders (who may also have been Masonic brothers) to discuss the events taking place in Texas. James Ramage's letter to Austin in October, 1835, refers to discussions with Austin while he was in New Orleans in the summer.[56] It is also possible that the accounts of the secret amphictyonic meetings became confused over time with meetings Austin may have had while in the city in July. Meetings took place in New Orleans, but little has been found to verify these as Masonic in nature.

Commercial exploitation and land speculation were certainly greater forces behind any meetings with Texian representatives with New Orleans businessmen and capitalists. The substance of the amphictyonic meetings in September, 1835, was not unlike the secret meetings between the New Orleans Association, a conglomerate of businessmen and leaders, and filibusters like James Long, José Felix Trespalacios, Xavier Mina, and Gutierrez de Lara, which took place twenty years earlier. Both sets of meetings arranged for the financial support of expeditions in exchange for commercial gain for the investors.[57]

George Fisher, another exile, who was forced to leave Matamoros for publishing inflammatory anticentralist remarks in his newspaper, arrived in New Orleans on October 9 or 11. Fisher wrote to Austin that he visited with both Mexía and Gómez Farías when he arrived in New Orleans. Fisher, a proponent of a northern Mexican coalition, reported that the governor of Tamaulipas conveyed to Fisher before his departure that a movement was underway for the secession of several northern Mexican states.[58] Fisher's news must certainly have raised the morale of the exiled federalists. Resistance to Santa Anna among the northern states still remained strong, and because of his talks with Gómez Farías and Mexía, Fisher felt that a public assembly should be called immediately. A meeting was scheduled for October 13 at Banks's Arcade. The gathering, however, would become the high-water mark for any alliance between American supporters and Mexican federalists.

3 § NACOGDOCHES LAND MEN

Nacogdoches merchants Adolphus Sterne and Albert Emanuel landed in New Orleans in September, 1835, with the hope of selling some of their Red River lands and other tracts they owned between the Neches and the Sabine Rivers.[1] The deteriorating situation in Texas precipitated drastic measures on the part of individuals like Sterne and Emanuel. Relying on past family connections in the city, Sterne turned to Edward Gottschalk and Maurice Barnett Sr., both New Orleans brokers, to advertise their lands.[2] Gottschalk published the following advertisement in the New Orleans *Bee* on September 18, 1835:

TEXAS LANDS

The subscriber offers for sale 65,300 acres of the most valuable land situated in Texas as follows:

4428 acres at Pecan Point, on Red River, above the raft,

4428 do 30 miles below said Point,

4428 do 15 miles above Jonesborough, on Red River,

4428 do on the waters of Sulphur Fork, about 12 miles from Red River, containing about 3500 acres alluvial prairies and the balance woodland, and is well watered;

4428 do about 10 miles from Galveston Bay,

And the balance of the tracts are situated on the waters of Trinity and Neches rivers.

The owner of the above described lands is now in this city, where he will remain for a few weeks. He has resided for eight years past in Texas, and being perfectly acquainted with the country, he has taken particular pains to make the choicest selections.

The Red River lands are very valuable, and will, as soon as the raft is cleared, and which is progressing rapidly, increase tenfold in value. The title is indisputable, and can be examined on application to the subscriber.

The above will be sold together, or in single tracts, on reasonable terms, and a liberal credit given for undoubted paper. Suitable goods would be taken in part payment.[3]

    Apply to   EDW. GOTTSCHALK, Broker.
                                        No. 100, Chartres street [sic].

Gottschalk and Sterne were old friends. Sterne, who had since moved to Nacogdoches, had given Gottschalk power of attorney to handle his deceased father's estate in New Orleans in 1828. As early as 1817 the teenaged Sterne had arrived in New Orleans with his family from Cologne, Germany. Either Adolphus's mother died or his parents divorced, for in succession records, Adolphus was identified as a son from a previous marriage, and Adolphus's father, Emanuel, and his second wife, Jeanette Hart Sterne, had a son Isaac. Emanuel Sterne and Adolphus's stepmother had a turbulent marriage. Jeanette Sterne filed for divorce in June, 1828, on the grounds of "being harshly treated." The month after the divorce petition was filed, both Emanuel and Jeanette died, leaving Adolphus to settle his father's debts from his new home in Nacogdoches.[4]

Emanuel Sterne was also a dry goods merchant and had difficulty succeeding in business in the bustling port. Emanuel, who declared bankruptcy by 1824, was also accused of defrauding his creditors. Adolphus had taken merchandise "upriver" for his father but, upon returning, had lost his pocket book and all of the money from the sale of the merchandise. M. Bullock, one of Emanuel Sterne's creditors, discovered that the merchandise, which Sterne had bought from him for the "upriver" trade, appeared in the hands of another local merchant, suggesting that Sterne had not been forthright in his business dealings. Sterne continued in business, however, and upon his death, Emanuel's estate included an inventory of dry goods from his business and other property, including slaves. All was auctioned off to settle his obligations, including a $900 debt to Edward Gottschalk. It appears that Adolphus went to Texas shortly after his father's bankruptcy, where he established himself as a merchant and land speculator in Nacogdoches. In 1829 Adolphus Sterne became a Mexican citizen, signing his name as "Nicolas Adolfo Sterne" and indicating the following: religion Catholic, age 28, married, occupation merchant. Sterne's application for citizenship reveals that he was willing to forsake the Jewish faith at least on paper in order to meet the specified Catholic requirement for citizenship.[5]

Albert Emanuel, the other Nacogdoches merchant who had arrived with Sterne in New Orleans, was also a Jew; his family was from Arolson, a town in the principality of Waldeck, which is in present-day Hesse, Germany. Emanuel arrived in New Orleans, much like Sterne had, as an immigrant looking for

a better life. By 1834 Emanuel had also made his way to the Mexican frontier settlement of Nacogdoches and was listed on the 1835 Nacogdoches census with his seventeen-year-old wife, Dorcas. He submitted his foreigner's
entrance certificate to the *ayuntamiento*, or governing council, of Nacogdoches
on March 23, 1835. A witness was required to legitimize the certificate, in which
stead Adolphus Sterne served. By May, 1835, Emanuel had begun buying Texas
land, including one league of land from Adolphus. The tract of land he bought
from Sterne was located along the south bank of the Red River, and upon his
arrival in New Orleans with Sterne, Emanuel wasted no time in selling his
newly acquired lands to eager buyers. On October 2, Emanuel sold his tract of
land to the partnership of Spencer Gloyd and Sylvester Gibbs Clark.[6]

Sterne had already sold Red River land to Spencer Gloyd and Isaac
Littlefield a week earlier. Both Sterne and Emanuel advertised the sale of their
lands to be "On reasonable terms, and a liberal credit given for undoubted paper."[7] In all of the land deals both men made while in New Orleans, most of
what was given as payment to them were one- and two-year promissory notes,
usually with the total sum split into several notes payable by each member of
the partnership who were purchasing the land. The means by which these partnerships agreed to pay both Sterne and Emanuel indicated very generous terms
for the day. Most promissory notes were for six months, twelve, or sometimes
eighteen months, but notes for two years were highly unusual. Why Sterne and
Emanuel agreed to these terms of long-term credit from their New Orleans
buyers is difficult to ascertain. It is possible that due to the need for quick sales
the men agreed to these terms, or they may have known these men before and
agreed to these terms as those that one might offer to a friend.

New Orleans was devoid of hard currency and relied upon paper, such as
promissory notes, to be loosely used for currency. Promissory notes would in
some cases be endorsed several times before the debt would be "called" for payment. Most of the notarial acts involving the sale of real estate did not specify
an interest rate. In this case, a customary interest rate of eight percent was as-
sessed only if the notes were not paid within the specified period for payment.
The men could use the promissory notes to purchase supplies or equipment, as
Sterne had done in 1826 for the Fredonian rebellion.[8]

Emanuel and Sterne conducted business with most of the same eager buyers. Gloyd and Clark, both of modest means, relied on several partnerships to
make their purchases. Spencer Gloyd was listed in the 1832 New Orleans city
directory as owner of "S. Gloyd and Company, shoe store, 7 Chartres Street."[9]
Sylvester Gibbs Clark was listed in the 1834 city directory as "S. G. and

C. Clark, grocers, 176 Bason."[10] Apparently Emanuel stayed in New Orleans longer than Sterne since on October 27 he sold two more leagues of land.[11] By the time Sterne left New Orleans on October 20, he had sold more than 21,000 acres of Texas land, and by October 27, Emanuel had sold more than 11,000. Sterne had made in excess of $13,000 from his sales, while Emanuel made more than $6,200.

Edward Barnett Sr., the other broker Sterne had used to advertise his lands, had traveled in Texas selling dry goods as far as San Antonio de Béxar. Barnett Sr. had lived in Baton Rouge earlier and was accustomed to traveling along the Red River. It is possible that on his trip into Texas, with his son Maurice accompanying him, he went through Natchitoches and then on to Nacogdoches along the Camino Real, or Spanish Royal Highway. Sterne, who was already in Nacogdoches, could have assisted Barnett with the necessary papers to trade in Mexican Texas. On his own, Maurice Sr. made "another prosperous expedition of the same kind" to Texas in 1831.[12]

The Barnetts and Edward Gottschalk were part of a close-knit Jewish community in New Orleans, which historian Bertram Wallace Korn describes as possessing an "irreducible residue of Jewishness."[13] Although Sterne and Emanuel had left the sheltering Jewish community of New Orleans to pursue the mercantile business in Nacogdoches, both men continued to look to many of their old Jewish friends in their business dealings and in the sale of Texas lands.[14]

Even though nativism poisoned the political atmosphere between Creoles and Americans in New Orleans in 1835, as an ethnic group the New Orleans Jewish community appeared to be relatively unscathed by the media attacks of the Louisiana Native American Association and received considerable acceptance from both the Creole and American populations.[15] Many Jewish men came to New Orleans independently and worked their way to financial respectability with little affiliation to their Jewish heritage. Many intermarried with Catholic families, and when the bylaws of the first synagogue in New Orleans were passed in 1827, several provisions had to be made to account for the intermarriage of Christian women.[16] In 1828 Sterne also married a Christian girl, Rosina Ruff, and professed, as a Mexican citizen, to support the Catholic church. Sterne kept a diary for several years and occasionally hinted at his Jewish heritage.[17]

Not long after Sterne arrived in Nacogdoches in 1825, he aligned himself with Haden and Benjamin Edwards in a dispute over land titles in Nacogdoches, which erupted into open rebellion. Empresario Haden Edwards had encountered the frustrating problem of determining original land titles within his own empresarial grant. Edwards's heavy-handedness in dealing with original settlers, requiring them to produce their titles or get new ones issued, prompted a stiff response from Saltillo, nullifying Edwards's grant. Edwards declared the area around Nacogdoches independent and even called it the Republic of Fredonia. Sterne was caught smuggling flints and other supplies in coffee barrels into Nacogdoches for the Edwards brothers. He was arrested and sentenced to be executed.[18] The records of the trial and sentence were sent to Saltillo for approval, and Sterne was kept in chains in the old stone fort in Nacogdoches awaiting final judgment.

According to Masonic tradition, however, Sterne's Masonic affiliations in New Orleans helped to secure his release.[19] John H. Holland, Worshipful Master of Etoile Polaire Lodge in New Orleans, a Scottish and French rite Mason, and Grand Master of the Grand Lodge of Louisiana, helped secure Sterne's release by appealing to Mexican General Manuel Miér y Terán, who was also a Scottish rite Mason. Sterne, a Master Mason, was a member of the Lafayette Lodge, number 25, and was also a member of La Triple Bienfaisance Lodge, number 7319, a French rite lodge.[20] Sterne worked in both the French and York rites while in New Orleans, and many Jewish Masonic brothers were also raised in one or several rites. Etoile Polaire Lodge included the York, Scottish, and French rites. Fellow Jews Samuel Hermann Sr. and Samuel Hermann Jr. were members of Etoile Polaire Lodge, as was Mexican vice-consul Pizarro Martinez, who may have had considerable influence in obtaining Sterne's release.[21] Sterne's pardon was granted on the condition that he never again participate in rebellion against Mexico. Conditions in Texas in 1835, however, prompted a new response from the German merchant from Nacogdoches. Sterne stayed in Nacogdoches, carried on in the mercantile business, and remained an active Mason for the rest of his life.

Gottschalk's September 18 advertisement for Sterne's lands proudly predicted that with the removal of the raft of debris and logs on the Red River, lands located along or near its shores would certainly increase in value. Most of Sterne's land was sold with the enticement that the Red River was going to be opened beyond Natchitoches and that anyone buying land in that northeastern area of Mexican Texas would certainly be able to send large crops of cotton to the New Orleans market. After returning from Texas in 1835, Mississippian Gideon Lincecum mirrored Gottschalk's claims concerning the Red River lands: "Which lies in Texas is at present most spoken of by travelers. The lands on that part of red river are, in the cotton and corn crops very productive, and high up the river good wheat may be grown. Like the rest of Texas, it is a prairie country with wide bottom lands covered with useful timber, affording first rate prairie pasturage[.] This part of Texas is now on account of the prospect which is anticipated on the opening of the raft on the red river much talked of by the capitalists of that country and Louisiana."[22]

There was another underlying expectation involved with the Red River land—one the advertisement did not reveal. The U.S. purchase of the Louisiana territory from France left a nagging question of ambiguity in some minds regarding the existing boundaries between Spanish territory and the newly acquired American lands. Public opinion, primarily in the South, believed that Texas should have been included in the Louisiana Purchase as well.[23] Texas had been the focus of American interest as early as 1803. President Thomas Jefferson argued that the Louisiana Purchase should have included the lands from the Perdido River in Florida to the Bravo (Rio Grande) in Texas due to French exploration and national claims.[24]

Southern filibusters and adventurers, such as Dr. James Long, with New Orleans support, attempted to lay claim to Texas in the name of republicanism—with disastrous results. Southern assistance came from New Orleans merchants and businessmen, several of them loosely known as the New Orleans Association, which consisted of men such as Edward Livingston, James K. West, Abner Duncan, and August de Castera Davezac.[25] With the independence of Mexico, the filibustering fever waned, and now as a part of the fledgling Republic of Mexico, Texas was politically joined to Coahuila in 1824.[26] Political upheaval and instability in Mexico caused a delay in the ratification of the Adams-Onís Treaty in its original form, and with a new, independent Mexican government, some saw an opportunity to renegotiate a new set of terms concerning Texas.[27]

In 1821 Texas was an expansive territory, known as the *despoblado*—the "empty" or "unpopulated land." Austin recalled in 1831 that the land he explored for his grant was "A wild, howling, and interminable solitude from Sabine to Béxar. The civilized population had not extended beyond the margins of the Sabine in that quarter; and was confined, on the west to the towns or villages of Béxar and La Bahia (the latter now called Goliad) which were isolated military posts."[28] There were many tribes of Native Americans. Some, such as the Cherokees, had immigrated from the United States; others, such as the Comanches and Kiowas, lived nomadically on the Texas plains on fast-moving ponies following herds of buffalo; and others, such as the Caddoes, had established civilized farming settlements in East Texas. While New Orleans basked in its commercial opulence, Texas remained a rich wilderness waiting to be tamed and civilized in the image of the southern United States. A minor number of Americans had begun encroaching into Spanish Texas in the early 1800s; some of them were United States army deserters and fugitive slaves, which only exasperated and alarmed the Spanish. Deserters suspected of spying were either sent back to Louisiana or ordered to move farther into the interior away from the border area. Foreigners were looked upon with a suspicious eye. A census of foreigners residing in Nacogdoches was compiled because of growing Spanish concerns toward anyone who was not a Spaniard.[29]

Irishman and horse trader Philip Nolan had prompted wary attention to his incursions into Texas to capture wild horses; his activity was considered a ruse for spy missions to map Texas for American General James Wilkinson in Louisiana. In 1801, ignoring Spanish warnings to not reenter Texas, Nolan and a band of horse traders were attacked by Spanish troops. Nolan was killed, and his men imprisoned. Additional problems festered over the gigantic territorial changes that occurred after the 1762 defeat of the French in North America. The Spanish received the Louisiana territory in 1762, but in 1800 Napoleon Bonaparte, now emperor of a strong French empire, once again claimed the territory for France. Napoleon, who needed money more than land, sold the territory to the United States in 1803.[30]

The young American republic coveted the Spanish lands in North America. Characteristic of American encroachment in the Spanish territory along the Gulf of Mexico, both Florida and Texas were the targets of filibustering expeditions from the United States.[31] Mexican expeditions, such as the one by Gutierrez and Magee with its Republican Army of the North, supported by Americans in New Orleans and Natchitoches, invaded Texas only to be crushed by Spanish troops in 1813. Finally, in 1819 a weakened Spanish government signed a treaty with the United States, providing the young republic with at least some of their coveted lands. In article two of the treaty, Spain ceded their Florida territories to the United States, and in article three, the United States agreed to relinquish all claims to Texas, establishing the Sabine River as the eastern boundary.[32]

In the twilight years of Spanish power in Texas, a change in Spanish policy occurred that created a generous colonization plan devised to encourage Americans to settle in Texas. The region had remained relatively uninhabited, and hard-working, industrious settlers from the United States would serve as a buffer from hostile Indians and other Spanish enemies. After Mexico had won its independence, plans to inhabit Mexico's northern frontier continued with even greater generosity. The Mexican National Congress offered foreigners "who may be desirous of settling in her territory security for their persons and property, provided they obey the laws of the country." The law also mandated that the individual Mexican states frame their own colonization plan "as speedily as possible" in conformity to the national colonization law.[33] In 1825 Coahuila and Texas enacted one of the most liberal colonization laws in the Mexican republic. It served as a model for other state colonization laws.[34] *Empresarios*, or land contractors, were contracted to bring in a certain number of families, each of whom usually received a league and labor of land (amounting to one league, or 4,428 acres, and a labor, or 177 acres). Taxes on these lands were deferred for ten years, and Americans had to agree to live on and cultivate their lands within six years, or the title to their lands would be revoked. Some empresarios, such as Stephen F. Austin and Green DeWitt, were successful in bringing in American families; other plans resulted in frustrating failure, either from lack of understanding of Mexican culture and politics or from personal setbacks that prevented them from finishing their grant.

Just as filibustering designs had failed to free Texas from Spanish hands in the twilight years of the Spanish empire, diplomatic attempts by the United States to acquire Texas also failed, with equally disastrous results with the Mexicans. When Andrew Jackson was elected president in 1828, one of his main diplomatic targets was the acquisition of Texas. He appointed Anthony Butler of Kentucky to serve as his ambassador in Mexico to replace the controversial Joel Poinsett, who had been at the post since 1825.[35] Poinsett had single-handedly polarized many in the Mexican government with his Masonic affiliation with the York rite lodges and the yorkino federalists in Mexico City. Mexican freemasonry took on a political dimension of intense proportions not known in the United States. when Poinsett aided in the establishment of York rite lodges in Mexico City, Mexican escosé (Scottish rite) leaders interpreted the move as a clear signal of foreign interference in Mexican politics. The Scottish rite lodges attracted the upper echelon of Mexican society, such as military officers, priests, and the *hombres de bien*, or landed aristocracy.

In light of the prevailing, continued American interest in Texas, Ambassador Poinsett's attempts at discussing its acquisition were looked upon with added suspicion, especially in view of the Fredonian rebellion in East Texas. Mexicans suspected that the United States was behind the revolt, whose timing crippled any chances Poinsett might have had of ever conducting serious negotiations for Texas. The members of the Escosés party in the Mexican government demanded Poinsett's recall, and President Jackson reluctantly obliged. From the outset, the mission of Poinsett's successor, Anthony Butler, was to find a means to acquire Texas from Mexico. Butler, a native of Kentucky, had been a business partner in mining lead with the Austins in Missouri. In 1828 Stephen F. Austin wrote that Butler was an "unprincipled man" and that Austin anticipated serious difficulties with him. Butler demanded Austin to pay him five or six thousand dollars, expecting returns from the later years of the partnership.[36] In 1835 Austin referred to Butler as the "worst enemy I have in Mexico," and some in Mexico believed that Butler was instrumental in prolonging Austin's imprisonment. Butler also blamed Austin for influencing the Mexican government to refuse his attempts at securing the cession of Texas to the United States.[37]

Butler's overtures concerning Texas did not fare any better with the Mexican government than did Poinsett's yorkino involvement. Butler had been able to develop a working relationship with Mexican Foreign Minister Lucas Alamán, but Alamán and his government were soon overthrown in yet another coup de état in 1832.[38] Butler's failure, according to historian Andreas Reichstein, was due to his conflict of interests. He was simultaneously ambassador for the United States and an agent for various land companies.[39]

Two land companies had offered Butler huge compensations to protect their interests in Texas. John C. Beales offered him 500,000 acres in land script from the Arkansas and Texas Land Company.[40] In a series of letters written to Butler in July, 1835, James Prentiss, Thomas Davis, Joseph S. Joseph, and Gilbert Thompson, making up the Trinity Land Company, offered $10 million for the jurisdictional cession of Texas to the United States; in return, the company requested the right to colonize 5,000 leagues of Texas land. Prentiss offered Butler ten percent of the ceded lands and an additional $5.00 for each league Butler secured for the company.[41]

Growing tensions—a result of the Fredonian rebellion in Nacogdoches in 1826—caused the Mexican government to send General Manuel Miér y Terán on an inspection tour of Texas in 1828 and 1829. Terán discovered a Texas that, due to a flood of immigrants, had become increasingly Americanized as one traveled northward. Mexican leaders were suspicious that the United States was behind the rebellion in Nacogdoches, and General Miér y Terán's report reflected the Mexican view that the United States was an avaricious power threatening Mexican territory. Terán observed a population of Americans, especially in East Texas, who did not abide by Mexican law. Some were criminals from the United States, and some had entered the province illegally or were residing within the prohibited twenty-league buffer, a border that had remained undefined because of diplomatic delays.[42]

Even though the Adams-Onís treaty of 1819 had set the boundary between the United States and Spanish territory as the Sabine, commissioners had never officially surveyed the border. Anthony Butler attempted to establish a new boundary between Mexican Texas and the United States. Some early Spanish maps had erroneously marked the Neches River as a tributary or branch of the Sabine. Butler declared that the Texas boundary should historically have been the "western branch" of the Sabine, or Neches, River and not the Sabine, a river that also emptied into Sabine Bay on the eastern coast of Texas.[43] In 1833 Butler wrote to President Jackson "[t]hat occupancy of the Country by placing a Garrison at Nacogdoches would be justifiable, and I do so, because we have at least as strong grounds for insisting on the Naches [Neches] as the true boundary as the Mexicans have for claiming to establish the line at what they call the Sabine, as a reference to the enclosed topographical sketch I think will prove; and if our pretensions are apparently as clear and as strong as theirs we have equal right to occupancy in the Disputed Territory, Nacogdoches being about midway between the Sabine and the Naches [Neches]."[44]

Butler's pretentious Neches River claim became a political issue for years, and even though some earlier Spanish and French maps had erroneously marked the Neches as the Sabine, the officially recognized map, made by John Melish, on which the treaty was based, clearly showed the Neches and the Sabine as two distinct rivers.[45] Anthony Butler was the perpetrator of the Neches River claim, and it seemed that the plan was a consolation effort for him. If the United States could not acquire all of Texas, then at least it could acquire some of it. Butler's own speculative interests also fell in the Neches area and surely figured into his motivation to lay claim to the area.

President Andrew Jackson also adopted Butler's boundary position, and years later it was reported that Sam Houston and Jackson had discussed the Neches claim before Houston came to Texas in December, 1832. Anson Jones provides an account from J. W. Houston, who states that he was present with Sam Houston when "Gen. Jackson agreed to claim the Neches as the true Sabine and as a boundary between the United States and Mexico under the treaty of 1819, with Spain, and that he would defend and fight for that line."[46] Jones claims that General Houston's retreat toward the Sabine River in 1836 was done with Jackson's claim in mind. By luring Santa Anna into the disputed territory, General Houston could intentionally have drawn the United States into the revolution. Jones states, however, that Houston's own troops changed the course of history by refusing to retreat northward toward Nacogdoches and marched southward toward Harrisburg and San Jacinto. According to Jones, the plan was strangely similar to events that occurred on the Rio Grande in 1846, except this time General Zachary Taylor's U.S. troops were involved: "That is, war by the act of Mexico, and with precisely the same want of truth."[47]

The United States Senate finally ratified a treaty of limits between Mexico and the United States in April, 1832, which also established the Sabine as the Texas boundary. The treaty stated that the boundary line began at the Gulf of Mexico "at the mouth of the river Sabine, in the sea, continuing north along the western bank of that river to the thirty-second degree of latitude."[48] Only five months after the treaty was ratified, however, President Jackson wrote to Butler in September, informing him that United States commissioners were being instructed to lay out the boundary "to begin at the Gulph of Mexico, and run up the west branch of the Sabine [referred to as the Neches River by Butler and Jackson], and continue up on the west side of its west fork, to the point designated in the Treaty," thus intentionally disregarding the official, agreed-upon boundary.[49]

Jackson was also willing to use the Indian problems in East Texas as a pretext for possible United States' invasion into Mexican Texas. Anticipating revolution in Texas as early as 1832, Jackson suggested a plan to invade Texas, supposedly to keep the Indians from raiding on the frontier. In September, 1835, the Nacogdoches Committee of Vigilance and Safety appealed to President Jackson over a feared admission of Creek Indians from the United States into East Texas by empresarios. Their petition set the stage for the justification of eventually sending U.S. troops into the disputed area to protect settlers. In 1836 Jackson used this excuse to send General Edmund P. Gaines and a company of U.S. infantry into Texas. Gaines and the army occupied Nacogdoches for six months, but the attacks and threats from Indians on the frontier proved to be unsubstantiated. General Gaines's timing in sending troops into the Nacogdoches area could have coincided with Houston's retreat across the Neches River and might have placed the pursuing Mexican Army in direct conflict with U.S. troops.[50]

In 1829 General Miér y Terán recommended prompt attention by Mexican leaders to reconsider their generous colonization policies toward American settlers. The decree of April 6, 1830, which emanated from Terán's report, was an attempt to gain control of an already losing situation in Texas. The Mexican government suspended Anglo-American immigration into Texas, leaving the established empresario grants in place. Mexican soldiers were sent to Texas to build forts; thus, by fortifying and establishing a greater military presence, Texas would remain a Mexican department. The decree alarmed and infuriated Texians and served to further deteriorate relations between Texians and Mexicans.

Southern Americans had also been allowed to bring in slaves from the United States, but in 1829 Mexican President Vicente Guererro abolished slavery in Mexico. Coahuiltexian leaders sought to make Texas a cotton kingdom with slaves, but Guerrero's pronouncement caused panic among Texians and other slaveholders in New Orleans who had an interest in Texas. Coahuiltexian leaders were able to ward off a crisis by obtaining an exemption for Texians. In the early 1830s relations between Texians and Mexico took several nervous turns. In 1832 conflicts in Velasco and Anáhuac over the forcible collection of customs duties, the move by Texian leaders to secure separate Texas statehood, and the volatile political changes in Mexico City all served to bring about tenuous conditions in Texas.[51]

In 1832 and 1833 the Texians held two conventions to formulate steps to petition the Mexican government for separate statehood. Stephen F. Austin, representative for the Texians, took their case to Mexico City. His attempts at meeting with Mexican leaders brought about progress in some areas of concern, but the key issue of statehood continued to be elusive. Austin's failure to secure statehood and his eventual imprisonment in a Mexican jail after his rash letter brought about further suspicion, which prompted yet another inspection tour, this time by Colonel Juan Almonte. Almonte observed that the government had neglected to enforce the terms of empresario contracts and that there was a great deal of "pernicious stock-jobbing" occurring in East Texas. Almonte determined that the Galveston Bay and Texas Land Company owned three-fourths of the lands in the Nacogdoches district and that individuals owned the rest. This news caused much bitterness among the settlers: "They resent the monopoly exercised by companies or persons who have acquired lands so cheaply not for the purpose of colonizing them, but merely for speculation."[52]

The ripples of political change in Mexico impacting Texas, however, began with the removal of the federalist yorkinos under Mexican Vice-President Valentín Gómez Farías. The undoing of their reforms sent shock waves throughout the country. In 1834 Santa Anna had embraced the Plan of Cuernavaca, repudiating all support of yorkino policies. Santa Anna also dissolved congress and disbanded state legislatures and ayuntamientos. Several Mexican states— Zacatecas, Coahuila y Texas, and the Yucatan—defied Santa Anna's move. Resistance by the state militia in Zacatecas was crushed by Santa Anna's troops in

May, 1835. Augustín Viesca took office as governor of Coahuila y Texas in April, 1835, in the midst of political disarray; Saltillo and Monclova were battling over which city possessed the mantel as rightful capital of the state. Augustín Viesca, the Coahuiltexian yorkino governor, and the legislature sided with Monclova, while centralist General Martín Perfecto de Cós, commander of the eastern internal provinces, sided with Saltillo. The Coahuila y Texas legislature moved to defend Monclova from national troops, precipitating additional antagonism.[53]

By March, 1835, the state legislature authorized the sale of 400 leagues of Texas land at the discretion of the governor. Robert M. Peebles, Francis W. Johnson, Samuel M. Williams, and John Durst of Nacogdoches were present in Monclova at the time of the virtual give-aways. All of them left the capital with numerous land titles in their pockets. The year before, James T. Mason, agent for the Galveston Bay and Texas Land Company, and George A. Nixon of Nacogdoches had also bought 300 leagues of Texas land through the state legislature.[54] In April, 1835, the Coahuila y Texas legislature also granted the governor powers to move the capital, and with that act the legislature adjourned. General Cós arrested Viesca and his entourage of Americans and Mexicans trying to escape to San Antonio de Béxar.

The sales of the four hundred leagues of Texas land to a handful of American speculators was made null and void by the national congress. Moreover, the act by the Coahuila y Texas legislature approving the sale brought an outcry of resentment from Texian leaders. In May, 1835, the Brazoria *Texas Republican* printed Governor Viesca's call to arms. Rather than defend the governor, the editor referred to the governor and the "vile" state legislature as bartering away the public lands "for a mere song."[55] The anger over the corrupt land deals appeared to be a major concern for many, and some even feared that it actually contributed to the call for more Mexican troops into Texas. Thomas Jefferson Green wrote in July, 1835, that "[t]he simple facts are these: the administration of the government of this state during the present year has been of the most shameful character. Poor Viesca was completely hoodwinked and deceived by a few ... whose only object was to use the government for their own private purpose. A law was obtained for the sale of Four Hundred Leagues of vacant land, and the most shameless acts of SPECULATION were committed against the state and the interests of Texas."[56]

Green indicated that several of the speculators had begun stirring up rebellion; he maintained that "[t]he movement of troops towards Texas has in my opinion no other object than to meet and counteract the revolution which the general government had grounds to believe would be attempted by those individuals."[57] Samuel M. Williams received so much criticism for his involvement in the four-hundred-league purchase that he published a series of letters in the Brazoria *Texas Republican* defending his actions. General Cós ordered the arrest of José María Caravajal, one of the fugitive deputies who approved the sale.[58] Eluding capture, Caravajal joined a local militia company in Victoria. He evidently had also circulated information calling for resistance, for James Kerr bitterly complained to Thomas Chambers:

> At San Felipe Williams, Johnson, Carbajal [sic], Bowie, and others cry "wolf, wolf, condemnation, destruction, war, to arms! To arms!" Williams says, "I have bought a few leagues of land from the government; but if they don't bring the governor to Bexar, I shall not be able to get my titles." What a pity; and with his terrible tales I am astonished to see that they have had the cleverness to excite some persons of that colony to a high degree.... There is not in my opinion, in all the country one single person, with the exception of the interested ones, who would wittingly seek his own ruin in order to save thousands like Williams and the others. But they have been able to deceive many persons and make them believe that an army is coming to destroy their property and annihilate their rights in Texas.[59]

J. G. McNeel also complained to J. F. Perry in June that "Our country is again assailed by aspirants and speculators, they are attempting to deceive the people by preaching to them of the dangers that await us at San Felipe. It [the consultation] was got up for the purpose of sustaining the *Mammouth Speculation*."[60] The sale of the 300 leagues by the Coahuila y Texas legislature in 1834 and the 400 leagues in 1835 received such negative attention from Texian leaders that the transactions were specifically nullified by the fledgling republic of Texas government in its 1836 constitution.[61]

In June, 1835, Texians clashed with Mexican troops at Anáhuac and Velasco over the reopening of customs offices. Although many Texians did not support the actions of the state legislature and the small group of men responsible for the unrest in Anáhuac, General Martín Perfecto de Cós's demand for their arrest received a defensive, cool response from Texian leaders. General Cós sent more Mexican troops into Texas to enforce his authority and to arrest the fugitive Monclova legislators and the men responsible for the trouble at Anáhuac. Events in Coahuila and Texas did not go unnoticed in the New Orleans newspapers. The *Bee* reported that "Troops have been sent to Texas under the pretext of acting against land speculators; but really to overcome the colonists—and marched over land that they might make a more safe and quiet descent on the province, and distribute themselves before resistance could prove effectual."[62] Upon hearing reports that Mexican troops were being sent into Texas to establish order, several settlements formed committees of safety and vigilance. Citizens in Columbia, Brazoria, San Felipe de Austin, and Nacogdoches all met to formulate a response to the Mexican threat.

One of the first meetings in Nacogdoches occurred on July 19, 1835. Frost Thorn was appointed the chair, and Thomas J. Rusk, secretary. A committee of vigilance and correspondence was formed, consisting of John Forbes, George Pollitt, Frost Thorn, Thomas J. Rusk, and J. Logan. The committee requested that Henry Rueg, the political chief of Nacogdoches, call a meeting of his department to determine a course of action.[63]

In August, Francis Johnson and Mosely Baker of San Felipe arrived in Nacogdoches to seek support for a convention, or consultation, against the Mexican centralists. A public meeting was held in Veal's Tavern on August 15. James Bradshaw was appointed the chair, and William G. Logan, secretary. Resolutions were passed, several of them renouncing the arrest of Governor Viesca and members of the state legislature as "the invasion of Texas by an army whose intentions are not avowed." A reference was also made to Austin, whose arrest and imprisonment were "contrary to the express provisions of the constitution and laws." The body voted to support a consultation to be held at San Felipe. Considerable attention was also given to a proclamation from Thomas Thompson, a self-styled officer in the Mexican navy, who warned citizens to not organize themselves into militia companies. A unanimous resolution denounced Thompson's pretentious orders. James Bradshaw, Sam Houston, Thomas Rusk, and Richard Sparks were also commissioned to meet with the various Indian tribes to "preserve the peace with them." The Nacogdoches committee consisted mostly of the Nacogdoches land men, and Sam Houston quickly became a dominant figure in the proceedings. Houston, who had arrived in Nacogdoches in April, 1833, had reportedly known Adolphus Sterne in Nashville.[64]

Although it is not clear how the two men met, it was evident that Sterne assisted Houston upon his arrival in Nacogdoches. Houston boarded with the Sterne family and became close friends with them. Mrs. Sterne served as his godmother when he was baptized into the Catholic church in Sterne's parlor. Immediately, Houston and Philip Sublett bought eleven leagues of land in 1833. Rumors of the Neches River claim and the stories that Houston brought with him from Washington and President Jackson must have influenced other speculators to begin buying up lands at a rapid pace. In the midst of the growing danger of Texian defeat in April, 1836, Houston reminded Henry Raguet, a fellow land speculator in Nacogdoches, "Don't get scared at Nacogdoches—Remember old Hickory claims Nachez [Neches] as "neutral Territory."[65] Houston's reminder to Raguet of Jackson's designs for East Texas and Nacogdoches indicate that there were no secrets between Houston and the other speculators.[66]

Sometime before the third meeting of the Nacogdoches vigilance and safety committee on September 15, Sterne, Albert Emanuel, and Thomas Breece, a local carriage maker, departed for New Orleans. The minutes of the August meeting do not indicate whether the men were being sent as commissioners to New Orleans. Indeed, it is unclear just what the trip was for. One can presume that the journey had a dual purpose—the purchase of supplies for the cause and the sale of land. It is evident that the men left around September 7 or 8, since Breese sold a league of land to Augustus Allen and William G. Logan just before his departure. The three men traveled along the former Camino Real to Natchitoches and then down the Red River to New Orleans. The Camino Real began in eastern Louisiana and extended from Los Adaes, the former Spanish capital of Texas, southward to San Antonio de Béxar and on to San Juan Bautista on the Rio Grande. By the 1830s this old Spanish road was known as the San Antonio-Nacogdoches Road, which travelers described as little more than a grass-covered trail. It became, however, a major artery through which American settlers traveled into the Mexican province of Texas. Established in 1779, Nacogdoches became a key stopping point for many travelers as they passed into the province west of the Sabine River.[67]

A sizable Indian population from the United States also dwelled in the Piney Woods area of East Texas. Cherokees, Choctaws, Kickapoos, Delawares, and Shawnees had made their way to Texas as refugees and found acceptance under the Spanish and Mexican empire. For the most part the tribes in East Texas remained peaceful and carried on a respectable trade in deer hides.[68] On the Louisiana side of the Sabine River, the United States had established an army post, Fort Jesup, mainly to deter Indian incursions from Mexican territory into Louisiana. About twenty-five miles eastward, the French-Spanish town of Natchitoches served as the port of entry for much cargo and many immigrants traveling to Texas. The little village of San Augustine was the first settlement that Americans came to upon entering Texas. Nacogdoches was located another twenty-five miles farther west. An area of thickly forested pine, oak, and walnut trees with intermittent prairies, or "openings," the East Texas lands were sprinkled with small streams and creeks.[69]

Land speculators, especially in the Nacogdoches district, enthusiastically adopted the Neches claim position. The years 1834 and 1835 saw a feverish buying frenzy of East Texas lands by Sterne, Henry Raguet, Frost Thorn, Henry Rueg, Albert Emanuel, and William G. Logan. Lands in East Texas were selling for 50 cents an acre, whereas land in the United States was selling for $1.25 an acre. Those buying Texas lands in the disputed area, namely between the Red, Neches, and Sabine Rivers, would have made at least one hundred percent on their investment if Mexico had ceded the disputed area to the United States. U.S. land prices elsewhere, however, would have remained steady with government-controlled prices.

Examining Nacogdoches archival records, one is struck by the staggering amount of land that was bought in the Nacogdoches district in the years 1834 and 1835. A handful of men who came to be known, in an uncomplimentary way, as the "Nacogdoches land men" bought more than 483 leagues (2,138,917 acres) of land in those two years.[70] Frost Thorn purchased 94 leagues, as compared to 29 leagues for the previous five years combined (1829–1833); twenty-four-year-old William G. Logan, who received large sums of money from friends in Natchez, Mississippi, to buy Texas land, purchased 80 leagues. Augustus and John K. Allen bought 108 leagues; George A. Nixon, 74 leagues; and Adolphus Sterne, 37 leagues, all in 1834 and 1835.[71] Sterne had purchased 11 leagues in 1833, but before that he had bought mostly town lots in Nacogdoches. Land purchases were being made in an area that was owned chiefly by the Galveston Bay and Texas Land Company. It is unclear how these individuals were able to purchase such immense amounts of land while large land companies, such as the Galveston Bay and Texas Land Company and the Trinity Land Company were also vying for the same tracts. Fraud may have played a part in the story. Immigrants were warned to be wary of speculators who would freely take their money and sell them land with a paper title that some other unsuspecting settler also possessed.

The vastness of the Nacogdoches district, estimated by Juan Almonte in his 1835 report, at 600 square leagues, evidently allowed both individuals and land companies to speculate with little accountability. Several of these Nacogdoches land men served as both supplier and seller of land to the companies and their agents. Nacogdoches land man Frost Thorn sold 10 leagues of Texas land to Samuel Swartwout, New York City collector of customs in January, 1835, and Thorn also acquired John T. Mason's power of attorney in New Orleans in July of that same year.[72] Swartwout was a stockholder in and Mason was a land agent of the Galveston Bay and Texas Land Company. Terán and Almonte both complained of the rampant land speculation and corruption that were taking place in the Nacogdoches district. Although the Coahuila y Texas government had approved the sale of 400 leagues of Texas land in a controversial move to raise funds for the liberal federalist government of Augustín Viesca, the amount of lands that were sold off in East Texas in 1834 and 1835 were equally controversial by comparison.

There was also uneasiness and concern over the northeastern Red River lands. The boundary had not been formally established, and there was confusion over which country, Mexico or the United States, had legitimate authority and claim over those lands. Arkansas territorial governor John Pope claimed the lands between the Sulphur Fork and the Red River as Arkansas territory and even ordered Benjamin Milam to desist from completing his empresarial contract granted by the Mexican government. Many of the land tracts that Sterne and Emanuel sold on their New Orleans trip were a part of these lands. The beneficial results of removing the log jam, or raft, on the Red River seemed to far outweigh the risks of what was going to result from the boundary dispute. Henry Morfit, whom Jackson sent to Texas in 1836, reported to U.S. Secretary of State Forsythe that he knew that the United States had planned to extend their territory all the way to the Pacific. In August, 1836, Morfit reported that "Speculative plans were laid for extending the commerce of the United States when those limits were first proposed. In New Orleans it was said, that steamboats could go to Natchitoches, a railroad should be constructed from that place through a gorge in the southern Rocky mountains."[73]

When the consultation suspended all Texas land sales and sought to take control of the land offices in November, 1835, the Nacogdoches speculators—at a meeting on November 29—balked. S. H. Everitt, who had been sent to Nacogdoches to take over the land offices, was alarmed at the obvious displeasure with the consultation's measures. He observed those who attended the Nacogdoches meeting: "Composed of Men who were all, or nearly all, engaged largely in clearing out Lands or who are deeply engaged in land speculations the following is a partial list of those present, John K. Allen, George A. Nixon, Charles S. Taylor, W. G. Logan, A. Sterne, Henry Rueg & all very largely engaged in Land operations as well as Mr. English, Mr. Burney and others from the U. States with many strangers in this Meeting. . . . Mr. Sterne is appointed Judge. I hope not, as he is deeply connected with the _Land Men_."[74]

Although Mexican land laws forbade the sale of land to foreigners, many speculators ignored the prohibitions. Accounts of the period warned immigrants to beware of land speculators who were waiting to abscond with the unwitting settlers' money.[75] This did not deter men such as Nathan Ware from pursuing an investment interest in Texas. Ware, a prominent Pennsylvanian who had established himself as a wealthy Louisiana sugar planter, had informed Henry Austin in 1831 that he was interested in establishing a cotton mill in Texas. Over a six-month period, Ware had discovered that James Bowie had already secured the rights to the cotton mill in Texas. Correspondence between Stephen F. Austin, Henry Austin, and Ware reveals that Ware became tired of waiting for a favorable response to his proposal and reinvested his money in a new plantation in Louisiana.[76] However, he sought out new opportunities through twenty-four-year-old William G. Logan, a Nacogdoches land speculator. One of Ware's partners was Andrew Hodge Jr., another transplanted Pennsylvanian who had become the president of the prestigious Orleans Bank. His brother, William L. Hodge, also became an investment partner. Logan contacted Ware, Hodge, Hodge's brother, and another of Ware's partners, a Mr. Fearn. He sold them choice Red River lands in April, 1835.[77]

At this same time, Logan also gave these men power of attorney to sell land for him in New Orleans, indicating a growing and healthy interest in Texas lands by this group and others in New Orleans.[78] William Hodge became a member of the New Orleans committee that coordinated support efforts for the Texas revolution. Sterne and Emanuel attended the eventful meeting at Banks's Arcade on October 13, and Sterne's and Emanuel's sales of Texas land in September and October indicated a continued appetite in New Orleans for Texas land, especially in light of the U.S. claim on the Neches River and the prospect that lands along the Red River would soon be opened to river traffic from northeastern Texas to New Orleans. This fired the imaginations of Louisiana capitalists and speculators in Texas.

Sterne, Emanuel, and other East Texas land men were in the right place at the right time. New Orleans businessmen who were looking for new investments viewed Texas as a bright prospect. With the growing tensions and instability in the province, these two groups exploited the weakness of the distant Mexican government and the growing American influence for their own economic gain. The Texas revolution was the opportune backdrop to accomplish their goals.

4 § THE BIG MEN

With life experiences already beyond his years, twenty-year-old Ambrose Cowperthwaite Fulton arrived in New Orleans in late 1831. Born in Chester County, Pennsylvania, he left his parent's farm in 1827 to work as an assistant to a Philadelphia builder.[1] Two years later he became a sailor, traveling along the Atlantic seaboard shipping routes. On one voyage in August, 1829, from Havana to Boston, his ship, the schooner *Thaddeus*, was attacked by Spanish pirates. The experienced captain of the *Thaddeus* outwitted the brigands by leading them into an area of sunken rocks, where the pursuing ship abruptly ran aground. The bandits abandoned ship, leaving it at the mercy of the rocks and the crew of the *Thaddeus*. The crew cautiously boarded the sinking pirate ship only to find, to their horror, the body of a young girl left to face an ocean grave when the ship sank. Fulton convinced the captain to give the girl a proper burial at sea before continuing their voyage to Boston.[2]

In 1831 Fulton followed his youthful wanderlust down the Mississippi River to Louisville, Kentucky, and on to New Orleans. On a second Mississippi River trip, Fulton traveled as a deck passenger on the famed steamboat *Yellow Stone* on the Yazoo River, which was "set adrift" in Mississippi. He arrived in Benton just in time to hear David Crockett, the Tennessee backwoodsman and congressional legend, give one of his stirring speeches. Fulton recalled that Crockett's speech instilled in him a sense of direction and hope in his then-dismal condition. The speech was filled with populist exhortations identifying greatness with the common worker, farmer, and builder. Crockett then "gave the Jackson Cabinet a broadside with his heaviest guns, and set into motion a tidal wave of eloquence which hoisted me aloft, to float upon an upper gently waving sea of bliss, from which I descended again to earth with bewildered eyes and regret."[3]

After Crockett's inspirational speech, Fulton traveled on to Vicksburg, Mississippi, and along the way slept in a massive Mississippi canebrake. Upon arriving in New Orleans, the young man took another job as a sailor, traveling to Haiti, Cuba, and Chile. In the early 1830s, on one such voyage from the Atlantic seaboard, Fulton met Simon Cameron, who was transporting Irish workers to New Orleans for work on the New Basin Canal.[4] In the mid-1830s, Fulton had acquired enough money to start his own construction business, so he returned to New Orleans.[5]

The year 1835 was an eventful one as Fulton became embroiled in a race riot and the explosive events in Texas. James H. Caldwell, owner of the St. Charles Theater, was finishing the building's construction when the issue of his hiring a free mulatto, B. Alexander, to oversee the finishing work, became a volatile issue. The white workers, who were scheduled to work under the mulatto supervisor, assembled outside the theater calling for his removal. Resolutions were passed denouncing the training of blacks in the building trades. Caldwell appealed to the workers, stating that if there were a white worker who believed he was qualified to complete the job, then he would fire Alexander and hire the white worker in his place. Fulton recalled that not one man stepped forward.[6]

The unrest continued in Lafayette Square (Fulton remembered the location as Jackson Square) the next day. The local militia companies from the Louisiana Legion and the city guard were sent into the plaza under the command of General B. Plauché, a veteran of the battle of New Orleans, to break up the assembly.[7] General Plauché marched his men into the square, slashing as they went. Curious bystanders were injured, including sailors who had walked over from their ships to view the assembly, and some of them were actually imprisoned. Fulton and his men were present and witnessed the legion's march into the square. William Christy was hired to defend the sailors who had been imprisoned merely for being in the wrong place at the wrong time. J. C. Pendergast, editor of the *Louisiana Advertiser*, asked Fulton to provide his observations on the incident. Fulton was critical of the actions of Plauché's men, and, as Louisiana historian Joseph Tregle Jr. describes it, "The editor of the *Louisiana Advertiser* published a few days later, a series of crude jokes ridiculing the militia unit's competence and commenting disparagingly on the national origin of its members."[8] It is unclear how much of editorial attack was based on Fulton's account, but the comments infuriated General Plauche's men. Plauche's militia ransacked Pendergast's newspaper office, sending the editor fleeing for his life. Shaken and fearful, Pendergast was placed in "protective custody." From this incident Pendergast clearly discovered the influence the Louisiana Legion enjoyed in the city. His life was saved only after the intervention of Louisiana's Attorney General Mazureau.[9]

Fulton worked on several city buildings, including Banks's Arcade in 1833. In October, 1835, only a month after the excitement of the Lafayette Square riot, his involvement with Banks's Arcade took on a much broader role than its construction. Fulton recalls, "When word arrived at New Orleans by vessel that the representatives of Texas who were Americans had been cast into prison at the City of Mexico, and that President Santa Anna had issued a manifesto requiring the Texans to leave the State, I felt that they were not properly treated, and that they merited aid."[10]

In early October Natchitoches was one of the first American cities to call a pro-Texas meeting.[11] General Sam Houston's request for volunteers was published in the Natchitoches *Red River Herald:* "If Volunteers from the United States will join their brethren in this section, they will receive liberal bounties of land. We have millions of acres of our best lands unchosen and unappropriated. Let each man come with a good rifle and one hundred rounds of ammunition and to come soon."[12]

The news electrified New Orleans. For many that heard the claim, the promise of land for service sounded too good to be true. George Fisher, who had himself arrived in New Orleans by October 11, met immediately with Gómez Farías and Mexía. He also met with some of Mexía's American friends, who may have been some of the same people at the secret amphictyonic meetings in September. A public meeting was called, and the New Orleans newspapers published notices. The *Bee* announced, "We are requested to announce a meeting of the friends of Texas, at the private committee room in Banks arcade, this evening at 7 o'clock—to deliberate on affairs of importance in relation to that country."[13]

Hermann Ehrenberg, a Prussian immigrant, recalled that signs with two-foot-high letters were posted on the streets and read "Public meeting," beckoning the city to take notice and attend.[14] George Fisher recalled that the meeting was originally intended to be preparatory, but when the hour arrived, a throng of people filled the designated committee room in the arcade. It was packed with well-dressed businessmen, many of them with their slave attendants; dirty and tired immigrant dock workers; dray operators, who had spent their day going back and forth from the wharves, carting the many items for storage in the warehouses; and modestly dressed customs clerks and countinghouse clerks, who attended with their ink-stained hands, having finished a long day keeping books in the thriving port city. Charles B. Bannister, whose barrel-making shop was located on Magazine Street near Banks's Arcade, obviously got caught up in the growing excitement throughout the day as people passed along the street. He also attended.[15]

The second-story committee room was decidedly too small, but the coffee-

Banks's Arcade, 1838. Printed in John Gibson's Guide and Directory of New Orleans, *1838. Courtesy of the Center for American History, University of Texas at Austin.*

house and the galleries above were also filled with attendees, so a decision was made to remain in the original meeting room. The air was thick and heavy with layers of cigar smoke from fine Havana cigars and the stench from the attending workers permeating the room, making breathing difficult. The swelling assembly was keyed up in anticipation of the forthcoming speeches. Those who were able to get inside Banks's Arcade stood in the coffeehouse expectantly, and in the upper-floor galleries overlooking the coffeehouse were excited, murmuring onlookers. Many of those who came late could only stand outside on Magazine Street under the dim flicker of the gas lights that lined the street or wait in the glass-covered arcade.

The meeting opened with the customary parliamentary call to order. Fulton remembered that when the meeting began, "The big men rushed in, took possession of the meeting, crowded the boys into the background."[16] The hustling takeover by the "big men" was obviously unexpected and intimidating to Fulton, and it appeared that these men had orchestrated their own agenda for the assembly several days earlier. William Christy, as in many assemblies before, was quickly appointed chair, and James Ramage was appointed secretary. Octave de Santangelo proposed several resolutions from the floor. A resolution committee consisting of William Bryan, William Bogart, and James H. Caldwell was nominated to write up the proposed resolutions. Wading through the sea of people, the three retired to another committee room to write their report. While the committee completed its task, Christy called on several people to speak.

Gustave Schmidt, a New Orleans lawyer and alderman; George Fisher, who was recently exiled to New Orleans; Octave De Santangelo, also a political exile from Mexico; and attorney Randall Hunt spoke to the huge crowd. Schmidt expressed support for the Texians and urged approval of the resolutions that had been proposed by Santangelo. Santangelo, editor of the *Correo Atlantico*, was also exiled for his position in favor of the Texians and had even been exiled twice from Mexico. The first time was in 1826 for the publication of his book, *Las cuatro primeras discusiones del Congreso de Panamá, tales como debieran ser*, which criticized Guadalupe Victoria's administration. Santangelo and his wife lived in New York City, where they ran a boarding school. They returned to Mexico in 1833 and began publishing the *Correo Atlantico*. Santangelo was expelled again in 1835 for his pro-Texas sentiments.[17] This time he moved to New Orleans. In August he and his wife received considerable attention in the New Orleans *Bee*. His case was played out for the public. As reports began to circulate from Mexico of Santa Anna's centralist takeover, Santangelo's claim of political persecution and of loss of property and livelihood due to his abrupt expulsion from Mexico made him a sympathetic figure.[18]

Fisher provided an exposé of Santangelo's expulsion and Santa Anna's ruthless plans. Others spoke, but their names were not recorded. Fulton stated that he spoke to the throngs but was petrified to speak to such a large crowd. It was no accident that Caldwell presented the proposed resolutions. From years of acting before large theater crowds, Caldwell had developed a strong, clear voice. The six proposed resolutions were as follows:

> Resolved, That this meeting warmly and sincerely sympathize with our brethren in Texas, now engaged in a war forced upon them for their rights and liberties as freemen.
>
> Resolved, That we will aid and support them by every means in our power, consistent with the duties we owe to our own government, to save them from the tyrant's military rule.
>
> Resolved, That a committee of six be appointed to correspond with the provisional government of Texas, and also with such other committees as may be appointed throughout the United States in favor of the same sacred cause which our fathers in '76 defended, and which we their descendants are assembled to support.
>
> Resolved, That said committee be authorized to receive such donations as may be given for the relief of our brethren in Texas, and appropriate the same in such manner as they or a majority of them may deem expedient for the interests of the noble cause in which they are engaged.

Resolved, That the president and secretary be added to said committees.

Resolved, That the offices of this meeting be authorized forthwith to open a list for volunteers to enter in the aid of the Texians for the defence of their rights.

W Bogart   J H Caldwell   W Bryan [19]

Predictably, all of the resolutions were approved. Lists for volunteers were opened in the multistoried coffeehouse. Hermann Ehrenberg recalled that these remained in the coffeehouse for a few days, and Adolphus Sterne was ecstatic at the response. William L. Hodge, James N. Niven, and Thomas Banks, with the resolutions committee of Bogart, Caldwell, and Bryan, along with the chair and secretary, were nominated as a new committee to correspond with the Texians and other committees of assistance in other U.S. cities. The assembly was so large that the business at hand was concluded, and the meeting was temporarily adjourned from the upstairs committee room. For the benefit of the throngs who had been waiting patiently for the results of the gathering, a new meeting was convened in the large coffeehouse and held de novo. The newly nominated committee posted themselves at tables to oversee the enthusiastic recruiting of Americans and immigrants alike. Santangelo, who was already in his sixties, ceremoniously stepped up to be the first to subscribe his name for service, taking the pen directly from Christy's hand to sign his name.[20]

The "big men" that Fulton described as taking over the meeting were indeed influential and powerful. Noticeably, no Creole businessmen were nominated to the committee. Christy and Caldwell, both accused of involvement in the Louisiana Native American Association, served on the correspondence committee to the Texian government. No Mexican federalists were nominated either, imparting the committee an exclusively American viewpoint to the conflict in Texas. Whereas the amphicthyonic meetings a month earlier were exclusively Mexican in terms of agenda and planning, James Ramage, writing to Stephen F. Austin only week after the October meeting, made it perfectly clear that the meeting at Banks's Arcade was "solely, purely, simply American in all their parts." He also expressed "doubts" about Mexía's and Fisher's presence at the meeting, indicating that more than one agenda was being presented on October 13 at Banks's Arcade.

A New Orleans notary public and attorney, William Christy became the dominant figure on the New Orleans committee. He was born in Georgetown, Kentucky, in 1793. Orphaned at age fourteen, he inherited a sizeable fortune from his parents. He began studying law and, when the War of 1812 broke out, joined Captain Uriel Sebree's Boone county volunteers in Scott's First Regiment of Kentucky volunteers.[21] Christy, like his Tennessee counterpart, Samuel Houston, became a war hero. Known as the "hero of Fort Meigs," Christy saved several of his fallen comrades in a battle against the famed Tecumseh outside the walls of the fort in present-day Ohio. He was appointed first lieutenant of the First U.S. Infantry, served as adjutant of both the First and Twenty-third Regiments, and became inspector of customs along the Canadian border. He was sent to New Orleans after the battle of New Orleans to serve as paymaster of his regiment. Christy resigned his commission in the U.S. Army on July 4, 1816, and in January, 1818, married Catherine Pauline Baker Cenas, widow of Blaise Cenas, deceased Orleans parish postmaster and businessman. He helped raise Cena's three sons. The Christys also had three children of their own—two sons and one daughter.[22]

Christy was purportedly involved in the republican movement in Spanish Texas with the Mina expedition and later with Dr. James Long, José Félix Trespalacios, John Austin, and Benjamin Milam from 1819 through 1822.[23] According to an 1853 account in *DeBow's Review*, John McHenry, a veteran of the Long expedition, recounted that in 1819 Dr. Long led a filibustering expedition to Texas from New Orleans, while Mexican General Trespalacios, who was considered "the nominal head of the expedition" and a Long ally, coordinated a landing near Tampico. McHenry identified Christy and Benjamin Milam as members of Trespalacios's forces.[24] The political climate in Mexico had changed by 1821, and though Dr. Long's forces were captured at La Bahía and marched to Mexico City as prisoners, the leaders and men of his and Trespalacios's expedition found themselves among political friends in the new nation's capital.

Trespalacios, Christy, John Austin (a distant relative of Stephen F. Austin's), and Milam eventually met once again in Mexico City. Even though Trespalacios was named as the new governor of Texas, he, according to McHenry, was "fired with jealousy" toward Long. Visiting the minister of Chile in Mexico City, Long "was confronted and shot dead by a soldier, as all believed the fired tool of Trespalacios." Indignant over Long's murder, Christy, Milam, and Austin left Mexico City for Monterrey, where they devised a plan to intercept Trespalacios as he was traveling through that city to San Antonio de Béxar. Their plot was discovered, and Trespalacios had the conspirators imprisoned in Saltillo. McHenry and others attempted to rescue the group, but Col. Christy [who had been a member of General Mina's celebrated expedition and had possession of important papers in relation to that as well as Long's] had deposited his papers with a Mexican officer's wife and would not leave without them. The plan was thus frustrated, first by the delay, and then by the prisoners' removal.[25]

The group was sent to a Mexico City prison. Several Americans were in Mexico City at the time, namely General James Wilkinson and others, but according to McHenry, "Wilkinson appeared cold to the unfortunate men, and never visited them."[26] Joel Poinsett, U.S. envoy, was able to obtain the men's release, and they were transported to Tampico. The U.S. naval sloop of war *John Adams* escorted the men to Cuba, where most of them chose to go on to Norfolk, Virginia. Strangely, and according to McHenry, Christy also chose to go to Norfolk, even though his business interests and his wife and family were in New Orleans.

Equally more puzzling is that Orleans parish court records reveal that Christy was in New Orleans by the first of the summer of 1822 and represented his brother, Urriah Christy, in an Orleans parish court case in June. The chronology of McHenry's account lands the released prisoners, including Christy, in Norfolk, Virginia, by December, 1821. This is evidently an error since James Long was not murdered until April, 1822. Historian John Henry Brown corrects the date to December, 1822, which would be more logical in the sequence of events. Poinsett recorded that he secured the freedom of thirty-nine prisoners, half of whom were Americans, on November 11, 1822.[27]

It appears that perhaps Christy was released earlier, possibly through the efforts of General James Wilkinson, a fellow Kentuckian who was also in Mexico City at the time. Even though General Wilkinson reportedly refused to see the prisoners in Mexico City, he could still have privately arranged for Christy's release, after which Christy went to St. Louis to improve his business prospects. While there, Christy wrote to Stephen F. Austin in 1826, recommending a settler for Austin's colony. Christy concluded his letter with "I should be glad to here [sic] from you when convenient, and tell me any thing you know of my old friend Genl Wilkenson."[28] The court records provide conclusive poof that Christy was in New Orleans by June. His distinctive signature on the court records indicates that he acted as counsel for his brother.[29] Either McHenry mistook Christy for another man named of the same name, or Christy was able to somehow obtain his freedom earlier than the rest of the prisoners and returned to New Orleans before Poinsett arranged for the freedom of the others in November, 1822. In the 1820s Christy's brother, Urriah, lived in New Orleans and worked in William's tobacco office.

A biography of William Christy, dated in the 1850s, strangely does not mention Christy's involvement in the Long expedition. The biography, however, appears to be taken from an interview with Christy, which gave him the latitude and discretion to emphasize or deemphasize parts of his past. Christy ran for governor in the mid-1850s, and a glowing image of the "hero of Fort Meigs" is emphasized in the biography. One could argue that the emphasis on Christy's War of 1812 record would certainly have attracted greater political support than the emphasis on his shady dealings as a filibuster and adventurer in his early years. Christy was also charged with irregularities in paymaster accounts in 1816 just before his resignation from the U.S. Army. His quick enlistment into the Xavier Mina expedition might therefore prompt speculation. Was his quick enlistment related to the pay irregularities? Was it motivation to stay out of military prison?

Christy quickly made his way into a business partnership as a tobacco merchant. In the mid-1820s he traveled to St. Louis to improve his connections with the western tobacco states, and while he was away from New Orleans, his partner declared bankruptcy. In 1827 Christy was appointed as a notary public and continued in that position for thirty years (in New Orleans an appointment as notary public was for life).[30] In 1826 he also published a digest of decisions of the Louisiana Supreme Court.[31] Like all notaries of the parish, he was responsible for recording contracts and deed conveyances, and he preserved these records in bound books that would be passed on to his successor. Christy's notarial records include many documents relating to business dealings with Texian and, notably, East Texas businessmen.

Christy also developed a plan to ship Kentucky paving stones to New Orleans. He presented his proposal to the conseil de ville in October, 1830. As an alderman in 1825, Christy had visited Kentucky at the request of the city's paving committee to look into the feasibility of shipping the stones. It is unclear why the proposal was not submitted until 1830, but the conseil de ville evidently hesitated to approve it. Christy then submitted a petition expressing support for his plan by prominent businessmen of the city. In June, 1831, he canceled the contract for unstated reasons and did not pursue the plan again.[32] Christy served on various committees and boards, including that of the New Orleans Gaslight Bank, and became involved in the Nashville and New Orleans Railroad project in 1835. He was a dynamic, energetic man who continued to be an entrepreneur in many new projects and proposals, including a railroad venture in Texas in the late 1830s.

Thomas Banks, owner of the famous Banks's Arcade, came to New Orleans in the early 1820s. He opened a boarding house and, from this initial investment, was able to acquire large holdings of real estate in the American sector by the early 1830s.[33] He commissioned Charles Zimpel to build Banks's Arcade in 1833 as a showcase of his success. Banks was also affiliated with Niven, Caldwell, and Christy on various boards and investments, including the board of the Gaslight Bank.

William (actually Wilhelmus) Bogart originally came to New Orleans from New York in 1815 looking for a better life.[34] He was a bachelor and also a member of many boards of directors for banks and insurance companies.[35] In 1835 he was a partner with Passmore Hoopes of Port Gibson, Mississippi, as commercial merchants. His office was located across the street from Banks's Arcade, on the corner of Natchez and Magazine Streets. As one of the largest shippers of cotton in the 1835 business season, Bogart and Hoopes shipped cotton from the LaFourche interior and Vicksburg.[36]

Bogart was also a land speculator. He sold a large tract of land on Commerce Street to Thomas Banks in 1833 for $45,000. Amazingly, Banks bought the property without any warranty or guarantee of title. In true speculative fashion, Bogart had owned the property before, selling it back to Banks a year later.[37] He also owned land in Jefferson parish. Several of the men on the New Orleans committee had been land speculators in the city's real estate and also had dealings with Texas land agents and speculators such as William G. Logan and Frost Thorn. Banks and Bogart also served on the board of directors of the Mississippi Marine and Fire Insurance Company and the Ocean Insurance Company.[38] Bogart also served on the committee of appeals for the New Orleans chamber of commerce with William L. Hodge in 1835.[39]

William Bryan was born in Duchess county, New York, in 1793. His brother, Joseph Bryan, served in the United States consulship in Brazil in the 1820s. Bryan eventually made his way to New Orleans. James Ramage was cashiered out of the navy in 1831, and in 1833 he wrote Stephen F. Austin expressing an interest in coming to Texas.[40] In April, 1835, Ramage was listed as an inspector of the Louisiana Cotton Seed Oil Factory and Insurance Company, which was incorporated by the state on April 2,1835, with Charles Briggs as president, James H. Caldwell, J. E. Hyde, Thomas Barrett, J. A. Barelli, and H. W. Palfey as board members.[41] By July, Jerome Bayon was questioning the company's practices:

> The stock of the Louisiana cottonseed oil factory and insurance company
> is below par; and certainly cannot account satisfactorily for such a misad-
> venture. It is a matter of surprize [sic] as well as regret. When we know the
> suspicious circumstances under which the company were likely to com-

mence operations; the whole of the stock being taken; the object of the company being likely to realize considerable profit; and the privileges conferred by the charter being of a lucrative nature—for the company are vested with all the privileges of insurance, and many of those of banking: such as trading bills of exchange. Having then the privileges of insurance and brokerage, of a profitable speculation in a patent invention, and all the stock being taken, we fear that there must be some mismanagement of the affairs of the company. Is there so?[42]

James Caldwell, a member of the board, challenged Bayon's accusations, asserting that Bayon had "wantonly" published incorrect information about the company. Two days later, on July 22, Bayon stood by his original assessment. Citing irregularities in the issuance of dividends Bayon stated, "Who has now falsified? Or do we write merely from personal pique towards Mr Caldwell? Does not a discount of 3 percent prove the stock is below par?"[43] In less than a year after its initial incorporation, the Louisiana Cotton Seed Oil Factory and Insurance Company was restructured as the Eagle Insurance Company in March, 1836, and the members of the board of directors remained the same.[44] It is unclear whether Ramage continued to work as an inspector with the new company or went on to some other endeavor.

Caldwell, one of the more prominent business leaders of the American district and also an alderman, was a theatrical developer who built several theaters not only in New Orleans, but also in Cincinnati, Nashville, St. Louis, and Mobile. Born in Manchester, England, in 1793, he came to the United States early in life and quickly became a noted actor. By 1836 he had built two theaters in New Orleans: the Camp Street Theater in 1824 and the St. Charles Theater in 1835. The latter opened only a month after the Texas meetings at Banks's Arcade.[45]

In 1833 Caldwell secured a twenty-five-year contract with the state of Louisiana to install gas lighting in New Orleans. The lighting company, like many improvement projects in Louisiana at the time, was given banking privileges in order to secure capital through investors.[46] The New Orleans Gaslight and Banking Company listed Edward Yorke as its president in October, 1835. The board members were James H. Caldwell, James N. Niven, Thomas Banks, Joshua Baldwin, Samuel Thompson, Thomas C. Cash, J. Berry, and Samuel Hermann Jr., son of Samuel Sr., whose establishment had issued Gómez Farías a three-thousand-peso line of credit upon his arrival in New Orleans in August, 1835. The New Orleans Gas Light Company bought slaves to run the gas lines and install the lamps.[47] In addition to the Gaslight Bank, Caldwell was also the president of the New Orleans and Nashville Railroad.

James Neil Niven was a junior partner of Hagan, Niven, and Company, commercial merchants whose offices were located at 83 Canal Street. Niven was also president pro tem of the Gas Light Bank in October, 1835, and was on the board with Caldwell and Banks.[48] He lived in the prestigious area near Julia Street Row at 137 Julia Street.[49] Niven was also a member of the New Orleans chamber of commerce in 1835.

William L. Hodge, a neighbor of Niven, Gustave Schmidt, and Edward Yorke in the fashionable Julia Street Row, and business partner with his brother, Andrew Hodge Jr., came to New Orleans from Pennsylvania in the mid-1820s with Andrew Sr., their father.[50] The 1830 federal census records show an Andrew Hodge Sr. residing in New Orleans and list with him two sons between thirty and forty years of age. William, whose office was located at 49 Common Street, was a commercial merchant and exporter of goods from Cuba and other parts of the Caribbean.[51] William also dabbled in the cotton trade but declared bankruptcy in 1831. He possibly looked to his older brother for help to reestablish himself in New Orleans as a partner.[52]

While William seemed to have early difficulty forging a successful business career, Andrew Jr. rose to the presidency of the well-established Bank of Orleans by 1830. In 1830 his bank lent New Orleans $100,000 for wharf improvements in the American sector of the city.[53] Andrew Jr. had also developed an interest in land speculation. He made a healthy profit from the sale of property to the New Orleans Construction Company for the Julia Street Row, which became row houses for wealthier residents in the American district.[54] He was also a partner with Nathan A. Ware, another Pennsylvanian who had established himself in the lucrative sugar industry of southern Louisiana. The Hodge brothers and Ware began buying and selling Texas lands in April, 1835.[55] William's membership on the New Orleans committee was definitely a step toward protecting their Texas investments. He was also a member of the committee of appeals for the New Orleans Chamber of Commerce in October, 1835, along with Niven and Bogart.[56]

Writing to Stephen F. Austin on October 20, only one week after the Banks's Arcade meeting, James Ramage, secretary of the New Orleans committee, commented on the men of the committee: "There are men engaged in your cause here, who by their power, wealth and influence can do almost anything—The excitement is still at its height—hundreds of applications are daily making to join the Rank—but we allow only those we choose to muster them."[57] In the same letter Ramage expressed open distrust of the Mexican federalists' presence at the October 13 meeting: "I forgot to mention[.] You will see in the inclosed [sic] paper that Gen Mehia [sic], a man named Fisher and others were at the meeting—we have our doubts—These expeditions are solely, purely, simply American in all their parts."[58]

The city's newspapers reflect the view that Texas should have justifiably been American soil in 1835. It appears early on that the restoration of the Mexican federation, including Texas, was not a part of the agenda of the "big men." In July, 1835, several newspaper editors, including Jerome Bayon of the *Bee* and Putnam Rea of the New Orleans *Commercial Bulletin*, openly echoed their sentiments. Both argued that Texas should have been part of Louisiana as a result of French explorer La Salle's landing in Texas in 1685 and a 1721 French report that claimed that Louisiana extended from the Perdido, between Mobile and Pensacola, to the Rio del Norte (Rio Grande). In actuality, according to Bayon, Texas had been American territory ever since the Louisiana Purchase, and the treaty of 1819 establishing Texas as Spanish territory was unconstitutional. How could the United States give up territory that was theirs in the first place? Bayon maintained.

However, he expressed the concern that many had concerning Texas: "We may therefore reasonably conclude that the treaty of 1819 was unconstitutional, in alienating the acquired purchase or possession of Texas. But how far the unconstitutionality of that alienation can now affect either party to that treaty is a topic of another kind. Spain obtained it in good faith, agreeably to a solemn treaty now in acquiescent existence for 16 years; and its dominion has been estranged from her by a government whose independence we recognized, and integrity secured. The Monroe administration was wrong; but how can we rectify its error?"[59]

Only a week later Bayon shifted the events in Texas to center stage. Reiterating the claim of his July 13 article, he continued his survey of the French-Spanish tug-of-war for Texas. He discussed the diplomatic mission of Louis St. Denis, who established French outposts in Texas in the late 1700s. He pointed out that Texas had been an uninhabited land; therefore St. Denis's incursion into Texas politically established a French presence in Texas. Out of alarm at St. Denis's incursion, Spain set out to reclaim Texas. Bayon maintained, "They could not openly obtain occupancy [of Texas], they [the Spanish] resolved to do so by stratagem." St. Denis was arrested as a smuggler intruding in Spanish territory. Bayon maintained that because of St. Denis's outposts, France had a just claim to Texas and that in turn Texas should have been a part of the Louisiana Purchase.

In a July 20 article and later in September, Bayon maintained that the Texians were "Fully justified in separating from the Mexican consolidated government; and in either declaring their state to be sovereign and independent, or seeking to be admitted as a member of the United States." But as long as the Texians' fight remained a struggle for Mexican statehood and federalism, Americans were not justified in intervening in the conflict. U.S. neutrality laws prohibited involvement in another country's civil war, "[b]ut they [the Texians] still profess to adhere to the Mexican government—which is certainly a drawback on our pretensions to the territory." [60]

This did not mean, however, that individuals could not offer assistance if the Texians declared themselves independent or sought annexation to the United States. No matter what, the U.S. government could not intervene. The Whig-dominated state government in New Orleans sought to suppress the pro-Texas activity, but to no avail. The Mexican consul, Pizarro Martinez, filed a formal complaint with Orleans parish district attorney Henry Carleton concerning the pro-Texas meetings. Carleton assured Pizarro that his government would prosecute any violations of the law, but he needed evidence from Martinez before he could lawfully press charges. Pizarro, in a response that was not altogether clear, pointed out that all he was authorized to do was to report to his own government any violations of the law and that he was unable to cooperate with Carleton. [61] Governor Edward White finally published a proclamation calling on Americans to refrain from involvement in the Texas struggle: "Whereas the United States are now at peace with the neighboring states of Mexico, in which some hostile movements have occurred between the existing government there and a portion of their people, in which contest there has been in the State of Louisiana, some manifestation of interest which might lead not only to an infraction of our laws, but to breach of national faith and honor . . . [n]ow, therefore, I, Edward D. White, Governor of the State of Louisiana, issue this my proclamation, calling upon all magistrates and other officers of justice, and upon all good citizens, to assist in preventing the violation of this law [second section of the act of Congress, April 20, 1818], and in bringing to punishment those who may offend against it." [62]

By the time Governor White had issued his proclamation, more than $7,000 in donations had been raised, and three groups of immigrant volunteers had cleared the port of New Orleans. East Texas land men, American busi-

nessmen in New Orleans, and, to a limited extent, Mexican exiles formed an alliance to wrest Texas away from the fledgling Mexican republic under the nose
of the district attorney and the governor of Louisiana. The goals of the Americans and the federalist Mexican exiles, however, would soon become apparently
different as arrangements for the volunteers' departure were made.

5 § IMMIGRANT SOLDIERS

Many of the men who had volunteered the night before at Banks's Arcade met the next morning at 7:00 A.M. at Customhouse Square. The New Orleans Customhouse had become an eyesore. The yellow-stuccoed building, which represented the commercial center of the city, was surrounded by a motley array of buildings enclosed in a walled compound. In May, 1835, Jerome Bayon complained of the inadequacy of the customhouse for New Orleans and said that not only should the merchants of the city petition Congress for a new customhouse, but also that "Churches, grogshops, customhouse, and all—be demolished; and that the whole square be appropriated for a new customhouse."[1] This was where this band first met to organize themselves into military companies.

Ebenezer S. Heath, who had recently been discharged from Company K, Third U.S. Infantry in July, was probably appointed to instruct the men in the most basic drill movements, since none of them had received arms yet. The infantry drill, ceremony, and the manual of arms of the training manual, *Scott's Infantry Tactics*, was used, and those who had served either in the regular army, in the militia, or in volunteer companies were also familiar with the rigors of the training from its pages. Some of the volunteers were veterans like John Cooke, a British naval gunner. Artillery crews would likely have been formed at this time as well since the New Orleans committee had acquired pieces of artillery to take with them to Texas.[2]

George Fisher wasted no time in being the first to publish an enthusiastic article in the local papers reporting the results of the previous night's meeting. His article provides one of the only abstracts available of the meeting and describes the proceedings, speeches, and the six resolutions that were passed. While the immigrant volunteers were preparing themselves, the New Orleans committee published an announcement. The committee would meet the volunteers at Banks's Arcade on Thursday night, October 15, at six o'clock "for the purpose of taking measures for organizing themselves, preparatory to an immediate departure; arms, and ammunition will be furnished them, and their passage paid as far as Natchitoches." Any additional volunteers who wanted to join could also attend. James N. Niven, William Bryan, William L. Hodge, and William Bogart were all commercial merchants, and the task of equipping these men was not altogether different from what their jobs partly entailed as factors—that of providing and equipping their planter clients. This time, however, their "clients" would require arms, including artillery. Adolphus Sterne, beaming from the sale of twenty-one thousand acres of his advertised Texas lands, purchased fifty muskets and bayonets on October 15 from Hyde and Goodrich, a partnership who advertised not only military equipment, but also jewelry and fine silverware.[3]

Thus the respective military companies were formed during the October 15 meeting at Banks's Arcade. While it is not clear exactly how they were organized, some accounts of the initial meetings indicate that Adolphus Sterne from Nacogdoches offered the first fifty men who volunteered the same muskets he had purchased from Hyde and Goodrich that very day. The October 15 notice by the New Orleans committee also promised that passage would be paid to Natchitoches; it indicated that the first group, Thomas H. Breece's company, which was also sponsored by Sterne, would travel through Nacogdoches via Natchitoches. Thomas Breece was a carriage maker and was listed on the Nacogdoches 1835 census with his wife, Ann Mariah, and his son Joseph.[4] Breece obviously was in New Orleans by mid-October and more than likely had traveled there with Sterne. Breece had sold one league of land to John K. Allen and William G. Logan on September 8 in Nacogdoches, only a month before the meetings in New Orleans. The timing of his land sale coincided remarkably with Sterne's departure to New Orleans. Were the proceeds from the sale meant to cover the cost of his trip to New Orleans with Sterne, or were the proceeds for his family? If Breece did go to New Orleans with Sterne, what were his plans and intentions for going in the first place? Breece is not mentioned in any of the proceedings of the Nacogdoches Committee of Safety minutes as being commissioned to go to New Orleans. Breece quickly became the recognized leader of Sterne's company.

In addition to Breece, records from the New Orleans notarial archives reveal that Albert Emanuel, another Nacogdoches resident, arrived with Sterne and Breece. José María Caravajal, a Tejano, was also in New Orleans. In 1823 he had been sent to Kentucky, where he was apprenticed to Littlebury Hawkins, a tanner. He also attended college in Bethany, Virginia, near Wheeling, where he was converted to Protestantism. Caravajal had also spent some time in New Orleans, where he became friends with Nathaniel Cox.[5] He eventually returned to Texas and became a surveyor for Martín DeLeón's colony. He was elected deputy from San Antonio de Béxar in February, 1835, to the Coahuila y Texas legislature and was appointed the secretary of that chamber just before the legislature approved the controversial sale of the four hundred leagues of Texas land to a handful of speculators. Caravajal left Monclova after a warrant was issued for his arrest in July. He was wanted for his support in the land sales and was also accused of inciting revolution.[6]

Caravajal had slipped away into Texas, where he stayed in seclusion. On October 9, he was listed as a member of Captain George M. Collingsworth's men from Victoria, but he probably did not participate in the capture of Goliad on October 10.[7] At about this same time Caravajal, Fernando de León (the son of Martín DeLeón), and Peter Kerr traveled to New Orleans to raise money for supplies and war materiel. New Orleans notarial records indicate that Caravajal sold Red River lands to a widow—Betsy Cohen Kokernot—and her son for $1,000.[8]

Caravajal appointed his old friend Nathaniel Cox as his power of attorney to sell choice Texas lands located along the Red and Trinity Rivers to prospective clients in New Orleans. One can only speculate from which funds the supplies were purchased. Was it from the proceeds of the sale of these lands? No notarial record exists to confirm that the land was exchanged or sold for the supplies. The fact that Cox had Caravajal's power of attorney to sell his lands suggests that Cox may have accepted promissory notes from Caravajal using the land as collateral.[9]

A few days before Caravajal, Kerr, and DeLeón returned on the schooner *Hannah Elizabeth* for Texas, the famous Reverend Theodore Clapp appointed Caravajal, with his power of attorney, to buy the minister a league of choice land "situate[d] in any part of the country by the name of Texas, in the said republic of Mexico."[10] The power of attorney does not indicate whether Clapp gave Caravajal any money to fulfill the commission, but when the three men from Victoria left New Orleans, they had purchased $35,000 worth of supplies and armament for the Texian army.[11]

Before he left New Orleans, Caravajal entrusted Cox with the sale of several selected tracts of Texas land. He, DeLeón, and Kerr escorted the supplies on the schooner *Hannah Elizabeth* on November 17. Two nights later, a Mexican patrol ship near Matagorda ran the *Hannah Elizabeth* aground. The Mexican crew captured Caravajal and DeLeón, and their cargo fell into the hands of citizens in Matagorda.[12]

On October 16 the *Bee* published a notice for another meeting for Texas to be held at the Free Port Hotel in the lower faubourg.[13] No time was announced for the meeting, and Jerome Bayon did not publish an abstract of the proceedings afterward as he had for the one at Banks's Arcade. James Ramage mentioned the lower faubourg meeting to Stephen F. Austin on October 21: "The creoles of the lower faubourg not to be outdone by us, have I am truly informed raised a corps of 150 men at their expense." It is likely that the 150 men Ramage referred to were men for General Mexía's expedition. He maintained that the efforts of the Banks's Arcade meeting were purely American, and the efforts of the creoles of the "lower faubourg" meeting were relegated to a lesser importance. Once again the ethnic strife between the two districts of the city segregated any attempts at a unified campaign for the Texians and Mexican federalists.[14]

On October 20 William Christy and James Ramage forwarded a letter to the officers of the Texas provisional government. It was already known that a consultation had been called to meet in San Felipe de Austin, and the visiting Texians such as Adolphus Sterne had probably briefed the committee on efforts to gather the representatives of the various municipalities to form a unified response to the Texas crisis. Some of the members of both companies had secured letters of introduction to accompany them to Texas. Sydney S. Callender, a young publisher, joined Morris's Greys. L. R. Kinney, an old acquaintance of Stephen F. Austin, who had commanded militia against the Fredonian rebellion in 1826, wrote a letter on Callender's behalf.[15] He stated that "The Bearer [Callender] . . . is one of the Young men who have volunteered to aid the people of Texas in defending their rights—He is a practical printer and was for sometime Editor of the Lafayette Gazette—Sympathizing in your Cause he has determined to make Texas his adopted Country and to fight in her defence."[16]

While Breece's company was scheduled to go through Nacogdoches, the other group of volunteers was scheduled to travel by way of the Gulf of Mexico. The committee in New Orleans appointed Edward Hall to escort the other company to Texas.[17] Not much is known about Edward Hall. In 1835 he was William Bryan's business partner in what Hall called the "Texas business". In 1850 Hall wrote about his involvement with Bryan and the early days of their participation in the war in Texas. Hall had been sent to Texas in 1835 to handle business for their partnership when he heard that Stephen F. Austin had been released from prison and that war was inevitable. He hurried back to New Orleans in time to be appointed agent of the New Orleans committee to the provisional government of Texas. He was appointed as "Inspector of cannon, arms, and other military stores," and he was called on to inspect ordnance and military stores purchased in New Orleans for the Texian army.[18]

Colonel William Christy, engraving, circa 1850. Courtesy of the Center for American History, University of Texas at Austin.

As word circulated throughout the city concerning the meeting for Texas, donations came into Christy's office at Banks's Arcade. By early November, Hall, upon his arrival in San Felipe de Austin, reported that $7,000 had already been raised and that more had probably been donated since his departure from New Orleans. His notarial office at Banks's Arcade became a beehive of activity as persons interested in Texas continued to come there. W. G. Latham, a clerk in Christy's office, kept a daily memorandum of those who came to Christy's office to sign up as volunteers or to donate supplies or goods. After Latham showed the lists to Christy, they were copied and then were destroyed at the end of the day. Christy kept a book for enlistments and one for donations. The enlistment book was used to record the names of those who offered their services as immigrant volunteers. The donation book, titled "Dr. William Christy, treasurer, in account with the Texian emigrants, Cr.," provided a detailed record of donors and the amounts or supplies they contributed. The volunteers who signed up after the Greys left later formed into another company associated with General Mexía's planned Tampico expedition, which had been discussed in the amphictyonic meetings the previous month at 103 Ursulines.[19]

Businessmen like J. W. Swain, a New Orleans druggist, gave a donation that prompted a published word of thanks from the volunteers upon their departure from the city. Several fledgling apothecary merchants joined the volunteers. In 1835 Francis Lubbock, a future governor of Texas, was in the apothecary business in New Orleans and was a good friend of both William G. Cooke and Robert Morris, who were also in the same business. Another young apothecary merchant, Vincent A. Drouillard, a nephew of William Christy's wife, had already experienced the embarrassment of bankruptcy in August with his business. Cooke spoke for many of the men, such as Drouillard, when he stated, "I saw that it was an opportunity for the enterprising to better their fortunes, and immediately stepped forward and enrolled my name." Francis Lubbock's younger brother, Thomas, who had joined the volunteers, was an energetic youth, "well up in all manly sports, quite an athlete, very strong and muscular, and full of fire and determination," and little could be done to convince him to stay in New Orleans. Older brother Francis "fitted him out, and bade him godspeed," acknowledging that their family in South Carolina would "censure" him for submitting to the arrangement. Francis was greatly disappointed in his brother's decision to join the volunteers since he had arranged to get Thomas a job with a Mr. Holmes in the cotton business in New Orleans.[20]

Moses Albert Levy, a Virginia physician, had lost his wife after she gave birth to their daughter Rachel and, brokenhearted and grieving, left for places that helped him forget his loss. He arrived in New Orleans in 1835 and joined Morris's Greys as the company's chief surgeon.[21]

Little is known about Robert Morris, one of the Greys' future commanders. Archibald Hotchkiss of San Augustine wrote to Sam Houston, recommending Morris to the general. Because Robert was an old friend and a relative, Hotchkiss attested that Morris was "a young man of firmness and a man that will not disgrace the grays."[22] J. W. Collins of New Orleans also sent a letter of introduction to Stephen F. Austin for Morris and recommended him as a "Soldier & Tactician."[23] Collins had served in a New Orleans militia unit, the Louisiana Guards, with Morris for five or six years.

Soon after the Banks's Arcade meeting, New Orleans district attorney Henry Carleton also came to see Christy about Christy's involvement with Texas. Carleton examined Christy's donation and volunteer books. After looking at them, Carleton stated that he could not charge him with filibustering, but he warned Christy that he would prosecute any movements of organizing troops for Texas as a violation of U.S. neutrality laws, and he warned Christy that he was keeping a close eye on his pro-Texas activities. Christy assured Carleton that he was simply trying to aid the besieged Texians and that he would do nothing to violate the law. Carleton informed U.S. Secretary of State John Forsyth on October 21 that he had already visited Christy's office.[24] Carleton wrote, "There can be no doubt that certain persons intend to proceed thither, to act in concert with the Texans, should an occasion present itself. Yet, when the matter is more narrowly investigated, it is difficult to apply to them the provisions of the second or sixth sections of the act of the 20th April, 1818; for it does not appear that any regular enlisting or entering as soldiers has taken place within the meaning of the statute, or that any definite or tangible military expedition or enterprise has been set on foot or begun."[25]

Carleton and Christy had known each other for years. Carleton had represented his brother-in-law Edward Livingston, one of Louisiana's prominent political leaders, in a lawsuit initiated by Christy in 1830. Christy won a judgment for $2,704 against Livingston for nonpayment of a debt. Unlike their predecessors, this committee seemed to be keenly aware of the ramifications of the label of "filibuster," especially since a Whig governor, who was opposed to any military movements, was probably keeping a close watch on events. Instead of calling the volunteers "soldiers," Ramage and Christy referred to them as "emigrants," carefully walking the proverbial tightrope to avoid an appearance of filibustering. The "emigrants," according to Lubbock, already knew who their leaders were before leaving New Orleans. Both Robert Morris and William Gordan Cooke were unofficially recognized as the leaders of the company going to Brazoria. Thomas Breece was recognized as the leader of the company going through Nacogdoches.[26]

Later in the day, "express wagons," possibly drays, were sent throughout the city to obtain donations of arms for the men. Ambrose Fulton recounts that many veterans of the Battle of New Orleans sorrowfully gave up rifles for the Texian cause that they had used in that eventful 1815 combat. Hermann Ehrenberg stated that the men from his company sought out durable clothing "suitable for the prairie" for the arduous campaign. Ebenezer S. Heath, the U.S. Army veteran and a member of Morris's company, wrote to his mother later in March, 1836, that his company had obtained suits consisting of a gray jacket and pants, and with the suit, many had obtained a sealskin cap.[27]

Herman Ehrenberg provides the clearest account of the procurement of uniforms. He recalls that "We all quickly purchased ourselves clothing, grey in color, suitable for life in the prairies, which we found ready made in the numerous stores, [the color] from which the name of our company was derived."[28] A claim by Private John Beldon of Morris's (Cooke's) Volunteer Greys in December, 1835, reveals that he had purchased a "uniform suit" in New Orleans costing $18.00, along with "a cloak taken from camp" for $15.00, and a blue cloth coat for $8.00. Beldon's dirk and pistol, costing $15.00, a small sword (broken) for $5.00, and a blanket for $3.00 were all evidently lost when Beldon was wounded in the taking of San Antonio de Béxar in December. 1835. In the coming months, the Texian government ordered various kinds of clothing, similar in description to Beldon's, from the New Orleans market, including cotton shirts, vests, roundabout jackets, and even red flannel shirts, "all to be of a cheap & durable texture," for the Texian Army. By March, 1836, much of their original "prairie clothes" were in tatters, and many resorted to wearing whatever they could find. William L. Hunter, another member of Morris's Greys, was described wearing a calico or gingham shirt, coat, and hunting shirt.[29]

Ehrenberg survived both the Battle of San Antonio de Béxar in December, 1835, and the Goliad massacre in March, 1836. Seven years later in Leipzig, he wrote his memoirs relating his experiences in Texas. In 1846 an abridged English translation and review that included Ehrenberg's description of their clothing were published in *Blackwood's Edinburgh Magazine* and eventually in *Little's Living Age*. The Greys, according to the English translation, "ransacked the tailor's shops for gray clothing such being the color best suited to the prairie, and thence they received the name of "the Greys."[30] Reuben Marmaduke Potter, a retired U.S. Army officer who was living in Matamoros during the Texas revolution, had interviewed Texian prisoners when they were marched into Matamoros with the retreating Mexican army. He remarked to artist Henry McArdle in 1874 that "There were probably no uniforms among the defenders of the Alamo, though, as there was among them a remnant of the New Orleans Greys, there were possible in the garrison a few specimens of the dress of that company, . . . It would be a just commemoration to idealize one or more soiled figures in plain grey jackets, trousers, and forage caps."[31]

Men who were not personally sponsored, such as Thomas Lubbock, were issued rifles, pistols, Bowie knives, and in some cases swords by the New Orleans committee. Most were also issued knapsacks, cloaks, and canteens. Many of the men in Breece's company received the fifty muskets and bayonets from Hyde and Goodrich, along with an array of other weapons. While much of the men's clothing consisted of ready-made durable civilian clothing, probably much of the weaponry was also bought from suppliers or merchants, such as Barbarin and Hill, Groning and Company, and Hyde and Goodrich, who sold to local militias; supplies were also donated by private citizens. In New Orleans one of the largest centers of militia companies in the South, advertisements for military supplies and militia insignia were commonplace in the local newspapers. Enough of the Greys in Breece's company were uniform in appearance in their civilian suits for Cherokee Chief Bowles in Nacogdoches to ask Adolphus Sterne "if they were Jackson's men."[32]

Adolphus Sterne secured passage with Captain Reed of the steamboat *Ouachita*, which had just arrived from Natchitoches on October 13 with 773 bales of cotton. Built in Cincinnati in 1834, the *Ouachita* had a carrying capacity of ninety-six tons and was owned by Thomas C. Cash, also a board member of the New Orleans Gaslight and Banking Company along with Niven, Banks, and Caldwell. The *Ouachita* continued in the Red River shipping and packet service until its sale in 1836 to satisfy a debt of Samuel Thompson. Edward Hall and William Bryan secured the *Columbus*, an eighty-ton schooner for Morris's Greys. Captain Leidersdorf of the *Columbus* was scheduled to depart for Brazoria on October 18. The schooner did not clear the port, however, until October 20. The New Orleans *Price-Current and Commercial Intelligencer* listed the cargo of the *Columbus* as dry goods, groceries, and provisions.[33]

Armed with fifty muskets and bayonets provided by Adolphus Sterne and with rifles and other arms, Breece's company departed on the *Ouachita* on October 17, only to be disabled by the breaking of her main shaft. Sterne flagged down a steam packet, the *Bayou Sarah*, to return to New Orleans for assistance. Sterne hired the *Romeo*, another Red River steamer, to tow the *Ouachita* back to New Orleans. She was taken back to a dock in the American district, and after extensive repairs to her, the anxious group finally got under way again two days later, on October 19. In addition to the fifty-five men of Breece's company, there were also two six-pound cannons mounted on small carriages. Sterne at this point decided to travel on ahead of the company (probably on the *Romeo*) to Natchitoches, where he would wait for the Greys to arrive.[34]

Charles Bannister, the cooper from Magazine Street, described the mood of the men in Morris's group as festive when they departed New Orleans. The schooner and its cargo waited across the Mississippi at Algiers, possibly for precautionary reasons. All on board received instruction on and drill in the use of the grappling hooks that Ambrose Fulton had provided in case Mexican patrol ships approached the *Columbus*.[35]

Hermann Ehrenberg recalls the sporting mood on board the *Ouachita*. The men tried out their new rifles on the alligators of the river. He stated that the volunteers preferred the rifles to Sterne's muskets. The musket was such a "contemptible weapon in the eyes of the volunteers" that the person who carried one inherited the same contempt as the weapon, which was "fit only for hirelings [mercenaries]."[36]

Ehrenberg provides one of the only accounts of Breece's departure and travels to Texas. With the newspapers of the area providing sporadic coverage of their travels through Louisiana, a picture unfolds of anxious, young, and energetic volunteers being heralded as heroes even before they arrived at the scene of war. As Breece's company traveled from one town to the next, the quartermaster of the company was given the dubious task of procuring a bivouac location and food and water for the men. If the quartermaster failed, according to Ehrenberg, he was removed, and another man was put in his place. Ehrenberg's opinion of Breece and Cooke was different, however. He spoke very highly of the carriage maker from Nacogdoches and the apothecary merchant from Virginia: "But I must say that we were never obliged to dispose our captains, as Captain [Thomas H.] Breece of our company and Captain [William G.] Cooke of the other company of Greys knew how to command respect, and the latter particularly was well liked."[37]

In Alexandria, Louisiana, the company acquired a new recruit, Nicholas Kelly. An old acquaintance of Stephen F. Austin, Thomas Hooper sponsored Kelly by providing him with "a uniform[,] a good rifle[,] 25 lb of good powder[,] and as much lead as he could carry—Blanket Butcher Knife &...."[38] Not only did Hooper sponsor the young man, he also attempted to secure eighty stands of arms in the care of Captain R. Anderson of Alexandria. Captain Anderson, who was a local militia commander, told Hooper he would turn over the arms if Hooper could raise a company and receive an officer's commission. "He also agreed that if he does not raise the company, that he will let me have the arms to send on by my becoming responsible to the United States for them and to stand between him and all damage[.] I told him I would do so. I will have to borrow them as he cannot sell."[39]

The New Orleans committee sent the specifics of the meeting at Banks's

Arcade to the Texian provisional leaders, who were meeting at San Felipe. Hall went on with Morris's Greys with money and provisions. Morris's group was given three-months provisions while, according to Hall, "The Fifty men [Breece's company] sent to Nacogdoches were furnished with Arms & Equipment only, trusting to the inhabitants of the Country through which they will pass for further necessary supplies."[40]

Breece's Greys arrived in Natchitoches on October 30, only ten days after leaving New Orleans. There the company received a hero's welcome as in many places along their journey. Adolphus Sterne was also waiting for them. The next day D. H. Vail of Natchitoches wrote of the Greys' arrival and of the support of and reaction from the Mexican consul:

> On yesterday we started a subscription, through the politeness of L. R. Linn Esqr. And have received about $800 in different articles. . . . The french [sic] population have held back and were quite cool until to day. Some of the leading characters have come out & subscribed liberally, and I believe all will eventually come out and assist, the company, from N. O. left to day at 12 o clk, But have left the P. Master and 7 men to guard the baggage waggons [sic]. I have sent them out this evening $100, in Blankets, clothing and provisions &c. Mr. Stern is consigning his men to the Mexican consul at this place. But the consul has torn down his signe [sic] and Stamped it under foot, and says he is with the people. The waggons [sic] have just arrived this evening at 8 o'clock. I shall load them with arms and baggage, of camp. No. 1 Texas volunteers and fill up the balance of the load with sundries.[41]

For Breece's men at Natchitoches, the trek became much more arduous at this point. Starting on foot, they faced an immediate challenge. As they traveled across the Camino Real into Texas, they had to circumvent Fort Jesup, a U.S. Army post. Citizens in Natchitoches warned them that they would be stopped if they were discovered marching into Texas. Quietly they made their way to the ferry crossing at the Sabine River. There were those, however, who knew of their arrival. Ehrenberg recalled that when Captain Breece's men set foot on Texian soil, a group of ladies was waiting to present a beautiful, blue silk flag to the company. An eagle with a banner in its beak heralding the motto "God and Liberty" was emblazoned on the flag. It was specially made for them, with the title "First Company of Texan Volunteers from New Orleans" neatly centered above and below the eagle. The men knelt down and kissed the soil of Texas and took the oath of citizenship. Captain Breece graciously accepted it on behalf of the company. The flag gained a much greater significance in March, 1836, as the only reported flag of the Texian garrison taken from the Alamo.[42]

Morris's company arrived off the coast of Texas on October 25 in the early evening with no apparent incidents from Mexican patrol ships. Fortunately, the grappling hooks that Ambrose Fulton made for the trip did not have to be used. With the exception of a few possible cases of seasickness, the schooner *Columbus* eventually made an uneventful arrival off the coast of Texas. Velasco and Quintana, which were nothing more than a few houses straddling the mouth of the Brazos River on the Gulf coast, were the destinations, and upon their arrival, the men of Morris's company officially elected their officers. Robert Morris was elected captain; William G. Cooke, first lieutenant; Charles Bannister, second lieutenant; Nathaniel Brister, first sergeant; Ebenezer S. Heath, second sergeant; George Stephens, third sergeant; Edwin Wrentmore, fourth sergeant; and Robert Ross, first corporal. Judge Edmund Andrews swore the men in as citizens, and a certificate was issued to each man attesting to his oath as an immigrant entering a new country. A roster was prepared and sent to General Houston by adjutant and first lieutenant William G. Cooke.

The tedious unloading of the cargo from the *Columbus* seemed to take longer than expected due to the men's anxious enthusiasm. A smaller steamboat took the men and their cargo up the shallow Brazos River to Brazoria, where its citizens greeted them as heroes. Mrs. Jane Long, widow of the filibuster Dr. James Long, welcomed them with expectant nostalgia, and a young Georgian who had just arrived in Brazoria, Mirabeau Bounaparte Lamar, who had been in Texas for a short time himself, spoke to the men and the banquet hosts: "Flowers were strewn at their feet; and their presence was welcomed by an address, better intended than executed, whilst the smiles of beauty and the cheers all imparted pleasure and animation to the whole scene."[43]

The arrival of Breece's men was long anticipated in Nacogdoches by Adolphus Sterne, who had gone ahead of the Greys to prepare for their arrival. On November 4, they arrived in the hamlet of San Augustine, about twenty-five miles from Nacogdoches. They waited there for two days for their wagons catch up with the band.[44] The Greys finally arrived in the outer edges of Nacogdoches with much of the company scattered out over several miles of the Camino Real. Finally, Breece, who had resided in the area, led his weary and disoriented men to Sterne's white frame house. Sterne greeted them warmly and welcomed them with a sumptuous meal with German wines from his cellar.

Though many were tired from the march, some went into Nacogdoches to visit a local coffeehouse with Sterne.[45]

The next day the Greys were treated to a banquet hosted by many of the citizens. Along with raccoons, squirrels, turkeys, and the hindquarters and the backbone of oxen, the centerpiece of the table was a large Texas black bear with a Mexican tricolor flag of the constitution of 1824 gripped in its teeth. Henry Reug, the political chief of the department of Nacogdoches, reported to Thomas Rusk that the local Tejanos were hesitant in supporting the war effort. Reug held a meeting with many of them, and some of the wealthier Tejano citizens "furnished horses and money for the equipmt [sic] of the N. Orleans company, and in order to have some benefit of them I have ordered a permanent guard of 25 men of them, for the protection of the families and properties of those who are absent, and keep up the order at home."[46] George A. Nixon wrote the president of the council of Texas that the citizens of both San Augustine and Nacogdoches "had provided the Volunteers from N. Orleans and San Augustin [sic] with necessary supplies by private subscription, . . . it must evidently appear to You that a great burden has devolved on this place, as we have already subscribed upwords [sic] of Ten Thousand dollars and are daily pledging ourselves and property for the purchase of Horses and other necessary supplies. The President of this Committee has been obliged to advance money and pledge his own credit to obtain Horses."[47]

Becoming a mounted company with the donation of horses from leading Tejanos and other citizens in Nacogdoches, Breece's men were able to travel more rapidly although still anxiously. The men made their way along the road to the rough-hewn settlement of Washington-on-the-Brazos, where some of their firearms were repaired; while waiting, the men visited the saloon and billiard hall of the frontier village. From Washington-on-the-Brazos the Greys arrived late in the evening in Bastrop to another large reception and a bonfire in the streets.

Thomas F. McKinney, of the prestigious mercantile firm McKinney and Williams, reported that Morris's Greys were in Columbia on October 28, only three days after their arrival in Texas. McKinney stated that the volunteers took a circular sent to him from the provisional government of Texas and that he was not able to get it back before they left. They marched on to Victoria, where they received another exuberant welcome from notables of the settlement. When they arrived in Goliad, they reported to Captain Philip Dimmit, commander of the garrison, and got their first taste of military duty. Dimmitt ordered Captain

Morris along with five other men to serve as an escort into Goliad for Governor Viesca, James Grant, Ewen Cameron, and Colonel Gonzales. When the fugitive governor Augustín Viesca arrived at La Bahía, the men entered a tempestuous scene. A mutiny nearly ensued over how the governor should be received. When Captain Dimmitt refused to welcome Viesca as the acting governor of Coahuila y Texas, some of his command were incensed at this treatment of Viesca. The scene ended with Dimmitt declaring martial law in the area to reestablish order. Dimmitt also pressed into service forty or fifty horses from a local Tejano rancher, Bartolo Pajas, for Morris's men. Some of the men, according to Dimmitt, were still without mounts as they left for Béxar. This was in stark contrast with the scene in Nacogdoches, where leading Tejanos voluntarily donated horses to Breece's Greys.[48]

By the end of November, approximately a month and a week after they had left New Orleans, Breece's and Morris's volunteers reported to General Stephen F. Austin at his Texian militia camp north of San Antonio de Béxar. Austin's entry on the day of Morris's arrival was simply, "Nov 22d, 1835. The company of volunteers from New Orleans commanded by Capt. Morris joined the Army on the 21st in the afternoon and the Capt. Reported his company ready for duty, this day."[49] The two companies, consisting of 120 men, with at least three cannons and a large supply of arms and other materiel reported none too soon. The Texian Army was wasting away from the frustrating indecision of its commanders regarding an attack upon General Martín Perfecto de Cós and the Mexican garrison in San Antonio de Béxar.

6 § DISASTER AT TAMPICO

General José Antonio Mexía had watched anxiously while his own plans of invading Tampico were overshadowed by the organizing and equipping of the New Orleans volunteers.[1] Mexía's and Fisher's appearance at the Banks's Arcade meeting on October 13 earned merely a footnote in New Orleans committee secretary James Ramage's letter to Stephen F. Austin on October 21. Yet, Ramage's excited letter seems to express support for the federalist cause: "It is with feelings of indescribable emotion, that all here, wait with intense anxiety for news from your Quarter—What have the division that went after Coss [sic] done? Where is Col. Austin? Have they declared a provisional Govt adhering to the Constitution of 1824???—Upon this last—'hangs all the Law and the Prophets[.]' Cos must be checked."[2]

Even though Ramage's letter appears to be profederalist, it also reveals distrust toward the exiled Mexican federalists in New Orleans. Ramage makes it clear that any support efforts made by the city's Creoles and the exiled Mexican federalists, Mexía and Fisher, at least, are not to be trusted. On October 20, the day before Ramage's letter to Austin, William Christy, the committee's chair, also wrote a letter reflecting a supportive position toward Mexía and his planned invasion, but his support was conditional as to how Mexía's invasion would serve the Texian cause, not the other way around. After informing the provisional government of the departure of the Greys, Christy added that,

> A Vessel, well armed, furnished and manned by about one hundred and fifty efficient emigrants, will sail for Tampico, under the command of General Mexía in about a week:—with such acquisitions to your present force and resources, we trust that matters will be brought to a speedy and glorious termination. God be with you—
>
> Wm Christy
> Jas Ramage   Acting Committee[3]

From the tone of Christy's letter, Mexía's invasion plan was indeed inclusive to the committee's efforts. Even Adolphus Sterne, who had arrived back in Nacogdoches in November, had relayed to Judge Henry Rueg that "Genl. Mejia was to start from N. Orleans in a very short time with 150 men to make an attack on Matamoros or Tampico having a combined plan with the most influential men of the State, having the governor [Viesca?] at their head."[4] Correspondence from Mexía, Gómez Farías, and court testimony in Christy's 1836 filibustering trial reflects, however, that Ramage's confidential expression of distrust and exclusiveness toward them would reveal itself in various forms, initially in a lack of financial support for the Tampico invasion from the New Orleans committee.

Mexía visited Christy at his notarial office at Banks's Arcade in the weeks after the public meeting there. William G. Latham, one of Christy's clerks, testified in 1836 that Mexía "called upon Mr. Christy as chairman of the Texian committee, to see if the committee could give him any pecuniary or other assistance." Christy informed Mexía that his duties as chair had ceased and that the committee had expended more for the Greys than had been donated. Mexía then asked Christy if he would influence some of Christy's friends in the city to help him. Christy bluntly responded "that he could not, that he had been already injured by his exertions in the cause of Texas."[5]

James H. Caldwell, chair of the corresponding committee and general member of the New Orleans committee, testified in February, 1836, that he overheard Mexía at the Banks's Arcade meeting on October 13 state that he already had means of his own for his expedition and that "[he] had come to New Orleans already prepared with means." Caldwell also claimed that the New Orleans committee did not provide Mexía with any money and that several who were involved with the committee's work believed that Mexía's expedition was a foolish plan.[6]

It is unclear how much influence the amphictyonic council continued to have after the American committee was formed. The public meeting at Banks's Arcade and the takeover of pro-Texian efforts by the New Orleans committee apparently nullified any initial plans made with the Louisiana capitalists between Mexía and Gómez Farías in September. Mexía and the exiled federalists were, for all intents and purposes, on their own in financing the Tampico invasion after the meeting at Banks's Arcade. Gómez Farías sanctioned Mexía to seek out loans to be pledged on the "credit of the nation," which would be paid "as soon as the federal government is reorganized, or before, if [Mexía could] find [himself] in a position to do so and the needs of war."[7] An 1840s' anonymous account titled "The Anecdotes of Santa Anna" states that Christy had secured volunteers for the invasion, but "The expenses were furnished by Mexía alone and his friend Colonel Peraza." Despite the refusal or inability of the New Orleans committee to finance the expedition, Gómez Farías still believed as late as November 7 that the Texians wanted to maintain the Mexican federation. Evidently, the lack of financial support from the committee had not affected Gómez Farías's view of Texian sincerity toward remaining a part of Mexico.[8]

Strategically, the plan to capture Tampico was meant to take one of the major ports from which General Cós received supplies and thus cut off his access to the monetary resources of the Tampico customs house. Matamoros was also a target for capture, and with the taking of both ports, the Texians would proclaim Gómez Farías as "the legitimate and constitutional Vice-President of the Mexican federation." It was also meant to take attention away from the revolt in Texas.[9] The Mexican federalists themselves were hoping the invasion would provoke an uprising of the northern Mexican states. George Fisher wrote to Stephen F. Austin on October 20 that the resistance in Texas against centralism was the lynch pin for further opposition throughout the rest of Mexico and that other states were beginning to object to Santa Anna's government. Fisher also revealed that some of the northern Mexican states were beginning to push for a complete separation from Mexico: "Tamaulipas, with the [lieutenant g]overnor Dⁿ Vital Fernandez is decidedly in favor not only of the Federation, as a measure to act in concert with Texas, Coahuila, Nuevo Leon & but even, for an intire [sic] separation of the northern Confederated States from Mexico. viz. From Rio Pánuco, drawing a line to San Blas on the Pacific Ocean,—This grand project has the warmest wishes and best desires of all the proprietors of Matamoros and Tampico, and of the w[hole] estados internos de Oriente and Occidente, Chihuahua y Nuevo Mexico."[10]

Austin actually supported an expedition against Matamoros. Writing to the provisional government only two days before the Tampico expedition departed from New Orleans, he said that "Nothing will aid Texas so much as an expedition from N. Orleans against Matamoros under Gen'l Mexia. It is all important. . . . If matamoros [sic] is attacked and revolutionized by Mexia, Bexar would fall as a matter of course, for all supplies of funds or Troops would be cut off . . . —even a rumor of such a thing would keep troops from being sent to Texas." George Robertson, American consul from Tampico, had also arrived in New Orleans, and he too offered support for the invasion and vital information on the status of the port to Mexía and Fisher.[11]

Those who continued to volunteer at Christy's office after the Greys had departed for Texas were relegated to join Mexía. It is likely that the pro-Texas meeting in the Creole lower faubourg on October 16 contributed at least some volunteers for the invasion. Mexía's expedition attracted Creoles, and a French company, the Company of Liberty, was organized as a part of his forces. Mexía also tried to "procure the liberty" of the crew of the infamous Captain Thomas Thompson, who had been arrested and was being held in New Orleans for piracy. It is unknown whether Mexía was ever able to secure their release. He sought out Mexican deserters from Colonel Piedras's battalion, originally garrisoned at Nacogdoches, and also included the soldiers who came with federalist Martín Peraza from Tampico. The intent of mixing the deserters and sailors with the crew and volunteers from New Orleans, according to Fisher, was to "give some colour of nationality, and not to appear entirely a foreign invasion."

John M. Allen joined the expedition only a few days before its departure. He was a native of Kentucky and an old friend of Christy's. He had also served in the U.S. Navy and in Greece in the 1820s. Allen was eventually elected as one of the captains of the expedition after it left the jurisdiction of the United States. He testified that Christy tried to discourage him from going, stating that "there were an abundance of men who wished to go, who had no particular business or occupation to keep them at home." Christy, in fact, reportedly spoke to the whole expedition two to three days before their departure and urged anyone who had a job to stay.[12]

Colonel Martín Peraza, former commandant of the Pueblo Viejo battalion, had arrived in New Orleans as an exile and quickly became Mexía's trusted second-in-command. The commissioners who were secretly sent to Tampico to infiltrate the garrison may have been officers from Peraza's command who had accompanied him to New Orleans.[13]

George Fisher wasted no time in creating for himself a key role in the preparations for the invasion. He was appointed secretary of the expedition and as such was given the rank of lieutenant colonel. A native of Hungary, Fisher had attended college in Carlowitz, now in Serbia, with the goal of entering the priesthood of the Greek Orthodox church. Fisher, "who became wearied with the monotony of student-life, and feeling a decided repugnance to taking orders," joined the forces of George Petrovich during the first Serbian uprising against the Turks. He and the rest of Petrovich's forces fled across the Danube when the Turks captured Belgrade in 1813. The Austrians sponsored the organization of the Slavonian legion to relieve their country of Serbian revolutionaries during the latter days of the Napoleonic wars. Fisher joined the legion, campaigning in Italy. The legion eventually was disbanded, leaving him with

George Fisher, lithograph. Date unknown. Courtesy of the Masonic Grand Lodge and Museum of Texas, Waco.

nothing else to do than to wander through Europe. He ended up in Amsterdam and boarded a ship bound for the United States, eventually arriving in Philadelphia in 1815. There he adopted his new American name, "Fisher."[14]

Fisher married and made his home in Mississippi. In 1825 he also traveled to Mexico City, where he met U.S. ambassador Joel Poinsett and became Poinsett's editor and compiler for the ambassador's book on Mexico. Fisher, also with Poinsett's influence, became actively involved in the newly formed York Rite lodges in Mexico City. When Poinsett was recalled, Fisher departed with Poinsett on the ambassador's last official voyage from Mexico to New Orleans.[15]

Fisher was eventually appointed collector of customs at Galveston, at which he served intermittently from 1830 to 1832. He became a controversial and volatile figure, seizing the schooner *Cañon* with its contraband goods in 1830, just before word came that the customs house at Galveston would be closed. The ayuntamiento of San Felipe de Austin publicly attacked Fisher in the *Texas Gazette* for the seizure. General Manuel Miér y Terán, general and inspector of the eastern internal states, issued a letter of support for Fisher's actions and by 1831 had reinstated Fisher as collector of customs at Galveston.

Fisher irritated conditions again by imposing unreasonable customs requirements on schooners that traded with merchants at the mouth of the Brazos River at Quintana and Velasco. Stephen F. Austin wrote Terán requesting Fisher's removal, and in 1832 Fisher was dismissed and the customs house was moved to Brazoria. One account offers another view: that Fisher clashed with Colonel Juan Bradburn over the seizure of goods from several American schooners and was forced to back down when Bradburn won the support of local citizens. Fisher, "[f]inding himself extremely obnoxious to the people and bullied by Bradburn, le[f]t the place & country in the schooner *Exert* for Matamoros." Fisher blamed Austin for stirring up opposition against him, and Fisher, in a heatedly written letter to Austin, threatened to "shake the foundation of [Austin's] Colony, and [Austin's] very welfare" and blamed Austin for instigating and promoting "all the mobs against [him] in Tejas." In 1831 Fisher had been hired as secretary of the San Felipe ayuntamiento while awaiting the reestablishment of the customs office at Galveston.

Fisher began secretly writing to the governor of Coahuila y Texas, disclosing inflammatory information against Austin and the governing council. Upon discovering Fisher's secret correspondence, the ayuntamiento fired Fisher, only to discover that he had taken a good many council documents with him. Eventually the council was able to retrieve all of the papers from him, even to the point of extracting one from his throat as he was attempting to swallow it. Fisher had also chastised James Breedlove, Mexican vice-consul in New Orleans, censuring him for not preventing a number of slaves, who had been expelled from Louisiana, from entering Mexico. Needless to say, Breedlove expressed a deep resentment at Fisher's censure since there was little he could do about the problem.[16]

Austin and Fisher reconciled their differences in 1832, and when Fisher was once again reinstated as collector of customs at Galveston in 1833, Austin wrote extensively to colleagues and Texian leaders to urge their support for Fisher.[17] Fisher later became an agent for the Rio Grande and Texas Land Company in 1834 and was commissioned by J. C. Beales, who had also commissioned Anthony Butler as an agent for his other land companies. Fisher moved back to Matamoros in 1834 and once again was appointed collector of customs, in addition to becoming commissary general and comptroller of customs for that port. Retiring from public service in late 1834, Fisher dabbled in publishing the newspaper *Mercurio de Matamoros,* and his outspokenness against the centralist government of General Cós brought about his expulsion from the country in October, 1835.[18]

Fisher arrived in New Orleans with letters from Governor Vitál Fernandez of Tamaulipas to Mexía and Gómez Farías. In 1832 Mexía had become acquainted with Fisher at Matamoros during Mexía's northern Mexico campaign, when Santa Anna ousted Anastasio Bustamante. Fisher's earlier censure of James Breedlove and Fisher's presence in New Orleans may have contributed to the lack of financial help from businessmen. Breedlove was not only the collector of customs for the port of New Orleans, he was also an old friend of Austin's and Christy's. Moreover, he was a merchant and banker located directly across the street from Banks's Arcade.[19]

Mexía knew Tampico well. In 1829 he had served as secretary and aide-de-camp to General Santa Anna at Tampico during the failed Spanish invasion of Mexico. He had also used Tampico as a launching point to attack the pro-Bustamante forces at Matamoros in July, 1832.[20] The port of Tampico was founded in 1823 and formally renamed Santa Anna de Tamaulipas in honor of Santa Anna's victory in 1829. Tampico had become a key port along the northern Mexican Gulf coast. The town itself was located inland, approximately ten miles from the mouth of the Pánuco River. Surrounded by tropical lagoons, the town was strategically situated along the river, which was the principal route into Tampico. At the bar along the Gulf coast a pilothouse and fort were located at the mouth of the Pánuco River. To get to the town, ships had to be towed over the bar by steamers, and in addition to the coastal fort, another fortress, Fort Andoñega, loomed from the northern side of the river. The town of Tampico was relatively small, consisting in 1835 primarily of a customs house and a town plaza.[21]

Mexía had participated in the Mexican revolution and had joined the Escosés Lodge. He was converted to the York Rite early in his career and actually became a recruiter himself to the Yorkino cause. Later he was appointed as collector of customs at Tuxpán, from which he generated a considerable fortune. As Santa Anna's aide-de-camp, Mexía also served as an interrogator of Spanish prisoners during the failed Spanish invasion of Tampico. He was sent with the captured Spanish battle flags to Mexico City and received notable recognition for his loyal service. Because he was conversant in English, he was sent in 1829 to Washington, D.C., as secretary of the Mexican legation.[22]

Mexía later returned to Mexico amid rumors of yet another attempt by the Spanish to invade Mexico. During this time he also began to buy Texas land. Mexía, Lorenzo de Zavala, Joel Poinsett, and Anthony Butler attempted to establish a colonization and land company, but with little success. He traveled with Zavala to New York en route to his continued appointment in Washington, D.C., and there Mexía and Zavala met with New York businessmen and lawyers, namely Anthony Dey, George Curtis, William Sumner, and Samuel Swartwout, customs collector for the port of New York City, to discuss a Texas colonization and land company plan. In October, 1830, the Galveston Bay and Texas Land Company was organized with Mexía serving as a principal agent and Zavala as principal stockholder. Mexía obtained several Texas land grants for himself, many of them in the names of his Mexican-born children. In 1832 he returned to Mexico to secure the northern Mexican states for federalism and Santa Anna and served as a deputy in the national congress for the 1833–1834 term. When Santa Anna abandoned the federalist cause and proclaimed his support for the plan of Cuernavaca, Mexía was exiled from the country and arrived in New Orleans in 1834.[23]

In the weeks prior to their departure, Mexía was able to compile respectable Creole support for the invasion. Fisher commented that they had sought "The Cucullos, Mirandas, and perhaps Merle & Co." for assistance. New Orleans committee member and Texian agent William Bryan also helped provide some of the essentials of war. In 1835 he had commissioned the *Mary Jane*, a copper-fastened, fast sailing schooner, for his trade business with Edward Hall to Brazoria. He too was able to secure the *Mary Jane* for Mexía's expedition. While the expedition was being organized, Mexía boarded thirty-five of the volunteers with William Cole. When some of Cole's servants became sick, Cole turned most of them over to his neighbor, a Mr. Nutter. Nonetheless, Cole kept six or seven of the men. Even though Edward Davis was Mexía's agent with Cole in making the boarding arrangements, Mexía personally paid Cole and Nutter for the entire boarding bill for the thirty-five men for four days.[24]

On October 29 Mexía notified Texian leaders that he had formed the expedition and had pledged his own credit, making "lucrative offers" to get the expedition underway. He had "armed a schooner, with a 12 pound cannonade and two eight pounders, and manned it with a crew of 50 men, armed and provisioned for 2 months, having also 150 men, armed and equipped, for land service, and all in good spirits." Mexía told them that if circumstances dictated a change from his Tampico invasion plans, he would turn northward to Matamoros, "in which place we may count upon a large party of friends from the interior, who will assist us." He urged Texian leaders to pay close attention to coastal defense and to establish a navy as soon as possible, which could capture other Mexican ports such as Veracruz and Campeche in order to secure the customs houses. He stated that he had received letters from his old friend Governor Fernandez in Tamaulipas, who anticipated a union with Mexía's forces after taking Tampico.[25]

Mexía and Fisher, flushed with confidence that Mexican federalists would aid their cause, sent commissioners to Tampico to persuade the garrison to support the planned invasion. Volunteers, equipment, and arms were finally assembled by early November. William Christy, while avoiding financial support for the expedition, managed to be present at the *Mary Jane* on several occasions before its departure. Remaining consistent with his earlier speeches and conversations concerning the sending of volunteers, Christy urged the men to avoid violating U.S. neutrality laws and to wait until they were on board and away from New Orleans before they elected officers. In testimony from his 1836 filibustering trial, he was quoted as telling the men that the expedition's destination was not Texas (though the actual destination was not recorded). Major Charles E. Hawkins, Mexía's aide-de-camp, spoke to the men who were assembled at the square near the U.S. Mint (possibly Jackson Square). At that time he admitted that he did not know where the expedition was going, either, but it was assumed to be bound for a destination other than Texas. The reason for the secretiveness was apparently to maintain an element of surprise.[26]

The expedition finally left New Orleans on the evening of November 6, with 150 well-armed adventurers who were virtually untrained in the art of war. James Breedlove, collector of customs, recalled that "The Mary Jane cleared at the custom-house of New-Orleans on the 6th of November, 1835, for Matagorda and Galveston. Richard Hall appeared as master of the Mary Jane, and signed the papers." The *New Orleans Price-Current and Commercial Register* listed the *Mary Jane* as clearing the port on November 7, commissioned by B. Rodriguez for Matagorda. The listed cargo was 10 barrels of flour, 20 barrels of beef, 10 barrels of pork, 6 barrels and 20 boxes of fish, 8 boxes of hardware, and 20 boxes of potatoes.[27]

Once the *Mary Jane* was beyond the Mississippi River, officers were elected. John M. Allen, George Dedrick, and F. Lambert were elected captains. Perhaps more with the hope that the men's opportunistic fervor would make up for their lack of training and experience, line companies were formed. Also organized was a company of grenadiers, sharpshooters, light infantry, and even a marine corps. According to Fisher's report on December 9, 1835, the expedition left New Orleans with a company of grenadiers that consisted of fifty-two men, including officers and noncommissioned officers; a company of sharpshooters consisting of forty-eight men; the Company of Liberty, consisting of thirty-three predominately French and Creole volunteers; and the marine corps, which consisted of fifteen men and included a captain of marines, eight seamen, a first mate, a second mate, two cooks, and two stewards. E. D. Davis, who had arranged for the boarding of the volunteers with Cole and Nutter, was made one of the orderly sergeants.

Several men who had found a place above deck discovered that some of the French and Creole volunteers were already armed and equipped and had claimed a spot for themselves on the quarterdeck. Five days out from New Orleans, the *Mary Jane* encountered a severe Gulf storm, and George Dedrick recalled that many of the men grew uneasy about how far the storm had blown them off course. Dedrick understood that the expedition was scheduled to land at Brazoria, but because of the bad weather, the force was now going to Tampico. The storm may have served as an excuse for Mexía's staff to give the volunteers the impression that they had been blown off course, conveniently making their destination Tampico, not Brazoria. Dedrick wrote that the leaders of the expedition told the volunteers that "We would have to Lan[d] But we Should Shurley take the town without much troble wen [sic] we would get plenty of Gold. With theas and maney more fair promises we at last Consented to go for there [was] no other alturnitive [sic] for us." [28]

On November 14, eight days after leaving New Orleans, Mexía and his volunteers arrived off the bar at the mouth of the Pánuco River. Around four o'clock in the afternoon, a steamboat routinely came along side the *Mary Jane* to escort the schooner over the bar. The sailors were ordered to open the schooner's ports to reveal the *Mary Jane's* true intentions as a "man of war" rather than a trading vessel. General Mexía was astonished to discover that the steamboat captain knew nothing of Mexía's plans. For Mexía, this was the first indication that something had gone wrong with his plan to send in the secret emissaries who had left New Orleans before him. The steamboat captain was informed of Mexía's arrival, was brought aboard the *Mary Jane,* and, according to Dedrick, was bribed to take the schooner over the bar. As the steamboat was preparing to escort the schooner across the bar, another Gulf storm ripped into the area. The *Mary Jane* ran aground, and with night coming on and the schooner taking on water, Mexía ordered some artillery to be thrown overboard and as much of the other supplies and equipment as possible to be taken ashore to lighten the ship's load.[29]

In the meantime, Captain John M. Allen and the captain of the ship, John Hall, went ashore in a longboat with six sailors to make contact with the fort. Dedrick recalled that the fort, with its three twenty-four-pound cannon and its twenty-four-man garrison, quickly surrendered to Mexía. Not only did the garrison surrender to Mexía, they also enthusiastically joined his expedition. The garrison quickly sent a rope along the shore to guide the volunteers onto shore in the darkness. The men had to jump into the sea and wade ashore, holding their muskets over their heads. Most of the arms and accoutrements were drenched by the time they reached the fort.

By 2 A.M. all of the men were on shore, and because they were wet and fatigued, the garrison had made a large fire so the men could dry their clothes. Their muskets and ammunition were also wet, and the men spent the rest of the night and the next day drying weapons and trying to find usable, dry gunpowder. The force stayed at the fort until 5 P.M. the next evening, when General Mexía ordered his men, along with the garrison, to march into Tampico. Using local guides, Mexía led his men about four miles inland and then took a circuitous route. What was considered only a direct, nine-mile march from the coast turned into a nightmare for the men, who marched eighteen to twenty miles through the tropical jungles and lagoons surrounding the city.

The garrison, under the command of Gregorio Gómez Palomino, knew of Mexía's landing and prepared for his attack by holding the customs house. The federalist emissaries who arrived secretly from New Orleans had failed to foment a revolt among the city's garrison. Two officers of the Tampico garrison took over the artillery barracks the night before Mexía's arrival, but to their misfortune, a company of the Tuxpán Battalion arrived, and with their assistance, Colonel Gómez was able to put down the rebellion.

Mexía's men, though fatigued and thirsty, finally arrived on the outskirts of the town. They quietly made their way through the streets and quickly arrived at the customs house. Firing commenced only when the sentinel outside the house discovered the attacking force. The garrison opened fire with artillery, killing two of Mexía's men. The volunteers rushed the cannon and killed three Mexican soldiers. A fierce volley of musketry ensued and forced the city garrison to retreat into an adjoining fort. The battle lasted about two hours, with Mexía's men capturing the custom house and two pieces of artillery. Because much of their ammunition had been lost when the *Mary Jane* ran aground, Mexía's men were limited to only five cartridges each, which were quickly used up. Mexía ordered the men to approach the enemy as closely as possible and to charge with bayonets to conserve ammunition. Lack of experience, lack of training, lack of ammunition, and fatigue from both the exhausting shipwreck the day before and the long march took their toll on the troops' morale and their will to continue the attack.

After conferring with Captains Lambert and Allen, General Mexía called for an orderly retreat under the cover of darkness. The withdrawal, however, became anything but orderly. According to George Dedrick, it was described as "Spedey." The dead were left in the streets where they fell, and rather than staying with their companies, some of the men attempted to make their way across the Pánuco River to escape along a perceived shorter route back to the fort. Colonel Gómez's soldiers captured many of these men, and those who were left wounded were placed in the military hospital. Mexía's men marched back the way they had come and reached the fort again at noon the next day. Several of the men continued to straggle in over the next two days. When Mexía and his officers called roll, they discovered that thirty-nine of their force were missing. Eight had been killed, and thirty-one had been taken prisoner. Mexía later disdainfully reported that twenty had deserted and that they made up the majority of the prisoners taken in town.[30]

Upon his arrival back at the fort, Mexía immediately tried to contact federalists in the interior, but because of a lack of horses, no messages were sent out, and Mexía did not want to run the danger of any of his dispatches falling into enemy hands. Defeat, fatigue, and lack of supplies, food, and clothing threw a pall of discontent over the men. Mexía held the fort for twelve days, and, strangely, no attacks came from the city to drive him off. Several merchant ships were anchored off the bar waiting to be towed down the Pánuco River. Mexía contacted the *Halcyon*, an American schooner, and persuaded her captain to charter his men and remaining equipment back to Texas for $2,000.[31] As Mexía's men prepared to depart on November 26, the Tampico garrison finally attacked the fort, but according to Mexía, "We saw the enemy advancing, but we dispersed them with a dozen well directed cannon shot, when within a short distance." Mexía's men took all of the available artillery ammunition found in the fort and then spiked the artillery, which were left behind.[32]

General Mexía arrived at Quintana, at the mouth of the Brazos River, on December 3. Thinking that Agustín Viesca was still governor of Coahuila y Texas, he immediately sent a report of the disaster to his old friend. Undaunted by his failed invasion, Mexía requested that Viesca or some other executive come to Brazoria to discuss plans for a further collusion with his expedition. Mexía had kept his force intact with four cannon, artillery ammunition, and other arms, but he had exhausted all financial means to provide his men with necessities in the field. He wrote that the men were growing discontented, and with conditions worsening, a sense of urgency and desperation can be read into Mexía's communiqués. On December 7 Mexía wrote to the new provisional governor, Henry Smith, requesting that he meet with him as soon as possible at Brazoria or Columbia and to help provide financial relief. [33]

During the time that Mexía was in Tampico, Mexican federalists in the interior sent Julian Miracle to meet with Texian leaders to discuss plans for a unified effort against the centralists. Miracle was also sent to ascertain Texian resolve in the federalist cause because further preparations by federalists in other Mexican states were conditional on what the Texians did.[34] The work of the consultation and the forming of the Texian provisional government reflected profederalist goals. With a quorum of fifty-five delegates from twelve municipalities, the consultation met at San Felipe de Austin in early November.

The participants approved a Declaration of Causes, proclaiming that Santa Anna had overthrown the Mexican federalist system and that the social compact between the Mexican government and the people of Texas was dissolved. The declaration further indicated that Texas was "no longer, morally or civilly, bound by the compact of Union; yet stimulated by the generosity and sympathy common to a free people they offer their support and assistance to such Mexicans of the Mexican Confederacy as will take up arms against military despotism." The declaration also stated that Mexican centralist leaders had no authority in Texas and "that they hold it to be their right, during the disorganization of the Federal System and the reign of despotism, to withdraw from the Union, to establish an independent Government, or to adopt such measures as they may deem best calculated to protest their rights and liberties; but they will continue faithful to the Mexican Government so long as the nation is governed by the Constitution." On November 13 the delegates also established a provisional state government, consisting of a governor, a lieutenant governor, and a general council.[35]

On December 6 the council received Mexía's first letter to Viesca. Without hesitation, the council passed a resolution to relieve Mexía and also sent William Pettus to secure military supplies from Thomas McKinney "to enable [Mexía] to proceed into the interior, etc., with the object of carrying the war into the enemy's country." Mexía was instructed to report in writing to the council, through Pettus, his "plan of operations." A committee was then formed to draw up a response to the federalists, and Pettus went onto Brazoria to meet with Mexía.

On December 9 Governor Henry Smith vetoed the council's resolution to assist Mexía, stating that the resolution had authorized assistance to Mexía before the council knew specifically what Mexía's plans were. Smith expressed a lack of confidence in both Mexía and the Mexican federalists because he had "no confidence in General Mexia's cooperating in the smallest degree in our favor. That his intention to make a descent on the seaports west of us for the purpose of robbing, to recuperate his own desperate fortunes, I have no doubt; but can see no advantage he would be to Texas." Smith also considered "It bad policy to fit out, or trust Mexicans in any matter connected with [the Texian] government," stating to the council that "I am well satisfied that we will in the end find them inimical and treacherous." [36]

Nevertheless, the council passed the resolution in its original form over Smith's veto. On the same day that Smith vetoed the resolution to aid Mexía, Mexía finalized his reports on the condition of his forces. At the beginning of the invasion he had an effective strength of 161 men. On December 9 he listed sixty-one men lost: eight who had died in action, twenty-five who had been taken prisoner (actually twenty-eight prisoners were taken), three who had died from sickness, ten who had been "dismissed from service as useless," and fifteen marines who had been discharged. The two companies of grenadiers and sharpshooters were united under the name of the Company of Grenadiers of the Federation, and John M. Allen was elected as its new captain. The force had been reduced to 113 rank and file. [37]

With new reports that large Mexican reinforcements were marching to besieged San Antonio de Béxar, the council quickly sent instructions to Mexía through James Power to march there immediately to reinforce Texian forces. Pettus had since arrived at Quintana and had resupplied Mexía's men and also advised Mexía to march to San Antonio. Reflective of the democratic nature of militias, most of Mexía's men agreed to go to San Antonio but refused to go by the quickest route, which was by sea to Copano Bay, then to Goliad to San Antonio de Béxar. Reaching Columbia, with a shortage of horses, Mexía's men were separated into two forces. Most of the Americans placed themselves under the command of Captain John M. Allen and went by land to San Antonio. The rest of the force, mostly foreigners, Mexicans, and a few Americans, went back to Quintana with General Mexía to secure transport to Copano Bay. [38]

On December 7 Governor Smith had appointed Stephen F. Austin, along with Branch T. Archer and William Wharton, to go to the United States to seek support for the Texian cause. As Austin was traveling to Velasco, he intercepted Mexía and Pettus at Columbia as they were going to San Felipe to confer with the council. Austin met with Mexía at length and, before traveling on, wrote to the council explaining Mexía's plans. Austin relayed that instead of going to San Antonio, Mexía should go to New Orleans, "where his presence is necessary for the furtherance of the plans and combinations that are made and maturing in the interior in favor of federalism and Texas." Mexía also disclosed that he had spent $18,000 for the expedition, including the purchase of artillery and ammunition. He offered the supplies and armament to the government if they would pay at least $1,000 for his personal expenses.

In contrast to Henry Smith's lack of confidence in Mexía, Austin expressed "full confidence" in him and wrote that Mexía requested that Austin report that "whether he goes to Orleans, or wherever he may be, he wished to be considered a citizen of Texas." Austin reiterated, "On calm reflection during a solitary ride down here, that the political position of Texas, should continue as established by the declaration of the 7th Novr. last. This declaration secures to Texas everything, and without any hazard, for it satisfies the federal party, and is sufficient to secure their support and cooperation, should the federal system fall, the 5 article is a declaration of independence as a matter of course."

By December 11 the general council issued a declaration assuring Mexican federalists that they were fighting "To sustain the Republican Principles of the Constitution of 1824." The statement noted that Texian leaders had been left with no government after the arrest of Viesca and members of the state legislature and that, for self-preservation and their own security, they had formed their own state government. In addition, "The Texians have therefore taken up arms in the defence [sic] of their Constitutional rights, in fulfillment of their duties to the Mexican Confederation, and of the most sacred obligations to themselves." Members of the council invited other Mexican federalists to sustain the "federal compact." [39]

On December 15, instead of going on to San Felipe, Mexía went with Austin to Quintana to arrange for transport of the remainder of his men to Copano Bay. He also wrote letters to the provisional government and to Viesca. [40] Once again he identified the federalist cause as his motive for being in Texas, and he stated that his men were marching to San Antonio to aid the Texian forces. Identifying health problems as his reason for not going to San Antonio, Mexía also wrote to Texian forces in Béxar, urging them to fight for the federalist movement because Texians also desired what the federalists desired: the

Constitution of 1824.[41] On December 17 James Power reported to the council about his conversation with Mexía at Columbia. Power stated that "Mexia had declined to go to Bexar to join with our people. His object is to go to Copano to join with two hundred Mexicans who are at Palo Blanco; and thence to take Matamoros, if possible. Mr. Fisher, who is acting Secretary to the General, stated to me that the General could not place his military character at stake by accepting a command under the Provisional Government of Texas, as Mr. Viesca is not Governor."[42]

Fisher's comments were not well received by the council, who hotly and secretly ordered Thomas McKinney to seize all of Mexía's military stores and armament and to them as security for supplies and essentials for his men. Writing for the general council, Lieutenant Governor J. W. Robinson wrote that that body was "Thoroughly satisfied that this man [Mexía] is not disposed to cooperate with us in the way that we can afford him any aid of the pecuniary kind and the advances of money, clothing & already made him must be paid in full for by him, before he can be suffered to remove the arms &, & alluded to no man can be received into our service unless he complies with the requisitions of the Government, and this Gen. Mexia refuses to do. The authority sent you will be used as circumstances may require, no money must be paid or advanced him on account of the Government by any of our agents."[43]

Austin's positive report on his meeting with Mexía arrived the next day, and the council scrambled to countermand the order to seize the stores. Mexía, however, had already received the first order and had turned over all of the military stores to McKinney. Realizing that he and the provisional government were no longer on cordial terms, Mexía wrote a dejected, exasperated letter to the council on December 23. He declared that he had complied with Robinson's order and had relinquished all of his military stores to McKinney. Because of the capture of San Antonio de Béxar by Texian forces in early December, he had decided to return to New Orleans to continue his plans to work for Mexican federalism. He also revealed his own frustration in dealing with the council: "Since my arrival in Texas on the 3d inst. I have communicated to Your Excellency all my movements, the views with which I came, the causes that prompted me to undertake the Expedition against Tampico, and finally that I was returning to this place, with the intention of sending my troops, cannon, arms, and ammunition to the Copano. During all this time I have not received a single official communication, and this circumstance, and the last success of Béxar does convince me that my services are neither of any utility in Texas, nor are they desired or necessary.[44]

Meanwhile in Tampico, a military court martial sentenced the thirty-one prisoners to death by firing squad on December 14. Local residents called for mercy for the men, even offering ransoms to secure their release, but the men were to serve as examples for those who dared to invade Mexican soil. Three of the men died, leaving twenty-eight to also face execution. Before their deaths, a local priest petitioned Commandant Gomez to spare the men, but was unsuccessful.[45] The doomed prisoners wrote letters to friends and family informing them of their tragic and untimely death. They also signed a declaration "as a farewell address to their friends in the United States," which was eventually published in the United States as part of a pamphlet that defended their innocence in the expedition. The declaration stated,

> We, the undersigned, prisoners of war, condemned to be shot on Monday next, at 7 P.M. by a military court martial, conformable to the established customs of the country, and composed of officers of the Mexican army, the sentence being read and interpreted to us on Saturday at 4 P.M. by Captain Alexander Faulac of said army, as our last dying words, do declare ourselves innocent of the charge of either participating or colleaguing with any person or party, having for its object the revolutionizing or disturbing in any manner the tranquillity [sic] of the government of Mexico, and that the testimony given before the honorable court of enquiry [sic] will corroborate this declaration, the facts and circumstances being briefly as follows:
>
> This opportunity afforded many in low pecuniary circumstances a passage free, which was readily embraced and accepted of. The terms agreed upon were, that it was optional whether the party took up arms in defence of Texas or not; that they were at full liberty to act as they pleased when landed on the Texas shore. That taking advantage of this favorable opportunity they accordingly embarked— [46]

The declaration went on to state that the men who surrendered did so "with a full determination not to act in concert with it [the invasion], but submit ourselves as prisoners of war, having no design or intention to fight, the undersigned, from motives of conscience and oppression, added to the shameful abduction or deception practised [sic] on us, choosing to throw ourselves on the clemency of the authorities."[47] The Mexicans evidently did not find their defense believable.

The pamphlet that accompanied the declaration was written anonymously by one of the prisoners and published in New York in 1836. Much of the account deals with the person's wayfaring experiences as a young man, the story ending with the teller's arrival in New Orleans and his participation with the Tampico Expedition. He claims that he and others on the expedition had been deceived into participating in the attack. The expedition, according to the doomed writer, was supposed to ship emigrants to Texas through William Christy and the New Orleans committee and not to go to Tampico. He discovered to his horror that "when after having been at sea a few days, I found it was not the intention of taking us to Texas, but we had to go to Tampico, and there against our own will, take up arms against the Mexicans." [48]

Many of the letters of the doomed men were eventually published in U.S. newspapers. James Cramp, writing to his brother, maintained that many of the men on the expedition were tricked into going to Tampico. Cramp stated that his sole reason for joining the band was to go to Texas "seeking to better their circumstances." Cramp claimed that when the *Mary Jane* was beyond the Mississippi, General Mexía was introduced to the men and "who in the course of the voyage had us all formed into companies of soldiers, a step against which, when I attempted to remonstrate, the only satisfaction gained, was an order "to go below." Cramp asked, "Will the United States permit their citizens to be abducted by men who are now in their bosom, in the midst of affluence and luxury? If not, then is Mr. Christy, notary public of New-Orleans, still answerable for this wholesale murder?" [49]

William McKay, another prisoner, wrote to a woman he had boarded with in New Orleans. He reminded her of his plans to go to Texas but added that he was "forced to land on the Bar of Tampico. I was taken prisoner, and now, in the face of death, declare my innocence!" Thomas Whittaker also stated that his belief was that the expedition was going to Texas, but he and his companions were compelled to march against a city he had never seen and to shoot down the inhabitants of a country that had never offended him. "Rest assured this was an order not very faithfully executed; the consequence of which was, that a great many prisoners were made. . . ." Isaac F. Leeds echoed James Cramp's judgment on the planners of the expedition. He wrote to his family that "your unfortunate brother, with thirty others, have been sentenced to be shot in twenty hours from this; have been treacherously deceived by Don Antonio Mexia or rather his agent, Mr. William Christy." [50]

Did any of the other men who survived back up the testimony of the men who were shot? At least two, George Dedrick and Francis W. Thornton, appeared to corroborate the doomed men's claims. Dedrick's letter to his wife in

February, 1836, from Goliad indicates that he boarded the *Mary Jane* "to Build forts—the object of the men on Board was to Go to Texas to Volunteer in aide of the Cause of Libertey [*sic*]." [51] Years later, Thornton also confirmed to Mirabeau Lamar that having arrived in New Orleans on the night of November 7, 1835, he was told that a ship was leaving that evening for Texas. Thirty minutes after dinner he went aboard the *Mary Jane,* thinking that he was "on [his] way to Texas." He also attested that several "murmured" when they found out that their actual destination was Tampico, but most were won over to the plan "on being told that it was as well to fight for Texas in Mexico as in Texas & also of the advantages to be gained in so doing. We all, with the exception of some one or two concluded that it was best." The U.S. consul at Tampico, George Robertson, interviewed the doomed prisoners the day before they were put to death. The men admitted to Robertson that "they were deserters from Mexia, and that they had been deceived, as they enlisted for Texas, and never for a moment supposed that they were coming to Tampico. The poor creatures it is said, met their fate with calm resignation." [52]

On December 5 the New Orleans *Bee* erroneously reported that Mexía had been successful in his invasion attempt and had become "master" of the state of Tamaulipas and of the rest of the "northern states of the Mexican Confederacy opposed like Texas to Centralism." Ten days after the incorrect report of Mexía's victory, Jerome Bayon issued a new report acknowledging Mexía's defeat. Bayon's second report, however, reflects a much more fatalistic view of the expedition, stating, "We confess that we do not regret the fate of this expedition; for it was one that should never have been projected; and whose results (as regards the commerce of this country) might have been decidedly injurious."

The Mexican government filed and published official protests in American newspapers complaining of the filibustering activities in New Orleans. On November 19 Mexican Foreign Minister José María Ortíz Monasterio issued an indignant letter to the U.S. secretary of state addressing the issue of "the notorious co-operation of a great number of the inhabitants of Louisiana with colonial insurgents of Texas." Monasterio complained that New Orleans supporters sought "to give a color of American nationality to what is, in fact, a mere speculation of different adventurers of all kinds.... The undersigned knows already that many of these acts have been committed, and are still committed, under the refuge of the liberalism of American institutions—without the local authorities or the government of the union having any power to oppose them."

In late December the Mexican war department issued a notice in the New Orleans *Bee* that warned Americans to refrain from further support of Mexican rebels and reminded them of the neutrality laws of the United States, which prohibited their interference in Mexican affairs. The notice also warned that any Americans caught on Mexican soil with the purpose of filibustering or aiding rebels would be executed as pirates. Bayon's editorial made it evident that New Orleans merchants were growing anxious over how the launching of expeditions would affect their commercial trade with Mexican Gulf ports.

Also in late December, several of the doomed men's letters were published in the New Orleans newspapers, and by January their story and letters were being printed in the eastern press. Also in late December, a sizable number of New Orleans insurance firms petitioned New Orleans district attorney Henry Carleton to stop the outfitting and launching of the schooner *Brutus* by Augustus Allen for the purpose of capturing Mexican vessels.[53] Carleton initially stated he could do nothing to stop the *Brutus* from departing, but after additional reports and witnesses, Carleton initiated an investigation into Allen's activities. After several witnesses, namely William Bryan and Edward Hall, most working closely with Texian leaders, Carleton reported that he could not arrest Allen since the allegations remained unsubstantiated.[54]

The publicity of the Tampico tragedy created a cloud over Christy's work with the New Orleans committee. Ironically, even though Christy had distanced himself from the financing of the expedition, the weighty words of the dead men implicated him as a conspirator in the invasion plan. James Cramp and Isaac F. Leeds both held Christy responsible for the deception connected to their claimed abduction, and some called for men like Christy to account for their alleged involvement in the tragedy.

Mexía's return to New Orleans signaled the beginning of the end of the cooperation between Texian leaders and Mexican federalists. Regardless of Austin's call for adherence to federalism and the general council's declaration to the people of Mexico, for all intents and purposes, the disaster at Tampico and Fisher's supposed, subsequent inflammatory comments concerning Mexía's refusal to serve under the provisional government drove a political and military wedge between them. Mexía left Texas realizing that the independence movement in Texas was gaining ground and that support for federalism in Texas was on the wane.[55] As a result, one could interpret the meeting at Banks's Arcade as a high-water mark for cooperation between Americans and exiled Mexican federalists in New Orleans.

Conversely, one could also interpret Mexía's departure from Texas in late December after relations between him and the Texians had deteriorated as the low-water mark of cooperation between Texian leaders and Mexican federalists. The general council attempted to depose Governor Henry Smith in January, 1836, "for violating the republican principles of the Federal Constitution of 1824." The second of several charges accused Smith of throwing up "obstacles and difficulties in the way of General Mexia, to prevent him from uniting in the general cause against centralism." Although the general council's action seemed to finally validate Mexía's efforts in Texas, the political climate was changing, and their measure to support Mexía was too little, too late.[56]

Did the New Orleans committee betray José Antonio Mexía? Even though the committee appeared to support the Tampico operation in its initial correspondence with the Texians, their support was promised only for as long as the expedition appeared to be a part of a larger plan to assist the Texian cause, not vice versa. The committee's refusal to finance the undertaking and to seek assistance for Mexía, followed by expressions of distrust by committee members, betrayed their true agenda, which was anything but support for Texas in Mexican federation.

The prevailing view in New Orleans was that Texas should be independent from Mexico. The newspapers reflected this view, and volunteers were heard on the streets of New Orleans before departure declaring that they were going to Texas to free it from Mexico. When Austin, Archer, and Wharton had arrived in New Orleans in January, 1836, the call for an independent Texas became even louder. Wharton wrote that the federal cause had become "flat" in New Orleans and that renewed assistance would come only if Texian leaders embraced the cause of independence. Austin also had to realize that the winds of political change were blowing toward independence and that American support would come only if independence were declared.[57]

Moreover, in keeping with the original agreement between Mexía and the New Orleans amphictyonic council (consisting of Louisiana capitalists), the initial, conditional support for Mexican federalism in New Orleans appeared to be commercially driven, rather than a sincere expression for Mexican federalism. An uninterrupted flow of trade was the goal, and in the end it seemed that Louisiana merchants were less concerned with who was in charge in Mexico than they were with their own profit-making interests. New Orleans insurance companies insured many ships in the Mexican trade, and the prospect of any commercial disruption or loss as a result of further expeditions into Mexico concerned them greatly. Reports of an embargo on American shipping into Mexican ports caused anxiety among New Orleans merchants, and the *Niles Weekly Register* published an anonymous letter from a Tampico merchant expressing indignation over the failure of the U.S. government to do more to stop the embarkation of expeditions into Mexico from New Orleans. The writer stated that, "New Orleans is the only place in the United States where the operations [expeditions] ... can be carried on effectively; and I am still more surprised at it, as the capitalists of that place will be the heaviest losers should American property in this country [Mexico] be placed in jeopardy. All sensible merchants in Mexico wish for peace, under whatever form of government the nation may think fit to adopt; and it is really vexing to think that our security and that of our property should be compromised at home."[58]

William Christy clearly discouraged Americans, such as his old Kentuckian friend John M. Allen and others who had jobs, from going with Mexía. One might argue that Christy and James H. Caldwell, who were accused members of the Louisiana Native Association, were willing to see and even encourage certain types of men who volunteered for the Tampico expedition to leave New Orleans and to rid the city of immigrant foreigners, Creoles, Mexican deserters, and the unemployed, who tended to be blamed for crimes committed in the city.

Evidence seems to support the accusations that many of the men who went with Mexía were deceived in believing they were going to Brazoria—not Tampico. How many of them who initially claimed they were tricked into going to Tampico is impossible to determine, but once the plan was explained to them, most of the men reportedly agreed to join the attack. Evidently only a few continued to protest, and apparently many of those who were taken prisoner and executed were indeed those who continued to feel they had been abducted and forced into an attack they did not endorse. The men of the Tampico expedition—Americans, foreigners, and Creoles—were relegated to being nothing more than cannon fodder for a cause that many of them neither understood nor supported. In comparison, their counterparts—the New Orleans Greys— were heralded as heroes, while many of the men of the Tampico expedition were denounced as deserters and pirates.

In the end, Mexía sailed from Texas, sick, exhausted, discouraged, and $18,000 in debt. His earlier plan to form a Southern republic between Louisiana and the northern Mexican states and his efforts to form a Mexican federalist alliance with Texians, with eventual reinstatement of Gómez Farías as the recognized political authority, were never realized. Mexía's status as a legitimate and trusted leader with the amphictyonic council, the New Orleans committee, and the Texian general council would never recover.

The legacy of the Tampico expedition, though tragic, would live on through the remnant of Mexía's original force that marched to San Antonio de Béxar in December, 1835. Although San Antonio was captured before they could arrive, many of them would eventually join the forces at Goliad under Colonel James Fannin's command. Many were eventually killed or wounded, and few witnessed the victory at San Jacinto. The fledgling Texas Navy would find its first commodore in Charles E. Hawkins, who was Mexía's aide-de-camp for the Tampico expedition. For William Christy, public and legal scrutiny over the tragedy would continue for some time.[59]

7 § SAN ANTONIO DE BÉXAR, LA BAHÍA, AND THE TEXAS NAVY

On November 21, after the disastrous defeat at Tampico, General Mexía's men continued to languish at the fort near the mouth of the Pánuco River. On the same day, Captain Robert Morris's company of the New Orleans Greys finally arrived in San Antonio de Béxar, with Captain Breece's company a few days behind. The company commanders reported to General Austin at his headquarters on the northeast side.[1] The American volunteers discovered a military camp filled with discontented and poorly disciplined citizen-soldiers. William G. Cooke recalled "We found the Texian Army in a state of insubordination caused by frequent orders from the Commanding General to make a night attack on the town, which were as often countermanded."[2] The volunteers from New Orleans were astounded at the lack of military discipline. Hermann Ehrenberg recalls the comical scene of morning roll call of one nearby company:

> The company that lay opposite was, like the others, called out of its pleasant occupation of roasting its meat on the spits furnished by nature. But soon a small number of not fully clad warriors stood in front of their sergeant, who was waiting with the list in his hand waiting for the arrival of the others. They were without firearms, and most of them had in one hand a friendly wooden frying spit ornamented with good smelling roast and in the other the famous Bowie knife. Several did not fall in line, as their partially roasted meat did not permit them to leave it to its own fate, or possibly the threatening condition of the coffee did not allow them to leave the campfire. These certainly were important reasons and the sergeant decided to begin even if all the men of the company were not altogether. Alternatingly, now from the ranks and then from the fires, sounded the sonorous voice of a backwoodsman. Once a muffled "Here!" broke forth from under a bundle of woolen blankets in a tent, followed by a general laughing of the company.[3]

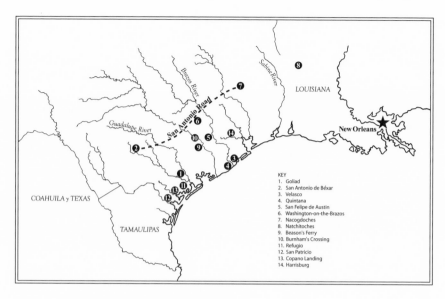

KEY
1. Goliad
2. San Antonio de Béxar
3. Velasco
4. Quintana
5. San Felipe de Austin
6. Washington-on-the-Brazos
7. Nacogdoches
8. Natchitoches
9. Beason's Ferry
10. Burnham's Crossing
11. Refugio
12. San Patricio
13. Copano Landing
14. Harrisburg

The Texas-Louisiana Frontier. Map by Gary Foreman.

General Martín Perfecto de Cós arrived in San Antonio on October 9. His forces consisted of more than 640 men, including 400 cavalry. Upon hearing of the capture of Goliad by the Texians, Cós centered his troops at San Antonio, garrisoning his command at the deserted and dilapidated mission called Mission San Antonio de Valero, also known as the Alamo. One of five Spanish missions built along the San Antonio River, San Antonio de Valero was the earliest, built in 1718. The presidio (or Spanish fort), San Antonio de Béxar, was built west of the mission across the river. Canary Islanders between Presidio San Antonio de Béxar and the west side of the river founded the first civil municipality in Texas, the Villa de San Fernando, in 1731. Various barrios, or neighborhoods, of the settlement continued to develop between San Pedro Creek to the west and the river to the east on into the early nineteenth century. Travelers described the settlement as a mixture of *jacales,* or huts, and flat-topped stone and adobe buildings. Two plazas were laid out with the parish church, San Fernando, located on the west side of Plaza de las Islas. Directly west of the church was the Plaza de Armas, which was originally used as a military parade ground for the Spanish soldiers, later Mexican, garrisoned at Presidio San Antonio de Béxar. By 1819 the governmental amalgamation of the Villa de San Fernando, Presidio San Antonio de Béxar, the Pueblo de Valero, and the surrounding barrios established the city of San Fernando de Béjar. Residents continued to call their village San Fernando de Béjar, or simply Béjar. By 1835 Anglos referred to the settlement as San Antonio de Béxar, San Antonio, Béjar, or Béxar.[4]

Mission San Antonio de Valero was secularized by 1794. Mission lands were granted to mission Indian families, Spanish soldiers, and civilians, and some stone from the mission walls and buildings were scavenged to build new buildings nearby. Spanish soldiers occupied the compound in the early 1800s, and the site became known as the "Alamo," the same name as the hometown of a company of light cavalry (compañía volante). The Second Company of San Carlos de Parras, from Alamo de Parras in Coahuila, occupied the compound for several years. When the troops under General Cós joined the small Mexican garrison in October, repairs began on some of the walls, and they were fortified with artillery. Although the mission had been secularized, the church of San Antonio de Valero continued to function as a parish church to locals until 1835. Preparing for the approaching Texas rebels, Cós also fortified the town, barricaded the streets, cut down trees, and placed artillery on the roof of San Fernando Church.[5]

Six weeks before, on October 2, Texians repelled Mexican cavalry near Gonzales. Colonel Domingo Ugartechea ordered his cavalry to confiscate a small cannon from the citizens of Gonzales. The cavalry, under Lieutenant Francisco Casteñeda, was driven off at the Guadalupe River, southwest of the village, without the cannon. Stephen F. Austin arrived soon after the engagement and was promptly elected commander of the growing militia force of farmers and merchants. Texian forces also captured Presidio La Bahía in Goliad on October 10, only days after General Cós had passed through the area. The final Mexican military bastion in Texas was San Antonio de Béxar.

Austin discovered that taking San Antonio would not be easy. Internal problems plagued him as much as Cós's cavalry, and perhaps more. Austin moved his force toward San Antonio on October 13, arriving three days later at Cibolo Creek, approximately twenty miles east of San Antonio. The cannon, which was defended at the Guadalupe by the farmers of Gonzales, was buried along a creek bank during the march because its carriage could not withstand the trip. A week after his troops arrived on the Cibolo, Austin cautiously moved them closer to Béxar, arriving at Salado Creek, east of the town. The South Texas prairies were more conducive to swift Mexican cavalry attacks, and the Texian volunteers were ordered to camp facing outward with their horses corralled in the middle. On October 20 Austin's troops inched their way from the Salado toward Mission San Francisco de Espada, south of the town, where they hoped to discover much-needed food and to discern "The disposition of the inhabitants to the [Texian] cause."[6] The atmosphere was tense as both sides sent out scouting parties to reconnoiter the other side, and occasionally skirmishes ensued with minimal casualties. Austin received additional reinforcements from the local Tejanos such as Juan N. Seguín, who brought with him a company of thirty-seven Tejanos. Juan Seguín's father, Erasmo, was the Mexican official who had greeted Stephen F. Austin when he arrived in Texas in 1821.[7]

James Bowie, brother of the maker of the famed Bowie knife, had also joined the "Army of the People" during this time. Born in Kentucky, Bowie became a Louisiana trafficker in slaves and a land speculator after the War of 1812. He had participated on a limited basis in the Long expedition. He came to Texas in 1830 and in 1831 married Ursula Veramendi, daughter of the vice-governor of Coahuila y Texas, Juan Martín de Veramendi. Ursula and Don Juan Martín both died in the 1833 cholera epidemic at Monclova. The death of his family threw Bowie into tragic despair, and he began to drink heavily. Austin's adjutant general, Warren D. C. Hall, was an old friend of Bowie's and had served with him in the Louisiana militia during the War of 1812 and later in the Long expedition. When Bowie arrived in camp, Hall and Bowie probably greeted each other with a warm handshake. Although Bowie continued to drink heavily to ease his grief, he continued to seek opportunities for economic gain in Texas. He had been a part of the enormous land sales in 1834 along with Ben Milam through the Coahuila y Tejano legislature and had bought more than 500,000 acres of Texas land. Serving as James T. Mason's agent, Bowie had acquired a ninety-five-league grant near Nacogdoches. Bowie was arrested along with Governor Viesca as the fugitive governor and his band attempted to make their way to San Antonio de Béxar. Bowie escaped to Nacogdoches and was blamed for inciting revolution in Texas by James Kerr and others. Bowie joined the army on October 19 on the Cibolo, where Austin appointed him a member of his staff.[8]

On October 27 Austin sent James Bowie and James Fannin with a small detachment of ninety men upriver to reconnoiter the outskirts of Béxar. Bowie and Fannin set up camp at a river bend near one of the sister missions of San Antonio de Valero, Mission Concepción, to establish a closer position for the Texian army.[9] The next morning, Mexican forces attacked the Texian position but were repelled and driven back into the town. Some of Austin's staff urged him to attack, but the majority of his officers advised him to be cautious. Austin moved most of his forces to Concepción the next day but still had no plans to attack.[10]

Austin attempted to draw Cós's forces out into the open. When the tactic

failed, Austin resigned himself to the view that a blockade was the most pru-
dent plan, even though he had no siege guns to carry it out. He split his force
into two divisions. Originally keeping his headquarters at Mission Concepción,
on October 31 Austin moved one division commanded by Edward Burleson to
an abandoned mill, known as the Molino Blanco or Zambrano's mill, on the
San Antonio River about a thousand yards north of the Alamo and near the
Camino Real (Nacogdoches-San Antonio Road) on the northeast side.[11] In
keeping with the democratic spirit of the U.S. militia system, Austin was delib-
erative in commanding the army. The officers of the northern division called a
meeting and considered two resolutions. The first one was to attack Béxar, but
a majority of the officers voted the proposal down. The second resolution—
that the army be united "above Bear [sic]"—was unanimously approved. On
November 14 Austin wrote to Fannin from headquarters at Mission Concepción that because of the resolutions, a move to reunite the army should be executed. The next day, the southern division, along with Austin and his headquarters staff, joined the rest of the army at the Molino Blanco.[12]

Austin knew too well of Ehrenberg's and Cooke's descriptions of his forces.
The militia became restless; food and supplies were low, and some who had
been with the force since Gonzales were anxious to attend to their families.
With winter setting in, the Texian army became dispirited. Discipline was poor
and getting worse, as guards left their posts without being properly relieved;
several guards were found asleep on duty. These difficulties prompted Austin to
issue stern, new orders threatening arrest and court-martial for such infrac-
tions. Men left camp at will and helped themselves to corn and cattle without
going through the quartermaster. The men also had to be ordered to tie up their
horses at night to avoid the risk of theft by the townspeople. Austin issued further orders for the men to stop gambling, firing off weapons in camp, and acting disorderly, with equally discouraging results. Alcohol in camp also vexed
Austin to the point that he wrote the government, begging them to not send
any more liquor to the camp.[13]

Austin's health (he was racked by bouts of dysentery) began to improve by
mid-November. In addition, he believed that fewer than half of his men were
willing to attack the city. He became resigned to the situation of keeping
250 men in winter quarters at the missions south of San Antonio "untill [sic] the
necessary regular force and guns and other supplies, come out."[14] On November 18 Austin received and accepted an appointment to go to the United States
to serve as a commissioner, doubting whether he could do any further good as
army commander. On the day after Morris reported his men ready for duty,

Austin wrote that he had submitted the question of storming the fortifications to a council of officers, who had uniformly decided against the action. The Texian general council officially called Austin, Branch T. Archer, and William H. Wharton to go to the United States to seek support for Texas.[15]

On November 24 Edward Burleson was elected as the new commander of the army. Also at this time Robert Morris was elected major; Nathaniel Brister was appointed army adjutant; and William G. Cooke, the apothecary merchant, was elected as the new captain of Morris's former command. On November 26 Burleson sent a force to attack a Mexican column from Laredo believed to be carrying silver for Cós's troops. After a spirited engagement, all that the Texian forces had to show for their efforts was a mule train of hay for Cós's horses and mules and no silver. Eager to join the fray, the New Orleans Greys warded off Mexican snipers and chased them back to the outer perimeter of the town. They were forced to retreat only after capturing much-needed cooking utensils in outlying houses.[16]

The majority of the officers, as with General Austin earlier and his successor, Edward Burleson, continued to be hesitant to attack the fortified town; with this indecision, morale continued to plummet among the farmers of the Texian militia. On December 3 Burleson called for a new plan to attack. Once again circumstances threatened to halt the latest attempt at taking the town. A Texian sentry reported that a mysterious figure had quietly left the Texian camp and made his way to the walls of the Alamo. Captain Cooke recalled that the news again plunged the commander and officers into a state of indecision. On December 4 Colonel Burleson called for the troops to move back to winter quarters. Upon hearing the order, many squads of ten to twenty men began to pack their gear and head eastward toward Gonzales for the winter. The ordered retreat all but dashed any residual momentum left from the earlier Texian victories at Gonzales and La Bahía. A last-minute development, however, infused life into the American volunteers. A Mexican who had deserted from Cós's ranks was brought to Burleson's tent. The defector reported that morale was not much better in Cós's camp. The American volunteers had not traveled move than five hundred miles to retreat to Gonzales for the winter. Thus, with the news of the low spirits in the Mexican camp, William Cooke took matters into his own hands.[17]

Cooke roused his men and began to march them through the dwindling militia encampment to drum up volunteers for an attack. He announced that he would rather stay in winter quarters at one of the local missions than retreat beyond the Guadalupe River at Gonzales. He went as far as to say that, if the army disbanded to the Guadalupe, Burleson might not see the Greys in the army the next spring. They would possibly leave Texas altogether since many of the men of them had given up good positions in New Orleans to join the fight, and they were not about to sit around until the spring in order to see action. Thomas Breece's Greys and a company from Mississippi joined Cooke, and he was able to raise more than three hundred men for the attack. Though many called on him to take the command, he refused and instead proposed Benjamin Rush Milam.[18]

Milam was an old empresario who had been caught in the political squeeze of the boundary dispute along the Red River in the late 1820s between the governor of the Arkansas territory and the Mexican government.[19] He later lost his empresario contract and ended up in Monclova in 1834. Milam acquired large tracts of land from the Viesca government at the same time that Bowie and others were buying up large sections of Texas land. He traveled with Governor Viesca, James Bowie, and James Grant when the governor opted to move the liberal Monclova government to San Antonio de Béxar. He was captured with Viesca and Bowie and then imprisoned but managed to escape into Texas, where he soon joined Austin's militia.[20]

At Cooke's practical recommendation, Milam was enthusiastically approved to lead the small force of three hundred volunteers into the town. Milam energized the group with his call, "Boys, who will come with Old Ben Milam into San Antonio?"[21] In spite of the Texas winter setting in and bands of Texians departing for Gonzales, the New Orleans Greys, led by Cooke and Breece, helped establish a renewed sense of purpose that set the stage for an attack on San Antonio. With Milam's rallying cry, a united force, though only a fraction of the original one, now remained at the Molino Blanco and began preparations for an assault.

A two-pronged attack took place the next.[22] Milam and Francis Johnson each commanded a division, and Burleson commanded the reserves at the mill. At 3 A.M. on the cold morning of December 5, the Texians, clad in woolen blankets, made their way to the launching point north of the town. A norther had blown in, causing temperatures to drop dramatically and rain to pelt the men. A Texian artillery crew, commanded by James Neill, fired on the Alamo, signaling the start of the attack and serving as a feint to distract the Mexican guards. Ignoring the cold, the Texian forces dropped their blankets and coats and hurried into the northern part of the town. The weather made the men numb and uncomfortable.

The first division—Milam's—consisting of six companies and fifteen artillerymen with two pieces of artillery, attacked down Acequia Street (now Main Street). Francis Johnson's second division, consisting of eight infantry companies, attacked down Soledad Street. Robert Morris served as Milam's second-in-command, and Cooke's and Breece's companies served in Johnson's division. The town's two main plazas, Plaza de Armas (Military Plaza) and Plaza de las Islas, were the Texian's main goals, and these were the points of stiffest resistance by Mexican infantry and artillery. In fierce fighting, the Mexican artillery controlled the two streets and forced the Texian forces to duck inside the flat-topped adobe houses along the streets. To avoid the crossfire, many of the Texian forces used hatchets, Bowie knives, and crowbars to hack their way through the adobe and limestone walls to move from one building to another; they cut portholes in the walls from which to fire. Mexican soldiers took full advantage of the high spots on the plazas to fire down on the Texians. Bannister recalled that Mexican sharpshooters made good use of the portholes: "From a distance of seventy or eighty yards they would shoot through our port holes, wounding several of the men." [23]

Hermann Ehrenberg witnessed two tragic scenes. Early on the two divisions lost sight of each other in the smoke and confusion. Ehrenberg, a member of Johnson's division, recalled that the men with Johnson tried to connect with Milam's men, who were seen firing while coming out of the houses across Soledad Street. A Mississippian named Moore attempted to make his way across the street to make contact, only to be shot by men in Milam's division. Thinking the movements from Soledad Street were Mexican soldiers, Milam's men took deadly aim at anyone who attempted to move down or across the street. Fortunately, according to Ehrenberg, Moore survived because of the lucky dollars he had secured in his vest pocket. Another Mississippian was not so lucky, however. As he attempted to cross the same path, a bullet tore his brain out of its cavity, splattering blood on the walls and the other men. The image of the man's body twitching for hours in the throes of death stayed with Ehrenberg for years to come. Making another attempt to connect with the other division, a German immigrant named William Thomas was also shot, although in the shoulder. Finally, after these three casualties, the second division was alerted of their mistake. [24]

A Tejana woman had found herself stranded in one of the houses with the advancing Texians. Rather than cower in fear of the ongoing battle around her, the woman showed great kindness by baking bread for the men. She fearlessly set out to retrieve water from the river for them as well. Dr. James Grant strongly advised her not to attempt the trip, but she assured them that as a woman she would be safe. Ehrenberg described the horrific scene that ensued. As the woman made her way back from the river to the house, she was riddled with musket balls. The Mexican soldiers shot her down, inciting indignation among the Texians, who witnessed the murder of a noncombatant. Many of the them defiantly went out to retrieve her lifeless body and then went to the river to draw their own water, placing themselves in the same peril the woman had faced.[25]

On December 7 the Texians sustained a severe blow to their morale. As Johnson, Milam, and other officers conferred on their position, a Mexican sharpshooter shot Milam in the head, killing him instantly. Milam's death threw a pall on the spirit of the Texian forces. Robert Morris was given the command of the first division, and the attack commenced. In addition to inflicting Milam's devastating death, additional Mexican reinforcements had also joined Cós's command at the Alamo. To establish a foothold on the main plaza, Johnson ordered Cooke's Greys to make a night attack. In some places his men had to crawl under the Mexican line of fire to advance onto the main plaza.[26] Under the most difficult circumstances, the men attempted to take the square. Ebenezer Heath wrote, "About 12 o'clock P.M. we entered the square in the face of three six-pounders, well loaded. We were able to spike one of them, but they made a rush and got them from us. Their officers tried their utmost to get their men to charge on us, but all their efforts were vain."[27]

Cooke's men established a position in which they could have a full firing position by daybreak. Realizing this, Cós decided to withdraw his troops from the plazas and concentrate them across the river at the Alamo. Francis Lubbock wrote that "The Grays led the advance to the plaza, and on the fourth night we forced an entrance to the priest's house, driving out the Mexicans. This decided the fight, as the next morning showed us the plaza abandoned, the enemy retreated to the Alamo Mission across the river."[28] Cooke had endeared himself to the men during the siege. When they began to grow hungry by the second day, he raced back to the reserves camp and ordered those who were not in the fight to gather firewood and to slaughter and barbeque cattle for the men. Thanks to Cooke, the meat was brought in, and most of the Texians gladly ate where they fought.[29]

On December 9 Cós sent a subordinate to negotiate a peace. William G. Cooke was the first to meet the Mexican officer and escorted him to Johnson. On the night of December 10, at a small house in Pueblo de Valero, a village south of the Alamo compound, a capitulation agreement was concluded at 3:00 A.M. and made official on December 11. The articles of capitulation stated that Cós and his men were allowed to keep their arms and personal property, ten rounds of musket cartridges, and a limited supply of arms to protect themselves and obtain food. All other military stores were to be inventoried and turned over to Burleson's command.

General Cós's men were required to evacuate the Alamo within six days after the ratification of the treaty. During this time Cós was allowed to occupy the Alamo, and Burleson's men occupied the town. Burleson provided Cós with as many supplies as he could spare to march to the Rio Grande. The Mexican sick and wounded would remain with surgeons and assistants, and no soldier in the Mexican army was to be molested for political beliefs in variance to the centralist government of Mexico. Above all of the liberal articles in the signed capitulation was the agreement that Cós would not oppose the reestablishment of the federal constitution of 1824 in Texas. On the same day that the prisoners at Tampico were shot, December 14, the Mexican army left San Antonio for the other side of the Rio Bravo del Norte (Rio Grande).[30]

On December 15 the Texian general council sent a letter of appreciation to the men of the army who had taken San Antonio. Proclaiming them "Brave sons of Washington and freedom," the letter also disparaged the Mexican soldiers, calling them "Hireling slaves of an usurper."[31] Benjamin Milam was heralded as a "precious gem from the casket of brilliant heroes." William G. Cooke was given honorable mention for his leadership in the attack.

Several of the Greys were either wounded or killed, many of them from Cooke's attacking squad. Francis Harvey of Captain Breece's company was killed; James McGee, Thomas Ward, John Cooke (no relation to William G. Cooke), George W. Main, Alexander Abrams (Abraham), William Thomas (the German who was shot by friendly fire), James Noland, James Cass, John Cornel, John Hall, and John Beldon were all wounded, some severely, some slightly. John Beldon lost an eye and part of his nose while attempting to spike a Mexican cannon during Cooke's final assault. Irishman Thomas Ward, who probably had seen his share of New Orleans canal work, lost his right leg when hit by a cannon ball early in the attack. John Cooke, the former British gunner, was also severely wounded and was probably a member of the same artillery crew with Ward.[32]

Burleson and others left San Antonio on December 18, leaving Francis Johnson in charge of the dwindling Texian force. Over the next few weeks more U.S. volunteers arrived to join the army, which began to lose its identity as an exclusively Texian force. The Mobile Greys, commanded by Captain David N. Burke; Captain Lawrence's Tennessee volunteers; and Thomas K. Pearson's artillery company all arrived by mid-December.[33] Many of the original volunteers who had joined the army at Gonzales went home to see to their families. Johnson reorganized the volunteer army of Texas on December 17 and named James Grant second-in-command and Nathaniel Brister, formerly of Morris's Greys, first adjutant. Dr. Albert M. Levy, also of Morris's former command and grieving husband from Virginia, was appointed as surgeon-in-chief. Cooke had already taken command of Morris's company, and the barrel maker from New Orleans, Charles Bannister, became Cooke's second lieutenant. Breece continued as captain of his old company, John J. Baugh became his first lieutenant, and William Blazeby became second lieutenant.[34]

The Texian army moved into the Alamo and discovered a large store of military equipment and supplies, some usable, others not. Mexican uniforms, left by the retreating Mexicans, were scornfully discarded. Ehrenberg states that the Texians would have chosen the apparel of the Indians rather than wear the surplus uniforms of the Mexican army.[35] Many of the men who had mounts spent the rest of December touring the area around San Antonio de Béxar. On one such outing Hermann Ehrenberg, Joseph Spohn, and Thomas Camp discovered a hidden cache of corn and supplies underneath a floor in the Mission San José compound, which, to the displeasure of local Tejanos, was quickly confiscated for the army.[36]

By December 18 Francis Johnson and James Grant had organized most of the remaining volunteers in Béxar for a new expedition directed at the Mexican port of Matamoros.[37] The Texian provisional government had officially supported an attack on Matamoros since November 13, when the consultation approved an attack and looked to Mexía's expedition to accomplish this goal. Mexía's defeat left a temporary vacuum in terms of an expedition against Matamoros. General Houston had also ordered James Bowie to command a force against Matamoros, but he evidently did not receive the communiqué. The notion of a northern Mexican confederation was still alive in spite of Mexía's failed attempt at taking Tampico.[38]

The conditional support of Mexía's expedition by the business interests of the New Orleans amphictyonic council for a republic of the South (described in chapter 2) may or may not have given the impetus for a northern Mexican confederation, but Dr. James Grant, a Scotsman who had made his fortune in Coahuila as a land speculator, had everything to gain by supporting such a political union to repossess lost land investments after the disbanding of the Coahuila y Texas legislature and the arrest of Governor Viesca. On December 21 General Sam Houston put Colonel Neill in charge of the small garrison

at the Alamo. Houston sent Thomas H. Breece on recruiting duty, leaving Lieutenant Baugh as acting commander of the Greys. Close to thirty members from
the two companies of Greys remained with the Alamo garrison under Baugh's
command.[39]

From the start, the expedition seemed fraught with controversy and obstacles. Before leaving for Matamoros, Johnson and Grant faced a crisis in late
December. The American volunteer companies of Captains Thomas Llewellan,
B. L. Lawrence, Thomas K. Pearson, John J. Baugh, David N. Burke, and William G. Cooke sent a petition expressing concern over a decree from the provisional government that subjected all auxiliary companies to the direction of the
commander in chief of the Texian army. Not only did the officers request that
their voices be heard, they actually curtly stated that neither they nor their men
would serve under the commander in chief. This petition revealed that most of
the volunteer companies viewed themselves as a semiautonomous force, run by
democratic principles and suspicious of any plan to place them in the control of
a commander in chief. It is not known what Johnson said to the commanders,
but he apparently calmed them down.

On December 30 the federal army of Texas left San Antonio de Béxar with
most of the supplies from the remaining military stores of both the town and
the Alamo. On the eve of departure, Robert Morris, who had made a meteoric
climb as a staff officer, wrote to General Houston declining a military appointment. He informed Houston that his position was with his men. He also revealed that the American volunteers, who now consisted of most of the remaining Texian army in San Antonio, would not consider entering into "any
service connected with the Regular Army, the name of which is a perfect Bug-
bear to them."[40] Most of Cooke's New Orleans Greys joined the Matamoros
expedition, and in the process they renamed themselves the San Antonio
Greys. Some of Breece's Greys, who chose to go with Grant rather than stay at
the Alamo, transferred to a new company, consisting primarily of David Burke's
Mobile Greys. The original band of New Orleans Greys was now scattered—
some to the Alamo and in two new companies, Cooke's and Burke's.

On December 25 Cós and his defeated troops wearily arrived in Laredo.
Ehrenberg recalled that many Texians left the army after the taking of Béxar,
thinking the war was over. However, reports began to arrive from Mexico that
Santa Anna was assembling an army to put down the rebellion in Texas. These
reports were true. Santa Anna, with the blessings of the centralist government,
arrived at San Luis Potosí on December 5 to begin organizing an army. By January 8 his army of operations had arrived at Saltillo. By the time he arrived at

the Rio Bravo del Norte (Rio Grande), Santa Anna's army consisted of more than six thousand men on two fronts.[41] U.S.-Mexican relations continued to deteriorate over the Texas issue. Anthony Butler, U.S. ambassador and the mastermind behind the Neches territory claim, agitated the situation even more by writing to President Jackson that Santa Anna was "Perfectly furious, mad, and had misbehaved himself in the most undignified manner, boasting of what he would do not only with the Insurgents of Texas but also with the United States, who he has identified with the Revolt, charging our Government and people with promoting and supporting that Revolt with sinister views, with the view of acquiring the Territory: He has sworn that not an Inch of the Territory shall be separated from Mexico, that the U. States shall never occupy one foot of Land west of the Sabine etc. etc."[42]

Butler went on to quote Santa Anna, who said that he would chastise the United States, and if resources were available, he would lay "Washington City in Ashes, as it has already been done before" because of the government's involvement in the Texas affair.[43]

Johnson and Grant's federalist army arrived at La Bahía (or Goliad) on January 5, only to face an awkward and tense predicament.[44] The commander at Goliad, Philip Dimmit, refused to cooperate with Johnson's men, causing a tense situation until, under pressure, Dimmit finally relented. Dimmitt had hoisted a flag for independence, while Johnson and Grant's expedition was federalist, flying the red, white, and green Mexican banner with the numbers "1824" emblazoned on it.[45] Cooke remembered that the expedition was not well received by Dimmit and that "Some difficulty occurred between the commandant of that place (Capt. P. Dimmitt who had hoisted the flag of independence) and Col Grant, and we all expected a fight with his forces—Dimmitt refused to furnish us with provisions, of which he had a large store, upon the grounds that we were acting contrary to the wishes of the people of Texas, in uniting with the Mexicans west of the Rio Grande—The next day however, he consented to furnish us with Coffee, Sugar & & for a three months campaign—During the time of the altercation both parties were kept in readiness for a fight—after the supplies were furnished we were permitted to exchange civilities."[46]

In December James Fannin of the battle of Concepción fame had been honorably discharged from the army and served as an advisor to the government in San Felipe. Sent to recruit and gather supplies for the army, on January 30 he arrived at the Copano Landing of Matagorda Bay after stopping at Velasco. On January 21 Fannin wrote acting governor Robinson that he had 250 men with him at Velasco and an additional 100 at Matagorda. Among that total, Fannin had recruited Captain Luis Guerra's artillery command left there by Mexía the previous month. Guerra, who had commanded the coastal fort with artillery, had joined Mexía's forces at the mouth of the Pánuco River. Fearing their execution if left behind, Mexía took Guerra's company with him to Velasco along with some of the artillery from the coastal fort. Arriving at Copano Bay Landing, Fannin and his men remained there until the next day, reaching La Bahía on February 13.[47]

The internal dissension between the governor and the council created confusion over the expedition. Johnson had traveled to San Felipe on January 3 to secure official authority from the government to carry out the attack. Smith opposed his appointment, and Johnson resigned three days later.[48] In the interim the general council appointed Fannin, who was soon arriving from recruiting duty, to take command of the expedition forces. However, Johnson changed his mind and once again accepted the commission. The confusion and strife continued. The growing distrust fostered by Mexía's failed federalist expedition to Tampico began to dampen the enthusiasm of many Texians to take the rebellion into the Mexican interior. On January 17, as Houston was preparing to leave for Refugio, he wrote to Henry Smith concerning the Matamoros expedition: "In an hour I will take up the line of march for Refugio Mission with about 209 efficient men, where I will await your orders from your Excellency, believing that the army should not advance with a small force upon Matamoros with the hope or belief that the Mexicans will cooperate with us. I have no confidence in them and the disaster at Tampico should teach us a lesson to be noted in our future operations."[49]

General Houston arrived at Goliad on January 14, under a cloud of conflicting orders from committees and officers of the provisional government. Robinson and the council had commissioned James Fannin to lead the Matamoros expedition even though Grant and Johnson had already taken upon themselves the task of organizing it. Preferring to put La Bahía under the command of regular troops, Houston ordered Lieutenant Thornton and the remnant of the Mexía expedition to the Goliad area. By late January, Thornton had arrived in La Bahía.[50] Fannin had arrived at the Copano Landing by late January with 350 men. Before landing, he had written to Lieutenant Governor Robinson from Velsaco that he had employed the schooners *Columbus* and *Flora* to transport his men and supplies to Copano. He also mentioned that he was bringing the two, brass four-pound cannon with him left at Velasco by General Mexía after the Tampico expedition.[51]

Houston was growing frustrated over the conflict in orders and expressed his concern openly to Governor Henry Smith.[52] Houston no longer believed that an expedition to Matamoros would be effective in swaying the Mexican federalists in Tamaulipas, Coahuila, and Nuevo León to support the cause. He had written his old friend John Forbes of Nacogdoches that independence was the only option to consider: "It is the project of some [who are] interested in land matters, very largely, for Texas to unite with some three or four of the Eastern States of Mexico, and form a Republic—This I regard as worse, than our present, or even our former situation. Their wars would be our wars, and their revolutions our revolutions: While our Revenues, our lands, and our lives would be expended to maintain their cause, and we could expect nothing in return; but prejudice, and if we relied on them disappointment.... Let Texas now Declare her Independence.... Were she to unite in such a confederacy; the preponderance, would have less influence if possible, than she has heretofore injoyed [sic] in the Congress of Coahuila and Texas."[53]

Upon his arrival at Refugio, the main staging point for the Matamoros expedition, Houston called the men into parade formation to disclose to them what he had already expressed to John Forbes—that the council did not sanction the expedition and that he urged them not to support the expedition to Matamoros. Many then chose to fall back to Goliad under Fannin's command.[54] Even though Houston had thwarted Grant's and Johnson's expedition plans, they were not deterred from traveling into Tamaulipas with a much smaller force. Captain Cooke was at Refugio guarding artillery and military stores. Grant, Johnson, and Morris, with seventy-five men, rode into Tamaulipas south of the Nueces River to rendezvous with Governor Vital Fernandez's troops. Cooke communicated to Fannin that only a few hours after Grant's departure, a Mexican federalist officer reported to him with a passport and letters from Grant and Morris to Fannin. Morris wrote to Cooke announcing that he "no longer intended to serve the Govt. of Texas—that he had received the appointment to the command of a Regiment in the Federal service of Mexico."[55] With these reports, Fannin ordered Cooke to fall back to Goliad. While in Refugio, several men of Cooke's command had grown disillusioned with the events in Texas. By January 21 Cooke had written more than ten discharges for men who wanted to leave the unit and return to New Orleans.

Fannin put the men to work at Presidio La Bahía, now Fort Defiance, preparing it for an attack. By mid-February Cooke was ordered to escort Mexican prisoners to Washington-on-the Brazos. William Fairfax Gray, who was attending the convention, wrote in his diary of Cooke's arrival at Washington-on-the-Brazos: "This evening two Mexican prisoners were brought here from

Goliad, charged with improper communications with the enemy and pointing out to them a place to build a bridge over the San Antonio. . . . They were brought under the care of Capt. Wm. G. Cooke, late of Fredericksburg, Va., who now commands the New Orleans Greys, and stands high in the army of Texas. Poor Cooke was very badly off for a wardrobe, and Waller and myself were happy in supplying him with such of ours as we could spare, which he received with thanks and without any false shame." [56]

General Houston assigned Thomas Breece, the Nacogdoches carriage maker, to recruiting duty on December 21, and when David N. Burke also left for similar duty, Burke's second-in-command, J. B. McManomy, was left in charge of the Mobile Greys. Charles Bannister, the barrel maker from New Orleans, was also assigned to the commissary for the Port of the Brazos, leaving Samuel O. Pettus in command of the San Antonio Greys. [57]

Several original members of both companies of Greys who returned to New Orleans included Sydney S. Callender, Frederick Proctor, Vincent Drouillard, William Christy's nephew, among others. The newspapers reported that several had become bitter about and disillusioned with the campaign. The *Niles Weekly Register* reported that "The gallant corps of volunteer greys from New Orleans had generally returned, disgusted with the service, saying that they would no longer fight to enrich a few Land speculators; they went to establish the liberty of the country." [58] The lure of the promise of land by the provisional government, however, drew many more volunteers to Texas to take their place. Edward Hall wrote to the general council on December 23 that "men are coming in every day from various parts of the Country bound for Texas, many however are without any means." He also relayed reports that Santa Anna was marching toward Texas with six thousand men and that Mexican ports were being closed to American shipping. In addition to this intelligence information, Hall also described the progress of the outfitting of Augustus C. Allen's ship and the making of a carriage for a howitzer. [59]

After escorting Morris's Greys to Brazoria, Hall went on to San Felipe to meet with the consultation. There he presented supplies, letters, and a report of the outpouring of support from the Banks's Arcade meeting. He left with a commission to be a purchasing agent for the consultation in New Orleans. Hall had difficulty getting passage back to New Orleans. When he finally arrived in New Orleans, he discovered that all of the funds originally donated to the Texas cause had already been expended by the New Orleans committee. Nonetheless, he wrote Houston on December 8 that he was sending on "a Company of Six Men whose object is to join the service." [60] Hall immediately published calls for more donations, and William Brookfield, a New Orleans merchant, gave an $1,100 loan, which Hall immediately used to equip fifty men from Georgia to sail to Texas. Brookfield was no stranger to Texas: He had bought ten leagues of land in the Nacogdoches area from Frost Thorn earlier in the year.[61]

Before and during the siege of San Antonio de Béxar, Austin had hoped for reinforcements from the United States, and by the latter part of December, companies were beginning to arrive off the coast of Texas.[62] The New Orleans newspapers had circulated the word throughout the United States that volunteers were needed and would be rewarded with Texas land for their military service. On December 8, even in the quiet little hamlet of Louisville, Mississippi, William Harwood wrote a friend in Baltimore, Maryland, that, "The great rage here is the cause of Independence in Texas. A great many young men are going from this country in expectation of acquiring homes and wealth in the cause. The government of Texas offers a large bounty in land for soldiers, and their lands I am assured by gentlemen who have visited the country are not surpassed by any in our Southern country for the cultivation of cotton, sugar, etc."[63]

On the day before Austin departed with Archer and Wharton for New Orleans, however, Austin wrote Francis Johnson a letter expressing worry over the coming flood of volunteers in the next months. He also explained how the pro-independence faction of the Texian government might use the new volunteers to establish a standing army to accomplish its political goals. Austin said, "I think it probable there will be some thousands [of] volunteers from the United States in a few months. They nearly all wish to join the regular army on the basis of volunteers. What shall we do with so many? How support them? I fear that the true secret of the efforts to declare independence is, that there must then be a considerable standing army, which, in the hands of a few, would dispose of the old settlers and their interests as they thought proper."[64]

Several of General Mexía's former officers quickly became assimilated into other positions in the fragmented Texian military. On December 17 John M. Allen returned with military contractor William Pettus to San Felipe, where he promptly received a commission as captain of the infantry in the regular army.[65] In addition to Allen, Thornton also eventually received a commission as first lieutenant.[66] It is not altogether clear what exactly happened at Columbia when Mexía and Allen split their forces. According to Pettus, many of the foreigners returned to Quintana (on the Texas coast) with Mexía, whereas many of the Americans of the Tampico expedition chose to remain with Allen at Columbia. Pettus stated in his report to the general council that the lack of horses and supplies and the weary condition of the men caused the split. It is possible that

Mexía's and Fisher's refusals to serve under the provisional government may have created a tense situation that caused some members of the companies to take sides. Needless to say, Pettus reported that the split was an amicable one.[67]

Allen's men, just as many others in the field at the time, were in desperate want of clothing and supplies. Pettus gave Allen $50 out of his own funds to help with needed supplies, but he also urged the government to send as much assistance as possible. On December 17 Allen met with the general council's committee on military affairs and was promptly made a captain of the infantry.[68] Also on December 17 Lieutenant Governor Robinson wrote to Thomas McKinney, instructing him to confiscate all military stores from General Mexía. He also mentioned that Allen was on his way back to resume his command at Columbia and requested that McKinney "encourage" the rest of his command at Quintana to join Allen's command. Evidently the men at Quintana were no longer looked upon as Mexía's expedition; they were now Allen's to organize into a company to march to San Patricio on the Nueces River. McKinney was informed that each of Allen's men would receive $8 per month, 800 acres of land, and a $24 bounty.[69]

Two days later, with word of the defeat of General Cós, General Houston ordered Allen and his men to Copano Bay to guard the landing and the military stores that were already there. Houston instructed Allen to select a good man to take command of his company, while Allen was ordered to go back to New Orleans to recruit another company. Colonel P. S. Wyatt was ordered to Copano Landing to relieve Captain Allen on December 28, allowing him to depart for New Orleans. First Lieutenant Francis W. Thornton took command of the small group of Tampico veterans.[70]

Houston then ordered Thornton to move the remnant of the expedition to Refugio, and in time he was ordered to La Bahía. By the time Thornton arrived at Goliad in January, 1836, what had once been the 150-man-strong Tampico expedition in November now consisted of only a fraction of that number. Houston made Thornton acting commandant of the presidio in January, and he continued as such until Fannin arrived the next month.[71] Neither Allen, Thornton, Breece, Cooke, nor Bannister would share the fate of their men at Goliad. Allen went back to New Orleans to recruit, and Thornton, who left his command to report to Washington-on-the Brazos on February 23, also eventually went back to New Orleans to do the same. Most of Thornton's men were absorbed into Captain Ira Westover's regulars when Thornton left for New Orleans. Robert Morris would not be so fortunate. His decision to join the federalist army would seal his fate with James Grant's small force.[72]

Charles E. Hawkins, Mexía's aide-de-camp, wasted no time in finding a position for himself after Tampico. He wrote Houston on December 9 asking for a command only six days after Mexía's expedition arrived at Velasco.[73] Hawkins traveled to San Felipe to meet with the governor and the general council. Houston, Governor Smith, and Lieutenant Governor Robinson all sent glowing recommendations for Hawkins. All of the leaders, who rarely agreed on the issues of the day, agreed that Hawkins was a premier candidate for a position in the Texian fledgling navy.[74]

On November 27 the general council had approved an ordinance to establish a Texas navy, starting with four schooners, two of twelve guns each, and two with six guns. All four schooners were ordered to be outfitted, manned, and armed and to rendezvous in Galveston Bay to await the governor's orders. Unofficially, the Texas navy had its origins with Nacogdoches land man Augustus C. Allen, who had presented a proposal to the consultation to purchase a ship and arm it for the purpose of preying on Mexican shipping in the Gulf. With the provisional government's blessing, Allen traveled to New Orleans and bought the *Brutus,* possibly with the proceeds from the sale of Texas lands to New Orleans committee chairman and treasurer William Christy.[75]

Alarmed at the prospect of shipping between New Orleans and Mexican ports being affected by Texian letters of marque and reprisal, New Orleans insurance agencies approached Henry Carleton to stop the arming and equipping of Allen's ship. Nevertheless, an inquiry by Carleton in New Orleans found nothing substantial in the charges against Allen and the *Brutus*. The schooner continued to be fitted for service and made its maiden voyage under the command of William Hurd. In September, 1835, Hurd had captured the infamous Mexican captain Thomas Thompson near Velasco and had captained several schooners commissioned by William Bryan, which had shipped between Texas and New Orleans for some time.[76]

On January 6 the general council approved the purchase of another schooner, the *Independence*. Formerly the U.S. revenue cutter *Ingham,* the *Independence* left the port on its maiden voyage on January 10, with Charles Hawkins as captain. Both Allen and Hawkins were the epitome of nineteenth-century adventurers. Both men had served in the U.S. Navy, and both had served in other countries' fights. Allen had participated in the Greek revolution, while in the Gulf of Mexico Hawkins had served in the Mexican navy under Captain David Porter's command, preying on Spanish shipping.[77]

By January, 1836, relations between the general council and Governor Henry Smith had grown so strained that the governor tried to dismiss the council; in turn, the council brought impeachment charges against Smith. On January 1, 1836, the new Texas commissioners—Austin, Archer, and Wharton—arrived in New Orleans. Encountering a flat response to the question of Texas's remaining a part of Mexico, the commissioners heard the loud and clear message that mercantile and financial support would be offered only when Texian independence was declared. Fortunately, new delegates had been called to Washington-on-the-Brazos to meet on March 1 to form an independent government.

Colonel Neill, who had commanded the Alamo garrison since December 19, left on February 11 to attend to family matters. This left the brash, young, twenty-six-year-old William B. Travis and a sick James Bowie to maintain an uneasy co-command of regulars and volunteers. Both men had ironically been ordered to evacuate and destroy the Alamo. Bowie, however, wrote to Governor Smith that "The salvation of Texas depends in great measure in keeping Bejar out of the hands of the enemy." He went on to say that he and Colonel Neill had "come to the solemn resolution that we would rather die in these ditches than give it up to the enemy."[78] Two men, formerly of Breece's Greys, assumed new roles in the Alamo garrison. John J. Baugh became the post adjutant for Travis, and William Blazeby became the captain, replacing Baugh. On February 13 Baugh informed Governor Smith of the split in command between Travis and Bowie and also harshly criticized the latter for interfering in civil and judicial matters, specifically of forcing the release of prisoners over the ruling of Judge Erasmo Seguín. Baugh also faulted Bowie for his drunkenness, "which has been the case ever since he has been in command."[79]

On February 23 Santa Anna's army arrived on the outskirts of San Antonio de Béxar, catching the Texian garrison off guard. The troops were able to make it to safety inside the Alamo, which ironically had been General Cós's headquarters only two months before. Within a week of their arrival, Mexican soldiers had virtually surrounded the Alamo. Travis sent urgent letters begging for reinforcements: "For God's sake and the sake of our country, send us reinforcements." He went on to request that certain companies be sent to the Alamo for help: "Capt. Allen's Co'y. under Lt. Thornton, now at Goliad, and the company of Regulars at Copano under comand [sic] of Lt. Turner, might well be ordered to this Post, as they could reach here in four days on foot."[80]

At Goliad (Fort Defiance), James Fannin had arrived by February 12 with approximately three hundred troops. He organized his small army into a single regiment consisting of two battalions—one from Georgia, which had recently arrived, and the Lafayette Battalion. Hermann Ehrenberg and the rest of the

Greys had settled in under Fannin's command as a part of the Lafayette Battalion. The cry for help from the Alamo left Fannin's men with a sense of urgency to go to their rescue. With a hesitant start, Fannin attempted to go to the Alamo's aid on February 25, only to return the next day after a council of war with his officers. Fannin's men lacked proper food and had a broken-down wagon, so the frustrated Texian force made its way back to the fort from which they had just departed.[81] Ehrenberg did not have a favorable impression of Fannin. He believed that Fannin's ambition to maintain his own separate command defending Goliad prompted him to remain at Fort Defiance. Ehrenberg maintained that Fannin never intended to go to the aid of the Alamo. Moreover, he was not willing to unite with Houston's forces, knowing that he would be outranked and thus subject to Houston's direct orders. Ehrenberg wrote that the men had repeatedly asked Fannin to reconsider reinforcing the Alamo, but to no avail, which created great discontent among the Greys.[82]

The Georgia Battalion had brought in a new flag, which now flew over Fort Defiance. Ehrenberg recalled that the blue flag with a white star was soon blown down during a Texas storm, and he mused years later that the abrupt action of the northerly winds howled a grim omen for Fannin and the Texian army.[83] Even with new volunteers from the United States, the month of March was one of darkest disaster from which the Texian army in South Texas would never recover. The original plans to take Matamoros and rendezvous with Mexican federalists and to establish a separate republic had become an elusive dream. General Urrea's formidable army was marching to intercept Fannin's troops at La Bahía.

8 § THE TEXAS AGENCY IN NEW ORLEANS

On New Year's eve, the residents of New Orleans ushered in the year 1836 with the usual fanfare. Children gleefully lit firecrackers in the streets, local militia units displayed their expertise in the public squares by moonlight, and people scurried about, attending the city's numerous dancing parties. The next day, January 1, the *Bee* broke the unofficial news that San Antonio de Béxar had fallen to Texian forces. The report came from an anonymous letter that was written to someone in the city and provided details of the attack, casualties, and the amount of Mexican military supplies captured. The writer of the letter voiced what many Texians were also hoping—that "our friends in the U States will send us all the aid in their power, as we have to maintain the ground on the other side of the Rubicon." [1]

On the same day that the *Bee* reported the victory at Béxar, Austin, Archer, and Wharton also arrived on the fifty-six-ton, armed schooner *Liberty* from Velasco. The three men, who had differed greatly on the question of Texas's future, now had the dubious task of raising funds for a beleaguered government, one that was becoming more fragmented every day because of the growing political chasm between Governor Smith and the general council. Within two weeks of the three men's arrival in New Orleans, Governor Smith had inflamed relations even further between himself and the general council by sending a harshly written letter ordering the council to adjourn. The council summarily impeached the governor and named Lieutenant Governor Robinson as acting chief executive. [2]

Austin had been the voice of moderation and an advocate for Mexican federalism even as late as December 22. He had expressed to a long-time friend, R. R. Royall, that he was suspicious of fellow commissioner William H. Wharton: "I am associated in a mission to the United States with a man that I cannot act with—a man whose conduct proves that he is destitute of political honesty, and whose attention is much more devoted to injure me than to serve the country. I mean Wharton." [3] Wharton, who had been appointed judge advocate of Austin's Army of the People after the battle of Gonzales, resigned in November in disgust at the "failure to enforce general orders and from an entire disregard of the grave decisions of councils of war." He believed that "No good will be achieved by this army except by the merest accident under heaven."[4] The Wharton family had supported independence early on when Austin still supported Texas statehood in a Mexican federation.

Austin also expressed doubts about Archer: "Dr. Archer, I believe, is governed by pure intentions, but he is very wild, as I think as to his politics, and too much inclined to precipitate this country into more difficulties than there is any necessity for. Associated with such men, what have I to expect? Or what has the country to hope?"[5] In spite of the apparent tension between the three men, their arrival prompted a stir of interest in their mission. The hotel in which Austin and Archer lodged, Richardson's, was filled with interested persons wanting to hear the latest from Texas. Traveler James B. Wallace, who had also arrived about the same time as the men from Texas, commented in his journal on their arrival: "Col. Austin. Do. Archer. W. Wharton, arrived last eve from Texas. . . . They are appointed Commissioners to negotiate loans for the purpose of carrying on the War."[6]

Wallace, who had no apparent connection to the Texas cause, was quickly made aware of their mission, which was to secure $1 million in loans "and as security for the payment of the same to pledge the faith of the Country, and if necessary to hypothecate the Public Lands of Texas."[7] The commissioners were also given the task of buying, equipping, and manning ships for a Texian navy and set out to accomplish the assignment among the friends of Texas in the city. They quickly discovered what had already been relayed the month before: The Texian cause had fallen flat among New Orleans supporters in spite of the fall of Béxar. As early as December 23, Edward Hall had written the government that "tis thought by the majority of our friends here that unconditional Independence will be necessary to obviate all difficulty."[8]

William Wharton wrote the Texas government that, upon his arrival in New Orleans, "Texas had not credit for 25 cents. This was produced by the opposition of certain Mercantile Houses, and Insurance offices, who had transactions with the ports of the interior of Mexico."[9] He also maintained that the political caution of maintaining Mexican statehood, with others in the government supporting independence, gave the Texian message an "indecisive tone." In addition, Mexía's failed expedition had dampened much of the enthusiasm and support expressed in the amphictyonic meetings of the previous September.

In spite of a directive from Governor Smith that made it clear that no more aid would go to Mexía or other Mexican federalists, the commissioners soon realized that the Mexía stigma still affected potential supporters.[10] The commissioners had to reassure their proponents that their cause was solid. They had to repair the damage done to commercial and business confidence as a result of the disaster at Tampico. Conversely, support from interested men in New Orleans now clearly required that Texas make a clean break and declare itself independent from Mexico.[11]

On January 6, another "friends of Texas" meeting was held. This time the assembly took place in the barroom at Bishop's City Hotel at Camp and Common Streets. Chair William Christy, James H. Caldwell, and the Texas commissioners were all present. The meeting was described as well attended. Unlike the meeting at Banks's Arcade the previous October, Virginian William Fairfax Gray, who attended this meeting, remarked that most of those present were residents of the hotel and that the wealthy and influential Americans of the city were absent.[12] As guests of honor, the commissioners were given seats beside Christy. Gray described the meeting's speeches as lackluster and not very "remarkable for information or eloquence." He continued his description with little excitement about the proceedings: "They [the speeches] all ran in the same circle, the wrongs of the Texans, and their noble resistance of tyranny, etc. and earnest and labored appeals to the feelings and sympathies of the people of the United States. The resolutions were carried by loud and enthusiastic acclamation, and when the noes [sic] were demanded not a no was heard, but a person in the crowd sang out yes, which caused the remark that the vote was unanimous and one over."[13]

Gray further observed the commissioners' reaction to the meeting: "The gentlemen from Texas are, or pretend to be, highly delighted with the result of this meeting. It certainly is proof of a pretty deep feeling of good will to the cause in the minds of those who attended." However, he acknowledged that it "would have been better if the wealth and respectability of the city had given it their countenance."[14] In the coming days, the commissioners' correspondence reflected the sense of good feeling Gray described. Austin, who, on December 22, did not believe that the time was right for a declaration of Texas independence, now wrote to friends, family, and Texas leaders after the January 6 meeting that independence was now their only course of action. In a letter to Henry Austin on January 7, he wrote, "There is great enthusiasm in favor of Texas in this city, and all over the U.S. . . . The universal opinion seems to be that, we ought to declare Independence immediately—it will give us aid of men of capital and high standing and character who wish for a more extensive field, than a mere party war in Texas."[15]

Austin had also received information from Mexico that many Mexican federalists had joined Santa Anna in his campaign and that "owing to what has already been said and done in Texas in favor of Independence, . . . does us no good with the Federalists, and is doing us harm in this country, by keeping away the kind of men we most need—were I in the convention I would urge an immediate declaration of Independence." [16] Wharton echoed these opinions to Governor Smith, stating that "The people of the U.S. look for this [independence], and nothing short of it will satisfy their expectations. If it is not done the sympathies, now so universally aroused in our favour, will certainly subside." [17]

In a very short time, the commissioners secured support from Andrew Hodge Jr. and the Bank of Orleans, announcing in the *Bee* that "All donations, or moneys intended for the government, will be received and receited [*sic*] for, and by the General Agent, and deposited in the Bank of Orleans." [18] Austin made it a point to see Hodge as soon as he arrived in New Orleans to deliver a letter. Henry Austin, a cousin of Austin's, had sent a letter to Hodge's business partner, Nathan Ware, but Ware was not in the city. In 1831 Ware had expressed interest through Henry Austin in investing in a cotton mill in Texas, but Ware had turned his attentions to buying a sugar plantation in Louisiana instead. [19]

Henry Austin had sent a letter to his cousin, proposing a loan to him to enable him to care for his family and to "Protect [Henry Austin] from the necessity of sacrificing [his] best property during [Austin's] present Difficulties." [20] In December the general council passed a resolution instructing the commissioners to divide any deposits they received between the Union Bank of Louisiana and the Bank of Orleans. It is not known why the funds were not deposited in the Union Bank of Louisiana, but it was quickly clear that Hodge's Bank of Orleans was the commissioners' first and only choice. [21] Andrew Hodge Jr. was the brother of William L. Hodge, a member of the New Orleans committee. They were partners in William's commercial merchant enterprises in the Caribbean and would remain so until March of that year. [22] The Hodge brothers, along with sugar planter Nathan Ware, former partner with Henry Austin, had become land speculators in their own right. The three investors had already bought eight *sitios* (parcels, or sections of land) out of eleven from Nacogdoches William G. Logan in April, 1835. [23] William, a member of the Texas Committee, had played no significant role in the committee's work since October, but his influence can be seen, however, in the selection of the Bank of Orleans, the bank in which his brother was president. Other notable members of the board of directors of the Bank of Orleans were Thomas Toby, the future Texas agent; T. R.

Hyde, a future member of the Louisiana Native American Association; and Hillary Breton Cenas, William Christy's stepson.[24]

January was the peak of the business season in New Orleans, and many merchants had arrived in the city. Others were traveling through New Orleans with the intent of exploring Texas lands. William Fairfax Gray, a land agent for Thomas Green and Albert T. Burnley of Washington, D.C., left his home in Fredericksburg, Virginia, in October, 1835, to seek out choice land for his clients.[25] As he traveled down the Ohio River and then down the Mississippi, he wrote of his visits and encounters with several men that he would eventually meet again in New Orleans. Gray arrived in New Orleans on December 28, lodging in Richardson's Hotel, across the street from Bishop's City Hotel at Camp and Common Streets.[26] In January and February, 1836, Gray, who kept copious notes in his journal, recorded whom he visited and in some cases provided abstracts of conversations with various parties in the Texas affair in New Orleans.

Texas men had also arrived in New Orleans in January. Land man Augustus C. Allen had arrived in the latter part of 1835. With a letter of marque and reprisal in hand from the general council, he bought the *Brutus*, equipping and arming her to prey on Mexican shipping in the Gulf of Mexico. However, because of an outcry from many of the insurance and merchant houses that did business with Mexico and also a subsequent investigation by district attorney Henry Carleton, Allen sold the schooner for $15,000 before it even set sail. The Texian government then bought the *Brutus* "at her Cash cost without interest on a credit which will equal Ten months."[27] Again, a commercial protest prompted the Texian government to reconsider the issuance of letters of marque and reprisal and to order a reexamination into the wisdom of their issuance.[28]

Not until January 11 did the general council act on the retraction of the letters, but by then, Governor Smith had angrily dismissed the council, and, in retaliation, the council had summarily impeached the governor, thus killing any chance at officially stopping the policy.[29] Not everyone in New Orleans supported or were even sympathetic to the Texas struggle. The *Brutus* controversy had revealed to Gray that there was "a strong monied party here opposed to the revolution in Texas on account of its endangering the trade with Mexico, in which they are largely concerned. The Messrs. Ligardi [Lizardi], Mexican merchants, residing here, said to be worth $15,000,000."[30]

District attorney Henry Carleton wrote a report on the *Brutus* for U.S. Secretary of State Forsyth. Providing several related documents, Carleton explained his handling of the controversy. Originally he had stonewalled an investigation into the dispute, stating that "proper affidavits" or lists of witnesses had not been provided.[31] Only when the story was published in the New Orleans *Union*, an anti-Texas newspaper, did he finally take action. Carleton stated that his investigation in Judge Preval's court found no substantial evidence against Allen, and "since these proceedings, nothing further has been said on the subject of such armaments, either in the papers or among the citizens."[32]

Almanzon Huston, the quartermaster general of the Texas army, and Dr. William Richardson, the surgeon general, were also in New Orleans. Both of them lodged at Richardson's Hotel ,where Gray was staying.[33] While awaiting the commissioner's arrival, Huston tried to sell Gray a league of land near the Sabine River for $5,000. Gray commented that "it is his own headright. Too high for me."[34] Only days later, Jeremiah Brown, captain of the schooner *Liberty*, offered to sell several leagues of Texas land to Gray, one of them adjoining Huston's Sabine league. Brown offered his land for fifty cents an acre—the entire league selling for $2,214, nearly half of Huston's price.

Other Texians who were in New Orleans offered Gray insights into the Texas land situation. Archibald Hotchkiss, an agent of the Galveston Bay and Texas Land Company and resident of Nacogdoches, believed that "old Mexican titles" could be bought for $1,000 per league.[35] Surprisingly, a New York attorney and Texas landowner, A. J. Yates, who had also traveled extensively in Mexico, provided Gray the most revealing information of all about Texas. He explained the system of government and slavery in Texas and also shared his plans of establishing a plantation on Galveston Bay, using Mexican indentured herders to build a cattle ranch. Yates explained that buying "native Mexicans, who have forfeited their liberty by debt, . . . they are the best for that purpose, being well acquainted with herding cattle, [and] are cheaper than blacks."[36]

Captains John M. Allen, formerly one of Mexía's officers, and Thomas H. Breece, formerly a commander of the New Orleans Greys, had also arrived in New Orleans in January to recruit new volunteers. General Sam Houston had ordered several talented and respected officers, like Allen and Breece, out of the field for recruiting duty. Eventually he would order Lieutenant Thornton to leave his command at Goliad and also recruit. Both Allen and Breece traveled to Mobile on January 24; from Mobile, Breece traveled on to Montgomery. Allen and a Lieutenant Milligan remained in Mobile while Breece recruited in Montgomery, and by early February, Breece, Allen, and Milligan went back to New Orleans with six new recruits. The recruiters checked into the Alabama Hotel, which became their recruiting headquarters.[37] Edward D. Davis, an orderly sergeant in the Mexía Expedition, came back to New Orleans with Allen. Once again, Davis became an orderly sergeant, this time for Allen. Davis had been Mexía's agent in securing lodging for volunteers in November. As before, Davis turned to William Cole, who had housed several of the Tampico volunteers, to lodge a new company of volunteers for Allen, including the six newcomers from Alabama. Upon their return to New Orleans, Allen continued to enlist new volunteers and also spent $110 for the making of a company flag.[38]

The commissioners also bought the schooner *Ingham* from Gregory Byrne for $5,000 on January 14. Charles H. Hawkins, who had been waiting to secure a naval command, was finally given the *Ingham*, which was renamed the *Independence*. The commissioners gave Hawkins $500 for "contingent expenses" to begin outfitting the schooner.[39] Jeremiah Brown, captain of the schooner *Liberty*, had already been in service with the transport of the Texas commissioners from Velasco to New Orleans. By the end of January, 1836, the commissioners and William Bryan could proudly announce that Texas had its first navy with three schooners: the *Liberty*, commanded by Brown; the *Independence*, commanded by Hawkins; and the *Brutus*, commanded by William Hurd. The *Invincible* would later become the fourth.

Gray continued to gather reports from whomever he could, weighing their information and their offers for sales of land with the others. He met young Nacogdoches land man William G. Logan, who offered to sell land for General Sam Houston, whose property was located thirty miles from Pecan Point near the Red River. Gray stated that Logan was selling the land for "Houston's toggery [wardrobe]." Gray kept careful notes, describing the land, the culture, and the laws, to send back to Green in Richmond.

Gray also noted that by January 14 William Christy, the chair of the New Orleans committee, "was getting out of favor with the Commissioners. He was offensive to them." Gray did not disclose what exactly Christy had done or said. However, Christy, who had been in charge of all Texas affairs in the city up to that time, even when there was no Texas government, felt he demanded more respect because of his role as committee chair. He was a dogmatic man and may have been painfully honest about the growing problems with Texian financial policy. In spite of the tension between him and the commissioners and with few New Orleans merchants stepping forward to assist the Texian cause, Christy, who had strong Kentucky ties, looked to several planters and merchants from the Ohio Valley who had recently arrived in the city to conduct business. He and the Texas commissioners were able to secure two sizable loans with several of these men. Those who joined in as lenders in the larger of the two loan instruments were merchants who had met Gray along their journey to New Orleans.[40]

The first loan, which was for $200,000 and reportedly negotiated by William Christy, was signed by Thomas D. Carneal of Covington, Kentucky (across the Ohio River from Cincinnati); Lewis Whiteman, James F. Irwin, and Paul Anderson, all from Cincinnati; James N. Morrison, Robert Triplett, and George Hancock, from Kentucky; William Fairfax Gray and James S. Brauder from Virginia; and one lone resident of New Orleans, Alfred Penn. All of them agreed to the generous conditions.[41] Triplett invested the largest amount—$100,000—with Thomas Carneal investing $40,000. Morrison, Penn, Gray, and Brauder each invested $10,000, and Whiteman, Anderson, Irwin, and Hancock each invested $5,000. Most of them were planters and speculators in their respective states, and some at the time considered the idea of securing rich Texas land a risky one. Nevertheless, if successful, the investment would bring sizable returns.

The loan, which was finalized at Christy's office in Banks's Arcade, consisted of fifteen articles, providing an immediate $20,000 advance to the Texians at eight percent per annum. The investors would receive scrip, "negotiable by endorsement," like private paper. The lenders were allowed to locate or select from any of the vacant public lands, and these lands had to be a minimum of 640 acres, unless a partial tract was available. The lenders could choose to take land directly in lieu of scrip and had to have the lands surveyed and platted six months after the Texian government opened the land offices, when they would make their final selections. The contract also stipulated that the lenders, if scrip were chosen, would lose their "right of priority selection" after the expiration of the six months, but their right to select lands would still be honored. Assuming the lenders agreed to continue the loan, the Texian government could repay the money at the end of five years; if it were not paid on time, the government would pay eight percent per annum in interest until the loan was paid in full. The government did not have the power to extend the loan without the lenders' consent.

A full reservation of priority for the land, located and claimed by the lenders, had to be maintained by the Texian government. The document stated that no public land sales would be offered until the lenders had selected their tracts. Their properties were exempt from surveying fees and would be free from taxation for one year from the time of the lenders' land selections. The lenders could either pay the remainder of the loan ($180,000), or the ten-percent advance could constitute the sole amount of the loan. Call for payment

was set at 60 days after the ratification of the contract by the constitutional convention, and upon the lenders' confirmation of the contract, the balance (with
installments at 60, 90, and 120 days) would be deposited in the Bank of Orleans. Each lender was responsible for only the amount invested, and any lender
could withdraw from the loan with a thirty-day notice. Any of the other lenders
also had the right to take the lender's place pro rata. The presence of two witnesses before the mayor, a judge, or a notary public of the city was required for
all sales of land by the lenders or sales by buyers of their lands.[42] A few days
later, the investors received scrip in proportion to their investment.

Robert Triplett, of Yellow Banks, Kentucky (now Owensboro), was a
wealthy businessman who had made a fortune in coal and land speculation. As
a young man, he had learned the coal business by managing his father's coal
yards in Virginia. He was eventually hired by a Richmond judge to go to Kentucky to settle several large estates there. He settled at Yellow Banks, where he
accumulated a large fortune in lands and coal. In the late 1820s, Triplett shipped
coal to Louisiana sugar planters, and when the sugar market softened, the demand for coal also decreased.

Triplett then went to New Orleans, where he sold coal to hotels such as
Richardson's and to local steamboats and cotton mills. Demand for coal became
so great that Triplett opened a coal yard on one of the wharves.[43] In 1835, an old
acquaintance, Thomas Green of Washington, D.C. (Triplett stated that Green
lived in Richmond), and Gray's future employer, proposed a joint speculation
venture in Texas lands. The suggestion "struck [Triplett's] fancy," and the men
entered into a business plan in which Green would put up the money and
Triplett would go to Texas to look for land. After sending his family back to Virginia with Green, Triplett left for New Orleans. By the time of the $200,000
loan, Triplett had already traveled to Nacogdoches. Land men Augustus C.
Allen and his brother John K. Allen had offered Triplett 300,000 acres of land
for sale, which Triplett had conditionally purchased with a $15,000 deposit.
Triplett confided in Gray that he did not believe that Allen's titles were legitimate, due to the location of the tracts, which were within the twenty-league
zone along the border established by the Mexican government. Returning to
New Orleans on December 30, 1835, Triplett quickly annulled the sale and got
his deposit back. Having invested the largest amount in the loan, he eventually
went back to Texas with Gray to search for land and to represent the lenders at
the March constitutional convention.[44]

Thomas D. Carneal, a former Kentucky state senator and a cofounder of
the town of Covington, Kentucky, had been a business associate of Christy's

former War of 1812 company commander, Uriel Sebree.[45] Gray had met Carneal while at Natchez, on his way to New Orleans. Gray recorded that Carneal, then fifty years old, had expressed concern for "the state of things" in Texas and preferred to speculate in U.S. lands. He stated to Gray that if he were twenty years younger, he might invest $10,000 in Texas lands. Carneal evidently changed his mind by the time he arrived in New Orleans.[46]

George Hancock, also of Louisville, and presumed to be an old friend of Christy's, was in the city on business as well. He had married the daughter of a New Orleans doctor named Davidson and would often visit his wife's brother, who was a doctor in Alexandria, Louisiana. Hancock was interested in Texas land from the outset and made plans to travel to the Mexican province.[47]

Little is known of the other investors, most of whom lent either $5,000 or $10,000. James L. Brauder, who represented James M. McCulloch and Company of Petersburg, Virginia, pledged $10,000, as did William F. Gray, who was an agent of T. Green and A. T. Burnley. Alfred Penn, the only Louisianan among the lenders, was a prominent cotton press owner and planter.

The lenders agreed not to sell any of their scrip until the constitutional convention ratified the contract. Until then, the scrip would be held at $1.25, giving the lenders a potential 150-percent return if sold at that price.[48] Most of the lenders chose to take lands as soon as possible at fifty cents an acre, and though the scrip was not issued, some of the investors set off for Texas to make their selections without waiting for the land offices to open.

A second loan was negotiated a week later. Though not as substantial as the first, it consisted of mostly New Orleans men. James Erwin, a Kentucky lawyer and planter who lived in New Orleans during the peak business season, assisted in recruiting a number of New Orleans investors to sign onto this loan. Erwin regularly traveled back to Kentucky in the summer with his family until his wife, Anne Brown Clay Erwin, died in childbirth the previous December.[49] Erwin's wife, daughter of statesman Henry Clay, married Erwin in Kentucky in 1823. Erwin, originally from Tennessee, became a good friend and beloved son-in-law of the Clay family. He maintained a plantation, called the Woodlands, near Clay's Ashland plantation so that his family could be close to his wife's when in Kentucky. Erwin and the Clays were devastated by the death of Anne Clay Erwin. Grief stricken and left with four children, Erwin tried to go on with life and business, stepping into the role of brokering the second Texian loan only one month after his wife's death.

Erwin at first offered $100,000 for land at fifty cents per acre outright, but the commissioners refused, stating they were neither authorized to sell lands nor willing to pledge the faith of the government beyond what had been agreed to in the first loan. The second loan, consisting of twelve lenders, contained much of the same language as the first one. The rights and privileges of the lenders of the first loan were preserved, meaning that they still had first choice in the selection of lands over the lenders of the second loan.

Five of the lenders were from out of state. Erwin, who was identified as from Lexington, Kentucky, was a winter resident of New Orleans. Jeremiah Morton, a Virginian from Orange County, lodged at Richardson's Hotel, keeping his family, according to Gray, at "Mr. Hagerty's on Canal Street." William F. Ritchie of Richmond and Howard F. Thornton of Rappahannock County, both Virginians, had traveled at least part of the way with Gray to New Orleans. Thornton had tried his hand at speculating in Mississippi land along his journey but with little success. He was further delayed when he became ill at Woodville, Mississippi, but finally arrived in New Orleans on January 10.[50] Triplett, who lent the largest amount for the first loan, pledged only $2,000 both to maintain an interest as a lender of the second and also to protect the rights of the first lenders.

The seven New Orleanians who became lenders were Gabriel W. Denton; Jacob Wilcox; James Huie; Thomas Banks, owner of Banks's Arcade and member of the New Orleans committee; Dr. Thomas O. Meux; Christopher Adams Jr.; and James Whital. Both Adams and Wilcox had served with William Bogart on the board of directors of the City Bank, and William Christy was listed as the bank's notary public.[51] Adams also served in the New Orleans Chamber of Commerce with both William L. Hodge and Bogart.[52] Several of the lenders also had offices at or near Banks's Arcade, suggesting that Christy or Banks was instrumental in bringing in some of their fellow commercial residents or neighbors.[53] Of the seven New Orleans lenders of the second loan, four were also members, or future members, of the New Orleans-based Western Gulf and Fire Insurance Company. Willcox, Adams, and Meux were current members, with Denton joining them by 1838. At about the time the second loan was being negotiated, one of the investors and a business associate of Erwin's, Gabriel W. Denton, also bought the old New Orleans Gaslight Bank building at Royal and Conti Streets for $50,000 with financial help from Erwin, Wilcox, and Adams. Denton's purchase of the Gaslight Bank building involved four $12,500 promissory notes to Adams, Willcox, and Erwin. The terms of the notes were generous: six percent interest per annum, payable in one, two, three, and four years. Andrew Hodge Jr., James H. Caldwell, and James N. Niven represented the Gaslight Bank in the deal.[54]

One of several insurance companies in the city who protested the outfitting of the *Brutus* was the Western Gulf and Fire Insurance Company. Even though several members of the company's board were investors in the second loan, they did not, however, seem to be affected by the company's protest when a good investment opportunity presented itself.[55]

The New Orleans investors who brokered the loans also received assurances from the commissioners that independence was on the horizon for Texas and that Mexican shipping would be affected only temporarily if at all. Austin confirmed this when he wrote Thomas Rusk on January 18 that "These loans are made on the firm belief that Texas will declare absolute independence in March—Otherwise they would not have been obtained—public opinion all over this country calls for such a declaration."[56]

The Texas commissioners also announced that they had officially appointed Edward Hall and William Bryan to be the Texas agents in the city.[57] At Hall's own insistence, the commissioners appointed Bryan as general agent. Hall and Bryan wrote to the Texian government on January 18 announcing their appointments.[58] Hall had come to New Orleans in the 1820s as a schoolmaster and English professor.[59] By 1835 he had become a partner with Bryan in the shipping business. Years later Hall recalled, "When I first became acquainted with William Bryan, I had money and credit & supposed he had his. His affable manners and apparent candor inspired confidence and induced me to engage with him in Texas Business, and I left New Orleans to visit Texas for that purpose, William Bryan remained and continued his other Business in New Orleans."[60]

Upon hearing of Austin's release from prison and his call for war, Hall quickly returned to New Orleans. The New Orleans committee appointed him to deliver supplies and escort Morris's Greys to Texas. When the Greys traveled on to La Bahía from Brazoria, Hall went to San Felipe de Austin to report to the consultation. Euphoric over the New Orleans committee's work, the government immediately sent Hall back to New Orleans to secure ordinance for the Texian army.[61] His commission to purchase ordnance was expanded, and, when the Texian commissioners arrived in New Orleans in January, they officially appointed him to the post. Despite Hall's and Bryan's new responsibilities, Bryan continued to operate their shipping business at 36 Old Levee Street. They had the added task of trying to rent out their old office space at 30 Old Levee Street.[62]

Before leaving San Felipe, the general council awarded Hall a league of Texas land on December 9, and by late January he had power of attorney for men in Texas to sell their lands to prospective buyers.[63] Even though the Texian provisional government had closed all land offices by late November, Bryan and Hall began to advertise Texas lands only days after their appointments.

To make matters worse, local Nacogdoches officials still issued large numbers of land titles in defiance of the consultation's closing of the land offices. Arthur Henrie, who had been appointed to take charge of the Nacogdoches land offices, wrote to Governor Smith on January 3, "The Alcalda [sic] has issued titles to more land within the three Last weeks, than ever were Issued by all the alcaldas [sic], of this place before, but I do not pretend to say what date they Bear."[64]

John Forbes wrote acting Governor James Robinson on January 12, stating that several Nacogdoches leaders had refused to surrender the departmental archives, thus refusing to acknowledge the authority of the provisional government. He also reported that the Nacogdoches committee of safety and vigilance had taken matters into their own hands by seizing the public funds and planning to reopen the land offices "for the purpose of getting the money they may pay in, to be used by themselves in Disbursements as they will say for the Use of the Volunteers."[65] Forbes also mentioned that he had administered the oath of allegiance to the famous David Crockett, along with a number of other Americans who were traveling through Nacogdoches.

On January 15, with the Texian government in disarray, the Nacogdoches committee of vigilance and safety met with the goal of appealing for aid separate from the Texian government at San Felipe. They passed four resolutions: First, a formal appeal was made to "The friends of Liberty in the United States for donations . . . of bread stuffs and articles of provisions." Second, a committee of three men was appointed to draft the address to the United States; third, John S. Turner and William Bryan of New Orleans were recommended to be appointed agents for Texas; and fourth, D. H. Vail was recommended to be appointed Texas agent at Natchitoches.[66] Many Nacogdoches leaders continued to operate on their own with little regard for the government at San Felipe, thus confirming Forbes's allegations.

Unlike their commercial counterparts, the New Orleans theatrical community had not yet offered their help for the Texian cause through benefit performances. James Wallace mentioned that he saw the commissioners at the January 4 performance of "The Fall of San Antonio, or Texas Victorious" at the American Theater on Camp Street. One can only speculate whether the play, which was written by twenty-three-year-old Nathaniel Harrington Bannister, was based upon actual reports of the siege. It could have been based upon information from any traveler arriving from Texas with unofficial news or possibly a returning member of the Greys with firsthand information.[67] The play was first performed on January 1; its second performance, on the night of January 4, was the one that Wallace and the Texian commissioners attended. In both January shows, the benefit yielded $150 in donations. On January 7 the American Theater announced that the profits from that evening's performance of "William Tell" would also be "Appropriated to THE TEXIAN CAUSE."[68]

William Gray, William F. Ritchie, and Robert Triplett attended another benefit performance, this time at Caldwell's St. Charles Theater on January 16. The play, "The Soldier's Daughter," was performed with a recital of patriotic prose afterward, followed by martial music to conclude the evening; Gray, Ritchie, and Triplett sat with the Texian commissioners. Gray commented that the crowd was small and the performance, poor.[69] Although Caldwell remained somewhat obscure in the ongoing Texian affairs, serving as the secretary of the committee, his handiwork in the theatrical world was evident in the performances for the Texas cause that winter and spring. Caldwell also presented Bannister's play at the St. Charles Theater five months later, which was renamed "Texas" by N. H. Bannister's wife.[70]

On January 17 William Wharton left for Nashville. The day before, Wharton went to Christy's notary office at Banks's Arcade to provide a power of attorney to the other two commissioners, should further business needed to be completed.[71] On January 20 Austin wrote to the impeached Governor Smith of the specifics of the loans and the appointments of Hall and Bryan as agents. He emphasized the urgency of declaring independence and ratifying the loans. He also enclosed a report of the receipts and disbursements made through the commissioners to several agents or officers who were now in the Texas service. Most of them had been sent to New Orleans to obtain arms, supplies, and ammunition. Austin stated, however, that "a considerable portion of the purchases were made by some of these officers without the intervention of the gen. agent which has caused some confusion in the manner of doing the business, & some of it owing to the want of a proper knowledge of the market." Austin recommended that all future purchases and expenditures go exclusively through the general agent to alleviate any further financial confusion.[72]

Austin also lamented the expenses of outfitting the schooner *Liberty*: "The Schooner Liberty has been expensive, and examination into her accounts may be necessary, and a strict accountability should be established."[73] Bryan also warned Governor Smith against the appointment of numerous "special agents" for particular purchases: "We [Bryan and Hall] can always make more advantageous purchases than a stranger, and gain more advantages on time, & that a municipality of Agents usually tends to injure the credit of the Government."[74]

By January 21 quartermaster Almanzon Huston had amassed $9,000 in orders for supplies, equipment, and ammunition.[75] John A. Wharton, the adjutant general of the Texian army and brother of William Wharton, had accumulated $5,500 in orders by January 11. Two outstanding bills had to be paid: $800 for expenses left over from the outfitting of the New Orleans Volunteer Greys and $208 for a six-pound, brass cannon, which went with the Greys. The commissioners had bought the schooner *Ingham* for $5,000 and advanced Captain Hawkins $500 for its outfitting. John M. Allen drew $4,000 for recruiting expenses.[76]

Bryan reported to Governor Smith the money on hand from the two loans: The $20,000 from the first loan and $40,000 from the second had been promptly spent. Bryan and Hall also quickly realized that their own credit would be required in order to complete future orders and pay for the growing, unforeseen expenses.[77] By January 21, in spite of the financial uncertainty, Hall and Bryan completed their first shipment of supplies. Divided among three schooners, the ninety-nine-ton *Tamaulipas*, the *Caroline*, and the fifty-nine-ton *Pennsylvania*, with the supplies going to either Matagorda or Brazoria and Velasco.[78]

The *Caroline* went to Matagorda, loaded with foodstuffs, such as flour, pork, coffee, sugar, cider vinegar, and ship bread (or hardtack). Tobacco, brandy, wine, and soap, blacksmithing tools, and utensils were also included in the cargo's inventory.[79] The *Tamaulipas*, which was destined for Brazoria, carried military cargo: bullet molds, kegs of musket balls, flints, pistols, sabers, carbines, U.S. muskets, cartridge boxes with straps, drums, bugles, fifes, canteens, copies of *Scott's Infantry Tactics*, and artillery tactics. Boots, brogans, leather, and writing supplies, including the cargo from the *Caroline*, were consigned to Texian Adjutant General John A. Wharton. Much-needed clothing, such as flannel shirts, kersey pantaloons, vests, peacoats and brogans, were shipped on the *Pennsylvania*. Valued at over $15,000, the cargo of the three schooners sailed out of New Orleans under the protection of the armed schooner *Liberty*. The convoy of ships landed off the coast of Texas on January 25.[80] By January 31, Bryan wrote Governor Smith that available cash funds had dwindled to only $500; he attributed the drain on Texian finances to the "appointing [of] special Agents at this place, for particular purchases."[81] Only two days later Bryan reported to Henry Smith that the Texian commissioners had ordered another transfer of $5,000 for Colonel T. D. Owings to raise a full regiment of volunteers.[82]

On January 16 an editorial on Texas was published in the *Bee*. Written by "Phoenix," the writer proclaimed "Texas, Texas, the all absorbing of the day is Texas. The curtain is raised, and a new scene is presented on the political theatre."[83] Though the focus of the newspapers continued to be on Texas, attention soon turned to a new crisis brewing in Florida. The news that Seminole Indians had massacred United States troops, commanded by Brevet Major Francis L. Dade, in Florida flashed through the city. On January 9—the same day that the $200,000 loan was completed—William F. Gray wrote in his journal that the news was being announced in the city's newspapers.[84] Two days later a public meeting was held, much like the friends of Texas gathering in October at Banks's Arcade. At the meeting, rivals on both sides of the nativist debate found themselves appointed to the same committee, whose charge was "To receive subscriptions for the relief of the widows and orphans of those who fell victims in the late massacre of the troops on their march from Tampa Bay to Fort King." The meeting gathered between $4,000 and $5,000 "for the purpose of procuring clothing and equipping volunteers."[85]

Upon receiving word of the massacre, General Edmund Pendleton Gaines, commander of the Western military district headquartered at New Orleans, requested that the governor and the militia commander call for volunteers. On February 3 General Gaines, Colonel Twiggs with three hundred regulars, and Colonel Persifor Smith with seven hundred Louisiana militia left for Florida from the U.S. barracks downriver from the city.[86] On January 23, while Gaines was preparing to go to Florida, U.S. Secretary of War Lewis Cass sent Gaines orders to march to the western frontier near Texas. Also ordering the U.S. Sixth Regiment to proceed to Fort Jesup, Cass ordered troops in western Louisiana, west of the Mississippi, and south of the Missouri River to join the movement. Maintaining neutrality, Cass ordered Gaines to prevent all of these parties from approaching the Mexican-United States border and from crossing into U.S. territory. Citing article thirty-three of the Treaty of Amity, Commerce, and Navigation, which allowed for the military prevention of Indian incursions into Mexico, he directed Gaines to faithfully enforce the treaty.[87] However, General Gaines did not receive the orders until February 9, when he was already at Fort Brooke in Florida. He refused to return immediately and, with Smith's Louisiana volunteers, marched on to Tampa. Gaines did not leave Florida until March, arriving back in New Orleans on March 28.[88]

East Texas leaders had also made the Indians an issue since the previous summer. In September, 1835, the Nacogdoches committee of vigilance and safety sent a letter to President Andrew Jackson expressing concern over a re-

General Edmund Pendleton Gaines, daguerreotype, circa early 1840s. Courtesy of Dr. Bill Schultz.

port that Archibald Hotchkiss and Benjamin Hawkins were planning to bring Creek Indians into Texas from the United States. Referring to these empresario plans as an "incursion," the committee appealed to President Jackson to prevent the Creeks from crossing into Texas, citing the thirty-third article of the 1831 treaty as a basis for their request.[89] Reports continued to circulate back to New Orleans that local Indians were allying themselves with the Mexicans through the incitement of secret agents. Cass's letter intimated that Indians from the United States were entering Texas with the intent of allying themselves against the Texians. U.S. troops were being sent to the western frontier to protect and, if need be, to infiltrate Mexican territory to stop any Indian abuses.

Back in New Orleans, the Tampico disaster would not go away. After several months of published letters from the prisoners of Tampico, a cloud of controversy continued to hang over Christy's head concerning his alleged involvement. The debate centered on the execution of men who were reportedly American citizens. On December 29, 1835, chargé d'affaires Anthony Butler submitted an inquiry to the Mexican government as to why thirteen of the Tampico prisoners, who were identified as Americans, were executed. José María Ortíz Monasterio, the Mexican foreign minister, replied on January 25. He defended the executions on the basis that the expedition was an invasion of Mexico's national territory, which was "under the orders of the traitor José Antonio Mexía." [90] Monasterio reported that Mexican authorities had considered the expedition an act of piracy, "as those adventurers belonged to no nation with whom the republic was at war, and fought under no acknowledged flag." [91] The authorities in Tampico, Monasterio wrote, had done nothing more than follow Mexican law. The next day Butler shot off a letter to U.S. Secretary of State John Forsyth that balked at Monasterio's reply.

Butler continued to perpetuate the reports that the Tampico prisoners were tricked into participating in an armed invasion. He believed that Mexía had abandoned the men and that they were "victims of the offended vanity and uncontrollable passions of General Santa Anna, merely because the people of Texas have dared to oppose his will in relation to the contemplated change of Government." He urged a stern reply to the executions: "Surely none better could present itself to justify us in teaching these semi-barbarians a lesson of justice and good faith." [92]

The Tampico prisoners' letters continued to be published throughout the United States. Several of the men had maintained that Christy had tricked them into going on an expedition they would have otherwise refused to be a part of if they had known what the true mission was before departing. In late February the negative attention forced District Attorney Henry Carleton to indict Christy on charges of "unlawfully setting on foot, and providing and preparing the means for a military expedition against the territory and dominions of Mexico." Carleton subpoenaed more than twenty witnesses for the trial. Even though several personal friends offered to serve as his attorney, Christy refused their offers and chose to represent himself in the trial.

Strangely, Mexía, who had returned to New Orleans in early January, was neither called as a witness nor deposed. Of the twenty-two witnesses who gave evidence, only John M. Allen and Elias Brush, former members of the expedition, testified. Charles Hawkins, who was now at sea as captain of the war schooner *Independence*, provided an affidavit, as did Allen, even though he had been a witness at the trial. Allen testified that the expedition's mission was unknown to him until the schooner cleared U.S. waters, but he believed that "the men entered willingly into Mexía's views." [93] He also maintained that Christy had remained outside the inner planning of the expedition and had even discouraged some men from going on the expedition, including Allen.

Elias Brush testified that Christy had discouraged him from going on Mexía's expedition. He maintained that he "knew the minds of the men as well as anybody, and he never heard any one say that he had been deceived by Mr. Christy, or make any complaint against him." [94] William Cole, who had boarded several of the men before they departed, testified that Orderly Sergeant Edward Davis, who at the time was Mexía's agent, had told him that their destination was Tampico, but he also believed that many of the men did not know that they were bound for Tampico. [95] Three newspaper editors— John F. Carter, R. M. Carter, and John Gibson—were called. Gibson, a good friend of Christy's, editor of the *True American*, and mouthpiece of the Louisiana Native American Association, stated that not only did he not know of "what was generally called Mexía's expedition," but he also did not know who had furnished the means or money for the expedition; he was especially unaware of either Christy's involvement with Mexía or the enlistment of any men for Texas. [96]

Even John F. Carter, editor of the anti-Texas newspaper, the *Union*, testified that he knew nothing of Christy's involvement with Mexía, even though he stated that he knew of Christy's role as chair of the Texas committee. [97] Many of the witnesses, including several merchants who had opposed the sailing of the *Brutus*, could not provide incriminating testimony linking Christy to Mexía's expedition. [98] The only witness who was outspoken against Christy and the Texas campaign was R. M. Carter. Carter at first refused to be sworn in, maintaining that there "was no trial before the court." When he was overruled by Judge Rawle, Carter testified that he first saw Mexía at a breakfast at Marty's coffeehouse, where Mexía gave a speech. Even though Carter admitted that he was not privy to any knowledge of Christy's involvement with Mexía, he criticized the war in Texas as a war of speculation and declared "the emigration there as injurious to our own country." He believed that all of the expeditions,

Mexía's and the sending of the Greys, were warlike and that Christy and others knew that they were. Christy, according to Carter, had told him that he had contributed money to the Texas cause.[99]

Amazingly, even though Christy and the other members of the Texas committee had committed questionable interference in Mexican affairs with their sponsorship of the Greys and the arming of ships to patrol against the Mexican navy, Carleton's and Judge Rawle's focus appeared to be on the Tampico expedition. Several witnesses—including William G. Latham, a clerk in Christy's office; Nacogdoches land man Augustus C. Allen; and John Brainard, the owner of Banks's Arcade Coffeehouse, and fellow committee member James H. Caldwell—all openly admitted to Christy's chairmanship of the Texas committee, but the sending of men to Texas was consistently defended as a lawful act of emigration, not the arming of military companies.

Those who had firsthand knowledge of the expedition, such as Allen, Brush, and Hawkins, stated that Mexía alone was responsible for the expedition and that Christy had nothing to do with it. According to Brush and Allen, Christy gave several speeches to the volunteers before departure, but that was the extent of his involvement. Second, even though the expedition's destination had been kept a secret until it had cleared U.S. waters, Allen's, Brush's, and Hawkins's testimony suggested that the majority of the men then agreed to participate in the attack on Tampico once briefed on the mission. Allen declared that he did "not know of Mr. Christy's having any pecuniary or personal interest in anything relating to Mexico or Texas." He went on to say that Christy owned lands in Texas, which he had purchased from Allen himself after Mexía had left.[100]

Even with such admissions, Carleton could not find anyone who could link Christy to Mexía. The apparent underlying view seemed to be that aiding Texas in its struggle was not the same as supporting the Tampico expedition. Judge Rawle then exonerated Christy from any involvement with Mexía. Not long after the trial, Christy had the proceedings printed by Benjamin Levy as a vindication of the charge of his alleged involvement with Mexía.[101] Jerome Bayon of the *Bee* wrote that he was not surprised at Christy's prosecution but that he predicted that Christy would be found not guilty. Bayon hoped that the trial would teach "forbearance to him and all other generous and spirited citizens, as regards the present struggle of the Texians."[102]

Undaunted by the trial, Christy continued to act as chair of the Texas committee and to receive reports of events in Texas from personal correspondence with Texian leaders at San Felipe. Acting Governor James W. Robinson wrote

Christy on February 5, enclosing a copy of a letter from Francis W. Johnson, reporting that he and Fannin had joined forces to march against Matamoros. Robinson also expressed his hope that the upcoming convention scheduled for March 1 would settle things in terms of the Texas's political future once and for all. Furthermore, he assured Christy that in spite of what he might have heard about Smith's impeachment, "The course of Texas is onward & . . . these clouds that hang upon the morn of her revolution will not, cannot retard her march to freedom & independence." [103]

On February 15 Christy bought fourteen leagues of Texas land from Nacogdoches land man Frost Thorn, who was in the city. He went in partnership with Kentuckian George Hancock, one of lenders of the $200,000 loan. The land, located near the Sabine River, was sold at fifty cents an acre and on terms of 12, 18, and 24 months. With the purchase price set at $30,996, Thorn threw in an extra *labor* (Spanish unit of measure) free of charge.[104] Writing to Richard Ellis, president of the constitutional convention, several weeks later, Christy apparently had entrepreneurial plans in Texas: "[Y]ou must not be surprised to see me among you, in a few months, if my present plans suceed [sic]. I shall soon have a large Cotton farm, perhaps several of them under weigh [sic] in Texas." [105]

On January 19 William F. Gray departed for Texas, traveling up the Mississippi to where it met the Red River. He stopped in Alexandria to visit George Hancock, who was visiting with his wife's brother. Hancock and James Irwin of Cincinnati traveled on to Natchitoches with Gray, where the travelers met the former governor of Coahuila y Texas, Agustín Viesca, and Nacogdoches political chief Henri Rueg. Gray also visited with D. H. Vail, Texas agent at Natchitoches, and received a Nacogdoches newspaper titled "Texan Emigrants Guide," which provided Gray with information on Mexico's colonization laws.

Both Hancock and Irwin appeared to return to New Orleans for some reason, but Gray went on. After visiting Fort Jesup, he traveled on to Texas, crossing over the Sabine River at Gaines Ferry, where he met Nacogdoches leader Frost Thorn at a local tavern. Arriving in Nacogdoches on January 30, Gray stayed there for a while looking at land titles. He witnessed a tense standoff between local citizens and incoming volunteers at the local election for delegates to the upcoming constitutional convention.[106] On February 7 Gray left Nacogdoches, traveling down the Camino Real, arriving on February 13 at the frontier hamlet of Washington-on-the-Brazos, where the constitutional convention was to open on March 1. As the delegates arrived, the weather turned bone-chilling cold. In the unfinished building that served as the meeting hall, sheets of canvas were tacked over the open windows to stop the north wind from piercing its way into the building.[107]

José Antonio Mexía and George Fisher returned to New Orleans to find that much of their respect and prestige of the previous November had evaporated. Fisher took a job with a local company, Koppenburg, Bleeker, and Company.[108] It is not known how Mexía was able to support himself and his family, but he remained at his residence at 62 Great Men Street in Faubourg Marigny.[109] As Santa Anna continued his march northward toward Texas with a large army, few federalists left to oppose him. The *Bee* confirmed that one of Mexía's and Goméz Farías's federalist allies, Governor Francisco Vitál Fernandez of Tamaulipas, had united with Santa Anna's centralist forces and had been named commander in chief of Mexican forces at Matamoros.[110]

Reports like these convinced Austin that the federalist cause was lost and provided him an additional justification of his new stance for independence. He wrote to Houston on January 16 that he had received reports that Santa Anna was at Saltillo with 3,000 men and that an additional 1,000 men were being transported from Tampico and Veracruz. Austin closed with this mention: "The federal party had united with Santanna [*sic*] to invade Texas. This, of course, leaves us no remedy but one, which is an immediate declaration of independence."[111] Father José María Alpuche y Infante, an old friend and exiled federalist ally of Mexía's, had visited Texas and the general council in November but had returned to New Orleans bitter and unconvinced that Texian leaders were sincere in their federalist declarations. Alpuche é Infante subsequently wrote his archenemy of federalism, Santa Anna, on January 18 from New Orleans and denounced the Texians. Santa Anna eagerly published the priest's letter in *El Mosquito Mexicano*, using it to bolster the march on Texas as a national war.[112] Totally disheartened and bitter, Alpuche é Infante then left for Europe immediately.

Former Coahuila y Texas Governor Augustín Viesca and Secretary of State Yrala arrived in New Orleans on January 29.[113] Jerome Bayon's *L'Abeille* reported that Viesca could no longer stay in Texas after witnessing the growth of the independence party. Former federalists like Governor Fernandez could no longer be trusted, and the war in Mexico, now a national war against Texas independence, unified both federalists and centralists. Mexía went back to face $18,000 in loans with a dwindling support base of friends and backers. Correspondence suggests that Mexía and Goméz Farías refused to accept defeat, but the support among American and even Creole merchants was at that point anything but certain.

Any perception of goodwill and cooperation between Texas leaders and Mexican federalist exiles in New Orleans had quickly eroded. Even more so, any impression that Christy and the Texas committee in New Orleans had any involvement with Mexía's Tampico expedition had been quickly dashed by Judge Rawle's ruling in favor of Christy. Nonetheless, the trial left more questions unanswered than it had answered. It did not deter Christy, however, from revealing that his main interest was as much Texas's lands as its struggle. All the while, Christy sought for himself a new role as a land speculator, plantation owner, and possibly even a Texian.

A NEW GOVERNMENT, MILITARY
9 § TRAGEDY AND TRIUMPH, AND
THE TEXAS NAVY

The Texian constitutional convention at Washington-on-the-Brazos convened on March 1, 1836. The weather was bitter cold, and the delegates huddled in the makeshift hall with their cigars and whiskey and made themselves as comfortable as possible. Following parliamentary procedure, the delegates established a quorum necessary to convene. Richard Ellis, a former delegate to the Alabama constitutional convention and Alabama state supreme court justice, was elected president of the gathering. Tennessean George C. Childress moved that the delegates draft a declaration of independence. His motion was seconded, and a committee to draft a document was appointed, with Childress as chair. The next day, a draft was presented to the convention that declared that their "political connection was now ended, and that the people of Texas do now constitute a FREE, SOVEREIGN, and INDEPENDENT REPUBLIC, and are fully invested with all the rights and attributes which properly belong to independent nations."

Childress had brought with him in his saddlebags a copy of the American Declaration of Independence, and he and the committee spent the night modifying it to fit the grievances against the Mexican government. Childress, whose family had been on friendly terms with Andrew Jackson, had crossed the Red River on December 13, 1835, only a few months before the convention, as an agent to deliver the proceeds of a pro-Texas public meeting that had been held in Nashville. He was also a land agent for New York speculator Samuel Swartwout and had arrived in Texas to inspect lands especially in the Red River area.[1] The declaration was approved unanimously on March 2, and all who were present the next day signed the document. Both Charles Taylor and John S. Roberts from Nacogdoches at first hesitated in signing, but according to Gray, they "finally yielded and signed their names."[2]

Although some of the delegates had not yet arrived, Ellis wasted no time in appointing committees to begin work on a constitution. Captain Cooke, Captain David Burke, and Lieutenant Francis Thornton had arrived with Mexican prisoners on the evening of March 5 and the next day were invited to "sit at the bar" and witness firsthand the workings of the convention. That same day Gray wrote that he was surprised to see Albert Burnley and Peter Grayson arrive at the convention. Gray had been an agent for Burnley, but with Gray at the convention on behalf of the lenders, he was unable to do much in scouting for lands. This had not stopped Burnley, who had just purchased $15,000 in lands on the Guadalupe and Lavaca Rivers.[3]

Robert Triplett finally arrived on March 11. He had remained in New Orleans to finalize a land deal that brought him a $5,000 profit. On the road to Washington-on-the-Brazos, Triplett encountered one of the Alamo couriers with a dispatch from Travis destined for the convention.[4] Over the next few weeks Travis sent several dispatches to the convention. The delegates remained on edge, awaiting each message. On March 6 Travis's dispatch of March 3 was received, apprising the delegates of his position. From February 25 to March 3, the Alamo had sustained a continual bombardment without any fatalities. Travis had heard of reports that Fannin was on his way to relieve him but admitted that he doubted the reports since he had sent several appeals to him with no sign of relief. He urged that reinforcements be sent from the colonies; otherwise he would have to fight the enemy on his own terms.

Robert Potter moved that the convention immediately form a temporary government and march to the aid of the Alamo. Gray wrote that "an interesting debate arose," but the convention adjourned for the day without any action. Houston, who had been at the convention as a delegate from Refugio, left instead as commander to organize the army at Gonzales, eighty miles from Béxar. Captain Cooke, Captain Tarleton, and others went with him as his general staff.[5] Cooke remained with Houston throughout the campaign as a member of his staff and a faithful assistant.[6]

Upon his arrival at the hamlet on the Brazos, Triplett found the village full of people—all of them anxious for news from the Alamo and Goliad. Triplett also found William Gray despondent. Gray expressed doubt about the delegates' support for the proposed loan. He observed that there was also much "log rolling" concerning the lands in Texas as well as jockeying for the "high offices of State." He also stated that there was still a "great hostility" toward the land sales by the Coahuila y Texas legislature, and this opposition caused some to call for the nullification of all land grants except headrights.[7]

On March 8 the loan issue was included in Governor Henry Smith's report to the convention. The report was referred to committee, and Gray lamented that "the subject was smuggled out of sight of the house, a course seemingly inauspicious to the confirmation of the loan." In light of conversations he had with the delegates, he had reason to be despondent. Dr. Stephen Everett complained to Gray that he believed the commissioners had overstepped their authority in negotiating the loans in New Orleans and viewed the conditions to be too harsh. Triplett's response to Gray's report was an observant one with regard to the perilous circumstances:"Men with halters about their necks are not in a humor to talk about loans, and their ratification will be of very little avail to us if they are conquered." Instead of accepting Gray's despondent report, Triplett suggested to him:" Let us, therefore, first render them what aid we can by clerking for them, while they are framing their constitution."

Triplett met many of the delegates, including Thomas Rusk of Nacogdoches, whom Triplett identified as a leading member of the convention. Triplett and Gray admitted to Rusk that they had a stake in the success of the proceedings and the revolution and offered to help in the copying of the convention's daily proceedings. They were promptly put to work copying at night.[8]

In the early morning hours of March 6, after a thirteen-day siege, Santa Anna's forces attacked the Alamo, overrunning the Texian garrison. Some Mexican military accounts provide a glimpse of the carnage, including the account that six to eight Texians had survived and called for quarter. Several accounts identify former Tennessee Congressman David Crockett as one of them. On Santa Anna's orders they were summarily executed, and the bodies were burned. Of the 200 or more men who were with Travis and Bowie, 25 of them had been members of Breece's company of New Orleans Greys. Nearly half of the original company that had left New Orleans in October had been killed in the early morning battle.[9] Included among the dead were their captain, William Blazeby, who had taken command on December 12, and John J. Baugh, who had become Travis's adjutant.[10]

Santa Anna's forces captured the Greys' flag, which Captain Thomas Breece's company had proudly carried from the Sabine River through the storming of Béxar. Other flags were flown at the Alamo and may also have been captured, but Santa Anna chose this one to send back to Mexico City with a note to Secretary of War and Marine José María Tornel:"The bearer takes with him one of the flags of the enemy's Battalions, captured today. The inspection of it will show plainly the true intentions of the treacherous colonist[s], and of their abettors, who came from parts of the United States of the North."[11] The Greys guidon, with the inscription"First Company of Texan Volunteers! from New-Orleans," served Santa Anna's political purposes well. It confirmed what many in Mexico already knew—that Americans were aiding the Texians in their revolution against him. Santa Anna's forces took the Alamo at a tremendous cost, however. It is estimated that Santa Anna lost at least 500 to 600 men, about one-third of his entire attacking force, in the early morning attack.[12]

Most of the women and children, possibly as many as twenty-five, who had entered the fort with husbands or family, had survived. Along with them, possibly five slaves from various owners, including Travis and Bowie, also survived. Most of the women were Tejanas, or native Mexican-Texians. The only Anglo woman, Suzannah Dickenson, was sent with a slave and her infant daughter to announce the morbid news of the Alamo to the Texian colonists to the east. General Houston, who had arrived at Gonzales, learned of the attack from her on March 11.[13]

On March 15 delegates finally received the news of the fall of the Alamo. Houston sent two letters to the convention, and San Antonio delegates Ruíz and Navarro received a letter relating the details from Juan Seguín. Some of the delegates refused to believe the reports. The next day, however, Dr. John Sutherland arrived from Gonzales and confirmed the news. A courier for Travis, Sutherland had actually seen the funeral pyres of the Texian dead and also lost his son William in the battle. The news left the delegates impatient and distraught, but most of them were determined to complete their work at hand.[14]

In less than three weeks, the convention established a constitutional government much like that of the United States, with three branches of government and a declaration of rights. The assembly agreed to a policy that provided land for the citizens of Texas who were legal residents before March 2, 1836 (up to one league and labor). All legally surveyed lands registered before the closing of the land offices by the consultation were declared valid, but reflecting the resentment left over from the previous year's sales of Texas lands by the legislature of Coahuila y Texas, the delegates nullified the sale of the eleven-league grants under the law of March 26, 1834, and the law of March 14, 1835, which the Mexican national congress had also nullified on April 25, 1836.[15]

John T. Mason became the target of the delegates' resentment. The acquisitions of land by Mason, an agent of the Galveston Bay and Land Company, and New York collector of customs Samuel Swartwout as well as all purchases of lands derived from those acts were declared null and void. All eleven-league grants located on the twenty-league buffer along the border with Texas and the United States were also declared invalid. Mason was targeted perhaps because he embodied the image of the American speculator, while those who had made Texas their home believed their lands should be for Texians, not for far-away investment interests in New York. For that reason alone the convention established the principle that no foreigner could hold land in Texas, except by titles directly issued by the government.[16]

At midnight on March 16, the convention finally ratified the constitution, and by four o'clock in the morning they had elected ad interim officers. David Burnet was elected president; Lorenzo de Zavala, vice-president; Robert Potter, secretary of the navy; Thomas Rusk, secretary of war; Bailey Hardeman, secretary of the treasury; and Samuel Carson, newly arrived in Texas, secretary of state.[17] The next morning, the issue of the New Orleans loans finally came before the convention when George Childress moved to allow Triplett to present the details. Triplett explained the specifics of the loans. Acknowledging the widespread opposition to the loans among the delegates, he stated that he was willing to offer an alternative to the original contracts. He also proposed to leave the decision to the president. With reports of Mexican cavalry only sixty miles distant, the delegates unanimously passed the resolution to allow President Burnet and his cabinet to consider the loans at a later date. Gray wrote, "They have blinked the question," acknowledging the need for money at the best terms, not rejecting the loan outright, but not confirming it either. Texas, according to Gray, was "an invaded, unarmed, unprovisioned country, without an army to oppose the invaders and without money to raise one, [and] now presents itself to their heretofore besotted and blinded minds, and the awful cry has been heard from the midst of the assembly,'What shall we do to be saved?'"The government was already in debt for $46,530.95, not including the debt incurred by Bryan and Hall in New Orleans and by other agents.[18]

When the convention adjourned, the delegates quickly scattered. Gray and Triplett traveled with Thomas Rusk and the government to Harrisburg, near the Gulf coast. Triplett, who had been allowed to sit in on many of their sessions and advise privately, waited for the chance to once again approach the cabinet concerning the loans. Burnet had polled his cabinet on the loans, and most of them objected to the terms for several reasons. They believed that the commissioners had exceeded their authority in negotiating the loans and that the fifth article of both loans—granting priority of location to the lenders—would paralyze the land sales. The cabinet also questioned whether the government actually had the right to set aside lands.[19]

Finally, Thomas Rusk, speaking for the cabinet, approached Triplett concerning the terms. Triplett asked Rusk what land was selling for. Rusk replied that the price had fallen to $12^{1}/_{2}$ cents an acre. Triplett responded that he would accept 25 cents an acre, twice the current rate, thereby acknowledging that he could have acquired lands at $12^1/2$ cents an acre based on the original terms of the loan. Rusk suggested a compromise to Triplett, and as negotiations went on, Triplett stated that he would take 135,000 acres at 50 cents an acre for what he and the other lenders had already "paid in" as the advance. Although the cabinet at first objected to the compromise, they finally agreed.[20]

Meanwhile, Edward Hall had also arrived from New Orleans to meet with the new government and offered a grim report of the financial conditions of their agency in New Orleans.[21] The cabinet also recruited Triplett as their new general agent for Texas in the United States. Triplett agreed, and the compromise to the original loan was settled, at least with Triplett and Gray. Triplett was given the power to appoint four secretaries throughout the United States and local agents as needed.

Triplett took charge immediately in purchasing cargo lying off Galveston Island. Burnet also issued Triplett $2,000 in land scrip to provide for much-needed operating funds. Triplett turned to his traveling companion, Dr. Sterling Niblett, who advanced him the money. With land scrip in hand, Gray, Triplett, and Niblett set off to Galveston Island, where Triplett and Niblett quickly surveyed off a section of land.[22]

Triplett and Gray took back a much different agreement from the one the commissioners had negotiated in January. All the original terms of the two loans were relinquished except for the mode of transferring scrip and titles. The ad interim government agreed to give 32 leagues of premium, unclaimed land at 50 cents an acre, to be divided among the lenders of the two loans, in proportion to the amounts they had invested. The scrip would be divided into shares of 640-acre sections. The lenders of the first loan had to relinquish their right to priority of land location over the lenders of the second loan. The lenders of the first loan would receive four shares, and the lenders of the second loan would receive one share of the 32 leagues. The lenders had the right to pay up the remainder of the loan if they so wished. They could also buy up to $100,000 from private Texian citizens after one year of the compromise agreement. Within ten years of the compromise agreement, the lenders were required to have at least one settler on their lands for every 1,280 acres.[23] Gray wrote with little fanfare in his journal, "at length the loan matter is concluded."

Meanwhile, at Goliad (Fort Defiance), Colonel James Fannin's situation grew worse by the day. Mexican General José Urrea's forces, which had marched northward from Matamoros through the grasslands of northern Tamaulipas, had closed in on the scattered remnants of Grant's and Johnson's forces. On February 27 Urrea systematically eliminated Johnson's force at San

Patricio. James Grant and former Greys commander, Robert Morris, were ambushed on March 2 at Agua Dulce Creek, approximately fifteen miles south of San Patricio.[24]

Fannin's force waited in vain for food and supplies located at Cox's Point on the coast. No carts, however, were available to transport them to Goliad. Expressing exasperation over the tenuous situation, Fannin leveled blame at the people of Texas for not coming to their aid.[25]

When Johnson, one of the survivors, made his way back to Fort Defiance with the news of his and Grant's defeat, the report created much anxiety among Fannin's men. To make matters worse, Fannin had received word from a local settler that colonists from Refugio and San Patricio had been left stranded in Refugio. On March 9 or 10, learning that some of the local Refugio rancheros had joined Urrea, Fannin sent Amon King and twenty-eight men to help with an evacuation. They arrived at Refugio on March 11 or 12.[26]

In the meantime, Houston had returned from a furlough during which he and Commissioner John Forbes had negotiated a treaty with many of the East Texas Indians. On March 4 Houston attended the convention at Washington, where the delegates named him commander in chief of all Texian forces. Upon his arrival in Gonzales, he immediately ordered Fannin to destroy Fort Defiance, take only a few of pieces of artillery, dump the rest in the San Antonio River, and retreat to Guadalupe Victoria. After destroying Gonzales to keep it from falling into the hands of the Mexican army, Houston fell back to Burnham's Crossing, on the Colorado River. On March 17 Houston once again ordered Fannin to fall back, this time to Cox's Point or Dimmit's Landing on the coast in order to protect military stores, with the ultimate goal of uniting with Houston's army.[27]

Once Fannin had committed men to the rescue of civilians at Refugio, he was forced to delay his withdrawal. While gathering the families near Refugio, King's men were attacked by local rancheros. King, with his forces and the colonists, withdrew to a local mission, Nuestra Señora del Refugio, to hold off approximately one hundred rancheros and Karankawa Indians.[28] King immediately sent a request to Fannin for help. In response, Fannin sent out reinforcements to help King. Lieutenant Colonel William Ward was sent to rescue King and the colonists. When Ward arrived at Refugio, his forces drove off the rancheros and Indians. With the arrival of Ward's men, more trouble ensued as the two commanders clashed over who should have rightful claim to the command of the forces.

At night, Ward's men attacked a Mexican encampment, killing twenty-five.

King raided local rancheros, while Ward remained at the mission after his nighttime attack. General Urrea arrived at Refugio, defeating King's small force and taking seven prisoners. Urrea went on to the mission where Ward's men were protecting the colonists. Realizing that he was outnumbered, Ward and his men escaped and arrived near Guadalupe Victoria six days later. Hoping to meet up with Fannin or Houston, Ward was surprised to discover that Mexicans already occupied the town. Many of Ward's men were either captured or killed. Ward and a remnant of the once-proud Georgia battalion attempted to make their way to the coast but were captured by Mexican cavalry and marched back to Goliad.[29]

Upon hearing reports of Urrea's victories near San Patricio, Captain Luís Guerra's men became alarmed. They knew that if they were captured, they would be shot as deserters or rebels. Guerra requested that he be allowed to take his men to Cox's Point on the coast and then to New Orleans. This came only days after a Mexican, stating that he was a local ranchero, had entered the fort to specifically talk to Guerra's men. Reportedly, the ranchero was actually a Mexican officer with a dispatch to Guerra from General Urrea. Urrea offered Guerra and his men a full pardon if they would rejoin the Mexican army. The alternative, however, would be capture and execution if they remained with the Texians. Guerra went to Fannin to explain his men's concerns.

Colonel Fannin expressed his understanding of their situation and granted them an honorable discharge. He then wrote a letter to José Antonio Mexía on March 11, obviously for Guerra and his men to take to New Orleans, recommending them to Mexía. Fannin included the latest intelligence on Mexican troop strength in Texas and informed Mexía that the convention in Washington-on-the-Brazos would soon declare Texas independent. He mistakenly assured him that the Texians would still support Mexía's aim of a federalist Mexico.[30] Guerra's small artillery company of eighteen men left Goliad and within days joined Urrea's men at San Patricio. It is not clear why Guerra did not go on to New Orleans. He may have truly intended to go to New Orleans but discovered that their route was cut off by Mexican cavalry. Rather than making a break for the coast, he and his men probably chose to join Urrea instead of risking capture. According to one report of the skirmishes around Refugio, the Texians discovered that one of the Mexican dead left on the field was Guerra.[31]

After Lieutenant Colonel Ward sent word of the situation at Refugio, Fannin sent orders for both forces to withdraw to Goliad and, if cut off, to march to Guadalupe Victoria. Fannin, now short 150 men, finally left Fort Defiance on the morning of March 19, with many of their provisions burned and the fort partially demolished. All of the artillery, except for two four-pounders, a mortar, and a smaller mortar, were spiked and left behind.[32] Only a short distance from the fort, according to Hermann Ehrenberg, additional supplies, provisions, and personal possessions were thrown into the San Antonio River because the few poor oxen teams and horses that had been commissioned to move Fannin's army were overloaded. Scouts were ordered to bring up the rear, looking for signs of Urrea's army. Both Ehrenberg and Thomas Kemp had joined Captain Albert C. Horton's mounted scouts and were the first to encounter the advance cavalry of the Mexican army coming up from behind the column approximately eight miles east of Fort Defiance.

Ehrenberg recalled that the main Mexican force was located to the front and left of Fannin's force and that the rear cavalry attack only detained Fannin from entering the local woods for cover. Despite frantic protests from officers and from many in the rank and file, Fannin stopped in the middle of an open prairie with no cover to form an effective defensive position. Ehrenberg stated that members of the Greys threatened to go to the woods on their own, but before they could do so, the Mexican army attacked. Ehrenberg made his way into the square, joining his comrades instead of fleeing with Horton's now dazed scouts.[33]

Surrounded by Mexican cavalry and infantry with Indian sharpshooters, Fannin's men maintained their poise under extreme conditions. The besieged army quickly formed a hollow square with wagons and carts centered in the middle. The respective companies were assigned a side of the square to defend. Artillery was placed on each corner, where artillery crews were able to direct a deadly cannonade that repulsed and disrupted the charge of the Mexican cavalry and infantry throughout the afternoon. Cannoneers took heavy losses, and the lack of water to sponge the cannon made the artillery so hot to operate that the remaining artillery crewmen had to resort to small-arms fire. Late in the afternoon, some of the San Antonio Greys manned the cannon.[34] The high, prairie grass helped conceal the attacking infantry, and in some cases, the Mexicans were able to advance to within reach of Texian defenders but were forced back. By sundown, Urrea's men were running out of ammunition, so the attack was halted until the following morning. Urrea had sent for artillery and ammunition, which finally arrived at six the next morning. He now had two, four-pound cannons and a howitzer.[35]

During the fitful, cool, drizzly night, the Texian wounded, who had no water to slake their thirst, cried and moaned for relief. Ehrenberg told of the death of one of his comrades, Conrad Eigenaur, a former member of Breece's company. As Ehrenberg roamed throughout the makeshift camp, a voice from the darkness called to him in German. The wounded man, Eigenaur, asked that a carpetbag be placed under his head, which Ehrenberg did. Ehrenberg spent the last moments with his comrade, talking with him and keeping him company until he died.

By the next morning, Urrea had readied his troops, and the Mexican artillery opened fire on the Texian force. Fannin immediately raised a white flag above the baggage. Most of Fannin's officers agreed that the only way to save the wounded was to surrender. General Urrea halted the artillery fire and sent out three of his officers under a white flag "to approach the enemy and ascertain their purpose." After a parley, Fannin asked for certain stipulations to his surrender. Urrea explained that he was authorized to accept only an unconditional surrender but that he would appeal to the Mexican government for their lives. Fannin agreed. Many of the members of the Greys and Red Rovers from Alabama cursed the decision, urging others to fight on rather than submit to the agreement set forth by Fannin and Urrea. Many expected to be butchered when captured by the Mexican forces. With many of their friends wounded, the Greys and the Red Rovers, however, yielded their positions on the line and gave up their weapons.

The Texians were marched back to Fort Defiance as prisoners of war while Urrea marched on to Guadalupe Victoria. For a week the Texians were crammed into the chapel of the presidio with little water or food. Upon hearing of the taking of Fannin's men at Coleto Creek, Santa Anna reprimanded Urrea and ordered Urrea's subordinate, Colonel José Portilla, to execute Fannin's men. Some of the Mexican officers assured the prisoners that they would be released, but much to Urrea's disapproval, on Palm Sunday, March 27, Fannin's men were divided into three groups. Weak and hungry, the men were marched out in three different directions and shot.[36]

Ehrenberg's group, consisting of Burke's and Pettus's men, were marched down the Victoria road, when suddenly the Mexican soldiers turned. With the command to fire—"Fuego!"—a volley of musket fire cracked the silence. In the midst of the smoke, Ehrenberg jumped up, his clothes now covered with the blood of Lieutenant J. B. McManomy, who had fallen next to him. Ehrenberg began running toward the San Antonio River. He took notice long enough to see Peter Mattern and George Courtman, now in the throes of death near where he and McManomy had fallen. In the midst of the smoke and the screaming, others also tried to escape. As Ehrenberg dashed to the river, a Mexican officer attempted to stop him with an abrupt saber blow to Ehrenberg's head and arm. Ehrenberg's determination to escape forced the officer to give way, and he was able to make it to the banks with musket balls whizzing around him. Miraculously, he swam across and avoided the Mexican cavalry waiting on the other side. The Grey's mascot, an adopted dog, was not so lucky. He too had jumped into the river only to be shot. He died in the waves.[37]

Ira Westover's company was in the group sent southwestward along the San Patricio road. The men who had endured the defeat at Tampico and the hardships with Mexía all died except Charles B. Stewart. William L. Hunter, a young attorney from Virginia, who had joined Morris's (Cooke's) Greys, was knocked to the ground. Feigning death, he lay still, only to be bayoneted in the shoulder. He was cut on the neck when camp followers were stripping off his hunting shirt to get to his coat. Discovering he was still alive, a Mexican soldier hit Hunter repeatedly over the head with the butt of a musket until he was left for dead. In the evening Hunter miraculously regained consciousness among the bodies of his dead comrades. Even though he was in tremendous pain and shock, he crawled to the banks of the San Antonio River, where he swam through the cool, muddy waters to the other side. For three days he wandered in the prairies until he found a local rancho, where he was kept at a settler's home and was able to recover from his wounds.[38]

Mexican officers spared some of the prisoners from the mass executions for utilitarian reasons. Members of the San Antonio Greys—John Voss, Joseph Spohn, Peter Griffin—were spared along with approximately twelve others to carry out various jobs for the Mexican Army.[39] Hermann Ehrenberg, William L. Hunter, John Rees, William Brennan, David Jones, Thomas Kemp—former members of the Greys and Charles B. Stewart, formerly of Mexía's expedition, all escaped. Joseph Spohn, who was conversant in Spanish, had served as a translator. A Mexican officer stopped him from marching out with the others.[40]

The losses from the Alamo and Goliad were staggering. Approximately 200 or more died at the Alamo, and those executed with Fannin were estimated at 342. Of the 38 volunteers in Burke's Greys, one was killed at Coleto Creek, 30 were killed on March 27, 4 were spared, and 3 escaped. Samuel Pettus's San Antonio Greys lost 19 men in the execution; 4 escaped and 3 were spared. Most of the Greys, who had so confidently left New Orleans only six months before, and many of Allen's (later Thornton's) men, who had experienced the disaster at Tampico, shared a common tragic fate with Fannin. The majority of Pettus's and Burke's companies, along with Westover's regulars, were shot. By the end of March, General Urrea's forces were in control of Refugio, San Patricio, Goliad, Guadalupe Victoria, and Copano Bay and were moving toward Brazoria.

General Santa Anna had taken San Antonio de Béxar and Gonzales and was marching on San Felipe de Austin. Another Mexican force captured Mina (now Bastrop) on April 1 on El Camino Real and continued moving toward Nacogdoches. The only thing that had slowed the Mexican army in Texas was the heavy spring rain that created widespread flooding, which made the crossing by large numbers of soldiers hazardous.[41]

Houston's men also marched and camped in the mud and rain, but the continual falling back only made them more ill tempered toward their commander and their circumstances. Santa Anna arrived in San Felipe de Austin on April 7, forcing a small Texian guard to withdraw. Texian forces in South Texas and Tamaulipas had been defeated, leaving Houston's army the only organized troops left to face Santa Anna's army of operations against Texas. Houston had fallen back to Burhnam's Crossing on the Colorado River by March 17 and would subsequently fall back to Groce's plantation on the Brazos River.[42]

Houston and the Texian army continued to retreat, creating much consternation among Texians as settlers ran eastward toward the Sabine to avoid the Mexican army. President Burnet wrote Houston, "The enemy are laughing you to scorn. You must fight them. You must retreat no further. The country expects you to fight. The salvation of the country depends on your doing so."[43] By April 13 Santa Anna's forces had taken Fort Bend. There he learned that the Texian ad interim government was at Harrisburg, only a short distance from his position. Hoping to capture Burnet and his cabinet, Santa Anna marched to intercept the fleeing government. On April 15 Mexican forces arrived in Harrisburg, only to discover that Burnet and his cabinet had escaped. On April 18 Santa Anna marched on to the village of New Washington to continue the chase. Burnet, his wife, and members of the cabinet barely escaped capture by leaping into a rowboat just as Mexican forces arrived. Turning his attention then toward Houston's army, Santa Anna ordered his forces to set out northward—for Lynchburg.[44]

Unaware of Houston's plans, the Texian army wearily approached the Nacogdoches road on April 15. According to several participants, the army foiled any plan to lure Santa Anna into a trap with General Gaines waiting on the Sabine River. Instead of marching northward toward Nacogdoches, the army took the fork southward to Harrisburg and toward Santa Anna. Anson Jones speculated in 1859 that Houston had planned to lure Santa Anna into Andrew Jackson's disputed Neches River area, which would have "afforded the Government of the United States a pretext for making common cause of Texas and produced the same state of things which was brought about ten years later by Gen. Taylor's advance to the Rio Grande." Jones called this the "war by the act of Mexico, and with precisely the same want of truth." Guy M. Bryan remarked that "Houston had everything to gain by ultimate success through desolation of Texas. Hence his policy to retreat across the Neches to the proximity of Genl. Gaines' army where he would be reinforced and aided by Gaines, and Santa Anna drawn so far into Texas as to make his escape impossible." Mirabeau Lamar recalled that as the army approached the Nacogdoches Road, Houston was told, "If he took the Nachadoches [sic] road the army would divide, that they were determined to meet the enimy [sic] that he must go down the river & fight: he accordingly took at the forks, the Harrisburg road." On April 20 Houston's and Santa Anna's armies skirmished with little result. Both settled into respective positions one mile from one another near the San Jacinto River and Buffalo Bayou. On the next morning, April 21, General Cós reinforced Santa Anna's position with an additional five hundred men.[45]

After a council of war with his officers and sounding out the rank and file with regard to a fight, Houston ordered his officers to prepare their men for attack. By four o'clock they were all ready. With the battle cry "Remember the Alamo! Remember Goliad!" and the playing of a contemporary love song, "Will You Come to the Bower?" the tired, angry Texian army attacked ferociously and, in only eighteen minutes, had gained possession of the Mexican army's camp, where the Mexicans were in total disarray. Mexican soldiers ran to escape the Texian onslaught. Some Mexican officers tried to rally their troops but failed. Houston was wounded in the ankle but continued to stay on the field of battle even though his boot had filled with blood and several horses had been shot out from under him.

The rest of the day and into the early evening, most of the vengeful Texians continued to hunt down the fleeing Mexican soldiers. In one case, however, Major John M. Allen, who had recently arrived with his company of fresh volunteers, saved several Mexican officers from certain death and prevented further bloodshed. On the field of San Jacinto, 630 Mexican soldiers lay dead, with 208 wounded and more than 500 captured. Texian losses were nine killed and twenty-eight wounded. Santa Anna had initially escaped when the battle started but was captured the next day. Ordered to write to his remaining armies to withdraw to appointed positions, General Filisola, second-in-command, ordered all of the Mexican armies back across Rio Bravo (Rio Grande).

Even though many of Houston's men wanted to execute Santa Anna for the atrocities at the Alamo and Goliad, Houston knew that the captured general was more useful alive than dead, for obvious reasons. Santa Anna still commanded the Mexican army of operations in Texas and could still send orders to his subordinates to keep them at bay. Mexican prisoners were shipped across Buffalo Bayou to Lorenzo de Zavala's home, where Texian doctors reluctantly treated them. The captured officers and men were shipped to Galveston Island to work on the new Fort Travis. Eventually Mexican officers were separated from the rank and file and sent to Liberty on the Trinity River. The rest of the prisoners were either left on Galveston Island or hired out as common laborers. On May 1 President Burnet arrived at San Jacinto, relieved Houston of duty, and sent him to New Orleans for medical treatment. Thomas Rusk was appointed the army's new commander.[46]

Santa Anna was sent with Burnet and his cabinet to Velasco, where they negotiated two treaties, one called the public treaty and the other called the secret treaty. Both stipulated that Santa Anna would cease to fight against Texas and that he would not influence the taking up of arms. A cessation of hostilities was called immediately, and all Mexican armies were required to "evacuate the Territory of Texas, passing to the other side of the Rio Grande del Norte." An additional secret treaty included some of the stipulations in the public agreement with one exception: that Santa Anna agree to encourage Mexican officials to accept a Texian delegation to settle hostilities and establish an official treaty recognizing the sovereignty of Texas. Later, instead of being released to go to Veracruz, Santa Anna was forced to stay on the war schooner *Invincible* when troops under Thomas Jefferson Green arrived, preventing the departure under threat of death by the angry volunteers.

Santa Anna spent the rest of the year as a prisoner of the Texas army at Velasco and was eventually moved near Columbia. The new Texas president, Sam Houston, released him to go to Washington, D.C., on November 20 to meet with President Andrew Jackson ("Old Hickory") to discuss a possible mediation of the war in Texas. Houston made arrangements for Santa Anna to leave Texas. Instead of traveling via the Gulf of Mexico to New Orleans, Santa Anna's escort took the general on the Opelousas Road and through the various channels and waterways to the Mississippi River at Baton Rouge; then they went on to Natchez, Mississippi, and ultimately to Washington City. One unlikely person who was instrumental in providing horses and supplies for the trip was William Christy. Christy had arrived in Texas in October and had already bought a cotton plantation on Oyster Creek on the Brazos River. Santa Anna and Juan Almonte also stayed with Christy one night before leaving for Washington City.[47]

The political and military situation continued to be uncertain for the Texians. Reports from travelers from Matamoros indicated that there were Mexicans calling for a reinvasion of Texas. The reports from Matamoros, however, also stated that Mexican soldiers there were hungry and deserting; many even refused to go back into Texas for another campaign. While still in New Orleans, Christy reported that Mexía and Gómèz Farías were once again planning a federalist overthrow of the Mexican government and that this time, if successful, they would invade Texas themselves.[48] Christy frustrated Mexía with the circulation of this rumor. In contrast, the officers of the Texian army made Christy a hero. They had sent General Cós's bridle and saddle to Christy along with a petition signed by most of the officers as an expression of their appreciation for his support for their cause. Houston's staffs took the saddle and bridle with them to New Orleans and presented the war trophies to Christy.[49]

Following the orders of their captured chieftain, the remaining Mexican armies in Texas withdrew to earlier staging points. The Velasco treaties were signed between the ad interim government and Santa Anna in June, 1836, but because Santa Anna was a prisoner, the Mexican government refused to seriously consider them. The Mexican army was too weak and the Mexican government too inept and too impoverished to carry out any more invasions of Texas for now.[50]

Several original members of the two New Orleans Greys companies survived to participate in the Battle of San Jacinto. William G. Cooke had been promoted to major and was on Houston's general staff at the time. Martin K. Snell, who had come to Texas as a private in Cooke's company, had been voted as first lieutenant in Captain Andrew Briscoe's company of regulars. John M. Allen was acting major of Colonel Henry Millard's regulars, and Robert McClosky, another Tampico veteran, was second lieutenant of Snell's company. Cooke, Snell, McClosky, and Allen had arrived at San Jacinto from totally different paths; Cooke and Snell had participated in one of the early Texian victories in the Battle for San Antonio de Béxar. Allen and McClosky, however, were survivors rather than heroes of the Tampico disaster. All now shared a common destiny in the victory at San Jacinto. Some members of Morris's (later Cooke's) Greys also joined the Texas navy after Béxar was captured. Albert Moses Levy, the surgeon in Cooke's company, left the army on February 10 and joined the crew of the *Brutus*. Hartwell Walker, also a member of Cooke's company, joined the navy as sailing master on Captain Jeremiah Brown's *Invincible*.[51]

In the early months of 1836, the Texas navy primarily served as military transport for volunteers to Copano Bay. Its ships also preyed on Gulf shipping. The *Liberty* captured the Mexican trading schooner *Pelícano* in early March. The captured schooner was wrecked near Matagorda Bay, and when the sailors boarded her, Texian authorities discovered that the barrels of apples and potatoes listed as her cargo were actually filled with 280 kegs of gunpowder for the Mexican army. New Orleans merchant James W. Zacharie had shipped the cargo, and when the report was released to the New Orleans newspaper editors, Zacharie denied knowing anything about the gunpowder. The *Liberty* had a lackluster and disappointing career as a Texian schooner of war. She escorted the *Flora*, which took General Houston to New Orleans, arriving there on May 22, where she was detained for repairs. Because the repair costs exceeded the schooner's value, the *Liberty* was subsequently sold in July, 1836.[52]

The *Invincible* had been ordered into the Gulf to oppose the Mexican war vessel *Montezuma*, later called the *Bravo*.[53] On April 3 the *Invincible* found the *Bravo* near the mouth of the Rio Grande, disabled by a lost rudder. The *Invincible* came alongside at noon, and Lieutenant William H. Leving boarded the *Bravo*. When the *Bravo* attempted to escape with Leving aboard, the Texians suspected foul play. With no rudder, the *Bravo* ran aground and received a broadside from the *Invincible*. The Mexican crew made it to safety on the beach with Leving as their prisoner. Meanwhile, while the *Invincible* was engaged with the *Bravo*, a brig, the *Pocket*, also appeared in sight of the *Invincible*. Captain Brown, turning his attention to the brig, captured the *Pocket* and escorted the vessel into Galveston. The crew of the *Pocket* was released on April 24, and the brig arrived in New Orleans on May 10, where the captain filed a complaint with the district attorney.

The seizure of the *Pocket* by the *Invincible* was denounced in New Orleans by many of the insurance companies. They wrote to Commodore Alexander J. Dallas, commander of the U.S. squadron in Pensacola, Florida, requesting naval protection. Dallas sent the sloop of war U.S.S. *Warren* into the Gulf, where it captured the *Invincible* on May 1 and escorted it to New Orleans. Forty-six of the crew were imprisoned and charged with piracy. Bryan hired three prominent lawyers to defend the crew: O. P. Jackson, Seth Barton, and Randall Hunt. The trial was scheduled to start on May 3 but was delayed until May 6 because witnesses for the prosecution had not yet appeared.

The defense questioned three officers of the sloop *Warren*. However, because the defense attorneys introduced no affidavits or evidence against the crew, Judge Edward Rawle dismissed the case and released the crew.[54] Bryan paid the attorneys $1,500 for their work, a rather large sum even for that day. The controversy continued with a letter from Thomas Urquhart to Commodore Dallas expressing concern over the continued capture of ships by the

Texian navy. Dallas then sent out ships to inform the Texas navy that the practice would not be tolerated. Public outcry against the *Pocket's* seizure prompted rebuke even from Jerome Bayon. The uproar from New Orleans merchants also prompted Burnet to revoke letters of marque and reprisals. It became abundantly clear to the ad interim government that their naval campaign against Mexican shipping could not be carried out without adversely affecting the support of New Orleans businessmen.

When Robert Triplett arrived in New Orleans on May 24, he found that the *Liberty* was being held for want of repairs and a lack of funding. He believed that the Texas navy, in its present form, was too expensive to maintain with so many small ships. Instead, he urged Burnet to purchase a large ship that could combat anything the Mexican navy had in the Gulf. In addition, if the war continued, a larger ship would be "indispensible [*sic*] other wise your whole force might be locked up or destroyed." Jeremiah Brown's crew on the *Invincible* were exceedingly "dissatisfied and insubordinate" at New Orleans. Brown was able to secure an order from Burnet that allowed him to sail to New York, claiming that the costs to outfit the *Invincible* would be cheaper there and that he wanted to get his crew out of New Orleans during the "sickly season." On August 10 Burnet ordered Captain Brown and the *Invincible* to New York for repairs to the vessel.[55]

On March 12 Charles Hawkins arrived in New Orleans, where he received word of his appointment as commodore. As the ranking officer of the tiny fleet, Hawkins patrolled the Gulf coast in the spring and destroyed several Mexican vessels. The *Independence,* which sailed into the Gulf in late March and early April, encountered both of the Mexican brigs of war, *Urrea* and *Bravo.* Hawkins's attack forced the ships to withdraw. Sailing to Galveston, Hawkins looked for both the schooners of war *Invincible* and *Brutus* to assist him in attacking the brigs. However, he discovered that both ships had sailed for New York for refitting without his permission.

Anticipating a major Mexican attack from the coast, Hawkins kept the *Independence* at Galveston. On April 28 the crew received news of Santa Anna's defeat. On May 5 President Burnet, the cabinet, and Santa Anna arrived in Galveston. Santa Anna was kept on the *Independence* and on May 8 sailed for Velasco. The *Independence* then left Velasco for New Orleans to be refitted. Grayson and Collinsworth were aboard and left for Washington City the next day. Texas agent Thomas Toby was quite impressed with Hawkins and his crew. He visited the schooner of war on June 15, commenting that Hawkins's crew was disciplined and the ship both clean and well structured.[56]

In contrast, Toby urged Burnet to dismiss William Hurd. At the end of the

July, Hurd had sailed to New York without orders, vexing both Burnet and Toby regarding his whereabouts. Toby recommended that Burnet keep Texian ships out of New Orleans and locate them at the southwest pass so that they would not be seized for payment of debts from Bryan's agency. Reports arrived from Matamoros that Mexican troops along with Indian allies were preparing to invade Texas once again. On July 21, to hamper the accumulation of supplies sent from New Orleans by pro-Mexican forces, Burnet ordered a complete blockade of the port of Matamoros. Jerome Bayon called Burnet's decree "high-handed." Bayon pointed out that "All would have been well" if Burnet's decree had singled out only Mexican ships. In response to accusations that he was pro-Mexican in the Texas conflict, Bayon retorted that New Orleans had received twice as much needed specie from Mexico the previous year; further, he believed that the United States would not "sit idle and see so fair a portion of our commerce destroyed." Captain Hawkins was given the dubious task of enforcing a blockade of Matamoros with only the *Independence* and four small privateers. The *Liberty* was detained in New Orleans and eventually sold; the *Brutus* and the *Invincible* remained in New York into the next year.[57]

On March 28 General Gaines returned to New Orleans from the Florida campaign, only to leave for Natchitoches immediately. Reports continued to circulate of Indian incursions into eastern Texas. Upon arriving at Natchitoches on April 4, Gaines wrote to Secretary of War Lewis Cass that he had received reports of Indian incursions into Texas and additional information that Santa Anna was marching straight for the Sabine. Gaines was convinced that an Indian force on the Trinity River would unite with him. Though he did not think that his forces were equal in numbers to any potential adversary on the frontier, his hope was to instill a sense of security along the border to encourage Texian settlers to remain at home. Gaines also viewed any future battles as a means to harm the enemy enough to gain their respect for the United States and any of their treaties.[58]

On April 20, with reports that Indians were driving Texian settlers across the Sabine, Gaines wrote to Secretary of War Cass that he had ordered eight companies of the Sixth Infantry and five companies of the Third Infantry to Camp Sabine, near the U.S. border. When Gaines arrived at the Sabine, he discovered several hundred Texian women and children, with some men, retreating into Louisiana from the Nacogdoches area. Though he did not receive any further reports of Indian incursions into Texas, he still sent a warning to Chief Bowles of the Cherokees and other tribes to remain peaceful.

U.S. Lieutenant Joseph Bonnell, who had been sent to meet with the

Caddoes in East Texas, reported to Gaines, however, that some individuals had been attempting to excite the Caddoes into hostilities. Bonnell reported that Mexican agents were working to get the Caddoes to turn on the Texians. On April 8 Gaines issued a call to the governors of Louisiana, Mississippi, Tennessee, and Alabama for additional troops; he requested enough men to compose three brigades and one battalion, with as many to be mounted as possible, and that they be sent to the frontier. He hoped that the mounted troops would arrive by May 1, when the prairie grasses would be sufficient to sustain the horses. The lessons of the Florida campaign, which was fought primarily by infantry, made Gaines more insistent on bringing in cavalry for his march into Texas.

On March 19 Henry Raguet, chair of the Nacogdoches committee of vigilance and safety, wrote to Archibald Hotchkiss, chair of the safety committee in St. Augustine, that he had received word that various tribes from U.S. territory were arriving in East Texas. He feared that, with sufficient spring grasses for their horses, these tribes would attack. He added that there would be more than one thousand Sauk and Fox warriors there soon. Raguet urged Hotchkiss to appeal to the commandant at Fort Jesup "to induce the Government of the United States to take measures to stop the Indians of that country from invading our frontiers." [59]

Hotchkiss and the safety committee at St. Augustine met on March 21 in response to Raguet's letter. They too acknowledged reports that Caddoes, Shawnees, Delawares, Kickapoos, Cherokees, Creeks, "and other renegade Indians from the United States" were assembling in Texas at the three forks of the Trinity River. The committee believed that their presence was, for one thing, "to make war upon the inhabitants of the frontier." They appointed Dr. G. Rowe and P. H. Sublett to go to Fort Jesup and to report Indian movements into Texas to the commander. [60]

John T. Mason, the despised speculator whose holdings from the Coahuila y Texas legislature were declared null and void by the constitutional convention, was also in Nacogdoches, and he too wrote to General Gaines, who had arrived on the western Louisiana frontier in late March. Mason was in Texas as a land agent for Samuel Swartwout, the New York collector of customs. On February 15 Swartwout wrote Sam Houston, asking him for mutual support in preserving Mason's and his own land interests. Swartwout wrote, "We have subscribed money, encouraged people to join your command and used every effort to make your beautiful Texas as free & prosperous, as it is salubrious & fertile. Defend us then & sustain our rights, as we have defended yours and upheld your cause."[61] On April 1 Mason declared to Gaines that the only warlike tribes in Texas were from U.S. territory. He called on Gaines to offer military protection under the mutual Mexican-U.S. treaty. Mason believed that only a small detachment of troops to Nacogdoches would be necessary "to prevent massacre and rapine."[62]

Less than a month after Raguet and others, many of them holding large tracts of land within the disputed Neches-Sabine area, had expressed fears of impending Indian attacks, the Nacogdoches committee of safety and vigilance wrote to President Burnet to urge him to come to Nacogdoches to make it the seat of government. Citing the healthful climate and the relative ease of access to the United States via the Camino Real, the committee offered to provide Burnet and his government with a cordial reception and to supply any necessary accommodations. The committee members understood that Houston's retreating Texian army would rally in the woodlands of East Texas; therefore the government at Harrisburg would be cut off. Once relocated, the government, according to the committee, could maintain proper communication with the army from Nacogdoches.

The committee, which was made up of Nacogdoches land men Frost Thorn, Henry Raguet, and Mason, may have known more than they admitted. On April 4 at Liberty, Samuel Carson wrote to Burnet that he had received a report that General Gaines was marching U.S. troops into Texas to protect Jackson and Butler's Neches River claim. Even though the report was false, it was evident that many in East Texas were hoping that Jackson would use U.S. troops to enforce the disputed line and thus save East Texas from Santa Anna's wrath. The expectation that U.S. troops would enter the disputed area prompted concern from Sterling Robertson on May 27 that men from East Texas would not fight, believing that "The U. S. will fight their battles therefore they are content and think the US calims [claims] to the Natchez [Neches] and they are safe."[63]

On April 11 the Nacogdoches committee of vigilance and safety appointed John Mason military commandant for the district. They authorized him to go to Fort Jesup to solicit the U.S. Army's aid for the protection of fleeing families. Mason accepted the commission with hesitation, still stung by the convention's action. As he stated, "I therefore shall expect and require a thorough cooperation; with which we may accomplish some good, but without which all efforts will be in vain."[64]

On March 14 diplomatic exchanges heated up between ambassador Anthony Butler and Mexican special envoy José María Ortíz Monasterio over the movement of U.S. troops along the U. S.-Mexico border.[65] In Washington City, Secretary of State John Forsyth attempted to assure Mexican special envoy Manuel Edwardo Gorostiza that Gaines's movement along the Texas-Louisiana frontier was not a hostile act toward Mexico; rather, it was intended to eradicate any danger from Indians for both Mexico and the United States.

An incident in New York City had further exacerbated relations. On September 1, when collector of customs Samuel Swartwout had allowed the Texian war schooner *Brutus* to enter the port, the Mexican consul loudly complained.[66] Swartwout, who was also a Texas land speculator, responded that the *Brutus* was a "national" vessel, with a commission from the president of the republic of Texas, that he had not received orders preventing the *Brutus* from entering the port, and that it was the port authority's practice to give entry to vessels from nations who had respectfully declared themselves independent. Swartwout also defended his allowing the *Brutus* into New York City harbor by pointing out that neither the Mexican consul nor the customs collector at New Orleans had openly opposed Texian ships from docking there.

Gorostiza replied that the Mexican consul at New Orleans had indeed protested, but his protests to the pro-Jackson customs collector, James Breedlove, had fallen on deaf ears. Secretary of State Forsyth defended Swartwout's actions, reminding the envoy that it was the practice of earlier U.S. administrations to allow Mexican ships to port at New York City when they were fighting for their independence. After weeks of apparent stonewalling by the Jackson government to his complaints, Gorostiza realized his efforts were useless, and on October 16, 1836, he demanded his passport and left Washington.[67]

On April 28 Gaines received the news of Houston's victory and also word that several of the Indian tribes, including the Cherokees, were returning to their villages to plant corn. Gaines withdrew his call for volunteers from Tennessee, Louisiana, Mississippi, and Alabama. He also sent messages to commanders of both Texian and Mexican forces that he would be willing to mediate the ending of hostilities. By June 7, however, he had changed his mind. Because the capture of Santa Anna had done little to win Texian independence and because of further threats of Mexican invasion, Gaines suspected once again that Indian tribes might be used to raid the frontier. He wrote to Tennessee Governor Carroll to keep his militia in readiness, and he ordered a detachment of U.S. Army regulars into Texas to occupy Nacogdoches. He wrote to the commanding officer to restrain any hostile Indians by force if necessary. By July 31 three companies of dragoons and six companies of the Seventh Infantry had arrived in Nacogdoches from Fort Towson.[68]

Jackson uncharacteristically ordered Tennessee Governor Carroll to suspend moving the Tennessee militia to the frontier. Gaines received a letter from Carroll telling him of Jackson's intervention. Gaines could not understand the change of policy. His orders were to take whatever action was necessary to subdue Indian attacks, and he believed that a strong and present danger still existed. At that point a new call for troops would be too late. Jackson suspected that Gaines was intentionally bringing in troops who would join the Texian army. Jackson wrote Carroll that his actions had "stopped it in the bud." Gaines expressed deep concern that, with insufficient forces on the Louisiana frontier, the same thing could happen there as in Florida. By September, however, the threat of Indian attacks along the frontier had not materialized. The commander of U.S. troops in Nacogdoches, Lieutenant Colonel Whistler, complained that there had never been a risk of Indian uprisings and that the presence of U.S. troops in the area assured settlers that there would be no danger. Gaines left the frontier in October to travel to Maryland for a military inquiry relating to his actions in Florida. On November 30, 428 U.S. troops still remained in Nacogdoches. On December 19, the last remaining detachment left Texas with little to show for their actions.[69]

Exiled Mexican federalists in New Orleans remained undaunted in their crusade against centralism. Most, however, also expressed fierce disapproval of the Texas declaration of independence and openly distanced themselves from the events there. Father Alpuche and former Coahuila Governor Viesca had openly expressed disgust with the Texians. In January, a Mexican exile, Martín Peraza, who was Mexía's second-in-command, wrote to his brother from New Orleans that he and other exiles were undaunted in the federalist cause and that he maintained his opposition to Texian separation. Blaming the "most influential colonists in Texas" of threatening the integrity of the Mexican territory of Texas, Peraza made clear their position "so that at no time could it be said justly that we promoted separation, we are abandoning that country and dispersing the members of our expedition, bringing the main body of them to this city."[70]

Mexía and Gómez Farías continued to receive letters from the Mexican interior. One such letter, to both Mexía and Gómez Farías, lamented that the liberal cause in Mexico needed only money, say 29,000 or 30,000 pesos, to overthrow the centralists, acknowledging that they barely had enough for subsistence. In truth, many of the exiles in New Orleans had little or no money to send and were themselves forced to depend on supporters in Mexico for financial support.[71]

Father Alpuche y Infante's letter to Santa Anna, written from New Orleans, was published in the centralist Mexican newspaper *Diario*. Visiting Texas, Alpuche had seen enough to rigorously support the centralist government's execution of the war in Texas, and although an exile himself, he claimed he had "secret information" for Santa Anna only and requested a private interview with him.[72] Even though Alpuche did not get his interview with Santa Anna, both sides used Alpuche's letter to further their cause. On March 16, even Jerome Bayon, who had remained sympathetic to Zavala, Gómez Farías, and Viesca in his French newspaper *L'Abeille*, warned the Texians of conspiracy from self-professed friends such as Alpuche.[73]

Christy capitalized on the change in mood toward the Mexican federalists. On May 14 he wrote to Burnet that he had received reliable intelligence that Mexía and Gómez Farías were plotting not only a federalist overthrow of the centralist government in Mexico, but also a continuation of the war against Texas. Mexía was planning to travel through Texas, where he had lands, and Christy advised Burnet " 'twill be well to have an eye upon him."[74] Before Christy could finish the letter, a courier arrived with a message from Mexía that strongly protested Christy's claims. Christy had been sharing the news with others in the city, and since Mexía knew the source of the news, he promptly responded to Christy. Mexía strongly declared that he had no intention whatsoever of invading Texas, but Christy's response was cynical: "Time and Circumstances will settle the matter." Two days later, Mexía was indicted by a grand jury for filibustering, but apparently he was never tried.[75]

George Fisher, who had maintained a low profile during the early part of 1836, once again joined the federalist cause with newfound enthusiasm. Mexía sent him to Galveston Island to visit the Mexican prisoners of war, whom he hoped to utilize for another federalist invasion. Fisher departed New Orleans on the schooner *Ocean*, along with Thomas Jefferson Green's 230 volunteers. and arrived at Galveston on May 25. Writing to Mexía from the prisoner-of-war camp, he described Cós as being nearly crazy.[76] The next day Fisher traveled to Velasco with Samuel M. Williams on the war schooner *Independence*. This was probably the first time Fisher and Hawkins had seen each other since the Tampico expedition.

Fisher, who had also taken up the cause for Santangelo's newspaper, *Correo Atlántico*, signed Hawkins up for a subscription before leaving the ship. Hawkins also extended to Mexía his wish for Mexía's success in his new plans. A few days later, Fisher once again went out to Galveston Island, where he interviewed prisoners, sending lists of officers and casualties to Mexía. Fisher also disclosed to Mexía that two treaties had been signed between Santa Anna and the Texian government. On June 9 Fisher wrote to Mexía with disheartening news for the exiles in New Orleans. He announced to Mexía that he was severing ties with the Mexican federalists and was joining the Texians.[77]

In June, Fisher returned to New Orleans with a renewed sense of purpose and resumed regular contact with Stephen F. Austin. Fisher wrote Austin on July 7, indicating his concern over the announced release of Santa Anna and the dampening effect the release would have on support for Texas in New Orleans. Fisher attempted to come to Santangelo's rescue, urging stronger Texian support for his newspaper, citing its value as a fomenter of revolution in Mexico. Fisher once again wrote Austin, informing him of reports that indicated that Vitál Fernandez, governor and commandant general of Tamaulipas, was poised to declare in favor of the Constitution of 1824. Fernandez, however, did not indicate any expression of support for the Texian cause. He had declared martial law in Matamoros on February 5 and established strict travel and passage restrictions to prevent movement into the "revolted colonies." Matamoros was the closest major Mexican port to Texas, and Fernandez was serious about preventing the town from being used as a clearinghouse for intelligence to the Texians.[78]

Mexía and many of the exiles remained in New Orleans throughout the summer. Gómez Farías, who had played a less visible role in Mexía's new efforts, had been instrumental in saving a black Mexican soldier from being sold into slavery in New Orleans. Mexican consul Pizarro Martinez had saved the soldier from an odious fate, and he, Gómez Farías, and other exiles had raised money for the soldier's return to Veracruz. Beginning in October, Gómez Farías spent the rest of the year in bed suffering from a "gangrenous tumor" and was unable to do much else for the federalist cause.[79]

By October 1836 the first Texas navy, consisting of four schooners, had dwindled to only one effective vessel, the *Independence*. The *Liberty* had been sold in New Orleans. The *Brutus* and the *Invincible* were still in New York City under seizure for unpaid bills for repairs. Even before the old navy had disappeared, efforts were already under way to create a new navy. On November 18, 1836, Houston approved a measure to buy new ships: one sloop of war, two steamers, and two schooners.[80]

William Christy and the committee were instrumental in driving a wedge between the Texian leaders and the Mexican federalists. From the beginning, independence was the goal. It took federalists such as Governor Viesca and

Father Alpuche to recognize this firsthand in Texas. Whereas Christy was a hero among the Texians, Mexía's tragic attempt to invade Tampico only vilified him more. Christy capitalized on this. Even though the federalists were neutralized, the Texian agents in the city still faced huge financial obstacles, and there was still confusion in Texas.

10 § CONFUSION AND THE CLASH OF THE TEXAS AGENCIES AT NEW ORLEANS

Financial difficulties continued to vex agents William Bryan and Edward Hall. Bryan wrote to the Texian government that the appointment of special agents had made their job exceedingly difficult. On February 26 he leveled specific criticism against Charles H. Hawkins, captain of the *Independence*. The Texian commissioners had given Hawkins total control of disbursements for the *Independence*, keeping Bryan and Hall uninformed of his expenses until he was ready to sail. Writing to the provisional government, Bryan complained to the Texian governor: "Your astonishment can hardly equal mine that Capt Hawkins should have gone to such an expense upon that small vessel."[1]

Voicing frustration over Hawkins's extravagance, Bryan made it very clear that the captain's expenditures had "troubled" him more than any other business. He also stated that the bills incurred by these special agents—Hawkins included—were not being received until it was nearly too late, leaving Bryan and Hall to find ways "To remedy the evil." Bryan and Hall had to pay the bills from the special agents, putting the Texian government credit at risk when the advances came due. Hall recounted the frustration he felt when he went to both Captain John M. Allen and Captain Hawkins to urge them to spend carefully. Hawkins responded that "He would have what He wanted for his vessel & looked to higher authority than the agents." In spite of Bryan's harsh criticism of Hawkins, he advanced $2,000 out of his own funds to get the *Independence* and the *Brutus* off, leaving another $1,000 in unpaid bills. Bryan and Hall had little clear authority from the provisional government but bore the responsibility for its bills.[2]

In February, Thomas McKinney was in New Orleans to raise funds and volunteers and wrote to the provisional government that he believed that the $10,000 that had been left by the Texian commissioners in January should be placed at Bryan's disposal, for "Without [funds], their credit and that of our country must suffer."[3] He wrote that even though he needed that money for his orders, the agency needed it more. McKinney's words would later be used against him. McKinney, of the mercantile house of McKinney and Williams, had been a commercial merchant in Texas since 1833. Located at Quintana, at the mouth of the Brazos River, the partners opened a commercial house that served several plantation owners such as Jared Groce and William H. Wharton. McKinney's partner, Samuel Williams, was harshly criticized for his involvement in the large land sales by the Coahuila y Texas legislature in the years prior to the revolution.[4]

The provisional government had attempted several times to commission McKinney to raise funds in the United States. Declining the commissions each time, McKinney allowed the government to draw on the mercantile house for $500 to $600 at a time until it could get additional funds. He remained at Quintana and also allowed the McKinney and Williams steamboats to be used to transport supplies and volunteers. McKinney had been appointed the captain of the schooner of war *Invincible* but chose Jeremiah Brown to serve in his place. While in New Orleans, McKinney met with Bryan and discovered that no funds were available. On February 13, in a show of support, McKinney wrote one letter and later, on February 18, coauthored another with Captain John M. Allen, both calling for government support for Bryan's agency. McKinney's actions in issuing $30,000 in bonds from the Bank of Orleans indicate that he was expecting to get the $10,000 when he arrived to make up the deficit for the $40,000 in supplies. None of Bryan's correspondence reveals that he knew of the bonds.[5]

Volunteers (Allen's company) were waiting for a charter to Texas, which Bryan stated would cost him another $1,500 out of his own pocket. The Seminole campaign in Florida was also affecting the availability of supplies in the city. Hall and Bryan were forced to consider buying ship bread in Cincinnati and New York since the bakers in New Orleans were engaged in baking for the army in Florida. On March 29 Bryan wrote that twenty to thirty more volunteers were being sent on the schooner *Congress* with 200 kegs of gunpowder. Bryan encountered a shortage of rifles in the city and had to send for more from upriver.[6]

Captain Allen had directed Hall to immediately charter a ship for his men and to supply provisions. Hall and Bryan chartered the schooner *Equity* at a very high price and got it ready for departure. Several days passed, however, yet Allen's men had not arrived. An exasperated Hall found Allen and advised him to send his men on another ship (the *Pennsylvania*) since Hall was holding an expensive charter on the *Equity*. Allen refused, stating that if he could not recruit the volunteers, then he would go alone on the *Equity*. He assured Hall that he would exonerate any blame leveled at Hall for the charter. Allen had problems of his own. A French Creole company under the command of Captain Girod refused at the last minute to board unless they were paid in advance. Allen had already had uniforms made for the officers of the company and twenty additional uniforms made for "cadets." At a much greater cost to Bryan and Hall, Captain Allen with his volunteers nonetheless departed New Orleans on March 12 on the *Equity,* still unable to convince Captain Girod's Creole French company to board. Allen brought a much smaller number of volunteers than originally claimed. It is not know whether he was able to get the French officers' and cadets' uniforms back before leaving since they had been paid for by government advances.[7]

Allen and his men—only 40, not 100—landed at Brazoria on March 28. After three days, Allen wrote to General Houston expressing frustration as to what to do with his military cargo. Quartermaster General Almanzan Houston had orders to move all provisions and arms to Galveston Bay and to fortify that place, whereas Colonel Warren D. C. Hall at Brazoria ordered Allen to return to Velasco to assist in fortifying the landing there. With the area deserted, many of the settlers had fled toward the Sabine River; Allen thus saw no need to remain there. Instead, informing General Houston that he would send the cargo back to Velasco, he set out to join the main army. Allen's men finally joined Houston's army on April 15. Allen, like Morris in December, was immediately elected acting major under Colonel Henry Millard's regulars.[8]

On March 16 Bryan wrote to the government that he had received two iron cannons from the citizens of Cincinnati, Ohio, and on behalf of the Texian government, Bryan expressed his appreciation. Hall left on the schooner *Pennsylvania* on March 19 with the two cannon and twenty-one additional volunteers. With no letters coming from Texas, Hall made the trip to there to establish a relationship with the ad interim leadership. Arriving in eight days, Hall found Burnet and his cabinet at Harrisburg; as for the two cannon, they were eventually sent on to join Houston's army by April 11. These two identical guns became known as the "Twin Sisters" and were used at the Battle of San Jacinto.[9]

Upon his arrival at Harrisburg, Hall found "everything in confusion," and much to his astonishment, he also found that "No communication had been rec'd & that Mr. Bryan & myself were not even known by the Government."[10] This should not have been a complete surprise to Hall since on March 9 Bryan had written to acting Governor J. W. Robinson that he had reason to believe that the provisional government had not received any of Bryan's and Hall's earlier correspondence. He had received a letter from Robinson on February 14 that indicated that Robinson's government did not even know of Bryan's agency. This should have been a forewarning. Nonetheless, Hall presented his report to the cabinet, providing them with a very dim view of the condition of the agency's financial affairs.[11]

Hall was also informed that Triplett had been appointed as the Texas general agent to the United States and had also been authorized to appoint local agents. On March 19 Burnet had appointed Thomas Toby, of Thomas Toby and Brother, as agent for Texas in New Orleans to sell 300,000 acres of Texas land to raise funds. Only five days later, the cabinet sent a nine-article commission to Toby, giving him the authority to sell land at no less than fifty cents an acre. It further specified that funds received from the sale of land be held and disposed of by order of the president and countersigned by the secretary of the treasury. The commission was explicit: "There shall be but one agent [Toby] possessing authority to dispose of the public lands of Texas." In spite of the fact that Triplett had been officially appointed general agent on April 3, it is doubtful that Burnet had informed Triplett of Toby's specific role to sell land, considering Triplett's reaction to the news when he finally arrived in New Orleans.

Instead of dismissing Bryan outright, Triplett wanted to withhold judgment on Bryan's agency until he arrived, thus making Bryan and Hall temporary purchasing agents. Triplett either did not know at the time, or if he did know, he evidently did not tell Hall that Burnet had already instructed him to "remove" Bryan when he arrived in New Orleans. Hall's trip at least secured a letter from Triplett authorizing Bryan and Hall to serve as temporary purchasing agents and a proclamation from the ad interim government to be published in the New Orleans newspapers. As Hall departed for New Orleans, he wrote Burnet admitting his concern about the lack of knowledge of their agency. He concluded the letter with the hope "That the Government will protect this agency thus far & if they should be found worthy, continue their confidence." Triplett informed Hall of the McKinney contract before he left Texas. Hall knew the damage it would cause and told Triplett so. One can only wonder whether Hall sensed the winds of change in the new government and what he was thinking when he made the journey back to New Orleans. What would be next for the beleaguered Bryan-Hall agency?[12]

Announcing on March 19 that the convention at Washington-on-the-Brazos had declared independence, Jerome Bayon considered how this bold move would affect business opportunities in New Orleans: "Speculation in Texian lands would now be available." He hoped that the United States would recognize the independence of Texas rather than offering to buy Texas from Mexico. Bayon further called on the United States to allow Texas to "Become a member of our federal republic. Let its boundaries be extended to the Rio Grande, and to California and the Pacific ocean—and we shall have an easy access to Asia."[13] The Mexican consul at New Orleans, Fernando Pizarro Martinez, also dutifully published the supreme government's latest pronouncements regarding Texas in the New Orleans newspapers. On March 21 he announced that all Texian ports were closed to foreign commerce, even though the decree did little to deter the Texas navy from wreaking havoc on Mexican shipping, while freely using Texas ports to unload cargo and volunteers.[14]

Two days after Bayon's prophecy, he published the Texas declaration of independence. In the same issue, C. A. Warfield, a local broker, wasted no time in fulfilling Bayon's prediction concerning Texas lands. Warfield announced on page one of the *Bee*, "TEXAS LANDS FOR SALE."[15] Nacogdoches land men continued their flurry of sales even though the convention agreed to keep the land offices closed. William G. Logan, who had traveled to New Orleans in December, 1835, made an aggressive effort to sell East Texas lands while in the city. Andrew Hodge Jr., who had purchased Texas lands from Logan the year before, once again bought lands from the young Kentuckian. Logan sold the banker eleven leagues (48,712 acres) of land on the Red River and Sulphur Fork for $6,500 in cash. He would ordinarily have sold lands for fifty cents an acre. In this case, however, Logan agreed to sell for thirteen cents an acre. In addition, he and Philadelphian Nathan Ware bought three more leagues of land for $1,750 on or near the Neches River.[16]

Tragedy struck only weeks after Logan finalized his deals with Hodge and Ware. As Logan made his way back home to Nacogdoches, he mysteriously died between Natchitoches and Nacogdoches. Logan's widow left Texas in 1837 with virtually none of her husband's wealth. Logan's business partner, Henry Raguet, assumed title to many of his lands and the business. Records do not reveal the cause of Logan's death, but the timing suggests that he may have carelessly revealed to the wrong person that he was carrying large amounts of cash; if he did, then his untimely demise was actually a murder.[17] Nonetheless, Mary E. H. Logan, later Gwin, sued Raguet and his family in 1855 to reclaim her first husband's lands and other assets from the mercantile house.[18]

On March 19 the Hodge brothers, William and Andrew, who had been associates for several years, announced the dissolution of their partnership. Both had pursued divergent commercial paths by 1836. Andrew continued as president of the Bank of Orleans and as a speculator in local and East Texas lands.

William, who had operated his commercial business primarily in the Caribbean, formed a new partnership with two other merchants, Thomas Oxnard and T. O. Stark.[19]

The Texas cause in New Orleans was just one more symptom of the ill feelings between the Creoles and the American district. Christy, Caldwell, and eventually Thomas Toby were all active in the Louisiana Native American Association. The tension between Christy and Mexía and the rivalry with the local Creoles and the American district, which had supported the Texas cause, ran deeper than just the commercial interests. The New Orleans committee's discrimination against Creoles and Mexican exiles reflected years of hard feelings and resentment on both sides. Creole merchants who had longstanding commercial ties with Mexico tended to side with the Mexican government, no matter who was in power. They sought Mexican specie, and it did not matter whether it came from a centralist or a liberal Mexico. For them, the Texian schooners of war were threats to their profits and business just as much as the American district was a threat to their local political and commercial prestige.

Hall and Bryan found it incredible that Burnet and the cabinet did not know of their agency. They had faithfully corresponded with the provisional government, to both Governor Smith and acting Governor Robinson as well as to the Texas commissioners. Bryan and Hall suspected foul play, surmising that their correspondence had been intercepted. In the early months of 1836, however, the provisional government could not even muster a quorum to carry on its business. The feud between Governor Smith and the council had paralyzed the government, thus shattering its effectiveness to govern even after Smith was impeached. On April 4 Bailey Hardeman, the new Texas secretary of the treasury, wrote Bryan and Hall a short letter instructing them to audit their books, assuring them that their accounts would be paid with "the first monies" deposited in the Bank of Orleans in the name of the Texian government.[20]

While Hall traveled back to New Orleans from his meeting with Burnet and Triplett, Bryan continued to keep the government's credit from faltering. Thomas Jefferson Green, a successful planter who had served in the state legislatures of North Carolina and Florida, had traveled to Texas to join the campaign. Green, who had been commissioned to recruit for his army of the reserve, arrived in New Orleans on April 6.

In hopes of obtaining funds and supplies, one of the first persons he sought out was Bryan. Seeing the financial straits Bryan and Hall were in, Green immediately wrote to Burnet urging the government to do everything possible to sustain Bryan and Hall's credit, stating that they had "Done everything they ought to have done to sustain our credit & our cause." Green's arrival also brought disconcerting news. On March 16 the finance committee of the constitutional convention recommended that the mercantile house of McKinney and Williams receive monetary relief as soon as the means were made available.[21]

With the quantity of supplies in Texas becoming critical and with an advancing Mexican army, Burnet contracted with McKinney to go to New Orleans to raise $40,000 in provisions. He was authorized to submit a draft on the Bank of Orleans for the remaining $10,000 left by the Texian commissioners in January, "Subject to the orders of the Govnt. which must be drawn for in the manner [of the commissioners'] instructions." McKinney in turn would transfer to Thomas Toby, of Thomas Toby and Brother, the funds necessary to forward the supplies.[22] The news prompted an immediate response from Bryan to Burnet. Bryan and Hall were already circulating $76,000 in government paper and were reeling from a total debt of $90,000. Understandably, Bryan was offended and shocked to hear of a move to take any remaining funds that could be used for their relief and give them to Toby.[23]

Bryan sought advice from Henry Austin, Thomas Green, and William Christy about what he should do. Before placing an injunction on the bank, Bryan went to see Toby to offer a solution. Bryan appealed to Toby, explaining to him what the move would do to the government's credit. Bryan offered to postpone the injunction if the contract were delayed for ten days or until they heard from Burnet, whichever came sooner. Toby refused. Bryan went to see Andrew Hodge Jr. at the Bank of Orleans and stopped the transfer of the $10,000 by placing an injunction on the check. That same day he wrote Burnet to explain his action.[24] A good deal of the available funds had already been designated for cash demands, including $5,000 that had been set aside in January for Colonel Thomas D. Owings for his Kentucky volunteers. Owings was reportedly preparing to depart for New Orleans and would expect reimbursement upon arrival. Bryan also pointed to Thomas McKinney's letters, which revealed that McKinney knew that the Texian agency was financially drained. McKinney's letter to the government on February 13 expressed support for Bryan and called for the release of $10,000 to Bryan's agency. McKinney, who, only a month before, had recommended that the funds be released to Bryan, was now presenting a check calling for the same funds be released to Thomas Toby in part to obtain $40,000 in supplies.[25]

Thomas J. Green indicated to Bryan that Burnet had mistakenly believed that Thomas Toby had actually been the agent who had outfitted the navy and had been sending supplies. Bryan believed that the government would not have granted the contract between McKinney and Toby if they had been properly informed of his agency. He further thought that either a suppression of papers sent from his agency or "misrepresentations" of the facts was at work. Using McKinney's own words, which called for the protection of the agent's and the government's credit, Bryan justified his decision to place an injunction on the funds.[26]

Hall arrived back in New Orleans on April 26 and informed Bryan of the new role he and his partner would now play under the new government. The $10,000 in government funds was frozen, and Triplett had yet to arrive. On May 1 Hall wrote Burnet about the financial standoff. People in New Orleans who sought to know whether the rumors were true turned to Hall to either verify or deny that Bryan was being replaced by Toby. Bryan also attempted to dispel panic by publishing a notice in the newspapers concerning the injunction. Hall's letter expressed the hope that letters that had been sent to the ad interim government explaining the facts would clear up the confusion and that the funds would be made available to Bryan's agency once again. Hall plainly stated that "If the business of your Government is not confined to one channel there can be no dependence placed in supplying future wants, No officers or Special Agents are required, 'tis Money! Money! Money! And I hope Col Triplett will be able to raise it." It was one thing to be replaced directly by the president, but to find out about their dismissal through rumor was distressing to both men. Bryan's and Hall's correspondence with Burnet increased at a feverish pace, as did their anxiety over exactly when Triplett would arrive back in New Orleans to straighten out the mess that President Burnet and the acting government had created.[27]

Triplett was still in Texas. He, Niblett, and others traveled eastward to the mouth of the Sabine River to find a boat leaving for New Orleans. Triplett was always looking for a good deal, and before going very far, he and Niblett had bought half a league of land with all of its improvements for only $600. At Sabine Lake, Triplett and Niblett parted ways with Gray. Gray went by land to New Orleans, while Triplett and Niblett both wanted to go by the Gulf.[28] Before their departure, however, they heard of Houston's victory at San Jacinto. Anticipating that the victory might change their instructions, Triplett decided to go on to San Jacinto, where he would hope to see the government. There he visited with Houston and met with both Santa Anna and Colonel Juan Almonte, who were being kept as prisoners. Mississippi volunteers under Captain John A. Quitman arrived while he was there, and according to Triplett, he and Quitman helped keep cooler heads over calls to execute Santa Anna. Triplett argued that "He could be executed at any time and he was a good trump to hold in any negotiation."

Some in Texas had criticized Triplett for unnecessarily delaying his departure for New Orleans. On April 19 Triplett wrote Burnet, believing the attacks were meant to force his resignation. Stung by the criticism, Triplett declared he would continue as general agent until a successor could be found, but he explicitly declared that, "On the first day of July next, you will consider my resignation as tendered." [29]

Triplett went on to Velasco where the temporary government had moved with Santa Anna. Before Triplett left for New Orleans, Burnet approached Triplett and asked him to temporarily annul the issuance of the land grant on Galveston Island, which Burnet admitted had created "great excitement." Triplett explained that Dr. Niblett, who was the co-owner of the grant, had already left for New Orleans, but that he—Triplett—would accept a temporary suspension as long as it did not injure his own rights. Triplett criticized Burnet for his "[t]imid dodging of responsibility," stating that he never regained his land grant on Galveston Island. The Texian government, according to Triplett, eventually sold his and Niblett's land grant to someone else. This was only the beginning of future problems for Triplett with Burnet's government.[30]

Government funds were kept frozen until Triplett could arrive at New Orleans, but this did not stop the demands for payment on the Texian accounts nor did it stop the controversy.[31] The pro-Mexican newspaper *Post and Union* scornfully commented that "Mr. Bryan, the agent of the Texas Provisional Government in this city, has commenced suit and taken out a writ of sequestration against all funds and property in this district belonging to the Provisional Government. It is very hard, in these degenerate times, to make 'Patriotism' and 'Pocket' meet on friendly terms." [32]

Bryan's injunction on the $10,000 had created much tension between him and Toby. The situation in New Orleans with the Texian agency went from bad to worse. William Bryan wrote Burnet on April 28 that the *Brutus* was in New Orleans awaiting repairs, and without Triplett, Bryan explained, he did not feel authorized to advance funds to refit the schooner. Furthermore, the *Brutus* was not the only war vessel in port waiting to be outfitted. On May 1 Hall wrote Burnet that "The Invincible, Brutus, San Jacinto and Kos[ciusko] are all here waiting the arrival of Col Triplett. The evil effects produced by the business with McKinney has paralised [*sic*] every thing and unless Col Triplett arrives and places funds immediately to the credit of this Agency, the worst consequences are to be feared." [33]

Bryan also reported to Burnet that they had received word from reliable sources that the crew of the *Invincible* was going to be arrested for their capture of the brig *Pocket*. Bryan sent provisions to the crew and urged them to leave the city immediately because they were about to be arrested on the charge of piracy. The capture of the *Pocket* had created much anxiety for Bryan, who feared that locking up the crew members would harm the Texian cause even further in the city. He wrote to Burnet that "The people of the United States are with us, but it will not be tolerated by the Government that we should capture even Mexican property under the American Flag, unless they should endeavor to return to a Mexican port after having been ordered off." Bryan admitted that "nearly all of the wealth of New Orleans" was against them, but he believed they were still up to the task of carrying on the work. He was also able to proudly announce to Burnet that all of the demands for payment that had come due had been satisfied.[34]

Nevertheless, in May the crew of the *Invincible* was arrested and put on trial for piracy. During the proceedings, $5,000 of government advances came due. Bryan once again attempted to compromise with Toby by meeting with him and Andrew Hodge Jr. over the $10,000. Bryan suggested that Toby "give his note" for $8,000 of upcoming advances, which were due before June 15. Then Bryan and Hall would endorse the note with their name and Hodge would agree to discount it at the bank, thus saving the government's credit. Bryan would in turn relinquish their claim on the $10,000. Toby refused, and Bryan was forced to allow "agency paper to be protested." Bryan shot off a letter to Burnet, announcing that "For the first time your paper is protested." In a veiled criticism of Toby, Bryan scornfully observed that "The friends of Texas are willing when they can [to] receive and disburse money & obtain a commission to be considered the patriots of Liberty; but when it comes to the trial they are found wanting. We wash our hands of the protest of the Government paper."

Hall, too, vented his frustration to Burnet on May 21, after being "severely taken to task" for issuing drafts on the government credit, with the open expectation that the provisional government had approved the loans. Hall did not identify who had reprimanded him, but he expressed concern that these drafts would now not be honored since no more monies were available. In a commercial city like New Orleans, Hall plainly said, the situation for Texas was "very bad." There were now two rival Texas agencies that could not work together; accounts were coming due, but no funds were available to pay them; ships were in port in need of outfitting; and the new general agent was still in Texas.[35]

On May 22 Burnet finally sent off a letter to Bryan explaining why the

$10,000 transfer was made to McKinney. Admitting that Bryan's agency had been only "partially known" by his cabinet, Burnet nonetheless still defended the transfer due to the "deranged condition of our home matters." He hoped that "this little affair" could eventually be adjusted but not at that present time.[36]

To Toby's credit, he bought the brig *Pocket* to appease the public backlash against the Texian cause in New Orleans. Toby and Bryan actually worked together this time to lessen the damage. Toby purchased the ship and its charter, and Bryan agreed to pay more than $800 in damages incurred by the officers and crew of the *Invincible*. Bryan once again believed that the "monied Aristocracy" in New Orleans had been behind the crew's arrest, noting that they had advised Commodore Dallas to escort the *Invincible* out to the Gulf of Mexico and send her to Key West for another trial. Bryan employed leading New Orleans attorneys Randal Hunt, O. P. Jackson, and Seth Barton to defend the crew. The case was held in Judge Rawle's court and lasted only three days. The seizure of the *Pocket* had come at a high cost to Texas. Not only had it hurt the Texians' image, but the Texas agents also had to pay the captain of the *Pocket* $35,000 to buy the brig as an appeasement for the capture in addition to the attorneys' fees to defend the crew.[37]

Triplett finally returned to New Orleans on May 24 and immediately set out to examine the condition of the government accounts, determining the current debt and remaining balances if any. He also went to see a bank president (probably Andrew Hodge Jr.) to negotiate a loan. If the bank approved the loan, according to Triplett, he offered to make the bank's notes the "circulation of Texas: receivable for government dues there etc." The bank president stated that his bank had made loans to individuals for Texas, and the papers had all been returned. There was no government revenue and therefore no "home demand for a circulation equal to the paper issued. The specie would all come to New Orleans."

Triplett went to another bank president but received the same response. After Triplett explained to both presidents his intent to seek loans in the north, each bank officer once again predicted that Triplett's attempts would be useless. Writing to Burnet concerning his discouraging meetings, Triplett resigned himself to the hope that Austin, Archer, and Wharton were the only ones left with a chance to obtain funds. Echoing what Bryan and Hall had wailed loudly before, Triplett also believed that the appointment of too many agents was harming the Texas cause in New Orleans.[38]

Triplett examined Bryan's and Hall's books and found that everything appeared to be in order. Writing to Burnet on June 2, Triplett made it clear that after examining their accounts, Bryan and Hall had "Manifested becoming zeal and devotion to the cause, and have done what they could to keep on the operations of the government." He also acknowledged what Bryan and Hall had been saying for months—that funds were "indispensable, to an amount to which [Bryan and Hall] cannot be reasonably expected to raise." When he met with Toby, however, he was provided with a report on the charters of the schooners *Flora* and *Good Hope*. Triplett was perhaps being overly demanding in instructing Toby to present the report in compliance with Triplett's "distinct shape." Toby refused to comply, stating he was not obligated to submit anything more to Triplett since he had already sent a report to Thomas McKinney. During the short time that Triplett remained general agent, Toby showed little inclination to cooperate with him.[39]

Seeing the overwhelming task of being general agent and having pressing personal business, Triplett informed Burnet again on June 2 that he would serve as agent only until July 1, acknowledging that whoever was general agent should reside in New Orleans. Triplett agreed to remain until any contracts or other "engagements" were finished or until he was notified of a change in agents by the president. Triplett had seen the personal financial strain the agency had put upon Bryan and Hall. Triplett admitted to Burnet, "I cannot venture to involve my private fortune—common prudence, and duty to my family forbid it."[40]

Triplett also called a meeting with the lenders who were still in New Orleans to discuss with them the compromise agreement. Gabriel Denton, Jacob Wilcox, Alfred Penn, Christopher Adams Jr., Thomas Meux (representing James Huie), and William M. Beal (representing James Erwin) attended the meeting held at the Arcade Exchange. They agreed to the compromise but found that the printed land scrip Triplett had brought with him from the government was not satisfactory. The lenders did not agree with the phrase "this certificate shall not be located, until by law, other persons are authorised to appropriate lands within the limits of this Republic." A committee was formed to propose an alternative form of the scrip to be consistent in wording with the terms of the compromise. The alternative phrasing stipulated that there "be a clear and explicit understanding in relation to their right to locate, before the lenders proceed any further with their investments."

Triplett and the lenders held two meetings, and on May 30 Triplett sent the minutes of the meetings and the amended scrip to Burnet with the expectation that the new scrip would be approved. Triplett asked that the new scrip be sent back in a sealed trunk to William Bryan. He explained that the scrip would in turn be sent to William Christy's office, at which time Christy would issue the scrip to the lenders proportionately. Triplett wrote Burnet that if the amended land scrip arrived before his departure, he would send on as much of it as possible to Washington City before Congress convened, thinking that it would sell there, so that Texas land scrip would "disseminate throughout the Union." Triplett was overlooking one thing: that the interim government might not approve the amended land scrip, thus jeopardizing the compromise altogether. Within a week of this letter to Burnet, Triplett would see the agreement completely fall apart as the result of a totally different and unexpected event.[41]

Sometime in the first week of June, Triplett was in Christy's office at Banks's Arcade and discovered that Texas land scrip was being sold of which he knew nothing. Learning that Toby was selling the scrip, Triplett went to Toby's office to demand an explanation. Toby confirmed what Triplett had seen at Christy's office. Burnet had granted him the authority to sell land scrip to raise funds. Triplett requested that Toby delay the issuance of the scrip until Triplett could get instructions from Burnet. Toby refused. Triplett pointed out to him that the issuance of more land scrip into the New Orleans market would make the lands issued to the lenders "worth nothing." Toby would not budge. Triplett had also tried to secure some of the $10,000 in government funds that was now at Toby's disposal, but Toby refused to surrender any part of the funds to him.[42]

Triplett became so sick after his meeting with Toby that he could barely sit up, but the expediency of the moment required that he write to Burnet. Triplett revealed that the prevailing rumors in New Orleans were that Toby was authorized to sell the 500,000 acres in land scrip, and whether true or not, the rumors were doing irreparable harm since Texas now had two agents selling land scrip in competition with one another.[43] Wishing to obtain official information on Toby's commission, Triplett wrote that he could get nothing from Toby. If the report was true, according to Triplett, then, writing as a lender, "the takers of the loans have no earthly inducement to prepare to take up the amount of their remaining instalments [sic]."

Four days later, reports confirmed Triplett's worst fears. In another letter to Burnet, Triplett, speaking for the lenders, stated emphatically that "when we invest money we do it with the hope of profit. As 500,000 acres more have been offered, we have no security that 1,500,000 will not follow." Toby explained to Burnet what had happened between him and Triplett on June 16. According to Toby, Triplett was doing nothing to address the current emergency created by the shortage of supplies while he waited for the ratification of the compromise agreement. Toby explained to Burnet that since Triplett was doing nothing to procure supplies, Toby was forced to start sales of some of the 300,000 acres of land scrip authorized by Burnet.

Toby also confirmed that Triplett wanted him to wait to hear from Burnet before selling any of the land scrip, but Toby replied, "If he had done anything we should have been satisfied, but the country might be in [a] state of starvation, before he could hear from you." Triplett had lent $5,000 of his own money to Bryan to meet some of the credit obligations coming due, but anticipating Bryan's removal as agent and in light of Toby's appointment to sell land scrip, he had withdrawn $4,000, leaving Bryan with only $1,000. The lenders had lost all confidence in Burnet's government and with the compromise, and there was therefore no more inducement to pay the balance of the loans. Around June 15, five days after Stephen Austin arrived in New Orleans, Triplett left for Kentucky, disgusted and bitter.[44]

Signaling the beginning of the end of Bryan's agency, Texian Secretary of State William H. Jack wrote to Bryan on May 27 that the president and cabinet made it "advisable to discontinue the Agency." Bryan received the letter on June 17. Believing that the order was for the suspension of his position as general agent, not as purchasing agent for Triplett, he responded that if the secretary's letter had accompanied a guarantee that the government would meet their outstanding debt, he would have cheerfully resigned. But in the present crisis, he could not resign with the many demands then facing the agency. Bryan said, "When the protection is granted[,] the slightest allusion will bring my resignation."

Responding to a complaint that he did not publish a proclamation that had been handed to Hall while in Texas, Bryan complained that he had never received any direct notices from Burnet to publish. He had received only three letters from Burnet, and all of the public documents that had been received indirectly were published. Bryan stated that his agency "should not be censured for the non execution of that which they have no orders to execute." Hall also came under criticism by his own partner, Bryan, for publishing a notice in the newspapers that no more volunteers were required. In a letter to Burnet, Bryan was noticeably irritated that, in publishing the notice, Hall had overstepped his authority. Stephen F. Austin, who had arrived in New Orleans, also reprimanded Hall for publishing the notice.

The growing squabble between Bryan and Hall reflected the frustration and confusion left over from the actions of the provisional government. No one in New Orleans, except perhaps Thomas Toby, knew exactly who was in charge and what their duties were. The large numbers of volunteers who had arrived in the city and the lack of supplies and clothing created an awkward situation for Hall. When Grayson and Collinsworth arrived in New Orleans, Grayson called on the office of the *Commercial Bulletin* to publish a similar announcement. Hall was merely following what Texian representatives had already done. Reflecting his hard feelings toward Austin for the reprimand, Hall wrote Burnet that if he had overstepped his authority, then he would submit to Burnet's censorship, not Austin's.[45]

On June 10 Burnet issued a decree authorizing Toby as the sole general agent in the United States. Burnet directed a part of the decree at Bryan and Hall. All other agencies with the power to contract for or borrow money or raise funds were officially revoked and declared null and void.[46] Bryan and Hall did not know of the Burnet proclamation until they read it in the newspapers on June 25. They wrote a discouraged reply to Burnet that "We flattered ourselves that the zeal shewn in the public Service . . . would have assured us the honour of a letter of advice from the Cabinet, naming such a change, and your reasons for making it."[47] They reminded Burnet that they had remained Texas agents during the darkest hours.[48]

On July 1 Bryan closed the books of the Bryan-Hall agency. One week later he sent Secretary of the Treasury Bailey Hardeman his statement of accounts, totaling $77,468.76. Bryan left out an additional $3,000 that had yet to be submitted for payment. He expressed his hope that their accounts would be considered of the utmost importance.[49] In Bryan and Hall's letter to the government on June 28, they bitterly recognized that "The face of affairs, is now changed!" In a parting shot at Thomas Toby, they wrote: "There is now honour and profit in the office, and those who have served you to the sacrifice & hazard of private credit, must give way to those who have friends at court, to promote their private advantage."[50]

Bryan, Hall, and Samuel Ellis (Triplett's secretary) published a pamphlet defending their agency. Burnet's June 10 proclamation made it clear that the powers of those agents appointed by the provisional government, including Bryan and Hall, were revoked and annulled. What alarmed and distressed Bryan and Hall even more was that Burnet's proclamation also warned that there were others who were defrauding donors in the name of Texas. Burnet basically lumped all of these into one category, thus establishing Toby as the sole agent.[51]

In order to distance themselves from any connection to Burnet's reference to fraud, Bryan, Hall, and Samuel Ellis presented their case to the public. They provided a pamphlet that set forth correspondence that supported their contention that they had been faithful to the trust placed in them and that they had also been unjustly treated. The former agents insinuated—without stating outright—that Thomas McKinney and the "lobby members of the Cabinet" in Burnet's government were behind the ploy to remove them as agents in order to "sustain the credit of a few favorites." Surprisingly, Bryan, Hall, and Ellis did not blame Burnet, stating rather that he was intentionally uninformed of their agency.[52]

McKinney in turn published his own defense titled "To All Who Have Seen and Read the Dying Groans of Wm. Bryan, E. Hall and Small. Ellis." McKinney's pamphlet, which was filled with sarcasm and name calling, referred to Bryan and Hall's defense as "the book of falsehoods." McKinney denied being behind any attempt at removing Bryan and Hall and presented his own case of being sent to New Orleans to purchase supplies in a desperate situation. He went on to state that he was given the authority to immediately draw on government funds. He lashed out at Bryan and Hall, accusing them of charging excessive commission rates and delivering inferior supplies and equipment.

Burnet wrote a short letter in McKinney's defense that stated that he had no knowledge of any attempt by McKinney or Williams to influence the government to remove Bryan and Hall. McKinney also accused Samuel Ellis of trying to swindle $120 from him when he was in New Orleans in February. McKinney left the city "without a suspicion in regard to Bryan's services," but he stated he "was done with Mr. Ellis, forever," not having confidence in a man who had tried to deceive him. McKinney also did not hesitate to comment on those who had come to Bryan and Hall's defense, calling Henry Austin, who had sent a letter of recommendation to Burnet, a "poor cracked brain citizen." McKinney closed his pamphlet with a challenge to Bryan, claiming that Toby and Brother had accrued more than three times Bryan's individual advances. McKinney offered Bryan $1,000 to disprove the allegation. The money, according to McKinney, would remain at the *Telegraph and Texas Register* office or at R. Mills and Company at Brazoria, waiting for Bryan to prove him wrong.[53]

Bryan attempted to respond to the accusations of inferior war materiel. Writing to Burnet, he explained that Toby had actually bought the ordnance and that he (Bryan) had paid for the freight. Bryan also maintained that they had bought powder "by sample" and that the samples appeared to be good. He lamented that "we cannot be expected to go nine miles to the Magazine & open kegs to ascertain if there has been deception, we do not (fortunately) stand alone, we have used all possible exertion to protect the Government from fraud."

Burnet was not convinced, however, and continued to believe that Bryan was guilty of sending inferior supplies. In a letter to Toby on June 20, Burnet claimed that "on more than one occasion, he [Bryan] sent us damaged and very indifferent Powder, Some of it really too worthless and inefficient to be used in ordinary salutes." Unless Burnet inspected the local warehouses in Velasco and Quintana himself, he would have had to depend on local agents such as McKinney and Williams or military inspectors to provide inspection reports of the supplies.

Complaints also came from the navy. Captain Hawkins criticized Bryan as being inefficient and unpopular. Surgeon O. P. Kelton of the *Invincible* attested that "matrasses, water-casks, powder, and blankets sent on board the Invincible, by the Agent of Texas, in February last, were of a very inferior order, and many of them damaged, and to the best of my belief would have been condemned under proper examination." An affidavit like this was difficult for Bryan to defend even though he tried. The damage to his reputation as agent had been done.[54]

Bryan also tried to justify himself to Burnet that the commission rates he charged were in accordance with those set by the New Orleans chamber of commerce. In actuality, McKinney and Williams and Toby also charged the same commission rates. The New Orleans chamber of commerce consisted of many of the city's leading merchants. Even though Bryan was not a member of the chamber, William Bogart and William L. Hodge—both members of the Texas committee—were. All commission merchants were expected to follow the standards set down by them.

As Triplett was preparing to leave New Orleans, he urged that the future general agent "should in no way be interested in profits upon Goods furnished to the Government, nor in commissions. He should stand aloof and keep guard for the Government."[55] This practice, however, was already in place, yet both agencies submitted charges for commissions for the shipping of goods and volunteers to Texas.

Bryan and Hall continued to serve in an unofficial capacity, reporting less and less to Burnet, and more to Austin, who lent them a sympathetic ear. Bryan and Hall wrote Burnet on June 28, informing him of the June 25 announcement in the local newspapers that Toby had been made sole agent. The former agents wrote that they expected better than this, receiving the news from the local newspapers. They stated that rumors were circulating in the city that the only objection to their agency was that they did not have the financial means to carry on the government's business. Bryan retorted: "In answer to [this] we would request your Excellency to point to any House, in the U. States that would have obligated themselves to the extent we have."[56]

The Texian commissioners, Austin, Archer, and Wharton, experienced much the same lack of government instruction as had Bryan and Hall. The only news they had received from Texas had been through Bryan. Reading from his letters of the desperate condition of the New Orleans agency, they were greatly distressed. They assured Bryan that they had agents in New York and other places seeking out "monied negotiations." Trying to encourage him, they wrote: "In Gods name Do hold on the good cause and strain every nerve to keep the public credit until we can relieve you."

Wharton had complained to Burnet that he had sent numerous letters to the government but had not received a reply from them since February 20. On April 3 Austin wrote to Burnet from New York that "the state of things at home, has embarrassed the labors of the Govt. agents in this country." He chided Burnet for the lack of correspondence, receiving news through the local newspapers that they had been "superceded" and that "we have no powers as agents etc." Austin urged that copies of the declaration of independence be sent since their work required official copies from the Texas government.[57]

On May 16 Austin wrote James Treat, an agent in New York, that Santa Anna had been captured. He acknowledged that he had received the news in a letter from William Bryan. Bryan saw the report in the *Commercial Bulletin*, which he enclosed with his letter.[58] Austin had tried to negotiate a $500,000 loan from Nicholas Biddle in Philadelphia, but Biddle could not accept Texas bonds as security. In New York, however, Samuel Swartwout and a number of other New York investors pledged financial support with a sizable loan of their own that rivaled that of the investors in New Orleans. Swartwout, who was already investing in Texas lands, pledged $2,000.[59]

Wharton had already met with various members of Jackson's cabinet and members of Congress. Attending a party at John C. Calhoun's home, he exhibited Texas bank notes and a map of Texas for the curious guests to see. Wharton also met with Jackson in private. Jackson asked him for diplomatic letters from his government; Houston's account of the Battle of San Jacinto; proclamations calling for settlers to return to their homes; and declarations that Texas ports were open. Wharton had none of these. Jackson chided Wharton: "Sir, . . . your President should send an express once a week to New Orleans to his agent and have published by authority the true situation of your country and everything that goes to show you are a *de facto* government. This is indispensable."[60]

The commissioners begged for someone to come to Washington to present credentials because their work and influence with Jackson's administration was only nominally effective until the proper documentation was forwarded to them.[61]

In their meeting, Wharton made it clear that he would not support a cession of Texas by Mexico. Texas was independent, and the very act of acquiring Texas from Mexico would nullify their declaration. Jackson admitted to Wharton that his government was guilty of mistakes regarding Texas. He believed that Anthony Butler's blundering in Mexico City had cost the United States its only chance of acquiring Texas before the revolution. However, he cautioned Wharton not to "be . . . surprised if I yet soon announce a cession by Mexico of Texas to the United States." Jackson assured Wharton that all that would be needed was a "quit claim" from Mexico and that the preliminaries would be worked out between Texas and the United States. Wharton, however, was adamant that Texas's independence be maintained; he did not believe that Texas should be an acquisition from Mexico that consummated a Texas-U.S. union.[62]

Burnet had also commissioned George C. Childress and Robert Hamilton to go to Washington City on March 19 to open negotiations with the cabinet. Childress wrote to Burnet at Natchitoches that he had read in the newspapers that Austin, Archer, and Wharton were in Washington and expressed concern that his arrival there would create "a very awkard [sic] situation." He requested that Burnet and the cabinet resolve the potentially embarrassing situation.[63]

On May 26 Burnet appointed James Collinsworth and Peter Grayson as commissioners to solicit Jackson's mediation in the war in Texas. Burnet also commissioned them to approach the U.S. government concerning the annexation of Texas with specific terms.[64] By June 10 three Texian representatives—Wharton, Childress, and Hamilton—were in Washington. Austin had already left Washington on May 24 for New Orleans. Childress and Hamilton met with U.S. Secretary of State John Forsyth, using only newspaper accounts of the Battle of San Jacinto for diplomatic credentials. By July 1 Texian Secretary of State Samuel P. Carson had also arrived in Washington; he dined with Jackson the next day. Jackson asked several probing questions, expressing concern over the release of Santa Anna. He asked what Texas would do if Santa Anna turned on the Texians. Carson responded that "It would not be six months till an army composed of your countrymen in part, and of Texians will be at the walls of Mexico, and ample revenge shall be had."[65]

Collinsworth and Grayson arrived in Washington on July 8, getting there barely in time to see Jackson before he departed for the Hermitage, his home near Nashville. Jackson told Collinsworth and Grayson that he had sent a "secret agent," Henry Moffitt, to Texas to represent the United States to the Texas government and report on conditions there.[66] Both commissioners also met with Secretary of State John Forsyth, and though cordial, he told them that they could not be treated as "accredited agents" without the proper paperwork from Burnet's government. Texas, however, had an unlikely ally in the Senate. Henry Clay, James Erwin's father-in-law, proposed a resolution before that body on June 24, calling for cautious American support for Texian independence. The Senate ceremoniously passed the resolution on July 4 before adjourning, leaving Grayson and Collinsworth with little to do.

They too left soon after their meeting with Forsyth to await further instructions at Louisville and Nashville. William Jack, Texian secretary of state, wrote to Grayson and Collinsworth on July 23, acknowledging reports of U.S. Congressional support for Texas independence. He also informed them that elections would take place in September, with the newly elected congress set to meet in October. Jack also admitted that a referendum on Texas annexation would also be presented to the voters, believing that a strong show of support for annexation would induce the United States to annex Texas. He expressed concern, however, that it would be disastrous for Texas if the arbitrary Neches River line were agreed to as the boundary. Jack maintained that if the United States were to take part of the territory, then it should take all it.[67]

Triplett's resignation, which went into effect on July 1, signaled the end of the Bryan-Hall agency. Afterward, Bryan's and Hall's complaints of injustice and betrayal fell on deaf ears. They were victims of a change in governments. Burnet and the interim government showed little regard for the work of the provisional government under Smith and Robinson. Thus they were forced to turn to persons they knew and the only resource Texas had left to obtain funds to purchase supplies quickly. On May 15 McKinney and Williams recommended that Burnet give Thomas Toby the authority to sell more land scrip than just the 300,000 acres. They pointed out that for them to advance any more for the cause of Texas would be "Adding fire to fuel by going any further in Expenditures."[68]

Concerning whether the cabinet had the authority to sell public lands, McKinney and Williams pointed out that they had already established that right by offering the thirty-two leagues to Triplett and the lenders in the compromise agreement. Not selling the public lands beyond this point was establishing priority of location for Triplett and the lenders by default. This was exactly what the cabinet was trying to avoid. A few days later, McKinney and Williams again wrote Burnet, urging him to authorize Toby to sell "a sufficiency of scrip" in sections of 640 acres at fifty cents an acre. A two-man executive committee of Lorenzo de Zavala and P. W. Grayson endorsed McKinney and Williams's recommendations, and on May 24 Burnet commissioned Toby as the sole agent to sell land scrip, increasing the amount to 500,000 acres at fifty cents an acre. Burnet concurred that the problems stemmed from the difficulties in obtaining funds through the loans.[69]

Toby's commission to flood the New Orleans market with Texas land scrip in essence negated the January loans and thus destroyed any perceived good faith between the government and the lenders. It nearly destroyed Bryan and Hall financially as well. Both had worked to maintain the government's credit, using their own personal credit at times, and in the meantime they continued to send supplies and volunteers even though they received little guidance from either the provisional government or Burnet's cabinet. They rightfully felt betrayed and indignant that fair-weather patriots under a cloud of indefensible accusations had taken their agency away from them. McKinney too had reason to take offense at charges leveled against him, since he had provided Texas with the financial resources necessary to initiate the revolution.[70]

In contrast to Bryan, Hall, and McKinney, Toby took on the role of agent much like he did in his mercantile house. He spent little time arguing and attacking, realizing that the loans were not going to bring quick relief to the beleaguered Texians and therefore land scrip was needed to obtain funds promptly. Toby received the new commission on June 16, admitting that some of the first scrip from the 300,000 acres had been sent to Philadelphia. He assured Burnet that it could be retrieved and the first issue declared void, for he was one of several merchants in New Orleans who had Philadelphia ties. The Hodge brothers and Nathan Ware were also from Philadelphia.[71]

Correspondence from Burnet was nonexistent with Bryan and Hall, but throughout the summer and the fall of 1836, Burnet and Toby maintained regular communication. In June, Burnet had ordered Triplett to announce that no more volunteers would be needed until the winter. Only a month later, Burnet wrote to Toby, urging him to send as many volunteers as possible. Reports were circulating that Mexican General Urrea was once again organizing a force to invade Texas. Burnet also urged Toby to sell as much land scrip as possible and to "Leave no means untried to dispose of it. Funds we must have, and Script is our only financial recourse." Toby received Burnet's letter requesting volunteers on July 12. He made arrangements for 100 volunteers from Louisville to leave on the *Flora* and 120 more on the brig *Good Hope* to depart by July 20. Both Colonel Edward J. Wilson's and Captain G. Lewis Postlethwaite's Kentucky volunteers had arrived in New Orleans the previous month and awaited transport to Texas.[72]

From July 11 through September 29, Toby also sent more than one thousand volunteers to Texas, relying on the schooners *Flora*, *Flash*, the *Congress*, the *Col. Fannin*, and the *Julius Caesar* to ship both volunteers and supplies to Texas. Plans to invade Matamoros prompted urgent requests from Burnet to send a significant amount of supplies to Texas.[73] As the invasion enthusiasm began to wane, however, Burnet issued orders on September 12, instructing Toby to cease providing "facilities or aid" to those who were volunteering for only three months' service. Calling them "mere Leeches," Burnet said that the government would accept only volunteers who enlisted for at least one year's service. The number of volunteers mentioned in Toby's correspondence began to drop off rapidly after Burnet's order.[74]

Burnet also sent an urgent request to get the Texian naval ships back into the Gulf: "The services of our little Navy are all important at this juncture." He asked Toby to "enable" Commodore Hawkins to finish the naval repairs as soon as possible. Both the *Independence* and the *Liberty* were being held until funds were available. When Austin arrived in New Orleans in June, he brought with him $5,000 that he disbursed for expenses of the two ships.[75]

Reports that a large Mexican force was again preparing to invade Texas dampened any enthusiasm for the purchase of the Texas land scrip. As of June 30, Toby had sold only 9,600 acres of scrip. He wrote that the only means available to his agency to obtain funds, under the current conditions, was through the final approval of the January loans. He urged that the scrip be sent as soon as possible. When he discovered that some of the holders of advances from Bryan's agency would accept payment in land scrip, he encouraged Burnet to send any audited accounts to be paid. Bryan and Hall's accounts, however, would not be audited until September, so on September 3 Burnet issued another order for Toby to sell an additional 500,000 acres of land scrip—a total of 1,000,000 acres.

Burnet also sent orders to Toby to pay individuals in land scrip upon their arrival in New Orleans. On September 22 Burnet sent James Morgan to the United States to obtain supplies. Toby was instructed to issue 100,000 acres of land scrip to Morgan upon his arrival. By September 1 Toby had issued a total of 372,120 acres of scrip out of a total 1,000,000 acres commissioned to him and his agents. In addition, Burnet's report to the new Texas House of Representatives in October revealed that the government had issued orders for 248,401 acres in land scrip to pay for recruiting expenses, naval repairs, and the purchase of arms and provisions.[76]

Burnet continued to write Toby, giving orders for scrip to be sold nearly up to Houston's inauguration. One of the last letters Burnet sent Toby as interim president was to inform him that Toby had forgotten to include the cognac in his last shipment. Houston was elected president of the republic of Texas and took the oath of office on October 22. Burnet had resigned early to allow Houston to take office rather than follow the constitutionally designated second Monday in December. Three days after he took office, Houston wrote to Toby, ordering a halt in the sales of land scrip. Later he modified the order by allowing Toby to finish existing contracts and to send the rest of the scrip back to Texas. Economic conditions were worsening in New Orleans, and sales of scrip were being made on one, two, and three years credit.[77]

In July, Bryan went to Natchez, presumably on business. On his return, Bryan sold Texas land for Fairfax Catlett on July 22 to Philo Goodwyn and to the partnership of John Fountain and William Martin. James Ramage, a member of the original New Orleans committee, wrote to his old friend Stephen F. Austin on July 27, noting that Bryan was on his way to Texas. Ramage defended Bryan, stating that he had been "shamefully treated by the existing government of Texas" and that public opinion in New Orleans was then running strong in Bryan's favor. In June, however, not all appeared lost. Bryan began publishing the sale of assorted goods and was once again attempting to reestablish himself as a commercial merchant. In spite of the temporary government's betrayal, Bryan also desired to become a citizen of Texas. He wrote to Austin, Archer, and Wharton that he had submitted a request for citizenship in 1834 to Samuel Williams, Austin's secretary at the time.[78]

With his commercial business crippled because of the heavy unpaid advances, Bryan sent a copy of his application to the former commissioners to renew his efforts to obtain Texian citizenship. Ironically, even though the Texian provisional government had deserted him, he still looked to Texas for a new beginning. on September 27 Bryan and Hall's accounts were finally submitted for audit.[79]

On July 20 Texian Secretary of State William Jack wrote to Thomas Meux, chair of the lenders' meeting, to inform him that the cabinet was mortified that the lenders still insisted on preserving their right to priority of location. Jack reiterated that the government could not in good conscience agree to this in view of their duty to their citizens to issue lands to them first. Though grateful for their original offer, Jack continued, "Still we recognize the doctrine that nations as well as men must be just before they are generous." He informed the lenders that the modified offer was officially withdrawn. The government expressed its willingness to pay back the advance as quickly as possible at a reasonable rate of interest. Jack allowed for future negotiation if the lenders would agree to the cabinet's compromise with Triplett and Gray.[80]

Upon receiving a copy of Jack's letter refusing acceptance of the agreement and the modified scrip, Triplett responded to the Texian secretary of state on August 19. Triplett was still bitter over his experiences in Texas and with the Toby land scrip. He wrote a long letter reviewing the events relating to the loans and criticized the ad interim government's handling of the compromise. Retorting that all that the lenders wanted was "Bare, naked Justice," he called on the Texian secretary to grant a compliance with their contract. The issue, according to Triplett, was not the compromise agreement; rather, it was the wording of the scrip. Giving the lenders any less than the terms of the compromise, according to him, would "Do more injury to your cause than ten thousand Bayonets of your Enemy, for who would afterwards Enter into any Engagement with a government which had failed to keep its faith."[81]

As late as October, Henry Austin, the "cracked brain citizen," wrote from New Orleans to Stephen Austin, informing him that there was still a glimmer of hope that the lenders of the first loans might agree to the compromise. Austin talked with collector of customs James Breedlove, who now had a share as an investor, in the hope that they might accept the agreement, "That is to be at liberty to locate their scrip when they please but without a preference."

Three days later, Thomas Muex, however, simply restated the lender's position of May 30. Muex maintained that the lenders would accept only the agreement set down by Triplett and Gray with the recommended changes in the scrip's wording.[82] Triplett wrote to Christy on October 4 that he had been in "perfect despair in regard to Texas," lamenting that the government had their money and were dictating the terms to the lenders. Warning of the pitfalls of operating in bad faith, Triplett predicted, "Capitalists will refuse to invest money in her lands—and they will be at so low, a price that a few resident monopolisers [sic] will get the whole for a song."[83]

The new secretary of state, Stephen Austin, wrote to the lenders on November 19 and urged them to accept the compromise as negotiated by Burnet's government. He defended the cabinet's offer, adding that the government was willing to settle the matter by issuing certificates of stock at twelve percent. Austin also pointed out to them that because the discussed annexation of Texas to the United States was a certainty, the return on their investment would be "very valuable."

Already by June, 1836, the Texian cause had become tiresome to some New Orleanians, none more than to William Christy's own family. One of Christy's in-laws, Francis R. Pierce, lamented to his sister, "You do not know how tired we are of the poor Texians."[84] Part of the weariness, according to Pierce, came from the two Texian factions vying for support: the independence faction and the Mexican statehood faction. Pierce's observations reveal that there were some, even in Christy's family, who viewed the conflict in Texas as a civil war.

John T. Mason, who had arrived in New Orleans in May from East Texas, awaited Houston's arrival. He visited Houston at Christy's home and immediately wrote to Samuel Swartwout concerning the status of their land investments. Mason gained Houston's support, referring to him as their "advocate and agent for our land business in Texas."[85] Mason gave Houston an advance of $2,000, drawing $1,000 from Christy as a loan to Swartwout. Mason proudly wrote that their surveys had been located between the Neches, Red, and Sabine Rivers. He predicted that their lands "will be embraced within the U. States if the Neches be declared the boundary—I had this in view in directing the locations."[86]

Perhaps to the relief of his family, Christy finally went to Texas and was present for his old friend's inauguration at Columbia. He did not come in military array as he had hoped, but he did receive Houston's recognition during his speech: "There sits a gentleman within my view whose personal and Political services to Texas have been invaluable. He was the first in the United States to respond to our cause. His purse was ever open to our necessities. His hand was extended in our aid. His presence among us and his return to the embraces of our friends will inspire new efforts in behalf of our cause."[87]

Christy must have felt great satisfaction in receiving these plaudits from his old friend, but they would soon be a bittersweet reward for his efforts for Texas. The first congress of the republic of Texas convened in September. Christy already knew that the constitution forbade foreigners from owning land in Texas, but he hoped Houston would secure an exception for him. Christy had wasted no time in buying a cotton plantation on Oyster Creek near Brazoria. With his land holdings with George Hancock in East Texas and the lands he had bought from Augustus Allen in February, Christy would have quickly become a major land owner in Texas and would also have realized his dream of a cotton plantation enterprise. He obviously had much to gain or much to lose, hinging on this one special act to preserve his holdings. Seeing the bill as a favor for one of President Houston's friends, opponents were successful in getting the measure defeated. Houston, however, was not resigned to accepting a total loss of his friend's lands. On December 10, Houston wrote a letter to Christy's sons, George and William, granting them a league and labor of land in the name of their cousin, New Orleans Grey Vincent Drouillard. Houston wrote that Drouillard would hold the land for their benefit "until provisions are made by law or otherwise, which will enable you to hold in your own names, which I trust will soon be the case."[88]

Christy was not deprived of other opportunities, however. He became an agent for the newly formed Texas Railroad and Banking Company. Former Texian commissioner to the United States Branch T. Archer was elected its president, and another former commissioner, James Collinsworth, was elected as a board member. Thomas J. Green, Christy, and Samuel M. Williams were appointed commissioners to negotiate funds for the company in the United States. In the petition to the bill, Green gazed into the future when he wrote "I look to the time, not distant, with as much confidence, when I shall see a trip made from the Gulf of California to the city of Orleans in ten days or less, . . . If I had an opportunity, I would call the attention of the city of Orleans to it, as she is equally interested in the work, and its accomplishment would fill the measure of her glory and grandeur." The proposed route would be strategically located near the northern Mexican states—with large silver deposits—and therefore "its discounts can always be large without the fear or danger of a run upon it for gold or silver." Jerome Bayon had proclaimed earlier in the year that railroads and land speculation must go hand in hand, and this applied nowhere more than in Texas. Nonetheless, Christy left Texas, disappointed that his efforts were not more appreciated. The prohibition against foreigners owning lands in Texas remained, but Christy still had a hand in the future development of the region. Like William Bryan, Christy's future would continue to be connected to Texas.[89]

Christy's friendship with Houston would serve both men for years to come. Eventually, in spite of new prohibitions on owning land in Texas and even at the risk of using his valuable political capital, Christy fulfilled his dream of becoming a plantation owner.

EPILOGUE

New Orleans was the major commercial center on the Mississippi River and the Gulf of Mexico, and it was also a launching point for revolutionary causes in the region throughout most of the nineteenth century. Beginning with the Hidalgo revolution in Mexico against Spain in the early 1800s and continuing with the Texas revolution in 1835 and 1836, New Orleans would continue to be a center for revolutionary causes in Latin America and the Caribbean on into the 1850s.[1]

The Committee on Texas Affairs in New Orleans was a mirror reflection of a previous committee, the New Orleans Association, which had also exploited instability in Mexico. Additionally, the 1835–1836 committee was a forerunner of future revolutionary movements in Latin America and Cuba in the 1850s and influenced pro-Texas movements in other areas of the United States. The perceived lethargic action by the U.S. government to stop these movements only confirmed Mexico's suspicions that the United States had ulterior motives to acquire Texas. The eventual annexation of Texas hastened the westward movement of the United States. Ten years later, as a result of the Mexican War, the United States gained the vast northern frontier of Mexican territory that extended to the Pacific Ocean.[2]

The Committee on Texas Affairs in New Orleans consisted exclusively of American businessmen, and the meeting during which the committee was formed was held in one of the opulent symbols of American commercial ascendancy, Banks's Arcade. Their work was exclusively American in purpose and goals. Although the committee existed for only a short time, several members emerged as central figures in Texas affairs for years to come: William Christy, William Bryan, and Edward Hall, to name a few.

Texian supporters in New Orleans made Texas independence a condition for their financial assistance or their influence to obtain backing from associates. In January, 1836, they influenced a moderate Stephen F. Austin to swing his support wholeheartedly to independence. From the start, members of the committee looked suspiciously at Mexican federalist movements in New Orleans.

Their early profederalist rhetoric at the Banks's Arcade meeting failed to raised the significant monetary aid the federalists needed to regain power in Mexico. William Christy clearly stonewalled requests for help from Mexía. In May, 1836, Christy did not hesitate to relay to the Texian government rumors that Mexía and Goméz Farías planned to invade Texas if they regained power in Mexico. The committee members viewed the conflict in Texas as a fight for independence with financial gain in mind, not for separate Mexican statehood or the restoration of the Constitution of 1824.

The Texas conflict also agitated an already-tense situation between Anglo-Americans and Creoles in 1830s' New Orleans. Creole merchants depended heavily on Mexican commerce for much needed specie. Christy and Caldwell, who had been recognized as leaders of the Louisiana nativist (antiforeigner) movement in New Orleans, were also central members of the Texas committee. It was a glaring reminder of the ethnic tensions in the city that no Creoles were nominated to the New Orleans committee. The various incidents of the Texian war schooners and privateers preying on Mexican shipping only exacerbated the situation. Apart from the October 16, 1835, meeting, the Creole population appeared to be indifferent to the Texian struggle.

The Texian provisional government, which was wracked with internal discord, made matters difficult for the New Orleans agents by sending numerous middlemen to purchase supplies and war materiel with little coordination, correspondence, or oversight with Bryan and Hall's agency. Burnet's ad interim government made matters worse by commissioning its own agents, thus leaving Bryan and Hall in a precarious financial situation.

Robert Triplett's appointment as general agent created a headlong clash of interests because of Triplett's personal interests as an investor in the two January 1836 loans and his civil duties. A crisis occurred when Burnet appointed Toby and Brother to sell off Texas lands for funds apparently without informing Triplett. Triplett, the investor, viewed the sale of the 300,000 (later 500,000) acres of land scrip as a breach of trust in allowing the lenders priority of choice. He also believed that Toby's sale of Texian lands would adversely affect the value of their investments. The clash between Bryan, McKinney, and Toby over the $10,000 in the Bank of Orleans and Toby's appointment as general agent paralyzed efforts in New Orleans to supply much-needed support and eroded public confidence in the legitimacy of the Texian cause.

Did the Burnet government deliberately betray Bryan and Hall? When taking office, Burnet maintained that he was not informed of Bryan's agency. It is entirely possible that Burnet was honestly unaware of the Texian commissioner's appointments. He also gave little recognition to his predecessor's actions or appointments. Unfortunately, it appears that Bryan and Hall had no one who endorsed their efforts. Thomas Toby, who replaced Bryan and Hall as general agent, already had name recognition with commercial allies such as McKinney and Williams. Furthermore, Burnet believed the complaints that Bryan's agency was shipping substandard supplies. The criticism of leaders such as Captain Hawkins also contributed to the growing doubts about Bryan's abilities.

In fairness to Burnet, his government faced the daunting task of winning a war against superior numbers, an assignment that required desperate measures. Nevertheless, with the abrupt change in agents, Burnet's failure to regularly correspond with Bryan and Hall as Texian agents was inexcusable and created confusion and ill will among some New Orleans supporters. Bryan and Hall, who were already weighed down by nearly $90,000 of debt on behalf of the Texas cause, were understandably offended and feared their own financial ruin in their efforts for Texas. The first congress of the republic of Texas repaid Bryan in land scrip in December, 1836. The Texian congress authorized him to sell "a sufficient quantity of Land Scrip to pay all of the demands." [3] Bryan was appointed as Texian consul at New Orleans in December, 1838. [4] He must have felt pleasure in relieving his predecessor, Thomas Toby, who had replaced Bryan as agent in 1836. [5] Bryan served intermittently as consul through 1842 prior to being succeeded by P. Edmonds. President Houston subsequently appointed Bryan and James Morgan to secretly sell the Texian navy.

Bryan and Hall continued in various partnerships, including a venture in making carriages. [6] Land speculation, however, remained a lifelong ambition for Hall. In 1839 Bryan assigned land scrip from his agency claims to Hall and another investor, Levy Jones. Hall and Jones in turn applied for patents for many of the unsold portions of Galveston Island. [7] In 1837 Michael Menard, along with Robert Triplett, William Fairfax Gray, Sterling Niblett, Thomas Green, Levi Jones, and William R. Johnson, had already been granted a patent for a league and labor on the island for $50,000. [8] After the Texas General Land Office refused to grant Jones and Hall their land patents, the partnership challenged the decision through court battles and appeals. The state legislature eventually granted them patents amounting to 18,215 acres of island land. [9]

After service as a naval commissioner, Bryan lived in Galveston, partly to oversee his and Hall's mutual land investments. In 1848 Hall discovered that Bryan had indeed been a poor businessman. When he visited Bryan in Galveston to determine the status of their partnership, he found Bryan in ill health and penniless. Hall disgustedly declared that Bryan "was not worth a picayune."[10] Bryan had been living a charade that finally caught up with him and his long-time partner. Even though Bryan admitted that he had not kept any books for their partnership or any of the funds, Hall offered to remain in the partnership and also supplied his old friend with the necessary funds to go to New York for his health. As Bryan was packing a borrowed trunk from Hall for the trip, he became seriously ill and died ten days later. Hall paid $59 for Bryan's funeral and $2.50 to have the grave dug.[11] Edward Hall, who had come to New Orleans as an English professor, became a successful land agent and commercial merchant in spite of the financial failings of his early partner, William Bryan. Hall also drew one of the first sketches of Austin, the new Texas capital, which was published as a frontispiece for A. B. Lawrence's *Texas in 1840*.[12] In 1860 Hall was living at 77 Common Street and was a partner in Hall, Kemp, and Company on Tchoupitoulas Street in New Orleans.[13]

Thomas Toby continued as general agent in New Orleans until December 25, 1837, when Houston proclaimed that all agents in the United States were officially recalled.[14] Toby and Brother presented their statement of accounts on April 23, 1837. By November, 1837, Toby's accounts exceeded $65,000 in outstanding payments. The Texas government made no provision to pay Toby. He was commissioned as consul in New Orleans on September 20, 1837, and served in that capacity until Bryan relieved him in December. Despite Toby's sacrificial service to the republic of Texas, he remained a successful merchant in the city and resided in the luxurious, suburban Garden District. Toby died in July, 1849, and his accounts remained unpaid; in 1874 his widow filed a claim for the unpaid bills. J. B. Shaw, who was hired to present her case, stated that the total amount owed to Toby's estate was $66,712.18 after $9,908.08 was deducted for overcharges.[15] In 1881 Toby's children once again presented the claim to the state of Texas for payment. Both houses of the Texas legislature then passed Resolution Forty-One, which provided for a settlement of $45,000, far less than Toby's original claim.[16]

Mexican federalist Goméz Farías and his family finally left for Mexico on February 3, 1838. Arriving at Veracruz, they returned to Mexico City, adding to federalist pressure on Mexican President Antonio Bustamante. When Goméz Farías again became president during the Mexican War, he challenged the power of the Catholic church once more by proposing to raid church treasuries to finance the U.S.-Mexican war. Santa Anna, who had also returned to Mexico, was sent to take command of the Mexican forces against the Americans.

Goméz Farías's proposal to take church funds created such a stir that Santa Anna again ousted Goméz Farías. Goméz Farías, however, witnessed the induction of a new Mexican constitution in 1857, one that censured the Catholic church in Mexico. He was carried into the Mexican congress so that he could be the first to sign the document.[17]

José Antonio Mexía continued to live in New Orleans and traveled to Central America in partnership with New Orleans attorneys Pierre Soulé and Achille Murat to build a canal in Nicaragua. José Urrea led a federalist revolt at Tampico in December, 1838. Assembling supplies and men, Mexía joined Urrea for the campaign. The two generals got as far as Puebla, where Generals Santa Anna and Gabriel Valencia defeated the federalist forces. Urrea escaped, but Mexía was captured. Santa Anna issued orders to execute him, and the command was carried out on May 3, 1839.[18] Mexía's family did however benefit from his vast Texas holdings. Maria Adelaida and Enrique, Mexía's children, received sizable tracts of land in Texas. Enrique rose to the rank of brigadier general in the Mexican army during the resistance against the French in the 1860s. He moved to Limestone County, where the town of Mexía was laid out in 1870. Enrique lived there until his death in 1896. Mexía's widow, Charlotte, died on September 25, 1864.[19]

George Fisher returned to Texas after his abortive attempts to recruit Mexican prisoners for a renewed federalist expedition. He and his wife, Elizabeth, had just purchased his wife's family plantation, but Fisher would not stay in Mississippi. Elizabeth's refusal to accompany him to Texas did not stop him from going there, and on January 23, 1839, the Texas congress granted Fisher a divorce.[20] In 1837 he opened a store in the new town of Houston, later forming the company of Fisher, Davis, and Lubbock. In 1839 he was appointed as justice of the peace in Harris County. That same year Fisher submitted his *Memorials* to the Texas congress, seeking relief for the members of the Tampico expedition. The committee, with Houston as chair, reviewed the petition but delayed action on the measure, and Fisher's petition for the Tampico veterans was all but defeated.[21]

The dream of a northern Mexican federalist confederacy resurfaced in 1840, when a convention met at Laredo and declared Coahuila, Nuevo León, and Tamaulipas as the Republic of the Rio Grande.[22] Centralist General Mariano Arista defeated Antonio Canales, the commander of federalist troops in Tamaulipas, on March 25, 1840, in Coahuila. The Rio Grande government sent General Juan Anaya to meet with President Lamar and other Texian leaders for financial aid. Their efforts achieved only moral support and virtually no monetary backing. The fledgling republic, however, collapsed when Canales surrendered to Arista in November, 1840.[23]

The amphictyonic council in New Orleans disappeared from record after Mexía's disastrous expedition in November, 1835. The council was more of a commercial and speculative venture than a fraternal one. Many of the capitalists at these secretive meetings, who had offered conditional financial assistance to Mexican federalists, might have been Masons, but money in this case was thicker than fraternal brotherhood. The introduction of Mexican federalist yorkino exiles into the multiethnic population of New Orleans was probably made through Masonic connections. Father Mariano Cuevas's assertion that Freemasonry and the yorkinos were conspirators, willing to sell Texas to their Louisiana Masonic brothers, cannot be substantiated from existing sources. Key leaders of the pro-Texas faction in New Orleans after the forming of the pro-Texas committee, namely Christy, Caldwell, Banks, Bryan, and Hall, were not Masons. The Masons have been given too much credit in fostering and financing revolutions, especially in the case of Texas.

The investors of the two New Orleans loans in January, 1836, openly anticipated a sizable return on their investments, but they did not foresee Texian governmental resistance to the original terms of the loans. The $50,000 New Orleans loan was actually settled before the first. James Erwin and the other lenders agreed to release the Texian government from the loan's conditions, which were considered "ruinous to the interests of the country." Congress set aside 20,000 acres to be issued in land scrip to the lenders in proportion to their investment. The lenders were given six months to file their acceptance of the contract. Any lender could surrender his scrip, and the secretary of the treasury would issue the lender a government bond for the principle and interest at the rate of $12^{1}/_{2}$ percent per annum.[24] The first New Orleans loan was finally settled on May 24, 1838, with the government once again using the compromise agreement as set down between Triplett, Gray, and the Burnet government as the final settlement.[25]

The numerous land contracts and powers of attorney found in the New Orleans Notarial Archives reveal that land speculation occurred in Texas by New Orleans businessmen and their associates before, during, and after the Texian Revolution. Many of them were ardent supporters of Texas independence and would eventually support Texas annexation.[26] Conversely, the Nacogdoches land men were eager to sell huge parcels of Texas land to these speculators in New Orleans, ignoring governmental freezes on such sales. William Christy, Edward Hall, William Bryan, William Fairfax Gray, Robert Triplett, George Hancock, and Andrew Hodge Jr. all capitalized on their partisan relationships with their Texian brethren.

It may be problematical to proclaim that Texas would have lost the revolution without its support base in New Orleans. Land was the only wealth Texas had to offer to finance their struggle. Rampant land speculation took place during the 1830s, and the ongoing political instability in Mexico and the revolution in Texas only fueled the hunger for more land. Many of those who became Texas's strongest supporters in New Orleans were also looking for new investments. Little did many of those who attended the October, 1835, meeting at Banks's Arcade imagine the outcome for them and for Texas. Those who left for Texas as volunteers and those who participated in the campaign as partisans and investors were forever changed; as a result, a continent was forever changed. The destinies of these men and that of Texas became intertwined as threads in a tapestry. In turn, the eventual annexation of Texas to the United States stimulated the westward movement of a new nation. New Orleans and its commercial interests hastened the removal of Texas from the Mexican nation.

NOTES

ABBREVIATIONS

Austin Papers	The Austin Papers
Blake	Robert Bruce Blake Research Collection
DCRT	*Diplomatic Correspondence of the Republic of Texas*
JBML	Jackson Barracks Military Library
Lamar Papers	*The Papers of Mirabeau Buonaparte Lamar*
Laws of Texas	H. N. Gammel, *The Laws of Texas*
NONA	New Orleans Notarial Archives
OCTR	*Official Correspondence of the Texas Revolution*
PTR	*Papers of the Texas Revolution*
QTSHA	*Quarterly of the Texas State Historical Association*
SHQ	*Southwestern Historical Quarterly*

INTRODUCTION

1. H. N. Gammel, ed., *Laws of Texas: 1822–1897*, 1:536; 927–28.

2. Carleton et al. to Preval et al., Jan. 4–5, 1836, John H. Jenkins, ed., *The Papers of the Texas Revolution, 1835–1836*, 3:480–89 (hereafter cited as PTR). The term "Texian" is used throughout this work to maintain the historical name for the inhabitants of Texas in 1835 and 1836.

3. Harris Gaylord Warren, *The Sword Was Their Passport: A History of American Filibustering in the Mexican Revolution*, 121–26.

CHAPTER I

1. New Orleans *Bee*, Aug. 18, 1835.

2. R. B. Way, "The Commerce of the Lower Mississippi in the Period 1830–1860," *Proceedings of the Mississippi Valley Historical Association*, 10 (1918–1921): 59; Henry C. Dethloff, "Paddlewheels and Pioneers on Red River, 1815–1915, and the Reminiscences of Captain

M. L. Scovell," *Louisiana Studies* 6 (summer 1967): 96–98; New Orleans *Bee*, July 2, 1835. Five steamboats that made the round trip from Natchitoches to New Orleans were the *Lady Washington, Romeo, O'Connell, Ouachita,* and the *St. Landres;* James E. Winston,"Notes on the Economic History of New Orleans, 1803–1836," *Mississippi Valley Historical Review* 11 (Mar., 1924): 208–10.

3. Ralph W. Haskins,"Planter and Cotton Factor in the Old South: Some Areas of Friction," *Agricultural History* 29 (Jan., 1955): 1–14; A. H. Stone,"The Cotton Factorage System of the Southern States," *American Historical Review* 20 (Apr., 1915): 557–65. Harry Mitchell in"The Development of New Orleans as a Wholesale Trade Center," *Louisiana Historical Quarterly* 27 (Oct., 1944). Stone asserts that the commercial merchant and the factor were functionally different occupations. Mitchell maintains that the factor was exclusively a "commercial merchant" for his planter clients (p. 951). Haskins, however, maintains that it was difficult to maintain a distinction. Haskins is consistent with Mitchell in that function played a major part in establishing a difference between the two roles. Haskins, however, maintains,"the former [factors] was an agent employed to market produce for a principal, in this case the planter; the commission merchant secured supplies of various kinds for his customers" (p. 1). Thus the factor became the commercial merchant for his clients in providing—in most cases—the supplies needed by the planter.

4. Robert E. Roeder,"New Orleans Merchants, 1790–1837" (Ph.D. diss., Harvard University, 1959), 4–5; Winston,"Notes on the Economic History of New Orleans, 1803–1836," 207.

5. Roeder,"New Orleans Merchants," 262.

6. Mitchell,"The Development of New Orleans," 953; Egal Feldman, *Fit for Men: A Study of New York's Clothing Trade* (Washington, D.C.: Public Affairs Press, 1960), 35–52; see also Way,"The Commerce of the Lower Mississippi in the Period 1830–1860," *Proceedings of the Mississippi Valley Historical Association* 10 (1918–1921): 62.

7. New Orleans *Bee*, Nov. 21, 1835.

8. Roeder,"New Orleans Merchants," 100, 235–36; 248; Roeder identifies Bullit and Shipp, N. and J. Dick, Fisk and Watt, John Hagan, John Linton, Reynolds and Byrne, and Maunsel White as the largest factorage houses in 1831 and 1832 based upon total bale receipts. Way,"The Commerce of the Lower Mississippi," 62. New Orleans *Price-Current and Commercial Intelligencer*, Oct. 17, 1835, and Oct. 24, 1835. An examination of available cotton bale receipts for 1835 indicates that Burke, Watt, and Co., Byrne and Hermann, Lambeth and Thompson, Thomas Barrett and Co., Bogart and Hoopes, N. J. Dick and Co., Buckner, McKenna, and Wright, and Buckner, Stanton and Co. made up eighty percent of bale receipts entering New Orleans for the last quarter of 1835.

9. J. Carlyle Sitterson, *Sugar Country: The Cane Sugar Industry in the South, 1753–1950* (Westport, Conn.: Greenwood Press, 1953), 187–91.

10. George D. Green, *Finance and Economic Development in the Old South, Louisiana Banking, 1804–1861,* 28; Mitchell,"The Development of New Orleans," 957.

11. Roeder,"New Orleans Merchants," 219–20; 254.

12. Green, *Finance and Economic Development,* 17, 29–30; New Orleans *Bee*, May 16, 1835; New Orleans *Price-Current and Commercial Intelligencer,* Oct. 24, 1835, 17.

13. Green, *Finance and Economic Development*, 22–23; Merl E. Reed, "Boom or Bust: Louisiana's Economy during the 1830s," footnote 15, 48.

14. *Niles Register*, Mar. 5, 1836.

15. Green, *Finance and Economic Development*, 33.

16. Reed, "Boom or Bust: Louisiana's Economy during the 1830s," 49; see also Merl E. Reed, "Government Investment and Economic Growth," 183–201.

17. John Gibson, *Gibson's Guide and Directory of the State of Louisiana and the Cities of New Orleans and Lafayette*, 286; Jo Ann Carrigan, "Impact of Epidemic Yellow Fever on Life in Louisiana," *Louisiana History* 4 (winter 1963): 5; Gordon Gillson, "Nineteenth-Century New Orleans: Its Public Health Ordeal," *Louisiana Studies* 4 (summer 1965): 89–90; New Orleans *Bee*, Oct. 12, 1835.

18. Theodore Clapp, *Autobiographical Sketches and Recollections, during a Thirty-Five Year Residence in New Orleans*, 120; Timothy F. Reilly, "Heterodox New Orleans and the Protestant South, 1800–1861," *Louisiana Studies* 12 (fall 1973): 547–51; Earl F. Niehaus, *The Irish in New Orleans, 1800–1860*, 37–58; see also Roger W. Shugg, *Origins of Class Struggle in Louisiana: A Social History of White Farmers and Laborers during Slavery and After, 1840–1875* (Baton Rouge: Louisiana State University Press, 1939; second printing, 1966).

19. John Martin, "The People of New Orleans as Seen by Her Visitors, 1803–1860," *Louisiana Studies* 6 (winter 1967): 366–67; Ambrose Cowperthwaite Fulton, *A Life's Voyage: A Diary of a Sailor on Sea and Land, Jotted Down during a Seventy-Year's Voyage*, 107–109.

20. Clapp, *Autobiographical Sketches and Recollections*, 244, 253–54; see also Fred R. Darkis Jr., "Madame Lalaurie of New Orleans," *Louisiana History* 23 (fall 1982): 389–90.

21. New Orleans *Bee*, Sept. 7, 1835.

22. Ira M. Leonard and Robert D. Parmet, *American Nativism, 1830–1860*, 49–73; Arthur C. Cole, "Nativism in the Lower Mississippi Valley," 258–75.

23. New Orleans *Bee*, Apr. 6, 1835.

24. New Orleans *True American*, Aug. 13 and Aug. 15, 1835.

25. *L'Abeille de Nouvelle Orleans* [New Orleans *Bee*], Apr. 11, 1835; Glenn R. Conrad, ed., *A Dictionary of Louisiana Biography*, 1: 51, s.v. "Jerome Bayon"; New Orleans *Bee*, Apr. 11, 1835.

26. New Orleans *True American*, Aug. 3, 4, 13, and 15, 1835.

27. New Orleans *Bee*, Aug. 1, 1835.

28. Ibid., Aug. 11, 1835.

29. Ibid., Aug. 10, 1835.

30. New Orleans *True American*, Aug. 21, 1835.

31. New Orleans *Bee*, Aug. 3, 1835.

32. *Address of the Louisiana Native American Association, to the Citizens of Louisiana and the Inhabitants of the United States*, 19–20.

33. New Orleans *Bee*, Feb. 13, 1836.

34. Ibid.; New Orleans *Bee*, Mar. 17, 1836; John Smith Kendall, *History of New Orleans*, 3 vols. (Chicago: Lewis, 1922), 1:135–39; Joseph Tregle Jr., *Louisiana in the Age of Jackson*, 303–308.

35. New Orleans *Bee*, Aug. 19, 1835.

36. Ibid., Aug. 12, 1835.

37. Ibid., Aug. 17, 1835.

38. *Gibson's Guide and Directory*, preface; Albert D. Kirwan, ed., *The Civilization of the Old South*, 77–94; D. L. A. Hackett, "The Social Structure of Jacksonian Louisiana," *Louisiana Studies* 2 (spring 1973): 324–53; Francis Burns, "The Graviers and the Faubourg Ste. Marie," 385–427; Grace King, *New Orleans, The Place and the People* (New York: Macmillan, 1895), 260; John Chase, *Frenchmen, Desire, Good Children . . . and Other Streets of New Orleans*, 206.

39. Albert A. Fossier, *New Orleans, The Glamour Period*, 10–12.

40. New Orleans conseil de ville, letters, petitions, and reports, vol. 3, 1821–Dec. 15. 1835, documents 721, 723, and 730.

41. Fossier, *New Orleans, The Glamour Period*, 12–13; see also Mary Louise Christovich, Roulhac Toledano, Betsy Swanson, and Pat Holden, *New Orleans Architecture, The American Sector.*

42. *Gibson's Guide and Directory*, 314; *Dictionary of Louisiana Biography*, 1:145, s.v. "James H. Caldwell"; Nelle Smither, "A History of the English Theatre at New Orleans, 1806–1842," 205–12; Nelle Smither, *History of the English Theatre in New Orleans*, 122–30.

43. W. B. Burkenroad Jr., president of J. Aron and Co., Inc., to William C. Shopsin, Feb. 26, 1979, from the files of Trapolin Architects, New Orleans; files and records of Banks's Arcade from Trapolin Architects, New Orleans; New Orleans Notarial Archives (hereafter cited as NONA), William Christy, notary public; Thomas Banks to the Washington Guards, lease, Oct. 26, 1835, starting Nov. 1, 1835, vol. 22, 329.

44. *Gibson's Guide and Directory*, 320.

45. *Proceedings in the Case of the United States vs. William Christy, on a Charge of Having Set on Foot a Military Expedition, in New Orleans against the Territory of Mexico, in Nov., 1835*, 27; *Western Americana: Frontier History of the Trans-Mississippi West, 1550–1900*; New Orleans *True American*, Aug. 8, 1835; New Orleans *Bee*, May 15, 1835; NONA, William Christy, notary public, Thomas Banks to John Gibson, lease, Nov. 4, 1835, and for Dec. 1, 1835, lease, vol. 22, 363.

46. *Gibson's Guide and Directory*, 89, 320, and 343; Darkis, "Madame Lalaurie of New Orleans," 390.

47. John Hope Franklin, *The Militant South, 1800–1861*, 170–92; "Louisiana Greys Historical Militia Data on Louisiana Militia, 1836–1842," Workers Progress Administration records, Jackson Barracks Military Library (hereafter cited as JBML); NONA, William Christy, notary public, Thomas Banks to the Washington Guards, lease, Oct. 26, 1835, starting Nov. 1, 1835, vol. 22, 329.

48. "Louisiana Greys Historical Data on Louisiana Militia, 1836–1842," vol. 58, Workers Progress Administration records, JBML.

49. Joseph G. Dawson III, *The Louisiana Governors, from Iberville to Edwards*; Joseph G. Tregle Jr., "Edward Douglass White (Baton Rouge: Louisiana State University Press, 1990), 113–18; Diedrich Ramke, "Edward Douglas[s] White, Sr., Governor of Louisiana, 1835–1839," *Louisiana Historical Quarterly* 19 (1936): 273–76.

50. Perry H. Howard, *Political Tendencies in Louisiana*, 36–45.

51. New Orleans *Bee*, Oct. 12, 1835.

CHAPTER 2

1. *L'Abeille de Nouvelle Orleans* [New Orleans *Bee*], Sept. 9, 1835.

2. J. Lloyd Mecham, "The Origins of Federalism in Mexico," *Hispanic American Historical Review* 18 (May, 1938): 164–82.

3. A good source for the expulsion of the Spaniards from Mexico is Harold Dana Sims, *The Expulsion of Mexico's Spaniards, 1821–1836*; Michael Costeloe, *The Central Republic in Mexico, 1835–1846*, 16–30. Costeloe provides a historical profile of the hombres de bien. Cecil Alan Hutchinson, "Valentín Gómez Farías: A Biographical Study" (Ph.D. diss., University of Texas at Austin, 1948), 29–31.

4. The early presidents of Mexico were Vicente Guerero, 1829; Maria Bocanegra, 1829; Pedro Velez, Luis Quintanario, and Luis Alamón, 1829–1830; Anastasio Bustamante, 1830–1832; Melchor Musquiz, 1832; and Manual Gomez Pedraza, 1833; Wilfrid Hardy Collcott, *Church and State in Mexico, 1822–1857* (Duke University Press, 1926, second reprint; New York: Octagon Books, 1971); Manuel Dublán and José Maria Lozano, *Legislación Mexicana; O coleccóon completa de las disposisciones legislativas expedidas desde la independencia de la Republica ordenada*, 2:689–90.

5. Waddy Thompson, *Recollections of Mexico*, 88; George L. Hammeken, "Recollections of Stephen F. Austin," *Southwestern Historical Quarterly* 20 (Apr., 1917): 374 (hereafter cited as *SHQ*); Farías, *The Farías Chronicles: A History and Genealogy of a Portuguese/Spanish Family*, 84; Cecil Alan Hutchinson, "Mexican Federalists in New Orleans and the Texas Revolution," *Louisiana Historical Quarterly* 39 (Jan., 1956): 5; Austin to Ayuntamiento of Béxar, Oct. 2, 1833, *Austin Papers* 2:1007–1008; S. F. Austin to S. M. Williams, Jan. 12, 1834; S. F. Austin to James F. Perry, Oct. 6, 1834, in "Some Texas Correspondence," *Mississippi Valley Historical Review* 11 (1924): 123.

6. Costeloe, *The Central Republic in Mexico*, 56; Hutchinson, "Valentín Gómez Farías," 243–45; Andres Tijerina, *Tejanos and Texas under the Mexican Flag, 1821–1836*, Centennial Series of the Association of Former Students, Texas A&M University, no. 54 (College Station: Texas A&M Press, 1994), 113–36, 245.

7. Ramón Musquiz to ———, Jan. 30, 1831, Béxar Archives at the University of Texas Archives, ed. Chester V. Kielman and Carmela Leal, reel 138, 369–71; Dublán y Lozano, *Legislación Mexicana*, 2:163; Tijerina, *Tejanos and Texas*, 116–18.

8. Costeloe, *The Central Republic of Mexico*, 31–32.

9. Costeloe, "Santa Anna and the Gómez Farías Administration in Mexico." *The Americas* 31 (1974): 18–21.

10. Dublán y Lozano, *Legislación Mexicana*, 3:15; Helen Mar Hunnicutt, "The Relationship between Antonio Lopez de Santa Anna as President and Valentín Gómez Farías as Vice- President of Mexico, Apr. 1833–Jan. l835" (master's thesis, University Texas at Austin, l925), 77–79; Hutchinson, "Valentín Gómez Farías," 342–43; A. Viesca to S. D. Valentín Gómez Farías, Parras, Mar. 19, 1835; A. Viesca to Thomas Jefferson Chambers, Parras, Mar. 19, 1835; A. Viesca to S. D. Valentín Gómez Farías, Parras, Mar. 25, 1835, Valentín Gómez Farías Collection, Nettie Benson Latin American Collection, University of Texas at Austin.

11. "1844 [M. B. Lamar, Richmond? Tex.] from Judge Toler," *The Papers of Mirabeau Buonaparte Lamar* (hereafter cited as *Lamar Papers*), ed. Charles Adams Gulick Jr., Katherine Elliott, Winnie Allen, and Harriet Smithers, 6 vols. (Austin: Von Boeckmann-Jones, 1924–1927), 4, part 1: 97.

12. Barragán to Cós, Mexico, July 4, 1835, *PTR* 1:188; David Glenn Hunt, "Vito Alessio Robles: Coahuila y Texas, desde la Consumacion de la Independencia hasta el Tratado de Paz de Guadalupe Hidalgo (Mexico, 1946), an Edited Translation of Volume II, Chapters 1–7," 6; Cós to Farías, Leona Vicario, Apr. 6, 1835, 2–3; Gómez Farías to Cós, Patagalana, Apr. 18, 1835, Gómez Farías Collection, Nettie Benson Latin American Collection, University of Texas at Austin; Hutchinson, "Valentín Gómez Farías," 362; (Baltimore) Niles Weekly Register, Sept. 19, 1835; New Orleans *Price-Current and Commercial Intelligencer,* Nov. 7, 1835.

13. Hutchinson, "Mexican Federalists in New Orleans," 3–4; John Winthrop, *Report of the Trial of Thomas M. Thompson for a Piratical Attack upon the American Schooner San Felipe, before the United States Court for the Eastern District of Louisiana* (New Orleans: E. Johns, 1835); John Winthrop, *Texas as Province and Republic, 1795–1845.*

14. Antonio Garay to Valentín Gómez Farías, Apr. 4, 1835, letter 347, trans. Robert M. Benavides, Valentín Gómez Farías Collection, Benson Latin American Collection, University of Texas at Austin; Hutchinson, "Valentín Gómez Farías," 287. Garay was a Veracruz commercial broker and probably had monetary connections with New Orleans businessmen for him to be able to make arrangements for a line of credit for Gómez Farías with Samuel Hermann Sr. See also John W. Batty, "M: W: Lucien Hermann, Grand Master, 1849–1850," *The Louisiana Freemason* 23 (July, 1994): 4–5; 34, 36. From the files of the Hermann-Grima House historic site, New Orleans; José M. Caravajal to Valentín Gómez Farías, Aug. 20, 1836, Valentín Gómez Farías Collection, Nettie Benson Latin American Collection, University of Texas at Austin; José María J. Carvajal to Valentín Gómez Farías, Aug. 20, 1836; Jorge Fisher to General José Antonio Mexía, May 27, 1836, Valentín Gómez Farías Collection, Nettie Benson Latin American Collection, University of Texas at Austin.

15. Valentín Gómez Farías to Juan Rolland, Feb. 2, 1837, trans. Robert M. Benavides, Valentín Gómez Farías Collection, Nettie Benson Latin American Collection, University of Texas at Austin.

16. Margaret Swett Henson, Lorenzo de Zavala: The Pragmatic Idealist, 72; New Orleans Bee, July 13, 1835; Lorenzo de Zavala, *Journey to the United States of North America,* 11–13.

17. Zavala, *Journey to the United States,* 29.

18. Ibid.

19. Ibid., 30; *Tableau des FF (Composant la T(R(L (de St. Jean de Jerusalem, sous le Titre Distinctif la Concorde, no. 3 (Anciens Maçons d'York)* (New Orleans: Roche, 1820), John Adems Paxton, *The New Orleans Directory and Register* (New Orleans: Leyman and Beardslee, 1827); *Michel's New Orleans Annual and Commercial Register,* 257; *Gibson's Guide and Directory,* 362; *New Orleans Directory, for 1841* (New Orleans: Michel and Co., 1840), 258.

20. *Tableau des FF (Composant la T(R(L (de St. Jean de Jerusalem, sous le Titre Distinctif la Concorde, no. 3 (Anciens Maçons d'York)* (New Orleans: Roche, 1820), 3, 4, 6; *Tableau des FF (Composant la T(R(L (de St. Jean de Jerusalem, sous le Titre Distinctif la Concorde, no. 3 (Anciens*

Maçons d'York) (New Orleans: Fourcand, 1822), 6, 8; files from Masonic historian Clayton Borne III, Metairie, La.

21. Cecil Alan Hutchinson, "General José Antonio Mexía and His Texas Interests," *SHQ* 82 (Oct., 1978): 121; Desalguilers, "Freemasonry in Mexico, Its Origin, & illustrated by Original Documents, Not Heretofore Published," *Masonic Review* (Aug., 1858): 1–8, in "Mexico, Masonry" file, Texas Masonic Grand Lodge Library, Waco, Tex.; Luis J. Zalce y Rodriguez, *Apuntes para la Historia de la Masoneria en Mexico*, 1:60–64; Leonard Durvin Parrish, "The Life of Nicolas Bravo, Mexican Patriot (1786–1854)," 165–66; Lillian Estelle Fisher, "Early Freemasonry in Mexico, 1806–1828," *SHQ* 42 (Jan., 1939): 199; Carlos W. Del Plaine, "Outline of Mexican Masonic History, Part I," *New Age* 65 (Nov., 19–?): 43; E. R. Turnbull, "Early Freemasonry in Mexico," *The Builder* (July, 1924): 205–206, in "Mexico, Masonry" file, Texas Masonic Grand Lodge Library, Waco, Tex.; Hutchinson, "General José Antonio Mexía and His Texas Interests," 121; Parrish, "The Life of Nicolás Bravo," 166; Biblioteca Nacional, Mexico City, Coleción Lafragua, no. 398, cited in Michael Costeloe, *The Central Republic of Mexico, 1835–1846*, no. 73, Cambridge Latin American Series (Cambridge: Cambridge University Press, 1993), 114–15.

22. Masonic Grand Lodge of Louisiana, *Report of the Committee appointed to inquire into the use of Free-masonry in Louisiana, and the accumulation of rites in by the State Grand Lodge, March 18, 1816* (New Orleans, n.p., 1816), 9.

23. Eugene C. Barker, "The African Slave Trade in Texas," *Quarterly of the Texas State Historical Association* 6 (Oct., 1902): 146–49 (hereafter cited as *QTSHA*); Clara M. Love, "History of the Cattle Industry in the Southwest, I," *SHQ* (Apr., 1916): 372; Joseph Carl McElhannon, "Imperial Mexico and Texas, 1821–1823," *SHQ* 53 (Oct., 1949): 125.

24. Frank Lawrence Owsley Jr. and Gene A. Smith, *Filibusters and Expansionists: Jeffersonian Manifest Destiny, 1800–1821*, 172–80; Warren, *The Sword Was Their Passport*, 119, 124, 131, 141, 181.

25. For studies on Southern filibustering activities in Latin America during the antebellum period see Warren, *The Sword Was Their Passport*; Franklin, *The Militant South, 1800–1861*; Owsley and Smith, *Filibusters and Expansionists*; and Robert E. May, *Manifest Destiny's Underworld: Filibustering in Antebellum America* (Chapel Hill: University of North Carolina Press, 2002).

26. Winston, "Notes on the Economic History of New Orleans, 1803–1836," *Mississippi Valley Historical Review* 11 (Mar., 1924): 208–10; New Orleans *Price-Current and Commercial Intelligencer*, Oct. 10, 1835. Exports and imports were reported from Oct. 1 to Sept. 30 of each year. For the same 1833–1834 reporting period, 307,421 bales of cotton were imported from the Louisiana interior and Mississippi, and 345,970 bales were imported in 1834 and 1835. North Alabama and Tennessee imported 135,542 in 1833 and 1834, and 148,132 bales were imported in the 1834–1835 reporting period. Texas exceeded Florida cotton imports by 320 bales (3,084 bales of Texas cotton to 2,764 bales of Florida cotton) for the 1834–1835 business season; Ramón Musquiz to ———, Jan. 30, 1831, the Béxar Archives at the University of Texas Archives, reel 138, 369–71; New Orleans *Bee*, July 22, 1835; shipping notices in 1835 New Orleans newspapers, namely the New Orleans *Bee* and the *Price-Current and Commercial Intelligencer*, reveal that William Bryan tended to ship to Brazoria, Galveston, and

Matagorda; E. W. Gregory tended to ship to Brazoria; Harrison, Brown and Company, and E. J. Forstall, and Cabellero tended to ship to Tampico.

27. Nettie Lee Benson, "Texas as Viewed from Mexico, 1820–1834," *SHQ* 90 (Jan., 1987): 280–81.

28. *L'Abeille de Nouvelle Orleans* [New Orleans *Bee*], Sept. 9, 1835; Jorge Fisher to José Antonio Mexía, May 27, 1836, Valentín Gómez Farías Collection, Benson Latin American Collection, University of Texas at Austin; NONA, Octave de Armas, n.p., vol. 24, 116, Apr. 6, 1835; Hutchinson, "General José Antonio Mexía and His Texas Interests," 120; James F. Perry to Austin, Oct. 27, 1830, Eugene C. Barker, ed., *The Austin Papers* 2:523.

29. *The Burr Conspiracy*, Workers Progress Administration Records, JBML.

30. Hutchinson, "General José Antonio Mexía and His Texas Interests," 127–34.

31. *Proceedings in the Case of the United States vs. William Christy*, 35; *Gibson's Guide and Directory*, 330–31.

32. Bibliotheca Nacionál, Mexico City, Coleción Lafragua, no. 398, cited in Michael Costeloe, *The Central Republic of Mexico, 1835–1846*, 114–15.

33. *The Federalist or, The New Constitution: Second Edition by Alexander Hamilton, James Madison, and John Jay*, ed. Max Beloff (New York: Basil Blackwell, 1947; 2d ed., 1987), "Number XVIII, Hamilton and Madison," 82–87; John Kaminski and Richard Leffler, eds., *Federalists and Antifederalists: The Debate over the Ratification of the Constitution*, Constitutional Heritage Series, vol. 1 (Madison, Wis.: Madison House, 1989), 20, 42.

34. (Mexico City) *El Mosquito Mexicano*, Dec. 11, 1835.

35. Ibid.

36. Ibid.

37. Ibid.

38. Ibid.

39. Farías to Mexía, New Orleans, Oct. 30, 1835, *PTR* 1:269.

40. Benson, "Texas as Viewed from Mexico," 279; Paul Leicester Ford, ed., *The Writings of Thomas Jefferson* 8:261–63, Thomas Jefferson to John Dickinson, Aug. 9, 1803, "We have some pretensions to extend the western territory of Louisiana to the Rio Norte, or Bravo; and still stronger the eastern boundary to the Rio Perdido between the rivers Mobile & Pensacola." See also *Jefferson and Southwestern Exploration: The Freeman and Custis Accounts of the Red River Expedition of 1806*, 25–26.

41. Ramón Musquíz to the governor of Coahuila y Texas, Mar. 11, 1833, San Antonio, in Vicente Filisola, *Memorias para la Historia de Tejas*, 2 vols. (Mexico, 1848–1849), I:321–22, cited in Hutchinson, "Mexican Federalists in New Orleans," 11–12.

42. Monterrey *Gazeta Constitucional de Nuevo León*, Dec. 3, 1829.

43. Eugene C. Barker, "Stephen F. Austin and the Independence of Texas," *QTSH* 13 (Apr., 1910): 271.

44. Translated letter or essay? 1833? Papers of Samuel M. Williams, Rosenberg Library, Galveston.

45. Gómez Farías to Barragán, July, 1835, Gómez Farías Collection, Nettie Benson Latin American Collection, University of Texas at Austin.

46. Hutchinson, "Valentín Gómez Farías and the Secret Pact of New Orleans," *Hispanic American Historical Review* 36 (Feb., 1956): 473–77.

47. Hutchinson, "Mexican Federalists in New Orleans," 10.

48. Mariano Cuevas, *Historia de la Iglesia en México*, vol. 5, 225–27.

49. Salvador Borrego, *América Peligra*.

50. Ibid., 172.

51. Ibid., 150.

52. Charles F. Zimpel New Orleans 1834 city map, in the Historic New Orleans Collection, New Orleans.

53. Dawson, *The Louisiana Governors, from Iberville to Edwards* (Baton Rouge, Louisiana State University, l990), s.v. "Pierre Auguste Bourguigrion Derbogny, Arnaud Julie Beauvais, Jacques Dupré," by Judith Gentry, 103–108; J. H. Young, *New Map of Texas with the Contiguous American and Mexican States* (Philadelphia: S. Augustus Mitchell, 1836); NONA, Louis Feraud, n.p., sale of property. Dufour to Dupré, Mar. 26, 1833, vol. 17, 113; NONA, A. Chiapella, n.p., Louis Decournau from the succession of Jacques Dupré, Apr. 15, 1848, vol. 14, 163, 388–90. Also from the personal research and files of Linda Burd and Mitch Burd, New Orleans, owners of the Dupré cottage. The author found specific Humble Cottage Lodge records and rosters in the Masonic Grand Lodge of Louisiana records dating back to the 1820s and membership rosters and minutes of New Orleans lodges in the 1820s and 1830s but found no mention of Dupré.

54. The author made a survey of Ursulines street addresses around 103 Ursulines in 1834, 1835, and 1838.

55. *Gibson's Guide and Directory*, 164.

56. Glenn Lee Greene, *Masonry in Louisiana, A Sesquicentennial History, 1812–1962* (New York: Exposition Press, 1962), 91. Also from the files of Louisiana Masonic historian Clayton Borne III, Metairie, La.; Ramage to Austin, New Orleans, Oct. 21, 1835, *PTR* 1:182–83.

57. Warren, *The Sword Was Their Passport*, 119, 124, 131, 141, 181.

58. George Fisher, *Memorials of George Fisher, late secretary to the expedition of Gen. José Antonio Mexía, against Tampico, in November, 1835* (Houston: Telegraph, 1840), 11; Winthrop, *Texas as Province and Republic*; Fisher to Austin, Oct. 20, 1835, New Orleans, typescript letter, George Fisher Papers, Center for American History, University of Texas at Austin.

CHAPTER 3

1. *An Abstract of the Original Titles of Record in the General Land Office, Printed in Accordance with a Resolution of the House of Representatives, Passed 24 May, 1838*, 95.

2. Bertram Wallace Korn, *The Early Jews of New Orleans*, 174–76.

3. New Orleans *Bee*, Sept. 18, 1835, and Oct. 7, 1835.

4. Sterne to Gottschalk, Oct. 18, 1828, Nacogdoches Archives, Robert Bruce Blake Research Collection (hereafter cited as Blake), from the archives of the office of the county clerk, Nacogdoches, Tex., book G, May 8, 1792–July 2, 1838, 4:38; Orleans parish probate and succession records, probate records for Emanuel Sterne, July 18, 1828 (microfilm) New Orleans Public Library; Orleans parish court, case 4997, *Jeanette Hunt Stern vs. Emanuel Stern*, June 20, 1828 (microfilm) New Orleans Public Library; Korn, *The Early Jews of New Orleans*, 192–206.

5. Korn, *The Early Jews of New Orleans*, 206, 329–31; *Book of Foreigners Settled at Nacogdoches with Date of Application for Citizenship and Action of the Authorities on Such Applications from 1827 to 1834*, Blake, 30:48–49; Harriet Smither, ed., "The Diary of Adolphus Sterne, XXIII," *SHQ* 35 (Apr., 1932): 321.

6. Henry Cohen, "Settlement of the Jews in Texas," *Publications of the American Jewish Historical Society* 2 (1894): 144–45; census records of Nacogdoches from Béxar Archives, Blake, 19:189, Apr. 30, 1835; certificates of entrance were required in order for a foreigner to remain in Texas under the colonization law of Coahuila and Texas, Mar. 24, 1825, Betty Fagan Burr, *Nacogdoches Archives: 1835 Entrance Certificates*, ix–xi; archives from the office of the county clerk, Nacogdoches, Tex., book I, J, May 7–Sept. 24, 1835, Blake, 5:155–59; 164–65; 170–71; NONA, William Boswell, notary public, Oct. 2, 1835, 36:1009.

7. New Orleans *Bee*, Sept. 18, 1835.

8. Interview with Mrs. Sally Reeves, Director and Archivist, NONA Research Center, Feb. 16, 2000. See also Richard Holcombe Kilbourne Jr., *Debt, Investment, Slaves: Credit Relations in East Feliciana Parish, Louisiana, 1825–1885*.

9. *The New Orleans Directory; Containing the Names, Professions, and Residences, of all the Heads of Families, and Persons in Business, of the city and Suburbs, with other useful information* (New Orleans: Stephen E. Percy and Co., 1832), 79.

10. *Michel's New Orleans Annual and Commercial Register*, 46.

11. Census Records of Nacogdoches from Béxar Archives, Apr. 30, 1835, Blake, 6:92–101.

12. Barnett merchant documents in Texas, Aug. 16, 1828–Mar. 24, 1832, Béxar Archives at the University of Texas Archives, reel 112, 302–12; reel 115, 995–96; reel 142, 753–57; Korn, *The Early Jews of New Orleans*, 104–109; New Orleans *Daily Picayune*, Dec. 6, 1898.

13. Korn, *The Early Jews of New Orleans*, 230–32.

14. The Sephardist Jewish sect was influenced primarily by Dutch, Spanish, and Portuguese Jews. New York Jew Jacob Solis, who had visited New Orleans in 1827 helped establish the Shanarai-Chassett synagogue; see Korn, *The Early Jews of New Orleans*, 192–208.

15. Ibid., 225–29.

16. Ibid., 209–16.

17. Smither, ed., "Dairy of Adolphus Sterne, IV," *SHQ* 31 (July, 1927): 65; Smither, ed., "Diary of Adolphus Sterne, IX," *SHQ* 32 (Oct., 1928): 165, 179; Smither, ed., "Dairy of Adolphus Sterne, XXVI," *SHQ* 36 (Oct., 1932): 221.

18. For further reading on the Fredonian rebellion see Eugene C. Barker, *The Life of Stephen F. Austin: Founder of Texas, 1793–1836, A Chapter in the Westward Movement of the Anglo-American People* (Austin: Texas State Historical Association, 1949), chapter 7, "The Fredonian Rebellion," 148–77.

19. ——, *The New Age* 20 (Jan., 1914): 101.

20. *Tableau des FF (Composant la T(R(L (Lafayette, no. 25) (Ancient Maçons de York)* (New Orleans: A. Peychaud, 1826), 5, 7; *Tableau des FF (Composant la T(R(L (La Triple Bienfaisance, no. 7319). (Rite Français.) Regulierement constituée à l'O (de la Nouvelle Orleáns, par la T(R(G(L (France).* (New Orleans: A. Peychaud, 1826), 5 (manuscript collection 895, Freemason

lodges in Louisiana, 1808–1933), manuscript department, Howard-Tilton Memorial Library, Tulane University.

21. *Tableau des FF (Composant la T(R(L (de St. Jean De Jerusalem, sous le Titre Distinctif L'Etoile Polaire, no. 5 (Anciens Maçons d'York) Regulierement constituée à l'O (de la Nouvelle-Orleans (Louisiane) par la T(R(G(L (de la Louisiane)* (New Orleans: M. Cruzat, 1825), 1–11, archives of the Grand Lodge of Louisiana, Alexandria, La.

22. A. L. Bradford, and T. N. Campbell, eds., "Journal of Lincecum's Travels in Texas, 1835," *SHQ* 53 (Oct., 1949): 198.

23. New Orleans *Louisiana Gazette*, June 24, 1835, 12; July 12, 1819, 7; Aug. 18, 1819; Natchez *State Gazette*, Aug. 14, 1819.

24. Dan L. Flores, ed., *Jefferson and Southwestern Exploration: The Freeman and Custis Accounts of the Red River Expedition of 1806*, 25. Flores cites Jefferson's pamphlet titled "The Limits and Bounds of Louisiana" in *Documents relating to the Purchase and Exploration of Louisiana*, 7–45. See also Ford, *The Writings of Thomas Jefferson*, 8:261–63, Thomas Jefferson to John Dickinson, Aug. 9, 1803, "We have some pretensions to extend the western territory of Louisiana to the Rio Norte, or Bravo; and still stronger the eastern boundary to the Rio Perdido between the rivers Mobile & Pensacola."

25. Warren, *The Sword Was Their Passport*, 119, 121, 124, 141.

26. Charles A. Bacarisse, "The Union of Coahuila and Texas," *SHQ* 61 (Jan., 1958): 341–49; Ernest Wallace, David M. Vigness, and George B. Ward, eds., *Documents of Texas History*, 61–62 (hereafter cited as *Documents of Texas History*).

27. William R. Manning, "Texas and the Boundary Issue, 1822–1829," *SHQ* 17 (Jan., 1913): 217–23.

28. Stephen F. Austin to Mary Austin Holly, Nov. 17, 1831, *Austin Papers* 2:705.

29. Odie B. Faulk, *The Last Years of Spanish Texas, 1778–1821* (London: Mouton, 1964), 115–22.

30. Marshall Sprague, *So Vast So Beautiful a Land: Louisiana and the Purchase*, 277–79; Richard R. Stenberg, "The Boundaries of the Louisiana Purchase," *Hispanic American Historical Review* 14 (1934): 32–64; Isaac Koslin Cox, "The Louisiana-Texas Frontier," *QTSHA* 10 (July, 1906): 1–75.

31. Owsley and Smith, *Filibusters and Expansionists*.

32. William M. Malloy, comp., *Treaties, Conventions, International Acts, Protocols, and Agreements between the United States and Other Powers, 1776–1909*, 1:1651–58.

33. Gammel, *Laws of Texas: 1822–1897*, 1:97–98.

34. *Laws and Decrees of the State of Coahuila and Texas*, 15–23.

35. For a classic but partisan study of Joel Poinsett's life see J. Fred Rippy, *Joel R. Poinsett: Versatile American*.

36. Austin to Emily M. Perry, July 24, 1828, *Austin Papers* 2:76–77.

37. Austin to Burnet, Apr., 1835, in Jacqueline Beretta Tomerlin, comp., *Fugitive Letters, 1829–1836, Stephen F. Austin to David G. Burnet*, 35; Barker, "Stephen F. Austin and the Independence of Texas," *QTSHA* 13 (Apr., 1910): 267–69.

38. Richard R. Stenberg, "Jackson, Anthony Butler, and Texas," *Southwestern Social Science Quarterly* 13 (Dec., 1932): 271–73.

39. Andreas V. Reichstein, *Rise of the Lone Star: The Making of Texas*, 96–97.

40. J. C. Beales to Anthony Butler, June 4, 1833, Anthony Butler Papers, box 2B179, general correspondence folder, 1828–1835, Center for American History, University of Texas at Austin.

41. James Prentiss to Anthony Butler, July 27, 1835, in ibid.

42. Manning, "Texas and the Boundary Issue, 1822–1829," 231–35; Manuel Mier Terán, *Texas by Terán: The Diary Kept by General Manuel de Mier y Terán on His 1828 Inspection of Texas*, 178; *Laws and Decrees of the State of Coahuila and Texas*, 16, 33.

43. Richard R. Stenberg, "Jackson's Neches Claim, 1829–1836," *SHQ* 39 (Apr., 1936): 255–74.

44. Anthony Butler to Andrew Jackson, Sept. 26, 1833, in John Spencer Bassett and David Maydole Matteson, eds., *Correspondence of Andrew Jackson*, 4:210.

45. Stenberg, "Jackson's Neches Claim, 1829–1836," *SHQ* 36 (Apr., 1936): 255; *Treaties, Conventions, International Acts, Protocols and Agreements between the United States and Other Powers*, 1:1082–84. The treaty of limits referred to the John Melish map as the official map source for determining the boundary, as did the Adams-Onís treaty of 1819.

46. Anson Jones, *Memoranda and Official Correspondence Relating to the Republic of Texas, Its History and Annexation*, 32, 82–83.

47. Ibid. For an opposing view of Jackson's involvement in the Texas issue see Eugene C. Barker, "President Jackson and the Texas Revolution," *American Historical Review* 12 (July, 1907): 788–809. Barker maintains that Jackson was the victim of inept and selfish agents in Mexico and that Jackson enforced neutrality laws to the best of his abilities and supported neither Sam Houston's revolutionary schemes nor General Gaines's incursion into East Texas.

48. *Treaties, Conventions, International Acts, Protocols and Agreements*, 1:1082–84.

49. Andrew Jackson to Anthony Butler, Anthony Butler Papers, Sept. 4, 1832, Center for American History, University of Texas at Austin.

50. Anthony Butler to Andrew Jackson, Jan. 2, 1832; Andrew Jackson to Anthony Butler, Feb. 25, 1832, and Mar. 6, 1832, *Correspondence of Andrew Jackson*, 4:390, 409–10, 415; Forbes et al. to Jackson, Sept. 11, 1835, *PTR* 1:611; Richard R. Stenberg, "The Texas Schemes of Jackson and Houston, 1829–1836," *Southwestern Social Science Quarterly* 15 (Dec., 1934): 245; *The Western Frontier, 1800–1836: Historical and Military Events of the Western Expansion of the United States Boundary to Texas and Mexico*, Workers Progress Administration Project, 1941, JBML, 110–87.

51. Dublán y Lozano, *Legislación Mexicana*, 3:15.

52. Juan N. Almonte, "Statistical Report on Texas," trans. C. E. Casteñada, *SHQ* 28 (Jan., 1925): 207.

53. Hubert Howe Bancroft, *History of the North Mexican States*, in *The Works of Hubert Howe Bancroft, 1801–1889*, 16:152–53.

54. Kate Mason Rowland, "General John Thomson Mason," *QTSHA* 11 (Jan., 1908): 194–96.

55. Brazoria *Texas Republican*, May 9, 1835.

56. Chambers to Miller, June 30, 1835, *PTR* 1:173–74.

57. Ibid.

58. Brazoria *Texas Republican*, July 25, 1835; Cós to Sabariego, June 20, 1835; Ugartechea to Cós, June 21, 1835; Kerr to Chambers, July 5, 1835; Ugartechea list, Sept. 3, 1835, *PTR* 1:155, 159, 206, 414.

59. James Kerr to T. J. Chambers, July 5, 1835, in Eugene C. Barker, "Land Speculation as a Cause of the Texas Revolution," *QTSHA* 10 (1906): 91.

60. J. G. McNeel to James F. Perry, June 22, 1835, *Austin Papers* 3:77.

61. *Documents of Texas History*, 104; see also David G. Burnett, *Opinion on the Four Hundred Leagues' Grant of Texas Land: By One of the Oldest Settlers of Texas* (New Orleans: William McKean, 1836), 1–12, Center for American History, University of Texas at Austin.

62. New Orleans *Bee*, Sept. 1, 1835.

63. Lois Foster Blount, "The Nacogdoches Committee of Vigilance and Safety, 1835–1836," in Blake, 68:190–96.

64. Adolphus Sterne, *Hurrah for Texas! The Diary of Adolphus Sterne, 1838–1851*, ix–xi; Newton J. Friedman, "Adolphus Sterne," unpublished article, Adolphus Sterne biography vertical file, Center for East Texas Research, Stephen F. Austin State University, Nacogdoches, Tex.; W. Zuber, "Captain Adolphus Sterne," *QTSHA* 2 (Jan., 1899): 211–12.

65. Sam Houston to Henry Raguet, Apr. 7, 1836, Amelia W. Williams, and Eugene C. Barker, eds., *The Writings of Sam Houston, 1813–1863*, 1:400.

66. Ibid.

67. *Nacogdoches Archives*, book J, in Blake, 14:124–26, May 19, 1835–Sept. 24, 1835.

68. *Texas by Terán*, 75–76.

69. Terry Jordan, "Pioneer Evaluation of Vegetation in Frontier Texas," *SHQ* 76 (Jan., 1973): 235–54.

70. A Spanish league equaled 4,428.4 acres, and a labor equaled 177.1 acres, *Categories of Land Grants in Texas*, Archives and Records Division, Texas General Land Office.

71. Records from the archives of the office of the county clerk, Nacogdoches County, Tex., books A–L, 1792–1836, Blake, vols. 1–6 reveal sales and purchases of lands in Nacogdoches district. In tabulating purchases, the author divided land bought by partnerships or groups by the total number of partners to determine shares of land.

72. Agreement between Samuel Swartwout and Frost Thorn, Jan. 28, 1835, in Samuel Swartwout Papers, Center for American History, University of Texas at Austin; NONA, William Christy, notary public, July 13, 1835, vol. 22, 65.

73. Morfit to Forsyth, Aug. 27, 1836, *PTR* 8:334.

74. Everett to Robinson, Nov. 29, 1835, *PTR* 3:25–26.

75. *Journal of a Tour in Texas; with Observations on the Laws, Government, State of Society, Soil, &, by the Agents of the Wilmington Emigration Society, 1835*, 14–15, Western Americana: Frontier History of the Trans-Mississippi West, 1550–1900 New Haven, Conn.: Research Publications, 1975 (microfilm); New Orleans *Bee*, Sept. 7, 1835.

76. Henry Austin to Austin, Mar. 4, 1831; Mar. 15, 1831; and Mar. 20, 1831; copy of a letter from the Mexican consul, Mar. 30, 1831; Austin to N. A. Ware, July 24, 1831; Henry Austin to Austin, Aug. 26, 1831, *Austin Papers* 2:605–606, 613–16, 619–21, 632–34, 681–82, and 690–91.

77. County clerk's office of Nacogdoches County, book I, May 19, 1835–Sept. 24, 1835, Blake, 5:136–37.

78. Ibid., 134–39.

CHAPTER 4

1. *Biographical History and Portrait Gallery of Scott County, Iowa* (New York: American Biographical Publication Co., 1895; reprint, Kokomo, Ind.: Selby, 1989), s.v. "Hon. Ambrose C. Fulton."

2. Fulton, *A Life's Voyage*, 26–34.

3. Ibid., 7–8.

4. Niehaus, *The Irish in New Orleans*, 44–47. Niehaus identifies Cameron as the same Simon Cameron who served as Abraham Lincoln's secretary of war in the 1860s. Fulton also identifies Cameron as Simon Cameron's brother.

5. John D. Tanner and Karen O. Tanner, "Ambrose Cowperthwaite Fulton, 1811–1903," 1993, unpublished biography in Ambrose Cowperthwaite Fulton Papers, 1895–1903, 1993, Center for American History, University of Texas at Austin.

6. Fulton, *A Life's Voyage*, 107.

7. Ronald R. Morazan, *Biographical Sketches of the Veterans of the Battalion of Orleans, 1814–1815* (Baton Rouge: Legacy, 1979), s.v. "Plauché, Jean Baptiste," 188–89.

8. Tregle, *Louisiana in the Age of Jackson: A Clash of Cultures and Personalities* (Baton Rouge: Louisiana State University Press, 1999), 304–305.

9. New Orleans *Bee*, Sept. 7, 1835.

10. Fulton, *A Life's Voyage*, 95. It is unclear whom Fulton is referring to as the Americans imprisoned in Mexico City. Since Stephen F. Austin had just left New Orleans on Aug. 25 after eighteen months in prison in Mexico City, it is probable that Fulton is referring to Austin.

11. Workers Progress Administration Records, JBML.

12. New Orleans *Bee*, Oct. 14, 1835.

13. Ibid., Oct. 13, 1835.

14. Hermann Ehrenberg, *Texas und seine Revolution*, 6; Freidrich W. von Wrede, *Sketches of Life in the United States of North America and Texas*, trans. Chester W. Geue (Waco, Tex.: Texian Press, 1970, English translation ed.), 8–9, 197.

15. *Michel's New Orleans Annual and Commercial Register* (New Orleans, 1834).

16. Fulton, *A Life's Voyage*, 95.

17. New Orleans *Bee*, Sept. 1 and Dec. 17, 1835; Ron Tyler, Douglas E. Barnett, Roy R. Barkley, Penelope C. Anderson, and Mark F. Odintz, eds., *New Handbook of Texas*, s.v. "Santangelo, Orazio de Attellis," by Luciano G. Rusich.

18. New Orleans *Bee*, Aug. 13, 1835.

19. Ibid., Oct. 14, 1835.

20. "1838 Apr. 22, O. de A. Santangelo. Petition to the Honorable Congress of the Republic of Texas," *Lamar Papers* 2:144–45.

21. National Archives Service Records, War of 1812, William Christy, private in Cap-

tain Uriel Sebree's company of riflemen, Aug. 17, 1812–Oct. 16, 1812. Christy's War of 1812 service records do not show when he joined the regular army. His letter to Andrew Jackson on Mar. 28, 1816, requesting permission to settle the U.S. First Infantry's paymaster accounts in Washington suggests that he was an officer by Mar., 1816 (in Harold D. Moser, David R. Hoth, and George H. Hoemann, eds., *The Papers of Andrew Jackson*, 4:426–27).

22. Conrad, ed., *A Dictionary of Louisiana Biography*, 1:179–80.

23. Lois Garver, "Benjamin Rush Milam," *SHQ* 38 (Oct., 1934): 85; John Henry Brown, *History of Texas from 1685 to 1892*, 1:75–82.

24. ——, "Captain John McHenry, Pioneer of Texas," *DeBow's Review* 15 (Dec., 1853): 578–79.

25. Ibid., 579.

26. Ibid., 579.

27. Brown, *History of Texas*, 1:82; Joel Roberts Poinsett, *Notes on Mexico, Made in the Autumn of 1822*, 122.

28. W. Christy to Austin, Feb. 10, 1826, *Austin Papers* 2, part 2:1264.

29. *U. Christy vs. Thomas Spooner*, Orleans parish court, June 28, 1822, New Orleans Public Library.

30. Edgar Grima, "The Notarial System of Louisiana," *Louisiana Historical Quarterly* 10 (Jan., 1927): 76–81; D. Barlow Burke Jr. and Jefferson K. Fox, "The Notaire in North America: A Short Study of the Adaptation of a Civil Law Institution," *Tulane Law Review* 50 (Jan., 1976): 318–45.

31. William Christy, *A Digest of Martin's Reports, of the decisions of the Supreme Court of the State of Louisiana: from its establishment in the year 1813, to Aug., 1826, Including those of the Supreme Court of the late territory of Orleans*.

32. New Orleans conseil de ville, letters, petitions, and reports to the conseil de ville, 1804–1835; no. 721, proposition, Christy to the New Orleans city council, Oct. 29, 1830; no. 723, petition, citizens of New Orleans to New Orleans city council, Dec. 7, 1830; no. 730, Christy to the New Orleans city council, June 2, 1831, New Orleans Public Library.

33. New Orleans *Bee*, Mar. 16, 1854; New Orleans *Daily Picayune*, Aug. 1, 1856.

34. New Orleans *Daily Picayune*, July 28, 1869.

35. Bogart was a major shareholder in the Hotel Exchange Company and a member of the Ocean Insurance Company, New Orleans *Bee*, Mar. 24, 1835, 7.

36. New Orleans *Price-Current and Intelligencer*, May 21, 1836.

37. NONA, William Christy, n.p., sale of property, William Bogart to Thomas Banks, Feb. 25, 1833, vol. 13, 221.

38. *Michel's Annual and Commercial Register*, 1834, 241.

39. New Orleans *Price-Current and Commercial Intelligencer*, Oct. 10, 1835.

40. United States National Archives, abstracts of service records of naval officers ("Records of Officers"), 1793–1893, microfilm roll 3, vol. E–F, Aug., 1813–Aug., 1825; microfilm roll 4, vol. G, Sept., 1825–Dec., 1831, James Ramage; William Dudley, ed., *The Naval War of 1812: A Documentary History* (Washington, D.C.: Naval Historical Center, 1985), 1:476–79; James A. Padgett, "Letters of James Brown to Henry Clay, 1804–1835," *Louisiana Historical Quarterly* 24 (Oct., 1941): 1138; James Ramage to Austin, Jan. 2, 1833, *Austin Papers*, correspondence log.

41. State of Louisiana, *Acts passed at the First Session of the Twelfth Legislature of the State of Louisiana, Begun and held in the City of New Orleans, the Fifth day of Jan., Eighteen Hundred and Thirty Five*, 92–112.

42. New Orleans *Bee*, July 20, 1835.

43. Ibid., July 22, 1835.

44. See note 40 above, 72–73.

45. Conrad, ed. *A Dictionary of Louisiana Biography*, s.v. "James Henry Caldwell"; *New Orleans Times Daily Picayune*, Sept. 22, 1863; Smither, "A History of English Theatre at New Orleans, 1806–1842," *Louisiana Historical Quarterly* 28 (Jan., 1945): 115–222; Henry Moehlenbock, "The German Drama on the New Orleans Stage," *Louisiana Historical Quarterly* 26 (Apr., 1943): 370–71.

46. See note 40 above, 92–112.

47. New Orleans *Price-Current and Commercial Intelligencer*, Oct. 24, 1835; New Orleans *Daily Picayune*, 1837.

48. NONA, William Christy, n.p., contract, Peter Ogier and the New Orleans Gas Light and Banking Company, Oct. 15, 1835, v. 22, 279–80.

49. Gibson, *Gibson's Guide and Directory*, 155.

50. NONA, William Christy, n.p., sale of lot 3, New Orleans Building Company to E. Yorke, May 10, 1833, v. 15, 121; sale of lot 4, New Orleans Building Company, May 10, 1833, v. 10, 125; lease of lot 6, New Orleans Building Company to W. L. Hodge, May 15, 1833, v. 15, 163; New Orleans *Daily Picayune*, Aug. 1, 1856; Gibson, *Gibson's Guide and Directory*, 155.

51. United States Federal Census, Louisiana, Orleans Parish, 1830, 64; New Orleans *Louisiana Advertiser*, Jan. 27, 1835; New Orleans *Bee*, Feb. 17, 1835.

52. NONA, William Christy, n.p., meeting of creditors of W. L. Hodge, June 28, 1831, v. 7, 593.

53. New Orleans conseil de ville, letters, petitions, and reports to the conseil de ville, 1804–1835, letter to the mayor and committee of finance from Andrew Hodge Jr., Jan. 29, 1830, no. 719.

54. NONA, William Christy, n.p., sale of property, A. Hodge Jr. to New Orleans Building Company, Apr. 11, 1832, v. 11, 477.

55. Archives from the office of the county clerk, Nacogdoches, Tex., book I, May 7, 1827–May 30, 1835, contract between William G. Logan, A. Hodge, and N. A. Ware, Apr. 27, 1835, Blake, 5:142.

56. New Orleans *Price-Current and Commercial Intelligencer*, Oct. 24, 1835.

57. Ramage to Austin, Oct. 21, 1835, New Orleans, *PTR* 2:182–83.

58. Ibid.

59. New Orleans *Bee*, July 13, 1835.

60. Ibid., July 20, 1835.

61. Carleton to Forsyth, Oct. 21, 1835, *PTR* 2:175.

62. New Orleans *Bee*, Nov. 17, 1835.

CHAPTER 5

1. Fulton, *A Life's Voyage*, 95; New Orleans *Bee*, May 11, 1835; "A View of New Orleans in 1835, from Joseph H. Ingraham, the South-West by a Yankee," in *Martin Siegel, ed., New Orleans: A Chronological and Documentary History, 1539–1970* (Dobbs Ferry, N.Y.: Oceana, 1975), 76.

2. Bill Walraven and Marjorie K. Walraven, *The Magnificent Barbarians, Little Told Tales of the Texas Revolution* (Austin: Eakin, 1993), 195; J. H. Eaton to Andrew Stevenson, Jan. 12, 1831, *The New American State Papers, Military Affairs*, ed. Benjamin Franklin Cooling, 19 vols., *Institutional and Military Society Ecology* (Wilmington, Del.: Scholarly Resources, 1979), 14:254–55. U.S. Secretary of War Eaton reported to House Speaker Andrew Stevenson that 60,000 copies of *Infantry Tactics* had been distributed to the respective states along with 5,000 copies of the U.S. artillery manual. Louisiana received 636 copies of the infantry manual and 51 copies of the artillery manual. They were distributed by Sept., 1829. *True American*, Sept. 15, 1836, in WPA Records, JBML, "[The Louisiana Greys] Marched to a convenient place, where they made the trial of skill, according to the usual form prescribed by the infantry tactics of the United States." Ornish, *Ehrenberg*, 156; James Ramage to Austin, Oct. 21, 1835, *Austin Papers* 3:197–98.

3. New Orleans *Bee*, Oct. 14 and Oct. 15, 1835; NONA, William Boswell, notary public, sale, Adolphus Sterne to Spencer Gloyd and Isaac Littlefield, Sept. 25, 1835, v. 35, 998; Republic of Texas audited claims, Adolphus Sterne, claim for $820.00, approved Dec. 19, 1839: Sterne listed $450 for fifty muskets and bayonets purchased from Hyde and Goodrich of New Orleans on Oct. 15, 1835; $250 expended in recruiting the "2nd Company New Orleans Grays commanded by Capt Breece," and $45 expended for the company after leaving New Orleans, totaling $820. Sterne's $820 claim was primarily expenses for recruitment and arming the Greys. Sterne submitted an additional claim for $950 in 1839 for the costs in transporting the Greys from New Orleans to Natchitoches. See also Sterne, *Hurrah for Texas!* 75; *Gibson's Guide and Directory*, 105.

4. Census records of Nacogdoches, 1835, Nacogdoches archives, translation, Blake, 19:385.

5. Nathaniel Cox to Austin, Mar. 22, 1832, *Austin Papers* 2:761; Austin to Mary Austin Holly, Jan. 30, 1832; ibid., 2:745; Ernest C. Shearer, "The Caravajal Disturbances," *SHQ* 55 (Oct., 1951): 201–204.

6. Chambers to Miller, June 30, 1835; Ugartechea to Cós, Aug. 8, 1835; Ugartechea to Sabariego, Aug. 13, 1835; Cós to Ugartechea, Aug. 31, 1835, *PTR* 1:173–74, 321, 335, 378.

7. Collingsworth et al., agreement, Oct. 9, 1835, *PTR* 2:76.

8. NONA, William Boswell, notary public, Oct. 12, 1835, 36:1023.

9. NONA, William Christy, notary public, procuration, Caravajal to N. Cox, Oct. 19, 1835, 22:293–94.

10. NONA, William Christy, notary public, procuration, Theodore Clapp to Caravajal, Nov. 16, 1835, 22, 396.

11. Fisher to public, Jan., 1836, *PTR* 2:211–23.

12. Ibid.

13. New Orleans *Bee*, Oct. 16, 1835.

14. Ramage to Austin, Oct. 21, 1835, *PTR* 1:182–83.

15. Austin to Richard Laurence Kenny, Sept. 6, 1825; L. R. Kenny to Austin, May 5, 1826, *Austin Papers* 2, part 2:1322.

16. L. R. Kenny to Austin, Oct. 20, 1825, *Austin Papers* 3:196–97.

17. (San Felipe de Austin) *Telegraph and Texas Register*, Oct. 31, 1835.

18. Statement by Edward Hall, Galveston, 1850? Edward Hall Papers, Alexander Dienst Collection, Center for American History, University of Texas at Austin.

19. Edward Hall to committee of the consultation, Nov. 5, 1835, San Felipe de Austin, *Official Correspondence of the Texan Revolution* (hereafter cited as OCTR), 1:54–55; *Proceedings in the Case of the United States vs. William Christy*, 24–25; (Mexico City) *El Mosquito Mexicano*, Dec. 11, 1835.

20. New Orleans *Bee*, Oct. 19, 1835; Harry Warren, "Col. William G. Cooke," *Quarterly of the Texas States Historical Association* 9 (Jan., 1906): 210; Francis Richard Lubbock, *Six Decades in Texas or Memoirs of Francis Richard Lubbock*, 28.

21. Saul Viener, "Surgeon Moses Albert Levy: Letters of a Texas Patriot," *Publication of the American Jewish Historical Society* 46 (Dec., 1956): 101–13.

22. Hotchkiss to Houston, St. Augustine, Oct. 29, 1835, *PTR* 2:265.

23. Collins to Austin, Oct. 20, 1835, *PTR* 2:173.

24. *Proceedings in the Case of the United States vs. William Christy*, 25.

25. Carleton to Forsyth, New Orleans, Oct. 21, 1835, *PTR* 2:175.

26. First judicial court (Orleans parish), New Orleans, case 8713, *Christy vs. E. Livingston*, Nov. 23, 1830, New Orleans Public Library; White proclamation, Nov. 13, 1835, *PTR* 2:404–405; Christy to government, Oct. 20, 1835, *PTR* 2:286–87; Lubbock, *Six Decades in Texas*, 28.

27. Fulton, *A Life's Voyage*, 96; Ehrenberg, *Texas und seine Revolution*, 7; Ebenezer S. Heath to his mother, Mar. 10, 1836, Fort Defiance, Goliad, Tex., Harbert Davenport Papers, Center for American History, University of Texas at Austin; Edward L. Miller, "The Texas Revolution, Civilian Suits, Whiskey-Loving Foreigners and the New Orleans Greys," *Military Collector and Historian* 48 (spring 1996): 33–37; Peter Stines and Edward L. Miller, "New Orleans Greys in San Antonio de Béxar, 1835," *Military Collector and Historian* 48 (spring 1996): 40–41; M. L. Crimmins, "The Storming of San Antonio de Béxar in 1835," *West Texas Historical Association Year Book* 22 (Oct., 1946): 102–103; Thomas Banks, owner of Banks's Arcade and member of the New Orleans committee, also owned property in other parts of the city. He leased No. 10 Chartres Street to James Evans, a New Orleans hatter, who in Nov., 1835, advertised a diverse selection of hats and, more specifically, sealskin caps; NONA, Jacob B. Marks, notary public, 1842–1843, 32, 102–91.

28. Ehrenberg, *Texas und seine Revolution*, 7–8, author's translation with assistance from Louis Brister, Southwest Texas State University, San Marcos.

29. John Beldon to the government of Texas, Jan. 19, 1836, comptroller of the public accounts records (304), Archives Division, Texas State Library; San Felipe de Austin *Telegraph and Texas Register*, Dec. 2, 1835; Clarksville, Texas *Standard*, June 29, 1883, and Nov. 12, 1886; John Russell Bartlett, *Personal Narrative of Explorations and Incidents in Texas, New Mexico, California, Sonora, and Chihuahua, Connected with the United States and Mexican Boundary*

Commission during the Years 1850, 1851, 1852, and 1853, 2 vols. (Chicago: Rio Grande Press, reprint, 1956), 1:29.

30. "A Campaign in Texas," *Littlel's Living Age* 8 (Feb., 1846): 413–22, in Earl Vandale Collection, Center for American History, University of Texas at Austin; see also James E. Crisp, "Sam Houston's Speechwriters: The Grad Student, the Teenager, the Editors, and the Historians," *SHQ* 97 (Oct., 1993): 203–37.

31. Marmaduke Potter to Henry McArdle, Aug. 13, 1874, McArdle Notebook, vol. 1, Manuscript Collection, Archives Division-Texas State Library.

32. Collins to Austin, Oct. 20, 1835, *PTR* 2:173; John K. Mahon, *History of the Militia and the National Guard*, Macmillan Wars of the United States Series (New York: Macmillan, 1983), 84–85; New Orleans *Bee*, Jan. 20, 1836; Henderson Yoakum, *History of Texas from Its Settlement in 1685 to Its Annexation to the United States in 1846*, 2:22–23.

33. New Orleans *Price-Current and Commercial Intelligencer*, Oct. 17 and Oct. 24, 1835; New Orleans *Bee*, Apr. 23, 1836.

34. Fisher to Austin, Oct. 20, 1835, typescript copy from original, George Fisher Papers, Center for American History, University of Texas at Austin.

35. Fulton, *A Life's Voyage*, 95–96; *Report of the Trial of Thomas M. Thompson, for a Piractical Attack upon the American Schooner San Felipe; Before the United States Court for the Eastern District of Louisiana* (New Orleans: E. Johns, 1835), 1–44; Winthrop, *Texas as Province and Republic, 1795–1845*.

36. Ehrenberg, *Texas und seine Revolution*, 165.

37. Ibid., 46.

38. Thomas Hooper to ——, Oct. 30, 1835, *OCTR* 1:31–32.

39. Ibid.

40. Hall to committee, Nov. 5, 1835, *PTR* 2:332.

41. San Augustine committee to council, Nov. 3, 1835, *PTR* 2: 307. Hotchkiss, who chaired the St. Augustine committee of safety, included the letter from Daniel H. Vail to the permanent council at San Felipe. Hotckiss's letter was used instead of Vail's to ——, Oct. 31, 1835, *PTR* 2:283.

42. Ehrenberg, *Texas und seine Revolution*, 9–10; Santa Anna to Tornel, Mar. 6, 1836, *PTR* 5:12.

43. (San Felipe de Austin) *Telegraph and Texas Register*, Nov. 7, 1835; "New Orleans Greys, 26 Oct. 1835, an Election of Officers by the New Orleans Greys in Quintana," adjutant general's records (RG 401), Texas State Archives and Library Commission; a copy of Robert Morris's roster can also be found in the JBML and in the M. L. Crimmins Papers, Center for American History, University of Texas at Austin; Villamae Williams, ed., *Stephen F. Austin's Register of Families* (Baltimore: Genealogical Publishing, 1984), 142–43; (Austin) *Texas State Gazette*, Nov. 16, 1850; on page 102 of the Nov. 16 issue, the "Historical Reminiscences" section featured a roster of Morris's Greys and the following statement: "On the 25th of Oct., 1835, about 5 o'clock p.m., E. Hall, landed at the mouth of the Brazos river, Texas, in charge of the Orleans Greys." "1838 June 16, M. B. Lamar [near Houston], to S. Whiting and J. W. J. Niles, Houston, Reply," *Lamar Papers* 2:166–67; (Brazoria) *Texas Republican*, Oct. 31, 1835.

44. Hotchkiss to council, Nov. 5, 1835, *PTR* 2:333.

45. Ehrenberg, *Texas und seine Revolution*, 13–24.

46. H. Reug to Colonel Thomas Rusk, Nov. 9, 1835, Thomas Rusk Papers, Center for American History, University of Texas at Austin.

47. Nixon to president, Nov. 10, 1835, *PTR* 2:375.

48. Joe B. Frantz, "The Mercantile House of McKinney & Williams, Underwriters of the Texas Revolution," *Bulletin of the Business Historical Society* 26 (Mar., 1952): 1–18; T. F. McKinney to R. R. Royall, Oct. 28, 1835, *OCTR* 1:19; Dimmitt to Austin, Nov. 13, 1835, *PTR* 2:389–92.

49. "General Austin's Order Book for the Campaign of 1835," *QTSHA* 11 (July, 1907): 53.

CHAPTER 6

1. Jorge Fisher to Col. S. F. Austin, Oct. 20, 1835, typescript letter, George Fisher Papers, Center for American History, University of Texas at Austin, 9–10.

2. Ramage to Austin, Oct. 21, 1835, *PTR* 2:182–83.

3. New Orleans committee to provisional government, Oct. 20, 1835, *OCTR* 1:9.

4. Henry Rueg to Thomas J. Rusk, Nov. 9, 1835, Thomas J. Rusk Papers, Center for American History, University of Texas at Austin.

5. *Proceedings in the Case of the United States vs. William Christy*, 21–22.

6. Ibid., 37–38.

7. Hutchinson, "Mexican Federalists in New Orleans," 23.

8. "The Anecdotes of Santa Anna," *Lamar Papers* 6: 190; Valentín Gómez Farías to Estevan Montezuma, Nov. 7, 1835, letter 370, Valentín Gómez Farías Collection, Benson Latin American Collection, University of Texas at Austin.

9. *Proceedings in the Case of the United States vs. William Christy*, 44.

10. Fisher to Austin, Oct. 20, 1835, George Fisher Papers, Center for American History, University of Texas at Austin, 4.

11. Austin to provisional government, Nov. 5, 1835, *Austin Papers* 3:240; Fisher to Austin, Oct. 20, 1835, George Fisher Papers, Center for American History, University of Texas at Austin, 9.

12. Fisher to Austin, Oct. 20, 1835, George Fisher Papers, Center for American History, University of Texas at Austin, 10–11, 17; *Proceedings in the Case of the United States vs. William Christy*, 42.

13. Fisher to Austin, Oct. 20, 1835, George Fisher Papers, Center for American History, University of Texas at Austin, 9.

14. Fisher, *Memorials of George Fisher*, biographical sketch, 1; see also Tim Judah, *The Serbs: History, Myth and the Destruction of Yugoslavia* (New Haven: Yale University Press, 1997), 48–52, and Vladimir Dedijer, Ivan Bozic, Sima Cirkovic, and Milorad Ekmercic, *History of Yugoslavia* (New York: McGraw-Hill, 1974), 262–75.

15. Fisher, *Memorials of George Fisher*, biographical sketch, 2; Eugene C. Barker, ed., "Minutes of the Ayuntamiento of San Felipe de Austin, 1828–1832, IV," *SHQ* 22 (Oct., 1918): 191.

16. Edna Rowe, "The Disturbances at Anahuac in 1832," *QTSHA* 6 (Apr., 1903): 272–75; Austin to Horatio Chriesman, June 19, 1832, *Austin Papers* 2:782–87; Austin to Terán, Feb. 5, 1832; Austin to Samuel M. Williams, Apr. 28, 1832, *Austin Papers* 2:747–48; 766–67; James W. Breedlove to Austin, Nov. 12, 1830; Fisher to Austin, Apr. 16, 1833, *Austin Papers* 2:947–50; [18–?, M. B. Lamar, Houston?] Fisher, *Lamar Papers* 3:285–86; James W. Breedlove to Austin, Aug. 11, 1831, *Austin Papers* 2:533–34, 688–89.

17. Austin to Wily Martin, May 30, 1833; Austin to ayuntamiento of Nacogdoches, May 30, 1833, *Austin Papers* 2:275–78.

18. Fisher, *Memorials of George Fisher,* 17–28.

19. Not only was Breedlove the collector of customs for the port of New Orleans, but he was also a commercial merchant and was listed as president of the Atchafalaya Railroad and Banking Company in 1837, located directly across from Banks's Arcade on Magazine Street (*Gibson's Guide and Directory,* 345).

20. F. H. Turner, "The Mejía Expedition," *QTSHA* 7 (July, 1903): 1–28; Austin to Samuel M. Williams, July 1, 1832, *Austin Papers* 2:808.

21. Hutchinson, "General José Antonio Mexía and His Texas Interests," 123.

22. Ibid., 121, 123; Zavala, *Journey to the United States of North America,* 8.

23. Hutchinson, "General José Antonio Mexía and his Texas Interests," 127–28, 136–40; John Austin to Austin, Jan. 5, 1831; William S. Parrott to Austin, Mar. 23, 1831, *Austin Papers,* 3:578–79, 629–30.

24. Fisher to Austin, Oct. 20, 1835, George Fisher Papers, Center for American History, University of Texas at Austin, 9; New Orleans *Bee,* July 3, 1835; *Proceedings in the Case of the United States vs. William Christy,* 31.

25. Mexía to consultation, Oct. 29, 1835, *PTR* 2:261–64.

26. *Proceedings in the Case of the United States vs. William Christy,* 16–17.

27. Ibid., 16–17, 29; New Orleans *Price-Current and Commercial Intelligencer,* Nov. 14, 1835.

28. *Proceedings in the Case of the United States vs. William Christy,* 45; a statement of the physical force of the expedition against Tampico, at the time leaving New Orleans, secretary of state records (RG 307), Archives Division-Texas State Library; "New Light on the Tampico Expedition," 157–58.

29. "New Light on the Tampico Expedition," 157–58.

30. Vicente Filisola, *Memoirs for the History of the War in Texas,* 2:86; Fisher, *Memorials of George Fisher,* 48, 53; "New Light on the Tampico Expedition," 160; Dedrick remembered that roll call revealed forty men either missing, killed, or captured.

31. Fisher, *Memorials of George Fisher,* 54.

32. Ibid.

33. Mexía to Viesca, Dec. 3, 1835; Mexía to Smith, Dec. 7, 1835, in Fisher, *Memorials of George Fisher,* 48–55.

34. Eugene C. Barker, "The Tampico Expedition," *QTSHA* 6 (Jan., 1903): 179–80.

35. *Documents of Texas History,* 91.

36. W. Roy Smith, "The Quarrel between Governor Smith and the Provisional Government of the Republic," *QTSHA* 5 (Apr., 1902): 300–301.

37. Mexía to Smith, Dec. 9, 1835, *PTR* 3:134–37.

38. William Pettus to the council, Dec. 17, 1835, *OCTR* 1:204–206.

39. Commission of Austin, Archer, and Wharton, Dec. 7, 1835; Smith to Austin, Archer, and Wharton, Dec. 8, 1835, in George Garrison, ed., *Diplomatic Correspondence of the Republic of Texas, Annual Report of the American Historical Association for the Year 1907*, vol. 2, part 1, 51–54 (hereafter cited as *DCRT*); Austin to provisional government, Dec. 14, 1835, *Austin Papers* 3:282–84; "The General Council of the Provisional Government of Texas to the Mexican People," in Fisher, *Memorials of George Fisher*, 30–32.

40. Mexía to Smith; Mexía to Robinson; Mexía to Viesca, Dec. 15, 1835, *PTR* 3: 202–204.

41. Mexía proclamation, Dec. 15, 1835, *PTR* 3: 205.

42. Barker, "The Tampico Expedition," 184.

43. J. W. Robinson to T. F. McKinney, Dec. 17, 1835, *OCTR* 2:207–208.

44. Mexía to Governor, Dec. 23, 1835, *PTR* 3: 302; Barker, "The Tampico Expedition," 185.

45. Anonymous letter, Dec. 14, 1835, *PTR* 3: 195.

46. *Interesting Account of the Life and Adventures of One of those Unfortunate Men, who was Shot at Tampico, with Twenty-Seven of His Companions, December 14th, 1835, with a list of all their names, together with the Letters which were written by the Sufferers*, 15; Winthrop, *Texas as Province and Republic, 1795–1845*.

47. *Interesting Account of the Life and Adventures*, 16.

48. Ibid., 14.

49. *Proceedings in the Case of the United States vs. William Christy*, 45–46.

50. Ibid., 50–52.

51. "New Light on the Tampico Expedition," 157.

52. [18–?] F. W. Thornton [Houston?], to [M. B. Lamar, Houston?], *Lamar Papers* 3:274–75; Robertson to Butler, Dec. 14, 1835, *PTR* 3: 191–92.

53. Merle et al. to Henry Carleton, Dec. 26, 1835, *PTR* 3: 331. The following insurance companies signed the petition: John A. Merle and Company; Cuculla, Lapeyre and Company; Chalaron, S. T. Hobson; and Company; Western Marine and Fire Insurance Company; Atlantic Insurance Company; Godfrey, Blossom; and Company; Louisiana State Marine and Fire Insurance Company; New Orleans Insurance Company; Merchant's Insurance Company; M. de Lazardi and Company; F. Gillit and Company; Kohn, Daron, and Company; Harrison, Brown, and Company; J. W. Zacharie and Company; Hermann and Company; Gasquet, Parish, and Company; G. Vance and R. Gamble; A. and R. Dennistoun and Company; J. Pratt and Company; A. M. Miranda and Company; J. M. Caballero; Francisco Tio; John Crosby; and R. and J. Curell. Hermann and Company lent Vice- President Gómez Farías $3,000 when he arrived in New Orleans in Aug., 1835.

54. New Orleans *Bee*, Dec. 5 and Dec. 15, 1835; Baltimore *Niles Weekly Register*, Jan. 16, 1836, 341; Eugene C. Barker, "The United States and Mexico, 1835–1837," *Mississippi Valley Historical Review* 1 (June, 1914): 12; Hutchinson, "Mexican Federalists in New Orleans," 27–28; *Proceedings in the Case of the United States vs. William Christy*, 44–55; Henry Carleton to Henry Forsyth, Jan. 21, 1836, *PTR* 4: 102–103.

55. Hutchinson, "Mexican Federalists in New Orleans," 36.

56. Smith, "The Quarrel between Governor Smith and the Provisional Government," 328.

57. *Proceedings in the Case of the United States vs. William Christy*, 32; New Orleans *Bee*, July15, July 20, and Sept. 16, 1835; John A. Wharton to Henry Smith, Jan. 26, 1836, *OCTR* 1:341; Stephen F. Austin to R. R. Royall and S. Rhoads Fisher, Jan. 7, 1836, *PTR* 3: 434.

58. *Proceedings in the Case of the United States vs. William Christy*, 27–28; Baltimore *Niles Weekly Register*, Jan. 16, 1836, 340.

59. James M. Denham, "New Orleans, Maritime Commerce, and the Texas War for Independence, 1836," *SHQ* 97 (Jan., 1994): 515–16.

CHAPTER 7

1. Crimmins, "The Storming of San Antonio de Béxar in 1835," 104; "General Austin's Order Book for the Campaign of 1835," *QTSHA* 11 (July, 1917): 53.

2. William G. Cooke to Dr. James Cooke, Aug. 7, 1839, Davenport Papers, Center for American History, University of Texas at Austin.

3. Ornish, *Ehrenberg: Goliad Survivor, Old West Explorer*, 132–33.

4. Alwyn Barr, *Texans in Revolt: The Battle for San Antonio, 1835*, 13; Hunt, "Vito Alessio Robles," 56, 78–79; Miguel A. Sanchez-Lamego, *The Siege and Taking of the Alamo*, 25. Sanchez-Lamego identified Plaza de las Islas as Plaza de la Constitutión in his 1836 map of San Antonio. Sanchez-Lamego identified Henderson Yoakum as his source for the name of the plaza on his map; Jesus F. de la Teja, *San Antonio de Béxar: A Community on New Spain's Northern Frontier*, 31–48; Gammel, *Laws of Texas: 1822–1897*, 1:572, 654, 687, 704; Austin to Burleson, Nov. 15, 1835, *PTR* 2: 417.

5. Tijerina, *Tejanos and Texas*, 9; Johnson to Council, Jan. 3, 1836, *PTR* 1: 413; O. C. Hartley and R. K. Hartley, *Reports of the Cases Argued and Decided in the Supreme Court of the State of Texas, at Austin, Texas, 1855*; Barr, *Texans in Revolt*, 16; "General Austin's Order Book for the Campaign of 1835," 17.

6. "General Austin's Order Book for the Campaign of 1835," 22.

7. Barr, *Texans in Revolt*, 15–16; Noah Smithwick, *The Evolution of a State or Recollections of Old Texas Days*, 75–76; Austin to the army, Oct. 23, 1835, *Austin Papers* 3:204; Jesús de la Teja, ed., *A Revolution Remembered: The Memoirs and Selected Correspondence of Juan N. Seguín*, 77–78; Frederick C. Chabot, *With the Makers of San Antonio: Genealogies of the Early Latin, An-glo-American, and German Families with Occasional Biographies, Each Group Being Prefaced with a Brief Historical Sketch and Illustrations* (San Antonio: Artes Graficas, 1938), 118–29.

8. William C. Davis, *Three Roads to the Alamo: The Lives and Fortunes of David Crockett, James Bowie, and William Barrett Travis* (New York: HarperCollins, 1998), 46, 434 (end-note 45), 595. Davis makes a good case for the probability that both James Bowie and War-ren D. C. Hall became friends while serving in the second brigade of the Louisiana militia during the War of 1812. Both men participated with James Long's expedition and would also have known William Christy and Benjamin Milam by the early 1820s; James Kerr to T. J. Chambers, July 5, 1835, in Barker, "Land Speculation as a Cause of the Texas Revolution," *QTSHA* 10 (1906): 91.

9. "General Austin's Order Book for the Campaign of 1835," 32.

10. Ibid., 15–26; Ruby Cumby Smith, "James W. Fannin, Jr., in the Texas Revolution," *SHQ* 23 (Oct., 1919): 85.

11. Austin to president of consultation, Nov. 3, 1835, *Austin Papers* 3:234. Austin requested mortars to be sent as early as November 3, but there is no record that they were ever sent. New Orleans purchasing agent Edward Hall discussed purchasing a howitzer, but it was already after the taking of San Antonio. No siege guns were needed after this event anyway. See Edward Hall to governor and council, December 9, 1835, *OCTR* 1:179. Hermann Ehrenberg mentioned that upon Fannin's final retreat from Goliad on April 18, 1836, several mortars were spiked and left behind at the fort, but it does not appear that these guns ever were at San Antonio in December, 1835; see Ehrenberg, *Texas und seine Revolution*, 117; Sanchez-Lamego, *The Siege and Taking of the Alamo*, 10. Sanchez-Lamego also called Molino Blanco mill, the Zambrano mill. In Austin's correspondence during the siege of San Antonio, he referred to the area as "Mill Station," Austin to Burleson, Nov. 15, 1835, *PTR* 2:417.

12. Fannin to Austin, Nov. 2, 1835, *Austin Papers* 3:231–32; Austin to Fannin, Nov. 14, 1835, *Austin Papers* 3:253–54. The original site of the Molino Blanco is located at Providence Catholic high school on S. St. Mary's Street. One mill wheel is mounted on a pedestal on the high school lawn, and the other is displayed at the Alamo Long Barracks Museum.

13. "General Austin's Order Book for the Campaign of 1835," 36, 44–45; Austin order, Nov. 16, 1835, *PTR* 2:434; Stephen L. Hardin, *Texian Iliad: A Military History of the Texas Revolution, 1835–1836*, 56.

14. Austin to James F. Perry, Nov. 22, 1835, *Austin Papers* 3:262–63.

15. "General Austin's Order Book for the Campaign of 1835," 50; Austin to Houston, Nov. 14, 1835, *PTR* 2:407–408; Austin to provisional executive, Nov. 18, 1835, *PTR* 2:450–51; Austin to James F. Perry, Nov. 22, 1835, *Austin Papers* 3:262–63; commission of Austin, Archer, and Wharton, Dec. 7, 1835; Smith to Austin, Archer, and Wharton, Dec. 8, 1835, *DCRT* 1:51–54.

16. Daniel Shipman, *Frontier Life, 58 Years in Texas*, 74–75; Hunt, "Vito Alessio Robles," 75; Ehrenberg, *Texas und seine Revolution*, 49–51.

17. Stiff notes, Nov. (Dec.?) 8, 1835, *PTR* 3: 389.

18. Ehrenberg, *Texas und seine Revolution*, 54–55; Warren, "Col. William G. Cooke," 211–15.

19. Robert W. Amsler, "General Arthur G. Wavell: A Soldier of Fortune in Texas," *SHQ* 69 (Oct., 1965): 188–92.

20. Hunt, "Vito Alessio Robles," 21; *Texas by Terán*, 183–84; Davis, *Three Roads to the Alamo*, 425.

21. Walter Lord, *A Time to Stand* (New York: Harper and Brothers, 1961), 57.

22. Ibid.

23. Ehrenberg, *Texas und seine Revolution*, 57–58; D. W. C. Baker, comp., *A Texas Scrap Book: Made Up of the History, Biography and Miscellany of Texas and Its People, Original Narratives of Texas History and Adventure* (New York: A. S. Barnes, 1875; reprint, Austin: Steck, 1935), s.v. "Northers," by W. J. Blewett, 366–68. Blewett describes Texas northers as "dreadful storms, which come on so suddenly and are so severe and extremely cold, that man and beast, caught out on the prairies a few miles from shelter, have been known to freeze to death in a very short time." Blewett identifies two types of northers, wet and dry ones. Evi-

dently from descriptions of the weather in early December, 1835, the norther that hit San Antonio was a wet one; Stiff notes, Nov. (Dec.?) 8, 1835, *PTR* 3:389; Johnson to Burleson, Dec. 11, 1835, *PTR* 3:160–61; Barr, *Texans in Revolt*, 71; Crimmins, "The Storming of San Antonio de Béxar in 1835," 110.

24. Ehrenberg, *Texas und seine Revolution*, 60–61.

25. Ibid., 62–63.

26. Barr, *Texans in Revolt*, 53–54; Warren, "Col. William G. Cooke," 214.

27. Ebenezer S. Heath to his mother, Mar. 10, 1836, Harbert Davenport Papers, Center for American History, University of Texas at Austin.

28. Lubbock, *Six Decades in Texas*, 31.

29. James De Shields, *Tall Men with Long Rifles*, 59–60.

30. Warren, "Col. William G. Cooke," 214; Cós's capitulation, Dec. 11, 1835, *PTR* 3:156–58; Burleson to Smith, Dec. 14, 1835, *PTR* 3:186.

31. Fellow citizens to Burleson et al., Dec. 15, 1835, *PTR* 3:199–200.

32. Stivers and Pollard to governor and council, Dec. 17, 1835, *PTR* 3:240. Francis Harvey appears to be a forgotten casualty. He does not appear on any of the reconstructed rosters of Breece's company. He may have been a volunteer who joined Breece's company just before the storming of San Antonio; Crimmins, "The Storming of San Antonio de Béxar in 1835," 111–12; Joseph E. Field, *Three Years in Texas: Including a View of the Texas Revolution and an Account of the Principal Battles, Together with Descriptions of the Soil, Commercial and Agricultural Advantages, Etc.*, 179. Bannister referred to a John Baldwin as the wounded volunteer. There were no volunteers with the name "Baldwin" under Cooke's command during the taking of San Antonio. One can assume that Bannister was referring to John Beldon; "Ward Information," research notes, Lois Fitzhugh Foster Blount Papers, box 31, file 7, East Texas Research Center, Stephen F. Austin State University, Nacogdoches, Tex.; see also Baker, *A Texas Scrap Book*, s.v. "Thomas William Ward," by compiler, 272; The *Telegraph and Texas Register* reported in its February 20, 1836, issue that "Mr. Ward, one of the volunteer greys, who was so unfortunate to lose one of his legs in the storming of Bejar, while bravely engaged with the cannon, is now in this place. Although his wound is not healed, we are happy to hear that it is doing well."

33. "[Feb., 1844, W. G. Cooke, Washington, Tex.] Written by Col. W. G. Cook," *Lamar Papers* vol. 4, part 1, 42.

34. Johnson to government, Dec. 17, 1835, *PTR* 3:226.

35. Ehrenberg, *Texas und seine Revolution*, 72–73.

36. Ibid., 77–79.

37. F. W. Johnson to the general council, Jan. 3, 1836, *OCTR* 1:267.

38. Smith, "The Quarrel between Governor Smith and the Council of the Provisional Government," 287–88; Houston to Bowie, Dec. 17, 1835, *PTR* 3:222–23.

39. Houston to Neill, Dec. 21, 1835, *PTR* 3:278–79; J. C. Neill to governor and council, Jan. 6, 1836, *OCTR* 1:272–74; Houston to Breece, Dec. 21, 1835, *PTR* 3:277.

40. Morris to Houston, Dec. 29, 1835, *PTR* 3:31–32.

41. Hunt, "Vito Alessio Robles," 86; Richard G. Santos, *Santa Anna's Campaign against Texas, 1835–1836*, 9–17, 23–25.

42. Butler to Jackson, Dec. 19, 1835, *PTR* 3:251–52.

43. Ibid.

44. In much of the correspondence of the day, the name for Goliad was also referred to as La Bahía. La Bahía was the Spanish presidio built to protect the mission of Espíritu Santo near the town of Goliad.

45. The unofficial flag of the profederalist movement in Texas was the 1824 flag. The eagle and serpent on the cactus centered on the Mexican red, white, and green national flag were replaced with the year "1824," signifying support for the Mexican constitution of 1824, which the centralist government had suspended in October, 1835. Philip Dimmit, the commandant of Goliad, who had at first refused to provide supplies to Grant and Johnson's federalist expedition, ironically had proposed a flag himself earlier, as a federalist, very similar to the one carried by Grant's men, except the words "The Constitution of 1824" were used instead of just the year. Purchasing agent Edward Hall had also recommended that all Texian ships use the 1824 flag in the Gulf of Mexico under the guidelines of the letters of marque and reprisal. See Hall to Henry Smith, Nov. 18, 1835, OCTR 1:94–95, and Gammel, *Laws of Texas*, 1:23.

46. "[Feb., 1844, W. G. Cooke, Washington, Tex.] Written by Col. W. G. Cook," *Lamar Papers* vol. 4, part 1, 42.

47. J. W. Fannin to J. W. Robinson, Jan. 21, 1836, OCTR 1:320–21; "Fannin and His Command," by Lewis M. H. Washington, 3, available at the Sons of DeWitt Colony website: http://www.tamu.edu/ccbn/dewitt/goliadwash.htm. According to Washington, one of Fannin's staff officers, Fannin accepted Guerra's tender of service a few days before Fannin departed for Copano Bay. Washington also indicates that Fannin accepted Guerra's services in order to secure the "double-fortified long sixes." He maintains that "their services were accepted by Col. Fannin, more for the purpose of obtaining the beautiful field pieces than on account of any real efficiency that was supposed to attach to the men as soldiers." Lewis M. H. Washington, "Fannin and His Command," *Texas State Gazette*, June 18, 1853.

48. John Henry Brown, *Life and Times of Henry Smith: The First American Governor of Texas*, 222–28.

49. Houston to Governor Henry Smith, Jan. 17, 1836, *Writings of Sam Houston*, 1:339.

50. Houston to Smith, Jan. 30, 1836, PTR 4:187; Thornton to Williams, Jan.? 1836, PTR 4:228; Lewis M. H. Washington, one of Fannin's staff members, stated that Ira Westover was commander at Goliad when Fannin and his forces arrived.

51. J. W. Fannin to J. W. Robinson, Jan. 21, 1836, OCTR 1:320–21.

52. Houston to Henry Smith, Jan. 6, 1836, *Writings of Sam Houston*, 1:332–33.

53. Houston to Forbes, January 7, 1836, PTR 3:436–37.

54. "[Feb., 1844, W. G. Cooke, Washington, Tex.] Written by Col. W. G. Cook," *Lamar Papers* vol. 4, part 1, 42–43.

55. Ibid. The only available correspondence in existence between Morris and Fannin is a letter written by Morris from San Patricio on February 6. In the letter Morris relays scouting reports from Placido Benavides indicating a growing Mexican army presence in South Texas and the defeat of federalist forces near Matamoros. Morris also expresses anxiety over Grant's absence with thirty men for two days. Nowhere in the letter does Morris state that he was considering accepting a commission in the federalist army, even though he states that the people of Tamaulipas were still generally in favor of federalism.

56. William Fairfax Gray, *From Virginia to Texas, 1835: Diary of Col. Wm. F. Gray*, 125.

57. Houston to Breese, Dec. 21, 1835, *PTR* 3:277; Bannister to Burnet, Apr. 15, 1836, *PTR* 5:479.

58. *Niles Weekly Register*, Mar. 26, 1836.

59. Hall to the provisional government, Dec. 23, 1835, *PTR* 3:300.

60. Hall to Houston, Dec. 8, 1835, *PTR* 3:117.

61. Hall to governor and council, Dec. 9, 1835, *PTR* 3:132; Blake, 6:126–54. Brookfield bought one league of land from each of the following ten persons on Oct. 14, 1835: William Smith, Elisha D. Spaine, Samuel Mondy, Russell Williamson, Thomas Oban, Hiram Blossom, Samuel Murphy, Aaron Poe, Henry Harper, and James Harris. Frost Thorn was the power of attorney for all of the sales. The land locations were all within the disputed Neches territory region.

62. Austin to committees of Nacogdoches and San Augustine, Oct. 4, 1835, *Austin Papers* 3:57; "General Austin's Order Book for the Campaign of 1835," 27.

63. Harwood letter, Dec. 8, 1835, Louisiana and Lower Mississippi Valley Collections, Louisiana State University Libraries, Louisiana State University, Baton Rouge.

64. Austin to F. W. Johnson, Dec. 22, 1835, *Austin Papers* 3:289.

65. Gammel, *Laws of Texas*, 1:678.

66. Ibid., 1:685. Allen recommended Thornton for a commission as first lieutenant on the same day Allen was unanimously approved as captain of the infantry by the general council. Thornton had to wait until December 20, however, for a vacancy to occur. John York resigned his commission in order to be promoted to captain, thus opening a slot for Thornton.

67. William Pettus to the council, Dec. 17, 1835, *OCTR* 1:204–205.

68. Gammel, *Laws of Texas*, 1:678.

69. Robinson to T. F. McKinney, Dec. 17, 1835, *OCTR* 1:206–207.

70. Houston to James Powers, Dec. 28, 1835, *Writings of Sam Houston*, 1:326.

71. Harbert Davenport, "The Men of Goliad," *SHQ* 48 (July, 1939): 13; Houston to Henry Smith, Jan. 30, 1836, *Writings of Sam Houston*, 1:345.

72. Davenport, "The Men of Goliad," 13.

73. Hawkins to Houston, Dec. 9, 1835, *PTR* 3:133.

74. Houston to Austin et al., Dec. 19, 1835, *PTR* 3:257–58; Robinson to Archer et al., Dec. 19, 1835, *PTR* 3:262; Smith to Austin et al., Dec. 20, 1835, *PTR* 3:274.

75. Gammel, *Laws of Texas*, 1:524–26, 931–32; *Proceedings in the Case of the United States vs. William Christy*, 14.

76. Carleton et al. to Preval et al., Jan. 5, 1836, *PTR* 3:480–89.

77. Alexander Dienst, "The Navy of the Republic of Texas, I," *QTSHA* 12 (Jan., 1909): 197; James M. Dunham, "New Orleans, Maritime Commerce, and the Texas War for Independence," 515–16.

78. Bowie to Smith, Feb. 2, 1836, *PTR* 4:237–38.

79. Wallace O. Chariton, *One Hundred Days in Texas: The Alamo Letters* (Plano: Wordware, 1990), 228–29.

80. Ibid., 226–27.

81. Fannin to Robinson, Feb. 26, 1836, *PTR* 4:443–44.

82. Ehrenberg, *Texas und seine Revolution,* 99.

83. Ibid., 106.

CHAPTER 8

1. Gray, *From Virginia to Texas,* 63; James B. Wallace Diary, Louisiana and Lower Mississippi Valley Collections, Louisiana State University Libraries, Louisiana State University, Baton Rouge; New Orleans *Bee,* Jan. 1, 1836.

2. New Orleans *Price-Current and Commercial Intelligencer,* Oct. 1, 1835; Jeremiah Brown, the captain of the schooner *Liberty,* formerly named the *William Robins,* described the schooner as armed with three mounted guns: one 12-pound pivot cannon and two 6-pound cannons, with two 12-pound cannons in reserve; Smith, "The Quarrel between Governor Smith and the Council of the Provisional Government," 322–38.

3. Austin to Royall, Dec. 25, 1835, *Austin Papers* 3:293.

4. William H. Wharton to Austin, Nov. 8, 1835, *Austin Papers* 3:247.

5. Austin to Royall, Dec. 25, 1835, *Austin Papers* 3:293.

6. Gray, *From Virginia to Texas,* 64; James B. Wallace Diary, Louisiana and Lower Mississippi Valley Collections, Louisiana State University Libraries, Louisiana State University, Baton Rouge.

7. Commission of Austin, Archer, and Wharton, Dec. 7, 1835, DCRT vol. 2, part 1, 51–52.

8. Hall to the governor and council, Dec. 23, 1835, OCTR 1:233.

9. Wharton et al. to Smith, Jan. 16, 1836, PTR 4:42.

10. Smith to Austin, Archer, and Wharton, Dec. 17, 1835, DCRT vol. 2, part 1, 54.

11. New Orleans *Bee,* Jan. 4, 1836; Wharton et al. to Smith, Jan. 16, 1836, PTR 4:42–43.

12. Gray, *From Virginia to Texas,* 68–69.

13. Ibid.; New Orleans *Bee,* Jan. 7, 1836.

14. Gray, *From Virginia to Texas,* 69.

15. Austin to government, Dec. 22, 1835, *Austin Papers* 3:290–91; Austin to Henry Austin, Jan. 7, 1836, *Austin Papers* 3:297. Austin also wrote to Sam Houston, R. R. Royall, S. Rhoads Fisher, and his cousin Mary Austin Holley, informing all of them of his political transformation in favor of Texas independence. See Austin to General Sam Houston, Jan. 7, 1836, *Austin Papers* 3:298; Austin to Royall and Fisher, Jan. 7, 1836, *Austin Papers* 3:299–300; Austin to Mrs. Holley, Jan. 7, 1836, *Austin Papers* 3:300–301.

16. Austin to Henry Austin, Jan. 7, 1836, *Austin Papers* 3:297.

17. Wharton et al. to Smith, Jan. 16, 1836, PTR 4:42–43.

18. New Orleans *Bee,* Feb. 13, 1836.

19. Henry Austin to Austin, Mar. 4, 1831, *Austin Papers* 2:605; Henry Austin to Austin, Mar. 15, 1831, 2:613–14; Henry Austin to Austin, Mar. 20, 1831, 2:619; Henry Austin to Austin, Mar. 30, 1831, 2:632–33; Austin to N. A. Ware, July 24, 1831, 2:681–82; Henry Austin to Austin, Aug. 26, 1831, 2:690–91.

20. Henry Austin to Austin, Dec. 15, 1835, *Austin Papers* 3:284–85. It is unclear what

sort of "present difficulties" Henry Austin was going through. Perhaps because of the revolution the value of his land and business was dropping, but he wanted to maintain his capital without completely selling out.

21. Gammel, *Laws of Texas: 1822–1897*, 1:629; New Orleans *Bee*, Nov. 4, 1835. The Bank of Orleans was chartered in 1811. The *Bee* reports that the bank "keeps its transactions secreted from the public and not even its stockholders have the privilege of inspecting more than the minutes of the board of directors."

22. *Louisiana Advertiser*, Jan. 27, 1835; New Orleans *Price-Current and Commercial Intelligencer*, Mar. 19, 1836.

23. Archives from the office of the county clerk, Nacogdoches, Tex., books I and J, Blake, 5:134–37.

24. New Orleans *Price-Current and Commercial Intelligencer*, Jan. 30, 1836. See also S. A. Trufant, "Review of Banking in New Orleans, 1830–1840," *Publications of the Louisiana Historical Society*, Proceedings and Reports 10 (1917): 25–40. In December, 1837, the Bank of Orleans reported a current credit balance of $12,811, with $500,000 in capital and $60,900 in real estate and other investments.

25. See note 24 above for Trufant, 33. A memo in Gray's journal states that Gray's instructions were to go to "Nacogdoches to get all the information about Texas lands, in what grants the titles are best, and where are the most desirable lands, headrights and 11 league grants. Do not be in too great a hurry, but examine well, and be very particular."

26. Gray, *From Virginia to Texas*, 60; Christovich, Toledano, Swanson, and Holden, *New Orleans Architecture, the American Sector*, 2:47, 70. Bishop's City Hotel was also located at the corner of Common and Camp Streets. Richardson's Hotel, though not identified in New Orleans city directories, must have been located on one of the adjacent corners of Camp and Common Streets.

27. William Bryan to Henry Smith, Jan. 28, 1836, OCTR 1:353; Denham, "New Orleans, Maritime Commerce, and the Texas War for Independence," 521.

28. Dienst, "The Navy of the Republic of Texas, I," 180–81.

29. Ibid., 181.

30. Gray, *From Virginia to Texas*, 62.

31. Carleton to Cuculla et al., PTR 3:341.

32. Carleton to Forsyth, Jan. 21, 1836, PTR 4:102–103.

33. Ibid., 61–62; A. Huston to Austin et al., Jan. 10, 1836, *Austin Papers* 3:301–302.

34. Gray, *From Virginia to Texas*, 61–62.

35. Ibid., 65.

36. Ibid., 65, 67–68; A. J. Yates to S. F. Austin, B. T. Archer, and W. H. Wharton, Jan. 19, 1836, OCTR 1:309.

37. Houston ordered Allen, Breece, Bannister, Burke, Cooke, and Thornton to New Orleans for recruiting duty; John M. Allen audited claim, Republic of Texas audited claims, comptroller of accounts (RG 304), Archives Division-Texas State Library. Allen et al. brought with them J. Waldon, William Donnington, Robert Oliver, William Thompson, Lewis Reeves, and B. Luster.

38. Ibid.; *Proceedings in the Case of the United States vs. William Christy*, 31.

39. Smith to Austin, Archer, and Wharton, Dec. 8, 1835, DCRT vol. 2, part 1, 52–53. The

commissioners were given four objectives from Governor Smith. The first was "To procure and fit out ... the contemplated armed vessel[s], calculated for protection of our commerce and Sea Coast. They should be well officered and manned and provided for, from four to six months cruise." The second objective was to "See that the necessary arrangements are made for the procuration of provision, arms, and munitions of war and that they meet with safe dispatch." Thomas F. McKinney was commissioned to secure a $100,000 loan. If the money became available, they were to "proceed to effect it for the immediate use of the Government." McKinney did not fulfill his commission. Finally, Austin, Archer, and Wharton would also be responsible for receiving "All monies proffer[e]d as donations, and all contracted for as loans and deposit them in the Banks contemplated [Bank of Orleans, Union Bank of Louisiana] by law." Hawkins receipt, Jan. 18, 1836, PRT 4: 57.

40. Gray, *From Virginia to Texas*, 76; Yoakum, *History of Texas*, 2:62; Yoakum states that Christy was the one responsible for negotiating the loans. He based his claim on a letter received from Christy, Jan. 18, 1836. The letter, which Yoakum alluded to, is no longer extant, so it is unclear exactly what role Christy claimed to play.

41. NONA, William Christy, notary public, vol. 23, 41–48, Jan. 11, 1836.

42. Ibid.

43. Robert Triplett, *Roland Trevor: or, The Pilot of Human Life, Being an Autobiography of the Author, Showing how to Make and Lose a Fortune, and then to Make Another*, 273–74, 284–87.

44. Ibid., 18–45, 52–56, 331–33; Gray, *From Virginia to Texas*, 63.

45. Richard H. Collins, *Collins's Historical Sketches of Kentucky*, 428, 773; United States National Archives, War of 1812 service records, William Christy. Captain Sebree's company of riflemen was transferred to Scott's first regiment of infantry, Kentucky militia, during the war. It appears that Christy actually served in Sebree's company for only two months (Aug. 17, 1812–Oct. 16, 1812) before he was transferred to Captain William Farraw's company, Johnson's regiment of mounted volunteers.

46. Gray, *From Virginia to Texas*, 58, 59.

47. Ibid., 83.

48. Ibid., 77.

49. Henry Clay to Jesse Burton Harrison, Sept. 11, 1833, in James Hopkins et al., eds., *The Papers of Henry Clay*, 8:400–401.

50. Ibid., 73.

51. *Michel's 1834 New Orleans Annual and Commercial Register*, 237.

52. New Orleans *Price-Current and Commercial Intelligencer*, Mar. 26, 1836.

53. New Orleans *True American*, Aug. 5, 1835; *Gibson's Guide and Directory*, 344, 353.

54. NONA, William Christy, notary public, Jan. 30, 1836, 23:169–71; New Orleans *Bee*, Feb. 10, 1836.

55. The only insurance company that did not sign the petition to attempt the launching of the *Brutus* was the Mississippi Marine and Fire Insurance Company. Thomas Banks and Andrew Hodge Jr. were both on the board of directors; Mirle et al., Carleton, Dec. 26, 1835, PTR 3:331; *Louisiana Advertiser*, Jan. 23, 1835.

56. Austin to Rusk, Jan. 18, 1836, PTR 4:53.

57. Austin and Wharton to Hall, Jan. 14, 1836, PTR 4:5.

58. Bryan and Hall to Smith, Jan. 18, 1836, *PTR* 4:57; statement of Edward Hall, circa 1848–1850, after the death of William Bryan in Galveston, Alexander Dienst Papers, Center for American History, University of Texas at Austin. Although Hall did not sign the statement, the historical details of the events in 1835 and 1836 seem to point to Hall as the author. Hall's statement is the only place known to the author in which Hall recounts his involvement in the early days of the revolution. It appears that Dienst has compiled a fairly large collection of Hall's papers, receipts, and court records dealing with his and Bryan's land holdings in Texas. The statement appears to be written for the purpose of explaining Hall and Bryan's land business. It may have been a copy of a deposition for court in Galveston to claim land in his partnership with Bryan after Bryan's death. Hall makes it clear he insisted on Bryan as general agent.

59. Edward Hall Papers, 1826–1829, Louisiana and Lower Mississippi Valley Collection, Louisiana Libraries, Louisiana State University.

60. Ibid.

61. Gammel, *Laws of Texas*, 1:529. Hall was authorized to purchase two long, mounted, eighteen-pound cannons with the necessary equipage, two hundred rounds of cannon balls and powder for each, and one mounted, twelve-pound howitzer with two hundred bomb shells.

62. New Orleans *Bee*, Feb. 13, 1836.

63. NONA, William Christy, notary public, Jan. 21, 1836, 23:111–13; NONA, William Christy, notary public, Jan. 23, 1836, 23:125–27; New Orleans *Bee*, Feb. 1, 1836.

64. Henrie to Smith, Jan. 3, 1836, *PTR* 4:412. Henrie was appointed as collector for the department of Nacogdoches by the general council in December, 1835; see C. B. Stewart to Arthur Henrie, Jan. 1, 1836, *OCTR* 1:261.

65. Forbes to Robinson, Jan. 12, 1836, *PTR* 3:496–98.

66. Nacogdoches meeting, Jan. 15, 1836, *PTR* 4:32–33.

67. Joseph N. Ireland, *Records of the New York Stage from 1750 to 1860*, 2 vols. (New York: Benjamin Blum, 1860; reissued, 1966), 205.

68. New Orleans *Bee*, Jan. 7, 1836.

69. Ibid., *Jan. 16, 1836*; Gray, *From Virginia to Texas*, 77.

70. New Orleans *Bee*, Jan. 7, 1836; Nelle Kroger Smither, *A History of the English Theatre in New Orleans*, 119, 128, and 336. The play "The Fall of San Antonio" was written by Bannister. Bannister was closely associated with James H. Caldwell and wrote several plays for Caldwell's theaters.

71. NONA, William Christy, notary public, 23:71, Jan. 16, 1836.

72. Austin to Smith, Jan. 20, 1836, *PTR* 4:79.

73. Ibid.

74. Bryan to Smith, Jan. 31, 1836, *OCTR* 1:369–70.

75. A. Huston to Austin et al., Jan. 10, 1836, *Austin Papers* 3:301–302.

76. Financial statement of Jan., 1836, New Orleans, secretary of state records (307), Archives Division-Texas State Library; William Bryan, Edward Hall, and Samuel Ellis, *A Vindication of the Conduct of the Agency of Texas in New Orleans*, 5.

77. For a comprehensive look at the credit system in Louisiana and New Orleans, see Kilbourne, *Debt, Investment, Slaves*, 26–48.

78. New Orleans *Price-Current and Commercial Intelligencer*, Oct. 1 and Nov. 14, 1835; Davenport, "The Men of Goliad," 20. The *Caroline* landed at Cox's Point on February 14.

79. Edward Hall to Henry Smith, Jan. 28, 1836, OCTR 1:355–62.

80. Ibid.; J. Brown to Henry Smith, Jan. 27, 1836, OCTR 1:342–43.

81. Bryan to Smith, Jan. 31, 1836, PTR 4:209.

82. Bryan to Henry Smith, Feb. 2, 1836, OCTR 1:379.

83. New Orleans *Bee*, Jan. 16, 1836.

84. Gray, *From Virginia to Texas*, 72.

85. New Orleans *Bee*, Jan. 12, 1836, and Mar. 3, 1836.

86. Historical Militia Data of Louisiana Militia, 1827–1837, 53:102–105, Adjutant General's Library, Louisiana National Guard, JBML, 106–107; New Orleans *Bee*, Feb. 4, 1836.

87. Cass to Gaines, Jan. 23, 1836, PTR 4:125–27; *Treaties, Conventions, International Acts, Protocols, and Agreements between the United States of America and Other Powers*, 1:1085–97.

88. John K. Mahon, *History of the Second Seminole War, 1835–1842* (Gainesville: University of Florida Press, 1965; reprinted, 1985), 143–50; New Orleans *Bee*, Mar. 28, 1836.

89. Forbes et al. to Jackson, Sept. 11, 1835, PTR 2:611.

90. Monasterio to Butler, Jan. 25, 1836, PTR 4:144–45.

91. Ibid.

92. Butler to Forsyth, Jan. 26, 1836, PTR 4:147–50.

93. *Proceedings in the Case of the United States vs. William Christy*, 15.

94. Ibid., 30.

95. Ibid., 31.

96. Ibid., 26.

97. Ibid.

98. John K. West, August St. Martin, James Curell, J. W. Zacharie, Placid Forstall, Thomas Urquhart, Thomas Toby, and James F. Hozey all consistently testified that they did not know of Christy's involvement other than from the newspapers.

99. *Proceedings in the Case of the United States vs. William Christy*, 35–36.

100. Ibid., 14.

101. Ibid., 7.

102. New Orleans *Bee*, Feb. 27, 1836.

103. Robinson to Christy, Feb. 5, 1836, PTR 4:265–66.

104. NONA, Hillary B. Cenas, notary public, 1:385–88, Feb. 19, 1836.

105. Christy to Ellis, Mar. 22, 1836, PTR 4:161.

106. Gray, *From Virginia to Texas*, 89–91.

107. Ibid., 121.

108. Mary Fisher Parmenter, Walter Russell Fisher, and Lawrence Edward Mallette, *The Life of George Fisher (1795–1873) and the History of the Fisher Family in Mississippi*, 56.

109. Jorge Fisher to General José Antonio Mexía, May 27, 1836, Valentín Goméz Farías Collection, Nettie Benson Latin American Collection, University of Texas at Austin; *Gibson's Guide and Directory*, 143.

110. New Orleans *Bee*, Feb. 8, 1836; Francisco Vitál Fernandez, General de Brigada del

Egercito Mejicano y Commandante Principal de las Armas en el Departmento de Tamaulipas, Feb. 5, 1836, micropublished in Winthrop, *Texas as Province and Republic, 1795–1845*.

111. Austin to Houston, Jan. 16, 1836, *PTR* 4:33.

112. Juan A. Padilla to the council, Nov. 25, 1835, *OCTR* 1:117–18; New Orleans *Bee*, Mar. 16, 1836; *El Mosquito Mexicano*, Feb. 9, 1836; Hutchinson, "Mexican Federalists and the Texas Revolution," 42.

113. New Orleans *Bee*, Jan. 30, 1836.

CHAPTER 9

1. Louis Wiltz Kemp, *The Signers of the Texas Declaration of Independence*, 57–63; Cornelia Hood, "Life and Career of George Campbell Childress," 58–68.

2. Gray, *From Virginia to Texas*, 124.

3. Wallace, Vigness, and Ward, *Documents of Texas History*, 99; Gray, *From Virginia to Texas*, 124, 125; James Woods and Andrew Briscoe did not sign the declaration of independence until March 10; Gammel, *Laws of Texas: 1822–1897*, 1:883; constitutional convention minutes, Mar. 6, 1836, secretary of state records (RG 307), Archives Division- Texas State Library.

4. Triplett, *Roland Trevor: or, The Pilot of Human Life*, 336.

5. Gray, *From Virginia to Texas*, 125.

6. Wallace, Vigness, and Ward, *Documents of Texas History*, 96–97.

7. Gray, *From Virginia to Texas*, 127; a *headright* was a special land grant issued to settlers who promised to live on and cultivate their land and who had legally entered Texas from 1821 through 1836; see Thomas Lloyd Miller, *The Public Lands of Texas, 1519–1970*, 29–36.

8. Gray, *From Virginia to Texas*, 126; Everett, who was a delegate for the municipality of Jasper, had been appointed as commissioner to Nacogdoches in November, 1835, to close the land offices there. He faced stiff resistance in getting the local land commissioners and agents to cooperate. He accused John K. Allen, George Nixon, Charles S. Taylor, William G. Logan, Adolphus Sterne, and Henry Rueg of "clearing out Lands" in east Texas. S. H. Everitt to J. W. Robinson, Nov. 29, 1835, *OCTR* 1:137–39; Kemp, *The Signers of the Texas Declaration of Independence*, 106–11; Triplett, *Roland Trevor: or, The Pilot of Human Life*, 336–37; Hobart Huson, *Refugio: A Comprehensive History of Refugio County, from Aboriginal Times to 1953*, 1:293–94, 337.

9. Ehrenberg, *Texas und seine Revolution*, 81; rosters of Breece's company were all reconstructed after a devastating fire at the Texas adjutant general's office in October, 1855. Some rosters show Breece's company with a total of 54 men. The author has identified 59 men in Breece's company at the time they reported for duty in November, 1835, at San Antonio de Béxar. Stephen Dennison, who has been identified as killed at the Alamo, was killed with Grant at Agua Dulce Creek. The total number of Texian Alamo casualties remains elusive. Several Mexican military eyewitness accounts, namely José Enrique de la Peña and Juan Almonte, estimate the Texian casualties at approximately 250. Texian accounts estimate them at 180 to 200; de la Peña, *With Santa Anna in Texas*, 54; "The Private

Journal of Juan Nepomuceno Almonte, Feb. 1–Apr. 16, 1836," *SHQ* 48 (July, 1944): 14; Smithwick, *Evolution of a State*, 96; Yoakum, *History of Texas* 2:78–81.

10. See de la Peña, *With Santa Anna in Texas*, 44–57; John S. Ford, *A Mexican Sergeant's Recollections of the Alamo and San Jacinto* (Austin: Jenkins, 1980), 22–23; Santos, *Santa Anna's Campaign against Texas*, 74–77; Sanchez-Lamego, *The Siege and Taking of the Alamo*, 50–53.

11. Santa Anna to José María Tornel, Mar. 6, 1836, *PTR* 5:12, 887; Timothy M. Matovina, *The Alamo Remembered: Tejano Accounts and Perspectives*, 74. Also see Joseph Hefter's article "The Flags of the Alamo," in Lemego, *The Siege and Taking of the Alamo*, 44–49.

12. Santos, *Santa Anna's Campaign against Texas*, 79–80; Hardin, *Texian Iliad: A Military History of the Texas Revolution, 1835–1836*, 155.

13. Matovina, *The Alamo Remembered*, 5; Houston to Collinsworth, Mar. 15, 1836, *PTR* 5:82–84. Recent sources for the siege and storming of the Alamo are Davis, *Three Roads to the Alamo*, and Hardin, *Texian Iliad: A Military History of the Texas Revolution, 1835–1836*.

14. Gray, *From Virginia to Texas*, 133.

15. Rupert N. Richardson, "Framing the Constitution of the Republic of Texas," *SHQ* 31 (Jan., 1928): 206–207; Barker, "Land Speculation as a Cause of the Texas Revolution," *QTSHA* 10 (July, 1906): 82.

16. Chambers to Miller, June 30, 1835, *PTR* 1:173–74; Rowland, "General John Thomson Mason," *QTSHA* 11 (Jan., 1908): 163–98; Barker, "Land Speculation as a Cause of the Texas Revolution," *QTSHA* 10 (July, 1906): 78–95; *Documents of Texas History*, 104; Richardson, "Framing the Constitution of the Republic of Texas," 206–207.

17. Constitutional convention minutes, Mar. 16–17, 1836, secretary of state records (RG 307), Archives Division-Texas State Library; Richardson, "Framing the Constitution of the Republic of Texas," 209. Mexican land policy also forbad ownership of lands by foreigners, except for those who emigrated to Texas and for empresarios, who were given grants of land to settle. Jose Antonio Navarro to Samuel Williams, Apr. 12, 1832, Samuel L. Williams Papers, Rosenberg Library, Galveston; Decree 16, *Coahuila and Texas: Laws and Decrees of the State of Coahuila and Texas, in Spanish and English*, 15–22.

18. Gray, *From Virginia to Texas*, 133; constitutional convention minutes, Mar. 14 and Mar. 17, 1836, secretary of state records (RG 307), Archives Division-Texas State Library.

19. Eugene C. Barker, "Texas Revolutionary Finances," *Political Science Quarterly* 19 (Dec., 1904): 631–32.

20. Triplett, *Roland Trevor: or, The Pilot of Human Life*, 343–44; Gray, *From Virginia to Texas*, 150–51. Triplett's demand of 135,000 acres is not clear, and Gray does not mention in his journal what the amount was. The compromise agreement was for 32 leagues, or 141,708.8 acres, to be divided among the lenders proportionately to their investment.

21. Triplett to secretary of state, Aug. 19, 1836, *PTR* 8:269.

22. Triplett, *Roland Trevor: or, The Pilot of Human Life*, 343–45; Gray, *From Virginia to Texas*, 156–57. Gray admits in his journal that there were already disputes relating to land on Galveston Island. Knowing this, it seems strange that Triplett and Niblett would have accepted the land grant. Possibly they believed that since Burnet's government was issuing the grant, their claim would be official and uncontested.

23. Gray, *From Virginia to Texas*, 150; "Contract containing terms of a compromise of the loan agreements of Jan. 11 and 18, 1836"; Winthrop, *Texas as Province and Republic, 1795–1845*.

24. The original state boundary between Coahuila y Texas and the state of Tamaulipas was the Nueces River; F. W. Johnson to convention, Mar. 8, 1836, *OCTR* 1:486; Davenport, "The Men of Goliad," 28–29.

25. William Corner, "John Crittenden Duval," *QTSHA* 1 (July, 1907): 49; J. W. Fannin to J. W. Robinson, Feb. 28, 1836, *Lamar Papers* 1:342.

26. Huson, *Refugio*, 293–94.

27. Houston et al., treaty, Feb. 23, 1836, *PTR* 4:415–18; Houston and Forbes to Smith, Feb. 28, 1836, *PTR* 4:461–62. The treaty was made with the Cherokees, Shawnees, Delawares, Kickapoos, Quapaws, Choctaws, Biloxis, Ionis, Alabamas, Coushattas, Caddos, Tahocullakes, and the Mataquos. The treaty essentially kept the different tribes out of the revolution with the promise of land for each tribe; Houston to Fannin, Mar. 11, 1836, *PTR* 5:51–52; Houston army orders, Mar. 17, 1836, *PTR* 5:122; "Account of W. I. E. Heard and Eli Mercer" (1860), in James M. Day, *The Texas Almanac, 1857–1873*, 315–16; Eugene C. Barker, "The San Jacinto Campaign," *QTSHA* 4 (Apr., 1901): 243; "Historical Notes. Lamar from William L. Hunter," *Lamar Papers* 5:376; Smith, "James W. Fannin in the Texas Revolution 4," *SHQ* 23 (Apr., 1920): 272–74.

28. Henry Stuart Foote, *Texas and the Texans: or the Advance of the Anglo-Americans to the Southwest*, 2:229; Huson, *Refugio*, 1:293–94.

29. José Urrea, *Diary of the Operations of the Division Which under the Command of General José Urrea, Campaigned in Texas*, in Carlos Casteñeda, trans., *The Mexican Side of the Texas Revolution* [1836] (Austin: Graphic Ideas, 1970), 240–41.

30. Fannin to Mexía, Mar. 11, 1836, *PTR* 5:47–48.

31. Lewis Washington, Fannin's assistant quartermaster at Goliad, states that Guerra went to New Orleans, leaving his men to join Urrea ([Austin] *Texas State Gazette*, June 18, 1853). Joseph W. Andrews, a member of Colonel William Ward's Georgia Battalion, states that Isaac Ticknor and Amon King's men near Mission Refugio routed Guerra and his men and that Guerra was killed in the attack. S. T. Brown, also a member of Colonel Ward's Georgia battalion, recalls that after Ticknor's night raid on the Mexican cavalry, the Texians discovered the next day that "[a]mong the slain was recognized a Mexican Lieutenant who had been with Col. Fannin at Goliad, pretending to have joined the Texians with eighteen men." Huson, *Refugio*, 1:295–96, 340; "Information Derived from J. W. Andrews," *Lamar Papers*, vol. 4, part 2, 238–39; S. T. Brown to Thomas Ward, Nov. 1, 1837, in Day, *The Texas Almanac, 1857–1873*, 362. Harbert Davenport states that a Lieutenant Blanco, also of Guerra's company, was killed in the attack; see Davenport, Notes from an Unfinished Study of Fannin and His Men, typescript (carbon copy), Brownsville, Tex., 1936, Center for American History, University of Texas at Austin, 16.

32. Ehrenberg, *Texas und seine Revolution*, 117; Urrea, *Diary of the Operations of the Division*, 230–31 (see chapter 9, note 29).

33. Ehrenberg, *Texas und seine Revolution*, 119–20; Foote, *Texas and the Texans*, 2:231–32, 237.

34. Ehrenberg, *Texas und seine Revolution*, 122.

35. Huson, *Refugio*, 340; Urrea, *Diary of the Operations*, 234–35 (see chapter 9, note 29). Urrea, in his report to Santa Anna, wrote after the battle that he had two six-pound cannons, not two four-pounders, as stated in 1838.

36. Santa Anna to Urrea, Mar. 3, 1836, *PTR* 4:501; Santa Anna to Urrea, Mar. 24, 1836, *PTR* 5:175; Portilla to Urrea, Mar. 26, 1836, *PTR* 5:205; Urrea, *Diary of the Operations*, 241 (see chapter 9, note 29); Santa Anna to Ignacio del Corrral, ministry of war and marine, May, 1837, in *The Mexican Side of the Texas Revolution*, 63 (see chapter 9, note 29); Ramón Martínez Caro, "A True Account of the First Texas Campaign," in *The Mexican Side of the Texas Revolution*, 107–108 (see chapter 9, note 29); Foote, *Texas and the Texans*, 2:238. Dr. Jack Shackelford, one of Fannin's officers recalled that a Colonel Holsinger (Shackelford's spelling, also spelled Holzinger), a German engineer in the Mexican service, announced to the Texian prisoners after a polite bow, "WELL GENTLEMEN, IN EIGHT DAYS, LIBERTY AND HOME!" (capital lettering from Foote's Shackelford account); Lewis Washington also confirmed that Fannin's men were assured that they would be released to go back to the United States ([Austin] *Texas State Gazette*, June 18, 1853). The centralist Mexican government had proclaimed on December 30, 1835, that all foreigners taking up arms in Texas would be treated as pirates and thus executed. Santa Anna was in conformity with this decree, Manuel Dublán and José María Lozano, *Legislacion mexicana: o coleción completa de las disposiciones legislativas expedidas desde la independencia de la República ordenada*, 3:114–15.

37. Both Peter Mattern and George Courtman were original members of Thomas Breece's New Orleans Greys. Both joined Captain David Burke's Mobile Greys in January, 1836; Ehrenberg, *Texas und Seine Revolution*, 143–49.

38. Bartlett, *Personal Narrative of Explorations*, 1:29; John J. Linn, *Reminiscences of Fifty Years in Texas: Original Narratives of Texas History and Adventure*, 190–91; Texas legislature, house of representatives, *Biographical Directory of the Texan Conventions and Congresses* (Austin: Book Exchange, 1942), 109.

39. John Milton Nance, "Abel Morgan and His Account of the Battle of Goliad," *SHQ* 100 (Oct., 1996): 207–33.

40. Davenport, "Men of Goliad," 37; *United States Telegraph*, Washington, D.C., Aug. 1, 1836; "Massacre of Fannin's Command" (Joseph H. Spohn's account), *Lamar Papers* 1:431.

41. De la Peña, *With Santa Anna in Texas*, 121. General Gaona was eventually ordered to San Felipe instead; Santos, *Santa Anna's Campaign against Texas*, 98.

42. Barker, "The San Jacinto Campaign," 243, 246.

43. Ibid., 330.

44. W. C. Day, comp., *History of the San Jacinto Campaign* (Lynchburg, Tex.: Author, 1923), 8; James W. Pohl, *The Battle of San Jacinto*, 26–27.

45. Jones, *Memoranda and Official Correspondence Relating to the Republic of Texas, Its History and Annexation*, 82–83; Stenberg, "The Texas Schemes of Jackson and Houston, 1829–1836," *Southwestern Social Science Quarterly* 15 (Dec., 1934): 246–50; Richard R. Stenberg, "Some Letters of the Texas Revolution," *Southwestern Social Science Quarterly* 21 (Mar., 1941): 308; "Notes on San Jacinto Campaign. Lamar," *Lamar Papers* 5:377; "Official Report of the Battle of San Jacinto, 25 Apr. 1836," *Writings of Sam Houston*, 1:416–20.

46. Marshall De Bruhl, *Sword of San Jacinto: A Life of Sam Houston*, 207–10; Day, *History of the San Jacinto Campaign*, 31–32; "Official Report of the Battle of San Jacinto, 25 Apr. 1836," *Writings of Sam Houston*, 1:419; San Jacinto list, Apr. 22, 1836, *PTR* 6:14–15; Santa Anna to Filisola, Apr. 30, 1836, *PTR* 6:132–33; Margaret Swett Henson, "Politics and the Treatment

of the Mexican Prisoners after the Battle of San Jacinto," *SHQ* 94 (Oct., 1990): 189–90, 196–98.

47. "Treaty of Velasco: Secret," *PTR* 6:275–76; Henson, "Politics and the Treatment of the Mexican Prisoners," 205–208, 223; "William Christy, New Orleans, Louisiana, the Hero of Ft. Meiggs," in *Sketches of Eminent Americans* (United States: n.p., 1857), 264; Millie Gray, *The Diary of Millie Gray, 1832–1840*, 127.

48. Henson, "Politics and the Treatment of the Mexican Prisoners," 189–90.

49. Billingsley et al. to Houston, May 3, 1836, *PTR* 6:152–53; Houston to Christy, May 4, 1836, *PTR* 6:169–70; Christy to Houston, May 28, 1836, *PTR* 6:395. The Cós saddle remained in the Christy family until the early twentieth century. It is unclear where it is now. The Christy family donated the saddle to a regional museum, but none of the regional Louisiana museums have any record of it.

50. Joseph Milton Nance, *After San Jacinto: The Texas-Mexican Frontier, 1836–1841*, 10–30.

51. Viener, "Surgeon Moses Albert Levy: Letters of a Texas Patriot," *Publications of the American Jewish Historical Society* 46 (Dec., 1956): 101–13; William Walker to Mrs. Sarah Hartwell, Feb. 26, 1836, used with permission from Bill Davis of Reston, Va., Texas navy website at http://www.hal-pc.org/~longhorn/tchest/letter.htm.

52. Day, *The Texas Almanac, 1857–1873*, 390; Dienst, "The Navy of the Republic of Texas II," *QTSHA* 12 (Apr., 1909): 249–50.

53. Ralph W. Steen, "Analysis of the Work of the General Council, Provisional Government of Texas, 1835–1836, IV," *SHQ* 42 (July, 1938): 29–31.

54. Neu, "The Case of the Brig *Pocket*," *Quarterly of the Texas State Historical Association* 12 (1909): 276–95.

55. Robert Triplett to D. G. Burnet, May 30, 1836, *OCTR* 2:724–25; D. G. Burnet to the senate, Oct., 1836, *OCTR* 2:1088–89; adjutant general records (RG 401), navy correspondence, Archives Division, State Archives and Library Commission.

56. Dienst, "The Navy of the Republic of Texas II," 265; Thomas Toby to D. G. Burnet, June 16, 1836, *OCTR* 2:789; Thomas Toby and Brother to D. G. Burnet, July 11, 1836, *OCTR* 2:850–51.

57. Burnet to Senate, *OCTR* 2:1088; Thomas Toby and Brother to D. G. Burnet, Aug. 13, 1836, *OCTR* 2:929–30; Burnet proclamation's of July 21 was published in the August 5 issue of the New Orleans *Bee*; New Orleans *Bee*, Aug. 6, 1836; Dienst, "The Navy of Republic of Texas II," 268–69.

58. New Orleans *Bee*, Mar. 29, 1836; Gaines to Cass, Apr. 8, 1836, *PTR* 5:373–374.

59. Raguet to Hotchkiss, Mar. 19, 1836, *PTR* 5:144.

60. Hotchkiss report, Mar. 21, 1836, *PTR* 5:153–54.

61. Swartwout to Houston, Feb. 15, 1836, *PTR* 4:346–47. Swartwout bought 48,443 acres at twenty cents an acre from Frost Thorn in January, 1835 (Samuel Swartwout Papers, Center for American History, University of Texas at Austin). Mason had close business ties with Thorn, granting Thorn power of attorney in New Orleans in July, 1835, "to carry on, manage and transact all and every kind of business which he may think proper in the said province of Texas as well as in any other part of or parts of the Republic of Mexico," NONA, William Christy, n.p., 22:65–66, July 13, 1835.

62. Mason to Gaines, Apr. 1, 1836, *PTR* 5:288–89.

63. Nacogdoches committee to D. G. Burnet, Apr. 6, 1836, *OCTR* 2:593–94; S. Carson to D. G. Burnet, Apr. 4, 1836, *OCTR* 2:584–86; Robertson to Rusk, May 27, 1836, *PTR* 5:392–93.

64. Nacogdoches resolutions, Apr. 11, 1836, *PTR* 5: 438; Mason to committee, Apr. 11, 1836, *PTR* 5:439.

65. Monasterio to Butler, Mar. 14, 1836, *PTR* 5: 78–79; Butler to Monasterio, May 15, 1836, *PTR* 5:79–80; Monasterio to Butler, Apr. 8, 1836, *PTR* 5:383–84.

66. Forsyth to Gorostiza, Sept. 23, 1836, *PTR* 8:517–18; Gorostiza to Forsyth, Sept. 23, 1836, *PTR* 8:518–19; Gorostiza to Forsyth, Sept. 12, 1836, *PTR* 8:444–50; Forsyth to Gorostiza, Sept. 20, 1836, *PTR* 8:505–507. When the *Brutus* and the *Invincible* were seized for nonpayment of expenses, Swartwout paid the outstanding bills and ensured their departure. The *Brutus* left on January 5, and the *Invincible* left on February 27, 1837; see George F. Haugh, ed. "The Texas Navy at New York," *SHQ* 64 (Jan., 1961): 377–79; B. R. Brunson, *The Adventures of Samuel Swartwout in the Age of Jefferson and Jackson*, 2:76.

67. Gorostiza to Dickens, Oct. 15 1836, *PTR* 9:92–98.

68. "Regulars" were often referred to as permanent forces, as opposed to the citizen-soldiers of the militia who were called out for service only when needed (Noah Webster, *An American Dictionary of the English Language*, 2 vols. New York: S. Converse, 1828; reprint, New York: Johnson Reprint, 1970, 2:54).

69. James W. Silver, *Edmund Pendleton Gaines: Frontier General*, 210–11, 213.

70. *L'Abeille*, Jan. 30, 1836; Martin to brother, Feb. 20, 1836, secretary of state records (RG Unprocessed Collection, miscellaneous manuscripts in Spanish, French, German, etc., oversize box 21), Archives Division-Texas State Library.

71. —— to Valentín Gómez Farías and José Antonio Mejía, Jan. 10, 1836, Valentín Goméz Farías Collection, Nettie Benson Latin American Collection, University of Texas at Austin.

72. New Orleans *Bee*, Mar. 16, 1836.

73. Ibid. Bayon had published favorable and sympathetic reports on the arrivals of Zavala, Goméz Farías, and Viesca (New Orleans *Bee*, July 13, 1835); *L'Abeille*, Sept. 9, 1835, and Jan. 30, 1836.

74. Christy to Burnet, May 14, 1836, *PTR* 6:257.

75. Ibid., *PTR* 6:257–58; National Archives and Records Administration, U.S. Federal District Court, Eastern District of Louisiana, general case 3797, "United States vs. William Christy, May 16, 1836 (microfilm); Eugene C. Barker, "The United States and Mexico, 1835–1837," *Mississippi Valley Historical Review* 1 (June, 1914): 15. The grand jury inquest is cited as "United States vs. William Christy," but the inquest was actually meant to investigate Mexía's involvement in the November, 1835, expedition.

76. Mexía to Fisher, May 12, 1836, Valentín Gómez Farías Collection, Nettie Benson Latin American Collection, University of Texas at Austin; George Fisher to José Antonio Mexía, May 27, 1836, Valentín Gómez Farías Collection, 1770–1909, Benson Latin American Collection, General Libraries, University of Texas at Austin; Parmenter et al., *The Life of George Fisher*, 56–57.

77. Parmenter et al., *The Life of George Fisher*, 58.

78. Fisher to Austin, July 7, 1836, *PTR* 7:378–79; Fernandez proclamation, Feb. 5, 1836, *PTR* 4:262–63; Fernandez to Smith, Feb. 17, 1836, *PTR* 4:374–79; Smith to Fernandez, Feb. 18, 1836, *PTR* 4:379–81.

79. (Mexico City) *Diairo de México*, Aug. 11, 1836; Hutchinson, "Valentín Gómez Farías: A Biographical Study," 409.

80. Gammel, Laws of Texas, 1:1090.

CHAPTER 10

1. William Bryan to the governor and council, Feb. 26, 1836, *OCTR* 1:458–59.

2. Hall to Bailey Hardeman, June 18, 1836, *OCTR* 1:797; William Bryan to the governor and council, Feb. 26, 1836, *OCTR* 1:458–59.

3. McKinney to Bryan et al., Feb. 13, 1836, *PTR* 4:324; Austin and Archer to Smith, Jan. 22, 1836, in *DCRT* 1:63.

4. Frantz, "The Mercantile House," *Bulletin of the Business Historical Society* 26 (1952): 4.

5. Eugene C. Barker, ed., "Journal of the Permanent Council (Oct. 11–27, 1835)" *QTSHA* 7 (Apr., 1904): 274–276; T. F. McKinney to R. R. Royall, Oct. 31, 1835, *OCTR* 1:36–37; T. F. McKinney to president of the council, Nov. 11, 1835, *OCTR* 1:65; J. Brown to Henry Smith, Jan. 27, 1836, *OCTR* 1:342–43; advisory committee to J. W. Robinson, Feb. 1, 1836, *OCTR* 1:375–76; McKinney to Bryan et al., Feb. 13, 1836, *PTR* 4:324; McKinney and Allen to agents, Feb. 18, 1836, *PTR* 4:377–78.

6. Edward Hall to the governor and council, Mar. 8, 1836, *OCTR* 1:489; Bryan to the government of Texas, Mar. 29, 1836, *OCTR* 1:558.

7. Hall to Bailey Hardeman, June 18, 1836, *OCTR* 1:797; John M. Allen, public debt claim, comptroller of public accounts records (RG 304) (microfilm) Archives Division-Texas State Library. A Lieutenant Girod was listed with Mexía's Tampico expedition and may have been the Captain Girod that Allen attempted to recruit; Allen receipt, Mar. 7, 1836, *PTR* 5:16; Bryan to governor and council, Mar. 14, 1836, *PTR* 5:74.

8. Allen to Houston, Mar. 31, 1836, *PTR* 5:245; Houston to Allen, Apr. 8, 1836, *PTR* 5:380.

9. Bryan to governor and council, Mar. 16, 1836, *PTR* 5:87–88; Bryan, Hall, and Ellis, *A Vindication of the Conduct*, 7; Foote, *Texas and the Texans*, 2:295–96; Ernest William Winkler, "The 'Twin Sisters' Cannon, 1836–1865," *SHQ* 21 (July, 1917): 61–68.

10. Hall to Burnet, Mar. 31, 1836, *PTR* 5:252.

11. William Bryan to the governor and council, Mar. 9, 1836, *OCTR* 1:490–91.

12. D. G. Burnet to Robert Triplett, Apr. 3, 1836, *OCTR* 2:579–80; Burnet proclamation, Mar. 19, 1836, *PTR* 5:142; Burnet et al. to Toby, May 24, 1836, *PTR* 6:138–39; Triplett, *Roland Trevor: or, The Pilot of Human Life*, 355; Bryan, Hall, and Ellis, *A Vindication of the Conduct*, 7; Hall to Burnet, Mar. 31, 1836, *PTR* 5:252; Hall to Bailey Hardeman, May 12, 1836, *OCTR* 2:66; Bryan to Burnet, June 17, 1836, *OCTR* 2:792.

13. New Orleans *Bee*, Mar. 19, 1836.

14. Ibid., Mar. 21, 1836; New Orleans *Price-Current and Commercial Intelligencer*, Mar. 26, 1836.

15. New Orleans *Bee*, Mar. 21, 1836.

16. Gray, *From Virginia to Texas*, 63, 66–76. Triplett nearly bought lands from Auguste Allen. After examining the lands, however, Triplett backed out the deal, fearing that Allen's titles were illegal under Mexican law, which required that there be a twenty-league buffer along the border with the United States. Allen's lands were located in this buffer zone; NONA, William Christy, n.p., 23:503–506, Mar. 23, 1836.

17. Carolyn Reeves Ericson, "Prelude to San Jacinto: Nacogdoches 1836," *East Texas Historical Journal* 11 (fall 1973): 36.

18. "No. 2264, William M. Gwin et al. vs. Henry Raguet et al.," Blake, 60:204–12.

19. New Orleans *Price-Current and Commercial Intelligencer*, Mar. 19, 1836.

20. Bryan, Hall, and Ellis, *A Vindication of the Conduct*, 8.

21. Ina Kate Harmon Reinhardt, "The Public Career of Thomas Green in Texas," 4–5; T. J. Green to D. G. Burnet, Apr. 6, 1836, *OCTR* 1:594; Collingsworth to the convention, Mar. 16, 1836, *PTR* 5:88–89.

22. Austin and Archer to Smith, Jan. 22, 1836, *DCRT* 1:63; Burnet to Hardeman, Mar. 21, 1836, *OCTR* 1:524.

23. Bryan to Burnet, Apr. 6, 1836, *PTR* 5:338.

24. Ibid., *PTR* 5:337–39; Bryan to Burnet, Apr. 8, 1836, *PTR* 5:370–72; Bryan, Hall, and Ellis, *A Vindication of the Conduct*, 10.

25. Austin and Archer to Owings, Jan. 18, 1836, *PTR* 4:54–55; Bryan to Burnet, Apr. 6, 1836, *PTR* 5:338; McKinney to Bryan et al., Feb. 13, 1836, *PTR* 4:324; Bryan, Hall, and Ellis, *A Vindication of the Conduct*, 9.

26. William Bryan to D. G. Burnet, Apr. 8, 1836, *OCTR* 1:608–609.

27. Hall to Burnet, May 1, 1836, *PTR* 5:142–43.

28. Ibid., 166.

29. Triplett to Burnet, Apr. 14, 1836, *OCTR* 2:673.

30. Triplett to Houston, *PTR* 5:290–91; Gray, *From Virginia to Texas*, 164–66; Robert Triplett to D. G. Burnet, Apr. 14 [May], 1836, *CTR* 2: 673; Triplett, *Roland Trevor: or, The Pilot of Human Life*, 350–52.

31. Hall to Bailey Hardeman, June 18, 1836, *OCTR* 2:797.

32. Alexander Dienst, "The New Orleans Newspaper Files of the Texas Revolutionary Period," *QTSHA* 4 (Oct., 1900): 150.

33. Hall to Burnet, May 1, 1836, *PTR* 6:142.

34. Bryan to Burnet, Apr. 28, 1836, *OCTR* 2:646–47.

35. Bryan, Hall, and Ellis, *A Vindication of the Conduct*, 10; Bryan to Burnet, May 18, 1836, *PTR* 6:324; Bryan to D. G. Burnet, Apr. 30, 1836, *OCTR* 2:647; Bryan to Burnet, May 18, 1836, *PTR* 6:323–24; Bryan to Burnet, May 19, 1836, *PTR* 6:329; Hall to Burnet, May 21, 1836, *OCTR* 2:699–700.

36. Burnet to William Bryan, May 22, 1836, *OCTR* 2:701.

37. William Bryan to D. G. Burnet, May 14, 1836, *OCTR* 2:676; Neu, "The Case of the Brig *Pocket*," 287.

38. Robert Triplett to D. G. Burnet, May 30, 1836, *OCTR* 2:723.

39. Triplett, *Roland Trevor: or, The Pilot of Human Life*, 355; Triplett to Toby, June 5, 1836, *PTR* 6:27–30.

40. Robert Triplett to D. G. Burnet, May 30, 1836, OCTR 2:726; Triplett to president and cabinet, June 2, 1836, PTR 6:503–504; William Bryan to D. G. Burnet, June 1, 1836, OCTR 2:734.

41. Thomas Green, *Memorial, and Documents concerning the First Texian Loan. Presented to the Congress of Texas, May, 1838*, xvi; Winthrop, *Texas as Province and Republic, 1795–1845*; Triplett to president and cabinet, June 2, 1836, PTR 6:503–504.

42. Triplett to Toby, June 5, 1836, PTR 7:27–30.

43. Robert Triplett to president and cabinet, June 9, 1836, OCTR 2:763–65.

44. Ibid.; Green, *Memorial, and Documents*; Robert Triplett to president and cabinet, June 13, 1836, CTR 2: 780; Thomas Toby and brother to D. G. Burnet, June 16, 1836, OCTR 2:789; William Bryan to D. G. Burnet, June 17, 1836, OCTR 2:792; Edward Hall to W. H. Jack, June 18, 1836, OCTR 2:798; Gregg Cantrell, *Stephen F. Austin: Empresario of Texas*, 347.

45. Jack to Bryan, May 27, 1836, PTR 6:388; William Bryan to D. G. Burnet, June 16, 1836, OCTR 2:791–93; Bryan to Burnet, June 17, 1836, OCTR 2:792; Hall to Burnet, June 17, 1836, OCTR 2:793–94.

46. D. G. Burnet proclamation, June 10, 1836, OCTR 2:768.

47. Bryan and Hall to government, June 28, 1836, PTR 7:293.

48. Bryan and Hall, June 28, 1836, PTR 7:293.

49. Bryan to Hardeman, July 8, 1836, PTR 7:386–87.

50. Bryan and Hall to government, June 28, 1836, PTR 7:293–94.

51. D. G. Burnet proclamation, June 10, 1836, OCTR 2:768; Bryan and Hall to the government, June 28, 1836, PTR 7:294–95.

52. Bryan, Hall, and Ellis, *A Vindication of the Conduct*, 14, 18; Winthrop, *Texas as Province and Republic*.

53. Thomas F. McKinney, *To All Who May Have Seen and Read the Dying Groans of Wm. Bryan, E. Hall, and Saml. Ellis, Ex-Agents of Texas; Who Have Made Their Appearance Recently in This Section of Country, in Pamphlet Form, Under the Following Title, viz: "A Vindication of the Conduct of the Agency of Texas in New Orleans,"* 1–15; Winthrop, *Texas as Province and Republic*; Henry Austin to D. G. Burnet, Apr. 7, 1836, CTR 2: 604–605.

54. Bryan to Burnet, June 6, 1836, PTR 7: 2–33; Burnet to Toby, July 20, 1836, PTR 7:210; Hawkins to the secretary of the navy, May, 1836, OCTR 2:694; McKinney, *To All Who May Have Seen and Read*, 14.

55. Triplett to president and cabinet, June 9, 1836, OCTR 2:764.

56. Bryan and Hall to government, June 28, 1836, PTR 7:295.

57. Austin, Archer, and Wharton, Mar. 31, 1836, *Austin Papers* 3:319; William F. Gray to D. G. Burnet, May 10, 1836, OCTR 2:664; Austin to [David G. Burnet], Apr. 3, 1836, *Austin Papers* 3:341; Jack to Austin and others, May 27, 1836, DCTR 1:91–92. The letter from Jack recalling Austin, Archer, and Wharton was the only letter the commissioners received from the ad interim government. See also Barker, *The Life of Stephen F. Austin*, 432; W. F. Gray to Bailey Hardeman, T. J. Rusk, and Robert Potter, May 15, 1836, OCTR 2:685–87.

58. S. F. Austin and W. H. Wharton to James Treat, May 16, 1836, OCTR 2:687.

59. Austin to Nicholas Biddle, Apr. 9, 1836, *Austin Papers* 3:328–30. Swartwout had longstanding connections with Texas. He was one of the investors of the New Washington

Association with agent James Morgan to bring colonists to Texas in 1834; Brunson, *The Adventures of Samuel Swartwout*, 2:69–79; Gammel, *Laws of Texas: 1822–1897*, 2:116.

60. Wharton to Austin, June 2, 1836, *PTR* 6:505–506.

61. Austin, Archer, and Wharton to the government of Texas, Apr. 6, 1836, *DCTR* 1:79–80.

62. Wharton to Austin, June 2, 1836, *PTR* 6:505–506.

63. Childress to Burnet, Mar. 28, 1836, *DCTR* 1:74.

64. Burnet to Collinsworth and Grayson, May 26, 1836, *DCTR* 1:90–91.

65. Austin to Burnet, June 10, 1836, *DCTR* 1:98; Childress and Hamilton to Burnet, June 10, 1836, *DCTR* 1:99–100; Carson to Burnet, July 3, 1836, *DCTR* 1:102.

66. Wharton to Burnet, Apr. 23, 1836, *DCTR* 1:86–87.

67. Grayson to Burnet, Aug. 2, 1836, *DCTR* 1:117–18; *Congressional Globe*, May 23, 1836, 485–89; June 13, 1836, 546–47; June 18, 1836, 564–65; June 24, 1836, 583; Jack to Grayson and Collinsworth, July 23, 1836, *PTR* 8:19–20.

68. McKinney and Williams to president and cabinet, May 15, 1836, *OCTR* 2:682.

69. Ibid., May 20, 1836, *OCTR* 2:695; Burnet to Toby, May 24, 1836, *PTR* 6:138–39; Burnet to Toby, May 25, 1836, *PTR* 6:369–70. Burnet actually increased the amount of land scrip to 500,000 acres in his May 25 letter; McKinney and Williams to president and cabinet, May 20, 1836, *OCTR* 2:695; Lorenzo de Zavala and W. Grayson to president and cabinet, *OCTR* 2:695–97; "1836 Oct. 4, D. G. Burnet. Message to Congress," *Lamar Papers* 1:455.

70. Bryan and Hall to government, June 28, 1836, *PTR* 7:293–94; Frantz, "The Mercantile House," 13–15.

71. Toby to Burnet, June 16, 1836, *OCTR* 2:789.

72. Burnet to Triplett, June 3, 1836, *PTR* 6:507; Burnet to Toby, July 2, 1836, *PTR* 7:335–36; Winston, "Kentucky and the Independence of Texas," *SHQ* 14 (July, 1912): 43–46. Colonel Wilson's volunteers arrived at Velasco on July 17, where Wilson reported to President Burnet. According to Wilson, Burnet was rude and guilty of "incivility" toward the colonel. Wilson and Postlethwaite left Texas disgusted, claiming that the Texas population consisted mostly of plunderers and was incapable of "a just idea of civil or political liberty."

73. D. G. Burnet to Thomas Toby and brother, Aug. 13, 1836, *CTR* 2:927; Nance, *After San Jacinto*, 22–24; Lillian Martin Nelson, "The Second Texas Agency at New Orleans, 1836–1838: Thomas Toby and Brother," 73.

74. Nelson, "The Second Texas Agency," 73.

75. Toby to Burnet, June 16, 1836, *OCTR* 2:788–89.

76. New Orleans *Bee*, May 11, 1836; June 7, 1836; June 16, 1836; Toby to Burnet, June 30, 1836, *OCTR* 2:833–34; Thomas Toby and brother to D. G. Burnet, July 13, 1836, *OCTR* 2:858–59; Brigham and Hudson to secretary, Sept. 29, 1836, *PTR* 9:26; D. G. Burnet to Thomas Toby, Sept. 3, 1836, *OCTR* 2:980; D. G. Burnet to James Morgan, Sept. 22, 1836, *CTR* 2:1029; D. G. Burnet to Thomas Toby, Sept. 22, 1836, *OCTR* 2:1029; Burnet to house, Oct. 12, 1836, *PTR* 9:80–83.

77. Burnet to Toby, Oct. 14, 1836; correspondence with Texas consuls (RG 307), Archives Division-Texas State Library; Stanley Siegel, *A Political History of the Texas Republic, 1836–1845*, 47–56; Gammel, *Laws of Texas*, 1:1075; Houston to Toby, Oct. 25, 1836, *Writings*

of Sam Houston, 1:454–55; W. M. Gouge, *The Fiscal History of Texas: The Fiscal History of Texas; Embracing an Account of Its Revenues, Debts, and Currency from the Commencement of the Revolution in 1834 to 1851–1852, with Remarks on American Debts,* 64.

78. NONA, James B. Marks, n.p., 3:38–40, 44–46; Ramage to Austin, July 27, 1836, *PTR* 8:47–48; New Orleans *Bee,* May 26 and June 1, 1836.

79. Bryan to Austin, Archer, and Wharton, July 11, 1836, *Austin Papers* 3:395–96; Brigham and Hudson to secretary, Sept. 29, 1836, *PTR* 9:26.

80. William Jack to Thomas Muex, July 20, 1836, secretary of state records (RG 307), Archives Division-Texas State Library.

81. Triplett to secretary of state, Aug. 19, 1836, *PTR* 8:272–73.

82. Austin to Austin, Oct. 7, 1836, *PTR* 9:65–66; Austin to Austin, Oct. 10, 1836, *PTR* 9:71–72.

83. Triplett to Christy, Oct. 4, 1836, *PTR* 9:59–60.

84. Francis Pierce to Mary E. Pierce, May 27, 1837, RG 37, box 1, folder 67, letter 2, Louisiana State Museum Historical Center, New Orleans.

85. John T. Mason to Samuel Swartwout, June 4, 1836, Samuel Swartwout Papers, Center for American History, University of Texas at Austin.

86. Ibid.

87. Houston's inaugural address, Oct. 22, 1836, *Writings of Sam Houston,* 1:451.

88. Christy to Houston, July 1, 1836, *PTR* 7:328–29; General S. Houston to William and George H. Christy, Dec. 10, 1836, unpublished typescript letter from the original, owned by Edmund Christy, Metairie, La.

89. "William Christy, New Orleans, Louisiana, the Hero of Ft. Meiggs," in *Sketches of Eminent Americans,* 263; *Charter of the Texas Railroad, Navigation and Banking Company; Together with Other Papers Therewith Connected, Passed by the Congress of the Republic of Texas, and Signed by the President of the Sixteenth Day of December, Eighteen Hundred and Thirty Six,* 11–12; Winthrop, *Texas as Province and Republic.*

EPILOGUE

1. C. Stanley Urban, "The Ideology of Southern Imperialism: New Orleans and the Caribbean, 1845–1860," *Louisiana Historical Quarterly* 39 (Jan., 1956): 47–73.

2. Ibid.

3. Gammel, *Laws of Texas: 1822–1897,* 1:1128.

4. Ernest William Winkler, ed., *First Biennial Report, 1909–1910; Accompanied by the Secret Journals of the Senate, Republic of Texas, 1836–1845,* 119–20; Gammel, *Laws of Texas,* 1:1128.

5. Houston *Telegraph and Texas Register,* Oct. 13, 1838, and Dec. 29, 1838; Alma Howell Brown, "The Consular Service of the Republic of Texas I," *SHQ* 33 (Jan., 1930): 210–11.

6. Edward Hall to M. B. Lamar, Aug. 8, 1841, *Lamar Papers* 3:562; Sam Houston to William Bryan, Jan. 24, 1843, *Lamar Papers* 4:502–503.

7. John Bordon to Lamar, Nov. 2, 1840, *Lamar Papers* 4:449; Charles W. Hayes, *History of the Island and the City of Galveston,* 252.

8. "Articles of agreement made and entered into this fifteenth day of June in the year

of our Lord one thousand eight hundred and thirty seven, between Michael Menard, a citizen of the Republic of Texas, of the first part, Robert Triplett, Sterling Niblett, and William F. Gray, of the second part, and Thomas Green, Levi Jones, and William R. Johnson of the third part"; Winthrop, *Texas as Province and Republic, 1795–1845*; Triplett, *Roland Trevor: or, The Pilot of Human Life*, 357; Bryan-Hall file, Alexander Dienst Papers, Center for American History, University of Texas at Austin; Hayes, *History of the Island*, 252.

9. Hayes, *History of the Island*, 252.

10. Edward Hall statement, Alexander Dienst Papers, Center for American History, University of Texas at Austin.

11. Bryan-Hall file, Alexander Dienst Papers, Center for American History, University of Texas at Austin.

12. A. B. Lawrence, *Texas in 1840, or The Emigrant's Guide to the New Republic; being the Result of Observation, Enquiry and Travel in That Beautiful Country, By an Emigrant, late of the United States.*

13. Ibid.

14. Nelson, "The Second Texas Agency," 63–65.

15. Ibid., 85–90.

16. Ibid., 92–93; Brown, "The Consular Service," 188.

17. Farías, *The Farías Chronicles*, 85.

18. Hutchinson, "Mexican Federalists in New Orleans," 46; Hutchinson, "General Jose Antonio Mexía and His Texas Interests," 141–42.

19. Hutchinson, "General Jose Antonio Mexía and His Texas Interests," 142.

20. Gammel, *Laws of Texas*, 2:72.

21. Parmenter et al., *The Life of George Fisher*, 68–69.

22. David M. Vigness, "Relations of the Republic of Texas and the Republic of the Rio Grande," *SHQ* 57 (Jan., 1954): 312.

23. Ibid., 321.

24. Gammel, *Laws of Texas*, 1:1289.

25. Gammel, *Laws of Texas*, 1:1498.

26. Elgin Williams, *The Animating Pursuits of Speculation: Land Traffic in the Annexation of Texas*, Studies in History, Economics and Public Law series, 86, 191–92.

BIBLIOGRAPHY

CORRESPONDENCE, PAPERS, AND COLLECTIONS

Anglada, George III. Correspondence and research files from Trapolin Architects, New Orleans.

Benavides, Robert M. John and Karen Tanner correspondence, 1993, San Antonio.

Borne, Clayton III. Correspondence and personal Louisiana Masonic research from Clayton Borne III, Metairie, La.; Membership records, Concorde Lodge, Perfect Union Lodge.

Center for American History, University of Texas at Austin. Austin, Stephen Fuller. Papers, 1676–1889; Blake, Robert Bruce. Research Collection; Burnet, David Gouverneur. Papers, 1798–1965; Butler, Anthony. Papers, 1810–1846; Crimmins, M. L. Papers; Fisher, George. Papers, 1795–1873; Fulton, Ambrose Cowperthwaite. Papers, 1895–1903; Hearne, Madge. Collection; Rusk, Thomas Jefferson. Papers, 1824–1859; Swartwout, Samuel. Collection, 1783–1856; Tanner, John D. and Karen O. "Ambrose Cowperthwaite Fulton, 1811–1903," 1993, Unpublished Biography; Vandale, Earl. Collection; *"William Christy, New Orleans, Louisiana, The Hero of Fort Meiggs." Sketches of Eminent Americans.* United States, n.p., 1857.

Christy Family. Papers and portrait, 1836. Edmund Christy, Metairie, La.

Cook, Richard O. Correspondence and personal family research concerning William G. Cooke, Stonewall, Tex.

Daughters of the Republic of Texas Research Library, San Antonio. Cooke, William G. Papers, 1835–1848; Blake, Robert Bruce. Research Collection.

East Texas Research Center, Ralph Steen Library, Stephen F. Austin State University, Nacogdoches, Tex. Baker, Karl Wilson. Papers; Blake, Robert Bruce. Research Collection; Blount, Lois. Papers; Sterne, Adolphus. Papers; Taylor, Robert S. Papers.

Grand Lodge of Louisiana, Alexandria, La. New Orleans Lodge Rosters, 1800–1845; Polar Star Lodge *(Etoile Polar)* no. 1 (French and Scottish Rite); Perfect Union Lodge no. 1 (York Rite); Concorde Lodge no. 3; Lafayette Lodge no. 25; Heritage Lodge no. 26.

Grand Lodge of Texas Library, Waco. Fisher, George. Files; Mexican Freemasonry. Files.

Hill Memorial Library, Louisiana State University, Baton Rouge. Lower Mississippi and Louisiana Collection: Alexander, John H. Letter, 1835; Wallace, James B. Journal, 1835–1836; Hall, Edward. Papers, 1826–1829.

Historic New Orleans Collection, New Orleans. Vieux Carré Commission Survey.

Howard-Tilton Memorial Library, Manuscript Department, Tulane University, New Orleans. Manuscript Collection 895 (Freemason Lodges in Louisiana, 1808–1933).

Jackson Barracks Military Library, New Orleans. Historical Military Data: 1811–1814, volume 338; 1818–1826, volume 340; 1827–1834, volume 342. Historical Militia Data of Louisiana Militia: 1815–1828, volume 50; 1827–1837, volume 53. Historical Militia Data: 1835–1842, volume 343. Historical Military Data, Louisiana Militia: 1835–1842, supplement; 1856–1857, volume 91. Louisiana Adjutant General Reports: 1806–1849. Louisiana Greys, Historical Military Data on Louisiana Militia: 1836–1842, volume 58. Louisiana Legion Historical Data of Louisiana Militia: 1837–1839, volume 57. New Orleans Greys. Vertical File. The Western Frontier, 1800–1836; Historical and Military events of the Western expansion of the United States boundary to Texas and Mexico. Texas History, 1835–1836, supplement.

Louisiana State Museum, New Orleans. Cenas Family (1780–1920). Papers. Record Group 37.

Nettie Benson Latin American Collection, University of Texas at Austin. Gómez Farías. Valentín Collection: 1770–1909.

New Orleans Public Library, New Orleans. First Judicial District Court Records; Orleans Parish Court Records; Louisiana Newspapers; New Orleans Conseil de Ville Records, 1819–1836.

Orleans Parish Notarial Archives, New Orleans. Notarial Records of William Boswell; William Christy; Hilary B. Cenas; Achille Chiapella; Octave De Armis; Louis Frerard; Joseph Benzaken Marks.

Polar Star (Etoile Polar) Lodge, New Orleans. Membership Records and Lodge Minutes. Courtesy of Worshipful Master Henry Thibodaux.

Rosenburg Library, Galveston. Williams, Samuel S. Papers.

Texas General Land Office, Austin. Republic of Texas Land Records.

Texas State Library and Archives Division, Austin. Republic of Texas Audited Claims; Secretary of State Records (RG 307); Adjutant General Records (RG 401).

GOVERNMENT DOCUMENTS

Abstract of the Original Titles of Record in the General Land Office, Printed in Accordance with a Resolution of the House of Representatives, Passed 24 May, 1838. Houston: Niles, 1838; reproduced, Austin: Pemberton, 1964.

Bexar Archives at the University of Texas Archives. Ed. Chester V. Kielman and Carmela Leal. Austin: University of Texas Library, 1967–1970. 172 microfilm reels.

Binkley, William C., ed. Official Correspondence of the Texan Revolution. 2 vols. New York: D. Appleton-Century, 1936.

Christy, William. A Digest of Martin's Reports, of the decisions of the Supreme Court of the State of Louisiana: from its establishment in the year 1813, to August, 1826, Including those of the Supreme Court of the late territory of Orleans. New Orleans: Lyman and Beardslee, 1826.

Coahuila and Texas: Laws and Decrees of the State of Coahuila and Texas, in Spanish and English. Trans. J. P. Kimball. Houston: Telegraph Power, 1839. Western Americana: Frontier History of the Trans-Mississippi West, 1550–1900. New Haven, Conn.: Research Publications, 1975. Microfilm.

Dublán, Manuel, and José Maria Lozano. *Legislación Mexicana; O coleccóon completa de las disponisciones legislativas expedidas desde la independencia de la República ordenada.* 34 vols. Mexico City: Impr. del Comercio, 1876–1904.

Fifth Judicial District Court Records, New Orleans, Original Court Documents, New Orleans Library.

First Judicial District Court Records, New Orleans, New Orleans Public Library. Microfilm.

Gammel, H. P. N., ed. and comp. *Laws of Texas.* 10 vols. Austin: Gammel Book, 1898.

Garrison, George P., ed. *The Diplomatic Correspondence of the Republic of Texas, Annual Report of the American Historical Association for the Year 1907.* 2 vols. Washington, D.C.: Government Printing Office, 1908.

Hartley, O. C., and R. K. Hartley. *Reports of the Cases Argued and Decided in the Supreme Court of the State of Texas, at Austin, Tex., 1855.* St. Paul: West, 1855.

Louisiana Legislature. *Acts passed at the First Session of the Twelfth Legislature of the State of Louisiana, Begun and Held in the City of New Orleans, the Fifth Day of January, Eighteen Hundred and Thirty Five.* New Orleans: Jerome Bayon, 1835.

Louisiana Legislature. *Acts Passed at the First and Second Sessions of the Twelfth Legislature of the State of Louisiana, 1835–1836.* New Orleans: Jerome Bayon, 1836.

National Archives and Record Administration. Abstracts of Service Records of Naval Officers, 1793–1893. Microfilm.

———. Abstracts of Service Records of Soldiers of the War of 1812. Microfilm.

———. Fifth Census of the United States, 1830. Kentucky, Louisiana, and Pennsylvania. Microfilm.

———. Fourth Census of the United States, 1820. Kentucky, Louisiana, and Pennsylvania. Microfilm.

———. Seventh Census of the United States, 1850. Kentucky, Louisiana, Mississippi, and Texas. National Archives and Records Administration. Microfilm.

———. Sixth Census of the United States, 1840. Kentucky, Louisiana, and Mississippi. Microfilm.

New Orleans Conseil de Ville Records, 1819–1836, New Orleans Public Library. Microfilm.

New Orleans Parish Court Records, New Orleans Public Library. Microfilm.

Texas Legislature. House of Representatives. *Biographical Directory of the Texan Conventions and Congresses.* Austin: Book Exchange, 1942.

Winkler, Ernest William, ed. *First Biennial Report, 1909–1910; Accompanied by the Secret Journals of the Senate, Republic of Texas, 1836–1845.* Austin: Austin Printing, 1911.

BOOKS, ARTICLES, THESES, DISSERTATIONS

Adams, Allen F. "The Leader of the Volunteer Grays: The Life of William G. Cooke." Master's thesis, Southwest Texas State University, San Marcos, Tex., 1940.

Address to the Public Authorities of the United States, by the Louisiana Native American Association. New Orleans: True American Office, 1836. Louisiana Collection, Howard-Tilton Memorial Library, Tulane University, New Orleans.

Address of the Louisiana Native American Association, to the citizens of Louisiana and the Inhabitants of the United States. New Orleans: D. Felt, 1839. Center for American History, University of Texas at Austin.

Almonte, Juan N. "The Private Journal of Juan Nepomuceno Almonte, February 1–April 16, 1835." *Southwestern Historical Quarterly* 48 (1944): 10–32.

———. "Statistical Report on Texas." Trans. C. E. Casteñada. *Southwestern Historical Quarterly* 28 (1925): 177–222.

"Andrew Jackson's Correspondence with James W. Breedlove." *Louisiana Historical Quarterly* 6 (1923): 179–88.

Bacarisse, Charles A. "The Union of Coahuila and Texas." *Southwestern Historical Quarterly* 61 (1958): 341–49.

Bancroft, Hubert Howe. *History of the North Mexican States and Texas, 1801–1889,* in *The Works of Hubert Howe Bancroft.* 39 vols. San Francisco: History Company, 1889.

Barker, Eugene Campbell. *The Austin Papers.* 2 vols. Washington, D.C.: Government Printing Office, 1924, 1928; 3rd vol. Austin: University of Texas, 1927.

———. "Land Speculation as a Cause of the Texas Revolution." *Southwestern Historical Quarterly* 10 (1906): 76–95.

———. *The Life of Stephen F. Austin: Frontier of Texas, 1793–1836: A Chapter in the Westward Movement of the Anglo-American People.* Austin: Texas State Historical Association, 1949.

———. "President Andrew Jackson and the Texas Revolution." *American Historical Review* 12 (1907): 788–809.

———. "The San Jacinto Campaign." *Quarterly of the Texas State Historical Association* 4 (1901): 238–345.

———. "Stephen F. Austin and the Independence of Texas." *Quarterly of the Texas Historical Association* 13 (1910): 257–84.

———. "The Tampico Expedition." *Southwestern Historical Quarterly* 6 (1902): 169–86.

———. "Texas Revolutionary Finances." *Political Science Quarterly* 19 (1904): 612–35.

———. "The United States and Mexico, 1835–1837." *Mississippi Valley Historical Review* 1 (1914): 3–30.

Barr, Alwyn. *Texans in Revolt: The Battle for San Antonio, 1835.* Austin: University of Texas Press, 1990.

Bartholomae, Edgar, "A Translation of H. Ehrenberg's *Fahrten und Schicksale eines Deutschen in Texas,* with Introduction and Notes." Master's thesis, University of Texas at Austin, 1925.

Bass, Feris A., and B. R. Brunson, eds. *Fragile Empires: The Correspondence of Samuel Swartwout and James Morgan, 1836–1856.* Austin: Shoal Creek, 1978.

Bassett, John Spencer, and David Maydole Matteson, eds. *Correspondence of Andrew Jackson.* 7 vols. Washington, D.C.: Carnegie Institution of Washington, 1926–1935.

Benavides, Adán, comp. *The Béxar Archives, 1717–1836: A Name Guide.* Austin: University of Texas at Austin for the University of Texas Institute of Texan Cultures at San Antonio, 1989.

Benson, Nettie. "Texas as Viewed from Mexico, 1820–1834." *Southwestern Historical Quarterly* 90 (1987): 219–91.

Binkley, William. *The Expansionist Movement, 1836–1850.* Reprinted. Berkeley, 1925; New York: De Capo, 1970.

Borrego, Salvador. *América Peligra.* Mexico City: Impressos Aldo, 1964. From the collection of Carlos Marbán, Mexico City.

Bradford, A. L., and T. N. Campbell. "Journal of Lincecum's Travels in Texas, 1835." *Southwestern Historical Quarterly* 53 (1949): 180–201.

Brown, Alma Howell. "The Consular Service of the Republic of Texas, I." *Southwestern Historical Quarterly* 33 (1930): 184–230.

Brown, John Henry. *History of Texas from 1685 to 1892.* 2 vols. St. Louis: L. E. Daniell, 1892. Reprint, Austin: Pemberton, 1970.

———. *Life and Times of Henry Smith: The First American Governor of Texas.* Dallas: A. D. Aldridge, 1887.

Brunson, B. R. *The Adventures of Samuel Swartwout in the Age of Jefferson and Jackson.* Vol. 2, Studies in American History. Lewiston, N.Y.: Edwin Mellon, 1989.

Burke, Barlow, Jr., and Jefferson K. Fox. "The Notaire in North America: A Short Study of the Adaptation of a Civil Law Institution." *Tulane Law Review* 50 (1976): 318–45.

Burnett, Arthur C. *Yankees in the Republic of Texas: Some Notes on Their Origin and Impact.* Houston: Anson Jones, 1952.

Burns, Francis. "The Graviers and the Faubourg Ste. Marie." *Louisiana Historical Quarterly* 22 (April, 1939).

Burr, Betty Fagan. *Nacogdoches Archives: 1835 Entrance Certificates.* Nacogdoches: Ericson Books, 1982.

Cantrell, Greg. *Stephen F. Austin: Empresario of Texas.* New Haven: Yale University, 1999.

"Captain John McHenry, Pioneer of Texas." *DeBow's Review* 15 (1853): 578–79.

Carter, James David. *Masonry in Texas: Background, History, and Influence to 1846.* Waco: Committee on Masonic Education and Service for the Grand Lodge of Texas, 1955; 2d ed., 1958.

Charter of the Texas Railroad, Navigation and Banking Company; Together with Other Papers Therewith Connected, Passed by the Congress of the Republic of Texas, and Signed by the President on the Sixteenth Day of December, Eighteen Hundred and Thirty Six. Texas as Province and Republic, 1795–1845. Based on the bibliography by Thomas Streeter. New Haven, Conn.: Research Publications, 1978–1979. Microfilm.

Chase, John. *Frenchmen, Desire, Good Children, . . . and Other Streets of New Orleans.* New Orleans: Robert L. Crager, 1949.

Christovich, Mary Louise, Roulhac Toledano, Betsy Swanson, and Pat Holden, authors and editors. *New Orleans Architecture, the American Sector (Faubourg St. Mary): Howard Avenue to Iberville Street, Mississippi River to Claiborne Avenue.* Vol. 2. Gretna, La.: Pelican, 1972.

Clapp, Theodore. *Autobiographical Sketches and Recollections, during a Thirty-Five Year Residence in New Orleans.* 1857; Freeport, N.Y.: Books for Libraries, 1972.

Cohen, Cohen. "Settlement of the Jews in Texas," *Publications of the American Jewish Historical Society* 2 (1894): 139–56.

Cole, Arthur C. "Nativism in the Lower Mississippi Valley." *Proceedings of the Mississippi Valley Historical Association for the Year 1912–1913* (1913).

Collins, Richard H. *Collin's Historical Sketches of Kentucky.* 2 vols. Covington, Ky.: Collin, 1882.

Condron, Stuart Harkins. "The First Texas Agency at New Orleans in 1836." Master's thesis, University of Texas at Austin, 1912.

Conrad, Glenn R., ed. *A Dictionary of Louisiana Biography.* 2 vols. New Orleans: Louisiana Historical Association, 1988.

Corner, William. "John Crittenden Duval, the Last Survivor of the Goliad Massacre." *Quarterly of the Texas State Historical Association* 1 (1907): 47–67.

Costeloe, Michael P. *The Central Republic of Mexico, 1835–1846, Hombres de Bien in the Age of Santa Anna.* No. 73, Cambridge Latin American Studies. Cambridge: Cambridge University Press, 1993.

————. "Federalism to Centralism in Mexico: The Conservative Case for Change, 1834–1835." *The Americas* 45 (1988): 173–85.

————. "Santa Anna and the Gómez Farías Administration in Mexico, 1833–1834." *The Americas* 31 (1974): 18–50.

Cotterill, R. S. "The Beginnings of Railroads in the Southwest." *Mississippi Valley Historical Review* 8 (1922): 318–26.

Crimmons, M. L. "The Storming of San Antonio de Bexar in 1835." *West Texas Historical Association Year Book* 22 (1946): 95–117.

Crisp, James E. "Sam Houston's Speechwriters: The Grad Student, the Teenager, the Editors, and the Historians." *Southwestern Historical Quarterly* 97 (1993): 203–37.

Cuevas, P. Mariano. *Historia de la Iglesia en Mexico.* 5 vols. First ed., 1928; reprint, Argentina: Editorial Porrua, 1992.

Daughters of the Republic of Texas. *Muster Rolls of the Texas Revolution.* Lubbock: Craftsman Printers, 1986.

Davenport, Harbert. "The Men of Goliad, Dedicatory Address at the Unveiling of the Monument Erected by the Texas Centennial at the Grave of Fannin's Men." *Southwestern Historical Quarterly* 48 (1939): 1–41.

Davidson, James D. "A Journey through the South in 1836: Dairy of James D. Davidson." Ed. Herbert A. Kellar. *Journal of Southern History* 1 (1935): 345–77.

Davis, William C. *Three Roads to the Alamo: The Lives and Fortunes of Davy Crockett, Jim Bowie, and William Travis.* New York: HarperCollins, 1998.

Dawson, Joseph D. III, ed. *The Louisiana Governors, from Iberville to Edwards.* Baton Rouge: Louisiana State University, 1990.

Day, James M., comp. *The Texas Almanac, 1857–1873.* Waco: Texian Press, 1967.

De Bruhl, Marshall. *Sword of San Jacinto: A Life of Sam Houston.* New York: Random House, 1993.

DeLa Peña, Enrique. *With Santa Anna in Texas: A Personal Narrative of the Revolution.* Trans. and ed. Carmen Perry. College Station: Texas A&M University Press, 1975.

De La Teja, Jesús. *San Antonio de Béxar: A Community on New Spain's Northern Frontier.* Albuquerque: University of New Mexico Press, 1995.

————, ed. *A Revolution Remembered: The Memoirs and Selected Correspondence of Juan N. Seguín.* Austin: State House, 1991.

Denham, James M. "Charles E. Hawkins: Sailor of Three Republics." *Gulf Coastal Historical Review* 5 (1990): 92–103.

————. "New Orleans, Maritime Commerce, and the Texas War for Independence, 1836." *Southwestern Historical Quarterly* 97: 511–34.

Desalguilers. "Freemasonry in Mexico, Its Origin, & illustrated by Original Documents, Not Heretofore Published." *Masonic Review* (1858): 1–8.

De Shields, James. *Tall Men with Long Rifles.* San Antonio: Naylor, 1935.

de Zavala, Lorenzo. *Journey to the United States of North America.* Trans. Wallace Woolsey. Austin: Shoal Creek, 1980.

Dienst, Alexander. "The Navy of the Republic of Texas." *Southwestern Historical Quarterly* 12 (1909): I, 165–204; II, 249–75.

————. "The New Orleans Newspaper Files of the Texas Revolutionary Period." *Quarterly of the Texas State Historical Association* 4 (1901): 140–51.

Edward, David B. *The History of Texas, or, the Emigrant's, Farmer's, and Politician's Guide to the Character, Climate, Soil and Productions of That Country: Arranged Geographically from Personal Observation and Experience.* Cincinnati: J. A. James, 1836; Fred H. and Emma Mae Moore Texas reprint series, Texas State Historical Association, 1990.

Ehrenberg, Hermann. *Texas und seine Revolution.* Leipzig: Otto von Wigand, 1843. "Western Americana: Frontier History of the Trans-Mississippi West, 1550–1900." New Haven, Conn.: Research Publications, 1975. Microfilm. Also republished as *Der Freiheitskampf in Texas im Jahre 1836* (1844) and as *Fahrten und Schicksale eines Deutschen in Texas* (1845).

Everett, Diana. *The Texas Cherokees: A People between Two Fires, 1819–1840.* The Civilization of the American Indian Series. Norman: University of Oklahoma Press, 1990.

Farías, George. *The Farías Chronicles: A History and Genealogy of a Portuguese/Spanish Family.* Edinburgh, Tex.: New Santander, 1995.

Featherstonhaugh, G. W. *Excursion through the Slave States from Washington on the Potomac to the Frontier of Mexico; with Sketches of Popular Manners and Geological Notices.* New York: Harper and Brothers, 1844. San Antonio Public Library.

Field, Joseph E. *Three Years in Texas: Including a View of the Texas Revolution and an Account of the Principal Battles, Together with Descriptions of the Soil, Commercial and Agricultural Advantages, Etc.* Boston: Abel Tompkins, 1836; reprint, Tarrytown, N.Y.: William Abbatt, 1928.

Filisola, Vicente. *Memoirs for the History of the War in Texas.* 2 vols. Trans. Wallace Woolsey. Austin: Eakin, 1987.

Fisher, George. *Memorials of George Fisher, late secretary to the expedition of Gen. Jose Antonio Mexia, against Tampico, in November, 1835. Presented to the Fourth and Fifth congresses of the Republic of Texas, praying for relief in favor of the members of said expedition.* Houston: Telegraph Office, 1840. "Western Americana: Frontier History of the Trans-Mississippi West, 1550–1900." New Haven, Conn.: Research Publications, 1975. Microfilm.

Fisher, Lillian Estelle. "Early Masonry in Mexico (1806–1828)." *Southwestern Historical Quarterly* 42 (1939): 198–214.

Flores, Dan L., ed. *Jefferson and Southwestern Exploration: The Freeman and Custis Accounts of the Red River Expedition of 1806.* American Exploration and Travel Series. Norman: University of Oklahoma Press, 1984.

Foote, Henry Stuart. *Texas and the Texans: or the Advance of the Anglo-Americans to the Southwest.* 2 vols. Original Narratives of Texas History and Adventure. Austin: Steck, 1935.

Ford, Paul Leicester, ed. *The Writings of Thomas Jefferson.* 10 vols. New York: G. P. Putnam's Sons, 1897.

Fossier, Albert A. *New Orleans, The Glamour Period, 1800–1840: A History of the Conflicts of Nationalities, Languages, Religion, Morals, Cultures, Laws, Politics and Economics during the Formative Period of New Orleans.* New Orleans: Pelican, 1957.

Franklin, John Hope. *The Militant South, 1800–1861.* Cambridge, Mass.: Belknap, 1956.

Frantz, Joe B. "The Mercantile House of McKinney & Williams, Underwriters of the Texas Revolution." *Bulletin of the Business Historical Society* 26 (1952): 1–18.

Fulton, Ambrose Cowperthwaite. *A Life's Voyage: A Diary of a Sailor on Sea and Land, Jotted Down during a Seventy-Year's Voyage.* New York: Author, 1898.

"General Austin's Order Book for the Campaign of 1835." *Southwestern Historical Quarterly* 11 (1907): 232–58.

Gibson, John. *Gibson's Guide and Directory of the State of Louisiana, and the Cities of New Orleans and Lafayette.* New Orleans: John Gibson, 1838.

Gouge, William M. *The Fiscal History of Texas: Embracing an Account of Its Revenues, Debts, and Currency from the Commencement of the Revolution in 1834 to 1851–1852, with Remarks on American Debts.* Philadelphia: Lippincott, Grambo, 1852; reprint, New York: B. Franklin, 1969.

Gray, Millie. *The Diary of Millie Gray, 1832–1840.* Galveston: Rosenberg Library Press, 1967.

Gray, William Fairfax. *From Virginia to Texas, 1835: Diary of Col. Wm. F. Gray, Giving Details of His Journey to Texas and Return in 1835–1836.* Houston: Gray, Dillaye, 1909; reprint, Houston: Fletcher Young, 1965.

Green, George D. *Finance and Economic Development in the Old South: Louisiana Banking, 1804–1861.* Stanford: Stanford University Press, 1972.

Green, Thomas. *Memorial, and Documents concerning the First Texian Loan. Presented to the Congress of Texas, May 1838.* Houston: Telegraph, 1838. *Texas as Province and Republic, 1795–1845.* Based on the bibliography by Thomas Streeter. New Haven, Conn.: Research Publications, 1978–1979. Microfilm.

Greer, Richard. "The Committee on the Texas Declaration of Independence, I." *Southwestern Historical Quarterly* 30 (1927): 239–51.

———. "The Committee on the Texas Declaration of Independence, II." *Southwestern Historical Quarterly* 31 (1927): 33–49.

———. "The Committee on the Texas Declaration of Independence, III." *Southwestern Historical Quarterly* 31 (1927): 130–49.

Grima, Edgar. "The Notarial System of Louisiana." *Louisiana Historical Quarterly* 10 (January 1927): 76–81.

Gulick, Charles Adams Jr., and Katherine Elliott, eds. *The Papers of Mirabeau Buonaparte Lamar.* 6 vols. Austin: A. C. Baldwin and Sons, 1921–1927; reprint, New York: AMS Press, 1973.

Hammeken, George L. "Recollections of Stephen F. Austin." *Southwestern Historical Quarterly* 20 (April, 1917): 369–80.

Hanna, Archibald, ed. *Western Americana, Frontier History of the Trans-Mississippi West, 1550–1900: Guide and Index to the Microfilm Edition.* 2 vols. Woodbridge, Conn.: Research Publications, 1980–1981.

Hardin, J. Fair. "Fort Jesup, Fort Seldon, Camp Sabine, Camp Salubrity, Four Forgotten

Frontier Army Posts of Western Louisiana, I–IV." *Louisiana Historical Quarterly* 16 (1933): 5–26; 279–92; 441–53; 670–80.

Hardin, Stephen. *Texian Iliad: A Military History of the Texas Revolution, 1835–1836.* Austin: University of Texas Press, 1993.

Haskins, Ralph W. "Planter and Cotton Factor in the Old South: Some Areas of Friction." *Agricultural History* 29 (1955): 1–14.

Haugh, George F., ed. "The Texas Navy at New York." *Southwestern Historical Quarterly* 64 (1961): 377–79.

Hayes, Charles W. *History of the Island and the City of Galveston.* Cincinnati: n.p., 1879; Austin: Jenkins Garrett, 1974.

Henson, Margaret Swett. *Lorenzo de Zavala: The Pragmatic Idealist.* Fort Worth: Texas Christian University Press, 1996.

———. "Politics and the Treatment of the Mexican Prisoners after the Battle of San Jacinto." *Southwestern Historical Quarterly* 94 (1990): 189–230.

———. *Samuel May Williams: Early Texas Entrepreneur.* College Station: Texas A&M University Press, 1976.

Hill, Jim Dan. *The Texas Navy: In Forgotten Battles and Shirtsleeve Diplomacy.* Austin: Statehouse, 1987.

Hogan, William Ransom. *The Texas Republic: A Social and Economic History.* Norman: University of Oklahoma Press, 1969.

Hood, Cornelia. "Life and Career of George Campbell Childress." Master's thesis, University of Texas at Austin, 1938.

Hopkins, James F., Mary W. M. Hargreaves, Robert Seager, and Melba Porter Hay, eds. *The Papers of Henry Clay.* 11 vols. Lexington: University of Kentucky Press, 1959–1992.

Howard, Perry H. *Political Tendencies in Louisiana.* Rev. and exp. Baton Rouge: Louisiana State University Press, 1960.

Huber, Leonard V., comp. *Notable New Orleans Landmarks: A Pictorial Record of the Work of the Orleans Parish Landmarks Commission, 1957–1974.* New Orleans: Orleans Parish Landmarks Commission, 1974.

Hunnicutt, Helen Mar. "The Relationship between Antonio Lopez de Santa Anna as President and Valentín Gómez Farías as Vice-President of Mexico, April 1833–January 1835." Master's thesis, University Texas at Austin, 1925.

Hunt, David Glenn. "Vito Alessio Robles: Coahuila y Texas, desde la Consumacion de la Independencia hasta el Tratado de Paz de Guadalupe Hidalgo (Mexico, 1846) (an Edited Translation of Volume II, Chapters 1–7)." Master's thesis, Southern Methodist University, 1950.

Huson, Hobart. *Refugio: A Comprehensive History of Refugio County, from Aboriginal Times to 1953.* 2 vols. Woodsboro, Tex.: Rook Foundation, 1953.

Hutchinson, Cecil Alan. "General José Antonio Mexía and His Texas Interests." *Southwestern Historical Quarterly* 82 (1978): 117–42.

———. "Mexican Federalists in New Orleans and the Texas Revolution." *Louisiana Historical Quarterly* 39 (January, 1956): 1–47.

———. "Valentín Gómez Farías: A Biographical Study." Ph.D. diss., University of Texas at Austin, 1948.

———. "Valentín Gómez Farías and the Secret Pact of New Orleans." *Hispanic American Historical Review* 36 (1956): 471–89.

Interesting Account of the Life and Adventures of one of those Unfortunate Men, Who was shot at Tampico, with Twenty-Seven of His Companions, December 14, 1835, with a List of all the Names, Together with the Letters which were written by the Sufferers. New York: n.p., 1836. *Texas as Province and Republic, 1795–1845.* Based on the bibliography by Thomas Streeter. New Haven, Conn.: Research Publications, 1978–1979. Microfilm.

Jenkins, John H., ed. *Papers of the Texas Revolution, 1835–1836.* 10 vols. Austin: Presidial, 1973.

Jones, Anson. *Memoranda and Official Correspondence Relating to the Republic of Texas, Its History and Annexation.* New York: D. Appleton, 1859.

Kemp, Louis Wiltz. *The Signers of the Texas Declaration of Independence.* Salado, Tex.: Anson Jones, 1959.

Keyes, Francis Parkinson. *The River Road.* New York: Grosset and Dunlop, 1945.

Kilbourne, Richard Holcomb, Jr. *Debt, Investment, Slaves: Credit Relations in East Feliciana Parish, 1825–1885.* Tuscaloosa: University of Alabama Press, 1995.

King, Grace. *Creole Families of New Orleans.* Vol. 8, Louisiana Classic Series. Baton Rouge: Harper and Row, 1950.

Kirwan, Albert D., ed. *The Civilization of the Old South: The Writings of Clement Eaton.* Lexington: University of Kentucky Press, 1968.

Korn, Bertram Wallace. *The Early Jews of New Orleans.* No. 5, American Jewish Communal Histories. Waltham, Mass.: American Jewish Historical Society, 1969.

Lack, Paul. *The Texas Revolutionary Experience: A Social and Political History.* College Station: Texas A&M Press, 1992.

Lawrence, A. B. *Texas in 1840, or the Emigrant's Guide to the New Republic; being the Result of Observation, Enquiry and Travel in That Beautiful Country, by an Emigrant, Late of the United States.* New York: William W. Allen, 1840.

Leonard, Ira M., and Robert D. Parmet. *American Nativism, 1830–1860.* New York: Van Nostrand Reinhold, 1971.

Letts, Bettie Lucille. "George Fisher." Master's thesis, University of Texas at Austin, 1928.

Linn, John J. *Reminiscences of Fifty Years in Texas.* Original Narratives of Texas History and Adventure. Austin: Steck, 1935.

Lubbock, Francis Richard. *Six Decades in Texas or Memoirs of Francis Richard Lubbock.* Ed. C. W. Raines. Austin: Ben C. Jones, 1900.

Mahon, John K. *History of the Second Seminole War, 1835–1842.* Rev. ed. Gainesville: University of Florida Press, 1985.

Malloy, William M., ed. *Treaties, Conventions, International Acts, Protocols, and Agreements between the United States of America and Other Powers, 1776–1909.* 2 vols. Washington, D.C.: Government Printing Office, 1910.

Manning, William R. "Texas and the Boundary Issue, 1822–1829." *Southwestern Historical Quarterly* 17 (1913): 217–23.

Marshall, Thomas Maitland. *A History of the Western Boundary of the Louisiana Purchase, 1819–1841.* Vol. 2, University of California Publications in History. Berkeley: University of California Press, 1914; New York: DaCapo, 1970.

Martin, François-Xavier. *The History of Louisiana, from the Earliest Period*. New Orleans: James A. Gresham, 1882.

Matovina, Timothy M. *The Alamo Remembered: Tejano Accounts and Perspectives*. Austin: University of Texas Press, 1995.

McCardell, John. *The Idea of a Southern Nation: Southern Nationalists and Southern Nationalism, 1830–1860*. New York: W. W. Norton, 1979.

McLean, Malcolm D., comp. and ed. *Papers Concerning Robertson's Colony in Texas*. 3 vols. Fort Worth: Texas Christian University, 1974–1977; 15 vols. Arlington: University of Texas at Arlington, 1977–1993.

Mecham, J. Lloyd. "The Origins of Federalism in Mexico." *Hispanic American Historical Review* 18 (1938): 164–82.

Michel's New Orleans Annual and Commercial Register, Containing the Names, Professions and Residences of All the Heads of Families, and Persons in Business of the City and Suburbs, for 1834. New Orleans: Gaux and Sollee, 1833.

Michel's New Orleans Annual and Commercial Register, Containing the Names, Professions and Residences of All the Heads of Families, and Persons in Business of the City and Suburbs, for 1835. New Orleans: Gaux and Sollee, 1834.

Mier y Terán, Manuel. Texas by Terán: The Diary Kept by General Manuel de Mier y Terán on His 1828 Inspection of Texas. Ed. Jack Jackson. Trans. John Wheat. No. 2, Jack and Doris Smothers in Texas History, Life, and Culture Series. Austin: University of Texas Press, 2000.

Miller, Edward L. "The Texas Revolution, Civilian Suits, Whiskey-Loving Foreigners and the New Orleans Greys." *Military Collector and Historian* 48 (1996): 33–37.

———, and Peter Stines. "New Orleans Greys at San Antonio de Bexar, 1835." *Military Collector and Historian* 48 (1996): 40–41.

Miller, Thomas Lloyd. *The Public Lands of Texas, 1519–1970*. Norman: University of Oklahoma Press, 1972.

Mitchell, Harry A. "The Development of New Orleans as a Wholesale Trading Center." *Louisiana Historical Quarterly* 27 (1944): 933–62.

Moser, Harold D., David R. Hoth, and George H. Hoemann, eds. *The Papers of Andrew Jackson*. 5 vols. Knoxville: University of Tennessee Press, 1994.

Muir, Andrew Forest. "Railroad Enterprise in Texas, 1836–1841." *Southwestern Historical Quarterly* 47 (1944): 339–70.

Nance, John Milton. "Abel Morgan and His Account of the Battle of Goliad." *Southwestern Historical Quarterly* 100 (1996): 207–33.

———. *After San Jacinto: The Texas-Mexican Frontier, 1836–1841*. Austin: University of Texas Press, 1963.

Nelson, Lillian Martin. "The Second Texas Agency at New Orleans, 1836–1838: Thomas Toby and Brother." Master's thesis, University of Texas at Austin, 1922.

Neu, C. T. "The Case of the Brig Pocket." *Quarterly of the Texas State Historical Association* 12 (1909): 276–95.

New-Orleans Annual and Commercial Directory for 1843, Containing the Names and Residences of All the Inhabitants of the City and Suburbs of New-Orleans. New Orleans: J. L. Sollee, 1842.

Newton, Lewis William. "Creoles and Anglo-Americans in Old Louisiana: A Study in Cultural Conflicts." *Southwestern Social Science Quarterly* 19 (1933): 31–48.

Niehaus, Earl F. *The Irish in New Orleans, 1800–1860.* Baton Rouge: Louisiana State University Press, 1965.

Ornish, Natalie. *Ehrenberg: Goliad Survivor, Old West Explorer, with the First Complete Scholarly Translation of the Fight for Freedom in Texas in the Year 1836 by Herman Ehrenberg.* Trans. Peter Mollenhaurer. Dallas: Texas Heritage, 1993, 1997.

———. *Pioneer Jewish Texans: Their Impact on Texas and American History for Four Hundred Years, 1590–1990.* Dallas: Texas Heritage, 1989.

Overdyke, W. Darrell. "History of the American Party in Louisiana, Chapter 1." *Louisiana Historical Quarterly* 15 (1932): 581–88.

Owsley, Frank Lawrence, Jr., and Gene A. Smith. *Filibusters and Expansionists: Jeffersonian Manifest Destiny, 1800–1821.* Tuscaloosa: University of Alabama Press, 1997.

Padgett, James A. "Letters of James Brown to Henry Clay, 1804–1835." *Louisiana Historical Quarterly* 24 (October, 1941): 921–1177.

Parker, A[mos] A[ndrew]. *Trip to the West and Texas.* Concord, N.H.: White and Fisher, 1835; New York: Arno, 1973.

Parmenter, Mary Fisher, Walter Russell Fisher, and Lawrence Edward Mallette. *The Life of George Fisher (1795–1873) and the History of the Fisher Family in Mississippi.* Jacksonville: H. and W. B. Drew, 1959.

Parrish, Leonard Durvin. "The Life of Nicolas Bravo, Mexican Patriot (1786–1854)." Ph.D. diss., 1951, University of Texas at Austin.

Partin, James Galloway. "A History of Nacogdoches and Nacogdoches County, Texas to 1877." Master's thesis, University of Texas at Austin, 1968.

Paxton, John Adems. *The New Orleans Directory and Register; Containing the Names, Professions and Residences of All Heads of Families and Persons in Business of the City and the Suburbs, with other useful Information.* New Orleans: Benjamin Levy, 1822.

———. *The New Orleans Directory and Register; Containing the Names, Professions and Residences of all Heads of Families and Persons in Business of the City and the Suburbs, with other useful Information.* New Orleans: John Adems Paxton, 1827.

Pohl, James W. *The Battle of San Jacinto.* Austin: Texas State Historical Association, 1989.

Poinsett, Joel Roberts. *Notes on Mexico, Made in the Autumn of 1822.* New York: Frederick A. Praeger, 1969.

Proceedings in the Case of the United States versus William Christy. Texas as Province and Republic, 1795–1845. Based on the bibliography by Thomas Streeter. New Haven, Conn.: Research Publications, 1978–1979. Microfilm.

Ramke, Diedrich. "Edward Douglas[s] White, Sr., Governor of Louisiana, 1835–1839." *Louisiana Historical Quarterly* 19 (1917).

Reed, Merl. "Boom or Bust: Louisiana's Economy during the 1830s." *Louisiana History* 4 (winter 1963): 35–53.

———. "Government Investment and Economic Growth: Louisiana's Antebellum Railroads." *Journal of Southern History* 28 (May, 1962): 183–201.

Reed, Merl E. *New Orleans and the Railroads: The Struggle for Commercial Empire, 1830–1860.* Baton Rouge: Louisiana State University Press, 1966.

Reeves, Carolyn Ericson. "Prelude to San Jacinto: Nacogdoches, 1836." *East Texas Historical Society* 11 (1973): 36–41.

Reichstein, Andreas V. *The Rise of the Lone Star: The Making of Texas.* Trans. Jeanne R. Wilson. College Station: Texas A&M Press, 1989.

Reinhardt, Ina Kate Harmon. "The Public Career of Thomas Green in Texas." Master's thesis, University of Texas at Austin, 1939.

Remini, Robert V. *Andrew Jackson and the Course of American Empire.* 3 vols. New York: Harper & Row, 1977.

———. *Henry Clay: Statesman for the Union.* New York: W. W. Norton, 1991.

Richardson, Rupert N. "Framing the Constitution of the Republic of Texas." *Southwestern Historical Quarterly* 31 (1928): 191–220.

Rippy, J. Fred. *Joel R. Poinsett: Versatile American.* Durham: Duke University Press, 1935.

Roeder, Robert E. "New Orleans Merchants, 1790–1837." Ph.D. diss., Harvard University, 1959.

Roland, Kate Mason. "General John T. Mason." *Southwestern Historical Quarterly* 11 (1908): 163–98.

Ruthven, A. S. *Proceedings of the Grand Lodge of Texas, from Its Organization in the City of Houston, Dec. A.D. 1837, A.L. 5837, to the Close of the Grand Annual Communication Held at Palestine, January 19, 1857, A.L. 5857.* 2 vols. Galveston: Richardson, 1860.

Sanchez-Lemego, Miguel A. *The Siege and Taking of the Alamo.* Trans. Consuelo Velasco. Santa Fe: Blue Feather, 1968.

Santos, Richard G. *Santa Anna's Campaign against Texas, 1835–1836.* Waco: Texian Press, 1968.

Shipman, Daniel. *Frontier Life, 58 Years in Texas.* 1879; reprint, Pasadena: Abbotsford, 1965.

Siegel, Stanley. *A Political History of the Texas Republic, 1836–1845.* Austin: University of Texas Press, 1956.

Silver, James W. *Edmund Pendleton Gaines: Frontier General.* Baton Rouge: Louisiana State University Press, 1949.

Sims, Harold Dana. *The Expulsion of Mexico's Spaniards, 1821–1836.* Pittsburgh: University of Pittsburgh Press, 1990.

Smith, Sam B., and Harriet Chappell Owsley, eds. *The Papers of Andrew Jackson.* 5 vols. Knoxville: University of Tennessee Press, 1980.

Smith, W. Roy. "The Quarrel between Governor Smith and the Council of the Provisional of the Republic." *Southwestern Historical Quarterly* 5 (1902).

Smither, Nelle. *A History of the English Theatre in New Orleans.* New York: Benjamin Blom, 1944; reissued, 1967.

———. "A History of the English Theatre at New Orleans, 1806–1842." *Louisiana Historical Quarterly* 28 (January, 1945): 85–276.

Smithwick, Noah. *The Evolution of a State: Recollections of Old Texas Days.* No. 5, Barker Texas History Series. Austin: University of Texas Press, 1983.

Sprague, Marshall. *So Vast So Beautiful a Land: Louisiana and the Purchase.* Athens: Ohio University Press, 1974.

Stenberg, Richard R. "The Boundaries of the Louisiana Purchase." *Hispanic American Historical Review* 14 (1934): 32–64.

———. "Jackson, Anthony Butler, and Texas." *Southwestern Social Science Quarterly* 13 (December, 1932): 264–86.

———. "Jackson's Neches Claim, 1829–1836." *Southwestern Historical Quarterly* 39 (1936): 255–74.

———. "Some Letters of the Texas Revolution." *Southwestern Social Science Quarterly* 21 (1941): 302–11.

———. "The Texas Schemes of Jackson and Houston, 1829–1836." *Southwestern Social Science Quarterly* 15 (1934): 229–50.

Sterne, Adolphus. *Hurrah for Texas! The Diary of Adolphus Sterne, 1838–1851.* Ed. Archie P. McDonald. Waco: Texian Press, 1969.

Stone, A. H. "The Cotton Factorage System of the Southern States." *American Historical Review* 20 (1915): 557–65.

Streeter, Thomas W. *Bibliography of Texas, 1795–1845.* 3 vols. Cambridge: Harvard University Press, 1960.

Thompson, Waddy. *Recollections of Mexico.* New York: Wiley and Putnam, 1846.

Tijerina, Andreas. *Tejanos and Texas under the Mexican Flag, 1821–1836.* No. 54, Centennial Series of the Association of Former Students, Texas A&M University. College Station: Texas A&M Press, 1994.

To All Who May Have Seen and Read the Dying Groans of William Bryan, E. Hall, and Saml. Ellis, Ex-Agents of Texas. Columbia, Tex.: Telegraph, 1836. *Texas as Province and Republic, 1795–1845.* Based on the bibliography by Thomas Streeter. New Haven, Conn.: Research Publications, 1978–1979. Microfilm.

Tomerlin, Jacqueline Beretta, comp. *Fugitive Letters, 1829–1836, Stephen F. Austin to David G. Burnet.* San Antonio: Trinity University Press, 1981.

Tregle, Joseph, Jr. *Louisiana in the Age of Jackson: A Clash of Cultures and Personalities.* Baton Rouge: Louisiana State University Press, 1999.

Triplett, Robert. *Roland Trevor: or, the Pilot of Human Life, Being an Autobiography of the Author, Showing How to Make and Lose a Fortune, and Then to Make Another.* Philadelphia: Lippincott, Grambo. 1853. Western Americana: Frontier History of the Trans-Mississippi West, 1550–1900. New Haven, Conn.: Research Publications, 1975. Microfilm.

Trufant, S. A. "Review of Banking in New Orleans, 1830–1840." *Publications of the Louisiana Historical Society* 9 (1917): 25–40.

Turner, F. H. "The Mejía Expedition." *Quarterly of the Texas State Historical Association* 7 (1903): 1–28.

Tyler, Ron, Douglas E. Barnett, Roy R. Barkley, Penelope C. Anderson, Mark F. Odintz, eds. *The New Handbook of Texas.* 6 vols. Austin: Texas State Historical Association, 1996.

University of Texas at Austin. Library. *Independent Mexico in Documents: Independence, Empire, and Republic.* Vol. 3, *Catálogo de los Manuscriptos del Archivo de Don Valentín Gómez Farías: Obrantes en la Universidad de Texas Colección Latinamericana.* Mexico: Editorial Jus. 1968.

Urban, Stanely C. "The Ideology of Southern Imperialism: New Orleans and the Caribbean, 1845–1860." *Louisiana Historical Quarterly* 39 (1956): 48–73.

Viener, Saul. "Surgeon Moses Albert Levy: Letters of a Texas Patriot." *Publications of the American Jewish Historical Society* 46 (1956): 101–13.

A Vindication of the Conduct of the Agency of Texas in New Orleans. New Orleans: Louisiana

Advertiser, 1836. *Texas as Province and Republic, 1795–1845.* Based on the bibliography by Thomas Streeter. New Haven, Conn.: Research Publications, 1978–1979. Microfilm.

Wallace, Ernest, David Vigness, and George B. Ward. *Documents of Texas History.* 2d ed. Austin: State House, 1994.

Warren, Harris Gaylord. *The Sword Was Their Passport: A History of American Filibustering in the Mexican Revolution.* Baton Rouge: Louisiana State University Press, 1943.

Warren, Harry. "Col. William G. Cooke." *Southwestern Historical Quarterly* 9 (1906): 210–19.

Wells, Tom Henderson. *Commodore Moore and the Texas Navy.* Austin: University of Texas Press, 1960.

White, Gifford. *1840 Citizens of Texas.* Nacogdoches, Tex.: Ericson Books; St. Louis: Ingmire, 1984.

Willborn, Alfred T. "The Relations between New Orleans and Latin America, 1810–1824." *Louisiana Historical Quarterly* 22 (1939): 710–94.

Williams, Amelia W., and Eugene C. Barker, eds. *The Writings of Sam Houston, 1813–1863.* 8 vols. Austin: Pemberton, 1970.

Williams, Elgin. *The Animating Pursuits of Speculation: Land Traffic in the Annexation of Texas.* New York: Columbia University Press, 1949.

Wilson, Rosa Belle. "The Mission of Austin, Archer, and Wharton to the United States in 1836." Master's thesis, University of Texas at Austin, 1937.

Winston, James. "New Orleans Newspapers and the Texas Question, 1835–1837." *Southwestern Historical Quarterly* 36 (1932): 109–29.

———. "New Orleans and the Texas Revolution." *Louisiana Historical Quarterly* 10 (1927): 317–54.

———. "Notes on Commercial Relations between New Orleans and Texas Ports, 1838–1839." *Southwestern Historical Quarterly* 34 (1930): 91–105.

Winthrop, John. *Report of the Trial of Thomas M. Thompson for a Piratical Attack upon the American Schooner San Felipe, before the United States Court for the Eastern District of Louisiana.* New Orleans: E. Johns, 1835. *Texas as Province and Republic, 1795–1845.* Based on the bibliography by Thomas Streeter. New Haven, Conn.: Research Publications, 1978–1979. Microfilm.

Yoakum, Henderson. *History of Texas, from Its First Settlement in 1685 to Its Annexation to the United States in 1846.* 2 vols. New York: Redfield, 1855.

Zalce y Rodriguez, Luis J. *Apuntes para la Historia de la Masoneria en Mexico.* 2 vols. Mexico, 1850.

Zuber, W. P. "Captain Adolphus Sterne." *The Quarterly of the Texas State Historical Association* 2 (1899): 211–16.

INTERNET SOURCES

Alamo de Parras. http://www.alamo-de-parras.welkin.org/.

Gammel's Laws, Government Documents Department, University of North Texas, Denton, Tex. http://texinfo.library.unt.edu/lawsoftexas/default.html.

Handbook of Texas Online, Texas State Historical Association. http://www.tsha.utexas
.edu/handbook/online/.
Maxey, H. Daivd. Index to Military Rolls of the Republic of Texas, 1835–1836. http://
www.mindspring.com/~dmaxey/.
Official Website of the Texas Navies. http://www.texasnavy.com/.
San Jacinto Veterans: Biographical Sketches of the Men Who Won Independence for
Texas. http://www.sanjacinto-museum.org/veterans.html.

MAPS

Robinson, E., and R. H. Pidgeon. Map of the City of New Orleans, Louisiana. New York:
E. R. Robinson, 1883, New Orleans Public Library. Microfilm.
Zimpel, Charles F. New Orleans City Map, 1834. Historic New Orleans Collection, New
Orleans.

NEWSPAPERS

Austin *Texas State Gazette*, 1850–1851
Baltimore *Niles Register*, 1835–1836
Brazoria *Texas Republican*, 1835
Clarksville (Tex.) *Standard*, 1856, 1882, 1886
New Orleans *Bee*, 1830–1836
New Orleans *Commercial Bulletin*, 1835–1836, 1846
New Orleans *Daily Delta*, 1849
New Orleans *Daily Picayune*, 1837, 1839, 1863
New Orleans *Louisiana Advertiser*, 1835
New Orleans *True American*, 1835
Mexico City *El Mosquito Mexicano*, 1835
Monterrey (Mexico) *Gazeta Constitución de Nuevo Leon*, 1829–1830
Philadelphia *National Gazette and Literary Register*, 1836
San Felipe de Austin (Tex.) *Telegraph and Texas Register*, 1835–1837

INDEX

Pages with illustrations are indicated by boldface type

ISBN 1-58544-358-1